AF228248

IN STRANGE COMPANY

IN STRANGE COMPANY

An American Soldier with Multinational
Forces in the Middle East and Iraq

COLONEL (RETIRED) ROLAND J. TISO JR., USA

Foreword by
GENERAL (RETIRED) ANTHONY C. ZINNI, USMC

CASEMATE

Philadelphia & Oxford

Published in the United States of America and Great Britain in 2023 by
CASEMATE PUBLISHERS
1950 Lawrence Road, Havertown, PA 19083, USA
and
The Old Music Hall, 106–108 Cowley Road, Oxford OX4 1JE, UK

Copyright 2023 © Roland J. Tiso Jr.

Hardback Edition: ISBN 978-1-63624-394-8
Digital Edition: ISBN 978-1-63624-395-5

A CIP record for this book is available from the British Library

All rights reserved. No part of this book may be reproduced or transmitted in any form or by any means, electronic or mechanical including photocopying, recording or by any information storage and retrieval system, without permission from the publisher in writing.

Printed and bound in the United Kingdom by CPI Group (UK) Ltd, Croydon, CR0 4YY.

Typeset in India by Lapiz Digital Services, Chennai.

For a complete list of Casemate titles, please contact:

CASEMATE PUBLISHERS (US)
Telephone (610) 853-9131
Fax (610) 853-9146
Email: casemate@casematepublishers.com
www.casematepublishers.com

CASEMATE PUBLISHERS (UK)
Telephone (0)1226 734350
Email: casemate-uk@casematepublishers.co.uk
www.casematepublishers.co.uk

This memoir is humbly dedicated to the memory of Lieutenant Colonels
Kim S. Orlando, Charles H. "Chad" Buehring, USA, and Major Hieronim
Kupczyk, Polish Army, who gallantly served God and country and
made the supreme sacrifice in Iraq, October–November 2003.

The closing ceremony ending the Peninsula Shield Force (PSF) mission in Kuwait was attended by several general officers and Kuwaiti officials including the minister of defense. General BaBa'eer, the PSF commander, directed me to stand with the PSF staff and proudly introduced me to the minister of defense as his "American adviser and LNO." Major General J. D. Thurman, USA, Combined Forces Land Component Commander (CFLCC) Chief of Operations (C-3), represented the CFLCC commander. General Thurman, a big man with a friendly, "good ole country boy" personality, warmly shook my hand and, with his characteristic broad smile, said,

"Tiso, I'd been told you were keeping strange company."

"Yes, sir," I replied, "You might say that."

Contents

Foreword by General (Retired) Anthony C. Zinni, USMC   ix
Author's Notes and Acknowledgements   xi

PART I: PLANNING AND TRAINING FOR WAR

1	Multi-Cultural Experiences in Old New York	3
2	United States Central Command and the Central Region	9
3	Leading U.S. and Multinational Forces in the Sinai	13
4	Fighting the Force-Protection Battle in Saudi Arabia and Afghanistan	31
5	Planning the Inevitable War	43

PART II: OPERATION *IRAQI FREEDOM* SPECIAL MISSIONS

6	Staffing Posthostilities Operations	61
7	Duty with the United Nations	71
8	Stability Operations in Iraq	85
9	Advising the Peninsula Shield Force	93
10	Reconnaissance of the Rumaylah Oil Field	109
11	Redeployment of the Peninsula Shield Force	119
12	Assignment to the Coalition Military Assistance Training Team	125
13	Building the Foundation of an Army	137
14	Making the Most of Scant Resources	155
15	Recruiting, Organizing, and Training the New Iraqi Army	163

PART III: SOLDIERING WITH THE MULTINATIONAL DIVISION (CENTRAL-SOUTH)

16	Preparing for Duty with a Combat Division	175
17	Serving with the Multinational Division (Central-South)	183

18   The Challenges of Multinational Command   207
19   The Power of the Theater Commander   223
20   Patrolling with the Ukrainians on the Iranian Border   229
21   Preparing the Occupation of Iraq   241
22   Indications of a Growing Insurgency in Central-South Iraq   253
23   Dealing with Generals   263
24   The War Comes to the Multinational Division (Central-South)   271
25   Defeating the Enemy with Overwhelming Force   281
26   Fighting the Battle for Central-South Iraq   291
27   Combat Action in Al-Kut   299
28   The American Bureaucracy in Baghdad   309
29   Developing a Strategy to Conduct the Long War   313
30   False Hope for Peace in Iraq   327
31   Christmas on the Iranian Border   333
32   Terrorist Attack and Tragedy in Kerbelâ'   343
33   Transitioning to a New Commander and Division Staff   349
34   Teaching the New Command to Conduct Combat Operations   355
35   A New Liaison Team Arrives at Camp Babylon   365

PART IV: GOING HOME: REFLECTIONS ON THE LONG WAR

36   Going Home via Poland   371
37   Epilogue   379

Glossary of Acronyms and Terms   387
Endnotes   391
Index   395
About the Author   402

Foreword

Much has been written, and will be written, about the events leading up to the war in Iraq and the conduct of the war itself. I don't know of anyone who can bring the perspective to these events that Roland Tiso can provide. He possesses a truly unique set of experiences from over a decade of service in the U.S. Central Command (USCENTCOM) region that is unmatched. He has served as the chief planner for USCENTCOM, in the Multinational Force in the Sinai, with the United Nations in Iraq, with Coalition forces during the war, and in numerous other capacities that have given him a degree of unparalleled knowledge, on-the-ground experiences, and strategy development participation. His depth of understanding of everything from the culture to war planning to the geography is exceptional.

I first met Roland when he came to my command headquarters in the early 1990s. I then commanded the Marine Corps' operational forces assigned to USCENTCOM. As the head planner for USCENTCOM, he impressed my staff and commanders with his extensive knowledge and willingness to assist us with our planning and decision making. His personal dedication and tireless commitment to aid us in the planning, wargaming, and exercises related to our USCENTCOM missions created a true sense of teamwork. I selected Roland as my executive assistant when I went on to command USCENTCOM. I knew firsthand of his passion for the region and his expertise in operating in it.

This is a rare, fascinating, and insightful work written from a most unique perspective. It provides a view of events that could not be given by anyone other than Roland Tiso. During this historic period, he has seen this critical part of the world through the multifaceted prism of a special set of experiences. This work is not theory or analysis from a thousand miles away. This is a firsthand account from someone who lived it in the sand.

Anthony C. Zinni
General (Retired)
United States Marine Corps

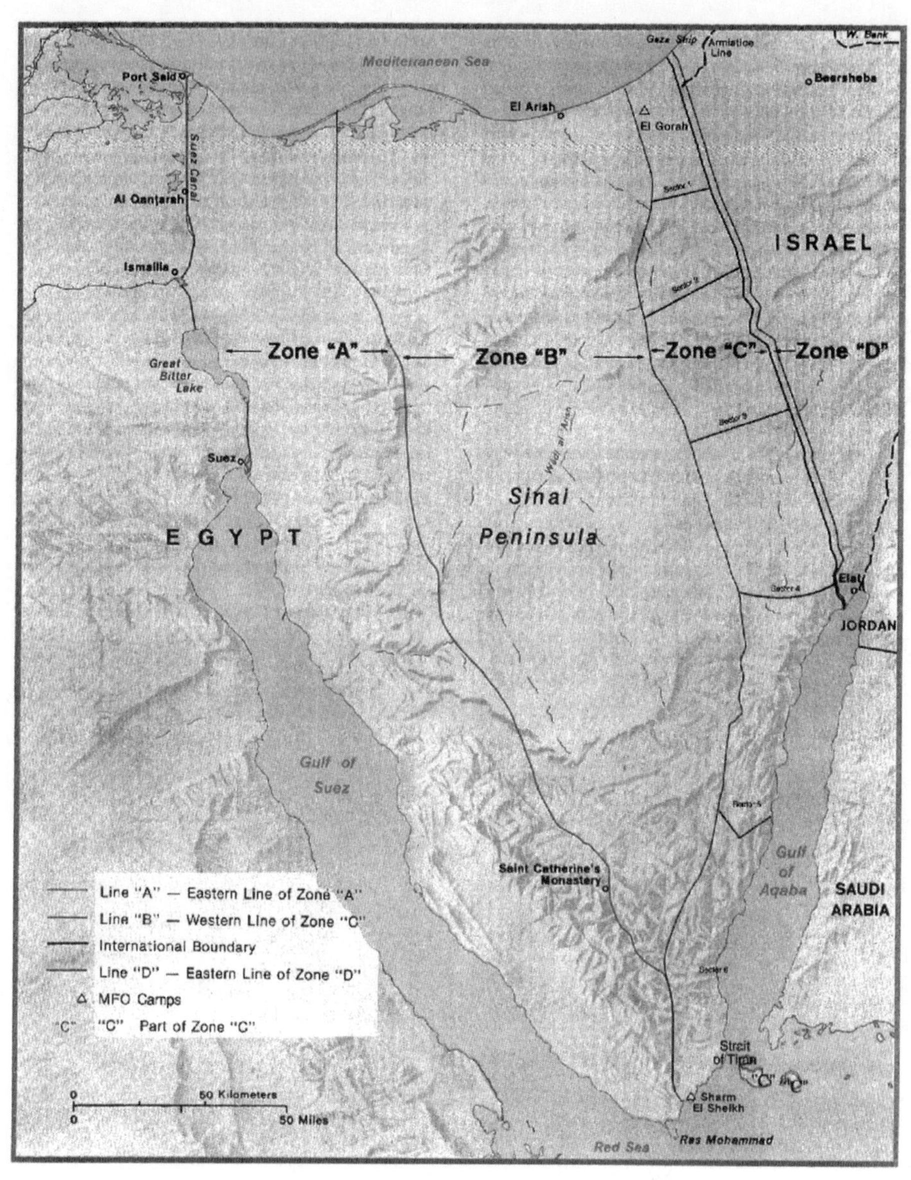

The Sinai Peninsula. (The Multinational Force and Observers, June, 1999)

Author's Notes and Acknowledgements

I participated in the U.S.-led invasion of Iraq in March 2003. The tumultuous year I spent in Iraq, several years in the Middle East that preceded it, and three years as an Iraq war planner constituted the most exciting and professionally challenging period of my military career. I was totally immersed in the issues confronting the United States in the Middle East. I watched America's experience in Iraq and the war on terrorism unfold over the last 10 years of my military career from a front-row seat in the halls of the Pentagon, U.S. Unified Command and Multinational Command Headquarters, to Africa and the Pakistan–Afghanistan border and, finally, to the deserts of Egypt and the Middle East. My command and staff assignments took me to all the region's hotspots including Somalia, Kuwait, the Sinai Peninsula, Pakistan, Afghanistan, Saudi Arabia, and Iraq. I worked closely with three exceptional theater commanders—Generals Peay, Zinni, and Franks—and learned a great deal about the Middle East and the challenges that confront the United States there. Before and during Operation *Iraqi Freedom*, I was assigned to, or worked closely with, the United Nations, the Multinational Force & Observers, the Arab Peninsula Shield Force, the Royal Marines, the New Iraqi Army, and the soldiers of over twenty nations that comprised the Polish-led Multinational Division (Central-South). These assignments, coupled with multiple staff assignments focused on war planning and Middle East policy issues, provided a unique perspective on the region and the war in Iraq, international organizations, and the strengths and weaknesses of numerous national militaries.

I was encouraged to write this book by several people who thought I had a unique story to tell. Many of them thought my experiences with multinational forces would be valuable to soldiers who are assigned to, or will work with, multinational forces in a command, advisory, or liaison role in the future. They thought I could provide an interesting perspective on the strategic and operational planning of the maneuver war and the occupation of Iraq, our initial efforts to develop a credible Iraqi Army, and the insurgency and sectarian violence that hampered our efforts to achieve a stable and credibly governed country.

I was deeply concerned throughout my tour in Iraq that our senior leaders failed to provide the forces so desperately required early in the Iraq war to occupy the country, secure its borders, and thwart a potential insurgency and sectarian violence in accordance with a decade of planning. I was disappointed by the under-resourced effort to recruit, train, organize, and deploy a New Iraqi Army. I was equally disappointed by the unimaginative, and often ineffective, way we integrated our allies into our operations. The combat effectiveness of multinational forces is dependent upon detailed planning and coordination of their employment, operational support, and material and technical assistance. In a constrained environment, our senior leaders in many cases proved either unwilling or unable to provide the personnel, expertise, operational support, and equipment multinational units required to achieve the combat effectiveness expected of them. The absence or disregard of our allies' opinions, coupled with our propensity to always do things our way, inevitably caused allied resentment of American senior leadership. My opinion of the bulk of the multinational units I saw in the field was fundamentally positive considering the national restrictions under which they served. I left Iraq with a profound respect for our Coalition partners and what they potentially bring to the asymmetric battlefields on which we now conduct modern Coalition warfare. This opinion was not shared by many of my contemporaries and superiors in 2003–04.

It was not my intent to write the definitive history of the war in Iraq, discuss the contributions of all the countries who contributed its soldiers and resources, or review all the challenges the Coalition encountered in its efforts to stabilize Iraq. The vast bulk of this memoir is taken from my personal journals, notes, papers, photos, and observations. It is my story, my small part of the Iraq War and key training and planning experiences that preceded it. It was a war that, for me, encompassed 10 years. The opinions I express are mine, shaped in large measure by my experiences in the Middle East and service in U.S. Central Command from 1994–2004. I have tried to "stay in my lane" and not second guess my commanders or higher echelons of command. Less than perfect decisions are the norm in extraordinarily difficult circumstances. The criticisms and observations I make are with full recognition of the complexity of war and the international and Iraqi environment. I believe, however, that many of our senior leaders never made a transition from peace to war and remained instead in a suspended state of crisis, a small but, I believe, significant observation that undoubtedly led to a lack of decisiveness on many key issues in the first year of Iraq's occupation and the events leading to the invasion. My experiences may cast additional insight on operational and posthostilities difficulties we experienced in Iraq, the challenges of recruiting, accommodating, equipping, and training the New Iraqi Army in the spring/summer of 2003, and the strengths and limitations of multinational forces.

I have written a lengthy, but vital chapter concerning Iraq war planning that will help the reader better understand the campaign conducted in the spring of 2003 and, more importantly, how and why our stability operations following the fall of Baghdad and the Saddam regime were under-resourced and less than successful. Military planning can be very technical, complicated, and no doubt confusing to an untrained soldier or civilian. I have tried to simplify the discussion of the development of the original Iraq war plan and focus on why senior-level decisions to not resource the posthostilities piece of the campaign may have set up the U.S. Army and the Coalition for the inevitability of a protracted insurgency and a less-than-satisfactory outcome.

There are a number of lessons learned throughout the book that may prove worthy of note to soldiers, government officials, diplomats, and concerned citizens. If my observations and thoughts contribute in any way to improving operational effectiveness and decision making, or enable an American soldier to engage with allied soldiers or indigenous people more successfully in the future, then I will have accomplished far more than simply telling a story of one man's war.

I am grateful to Generals J. H. Binford Peay III, USA, and Anthony C. Zinni, USMC, for sharing their knowledge and wisdom of our profession and the Central Region with me and countless other officers who served under their command. I am grateful to General Tommy Franks, USA, who provided me the opportunity to serve in Iraq under unusual and challenging circumstances. I am grateful for my friendship with Major General (Retired) Paul Eaton, USA, and his superb leadership in Baghdad with the New Iraqi Army project. I can never forget the exceptional service of my marines in Baghdad, Colonels Michael D. Greer, Bob Sommers, and Joe Moore, USMCR, and three outstanding young officers who served on the liaison team I led with the Multinational Division (Central-South), Major Tom Lowman, USA, Major Ken Owens, USMC, and Captain Britt Reed, USA. The United States should never forget the exceptional contributions of these men and countless thousands like them. I am grateful to Colonel (Retired) Richard L. Stouder, USA, the brilliant U.S. Central Command war planner who provided me with invaluable insights on the Iraq war planning effort from 1992–98. The success I enjoyed as his successor as the chief of U.S. Central Command's War Plans Division was due in large measure to his mentorship. Colonel (Retired) Mike Greer, USMC, Colonel (Retired) Barry Hammill, USAF, and Colonel (Retired) Michael D. Fitzgerald, USA, edited the initial drafts of this book, advised me on numerous administrative and legal matters concerning its publication, and identified classified information that required editing or removal. Lieutenant Colonel (Retired) James R. "Duke" Briley, USA, and Mr. Aaron Koch provided valuable technical assistance. I am grateful to all these gentlemen for their support.

I extend a special thanks to a dear friend and an exceptional officer, Colonel Douglas G. Schnelle, USAR, who, more than any other person, encouraged me to record my experiences and thoughts. Colonel Schnelle passed away shortly after he was demobilized from active duty at U.S. Central Command in 2005. He was a brilliant historian, a superb leader, a dedicated patriot, and a Christian gentleman.

I could not be prouder of my wife Judie and our daughters Catherine and Alexandra who endured long periods without a husband and father and excelled in every measurable way. More than a memoir of my 10-year war and multinational experiences in the Global War on Terrorism and Operation *Iraqi Freedom*, this book is a legacy for my daughters who I hope will better understand what their dad was doing during his long absences. For them, for those who encouraged me, and those who read it, I hope this book proves to be a noble and worthwhile effort.

Roland J. Tiso Jr.
Colonel (Retired)

PART I

PLANNING AND TRAINING FOR WAR

CHAPTER I

Multi-cultural Experiences in Old New York

Make your mark in New York and you are a made man.

—MARK TWAIN

Growing up on the streets of the old Bronx and the City of Mount Vernon in the fifties and sixties gave a young person an appreciation for the ethnic and religious diversity of the world. The neighborhoods of the day were ethnically dominated and seemingly segregated, but people moved about freely and without fear of each other. It was not unusual to hear many foreign languages spoken in the marketplaces. My family was of Italian ethnicity and Italian was spoken in our home, though my brothers and I were discouraged from learning the language. The elders did not want their boys to grow up with an Italian accent but rather be Americans who could speak good English and compete in business and the professions. It seems silly today, but it was a particular concern of my mother. She had immigrated in 1936, barely escaping the Mussolini regime that denied all departures shortly after she made her way to America. My father's family had immigrated to the United States in 1919. No one spoke English, but my grandfather was a trained and talented mason who quickly established his business and built a house for his growing family in Mount Vernon. He and his wife Anna would have six boys, five of whom would fight in Europe and in the Pacific in World War II.

Grandpa Tiso built his house with several floors that enabled it to serve as an extended family home. The basement served as a family dining room and kitchen, very typical of the Italian way of life at the time. My parents occupied the top floor of the house when they were married in 1947. It was the first home in which my two brothers and I would live. Though the street on which we lived was predominantly Italian, the adjoining street was a predominantly black neighborhood. The American Legion Post across from our home was comprised of black veterans who had served in World War II. My father knew most of these great guys who never failed to have a good time at their meetings. Pop was frequently invited to attend their parties. The booze flowed freely, and he always said he had a good time. Several buildings further down the street included a vegetable market that served as a black people's church on Saturday evenings. I was impressed by the way the attendees dressed. Suits and top hats and even spats were worn by the gentlemen and the ladies were always dressed "to the nines." Nothing was too good to worship the Lord. I used to sit on the front porch of our extended family home and listen to the loud music coming from the church. Pop told me it was their way of driving the devil from the church. There was never a shortage of horns and various other instruments to do the job. I gained an appreciation for music from that experience that I hold to this day. Far more subdued was the Catholic church we attended. Mount Saint Carmel was predominately attended by the Italian community, though a significant number of Hispanic people attended mass on Sundays. My parents were married in this church. Italian and Spanish were commonly spoken; English was a second or third language for most of the elders. Father Martin had served in Europe during World War II as an Army chaplain, and he was naturally very popular with the men of the church, most of whom had served in the war.

I remember very well the Catholic feasts of the day celebrated on the streets of Mount Vernon. My mother often participated in these events. Regardless of ethnicity, the women of the day were all about their homes and their families. They were a dominant force bent on the preservation of their families and the safety of their sons. The food in various booths along the parade routes, that featured large balloons and religious floats honoring various saints, gave a person an appreciation for the world; Italian, Spanish, Irish, Polish, German, and Hispanic fare lined the streets. Music and folk dancing reminiscent of the "old countries" added to the festive mood of these events. When I questioned my mother about why the women did not wear shoes in several of the church parades, she would say, in her beautifully accented and often broken English, that going shoeless replicated a mother's pain in childbirth or various other painful trials of a woman's life. My mother had come to America with no formal education to speak of and no knowledge of English. She had had a tough crossing aboard the ocean liner *Conte Savoia* and her reception at Ellis Island had been stressful. Like most of the immigrants of the day, she was tough and determined. She learned enough English to survive and "get around town," and met my father, Roland senior, shortly after he returned from Europe in the spring of 1946. They were married in 1947.

The neighborhoods were, in retrospect, somewhat on the poor side, and Italian mothers were always concerned their boys could end up on the wrong side of the law. I was very aware of the presence of the mob in New York City and the tentacles of organized crime reached well into the suburbs. The "numbers racket," or illegal off-track betting, was very common in all the ethnic communities and, like so many young boys of the day, I would unknowingly run the bets and the packaged money from one store front to the next for petty change. The cops seemed to turn a blind eye to this activity and no doubt played a few rounds themselves.

I frequently accompanied my mother to the marketplaces. The "hustle and bustle" of Gramatan Avenue, main street Mount Vernon, was fascinating. Not surprisingly, the market was a cacophony of foreign languages, including Yiddish and "Pig Latin." People were seemingly always fighting "tooth and nail" over the costs of vegetables, fruit, and other foods. I was amused even then at how such banter could result over a nickel or a dime. It was all about culture. One was to believe all the vendors were crooks but, at the end of the day, everyone knew bartering was endemic to the culture, and it was common to see these "knock down drag out" arguments end amicably.

The marketplace also gave you an appreciation of the human cost of World War II. It was common to see men in their late twenties or early thirties on crutches with a pants leg pinned up; men with hooks for hands and artificial arms were everywhere. My father seemed to know a lot of guys who had been permanently scarred in the war and he frequently stopped to speak with them on the street. There was one gentleman who appeared in a daze walking down the street constantly moving his head from side to side. I laughed at his strange behavior until my father explained he had survived the battles on Bataan, and the death march that followed in 1942, and did not fully recover from his psychological wounds. I was taught to respect our soldiers and hold all veterans in high esteem.

The extended Tiso home was a gathering place for the entire Tiso clan in the fifties and early sixties. The small yard in the back of the house still served as Grandpa's "victory garden," where all sorts of vegetables were grown, along with an olive tree. There was also a grape vine that provided shade, and under it was a picnic table where Grandpa met with his boys. I was taken by the conversation that always seemed to focus on their experiences in the war. My uncles would speak both English and Italian to accommodate Grandpa whose English was never very good. He was a brilliant mason and stone cutter who had made his way in the construction business. He had immense physical strength and was known to walk about with 100-pound cement bags under his arms when the job called for it. Grandpa was a hero in his own right, having been decorated for his actions on the Southern Front during World War I at the Battle of Caporetto. Pop and my uncles would swap stories that spanned the theaters of war from North Africa to Normandy and Central Europe, to Guadalcanal and Okinawa in the Pacific. They were my heroes and I listened to every word. Their stories were a form of oral history that was often exciting and comical. The laughter hid the more gruesome tales of combat that saw several of them wounded. Their stories convinced me that my calling in life was to be a soldier.

In New York, people tended to congregate by ethnicity. It wasn't segregation as much as it was personal choice. Sports were a big deal, perhaps more so than today at the community level. The WWII veterans enjoyed playing organized softball and big crowds came to watch them. I learned about the competitive black football leagues in the Bronx and Mount Vernon from my father. I was very young, barely 10 as I recall, but I was big for my age, and I took to football and baseball very quickly. My father asked the guys at the Black American Legion Post, who were coaches, if they would allow me to play on one of their teams; they quickly agreed. It didn't matter I was the only white kid on the field, and it never occurred to me. I had a helmet and a pair of shoulder pads and that was all that mattered. I was fast and I told my coaches I wanted to be a halfback like my father had been in 1939 when he played for Davis High School in Mount Vernon. Playing football and baseball in the tough city leagues was a great way for a young boy to develop as a man athletically and physically, and I was taken by the hard-nosed leadership and discipline inspired by these superb coaches. They were very harsh and used racial slurs that are all but forbidden in modern society. It was a tough environment for any kid who quickly learned to give everything he had and pursue excellence. I came to understand the toughness, physical fitness, and hard-nosed discipline of these exceptional black coaches were characteristic of many of the veterans who worked with young boys and men in sport. My high school coaches were nearly all combat veterans who were as tough as they were knowledgeable of the game. It seemed to me the big war had been a great equalizer that had provided an environment where discipline, toughness, fitness, and training were the "callsigns" of success.

Equally tough and unforgiving of legal or disciplinary faults were the cops. The streets have always been a tough place for a young kid in New York, and Mount Vernon was a tough town. It seemed to me like the police force was made up of mostly Irish guys. Like most of the boys on the street at that time, I was introduced to the Police Athletic League (PAL). The gyms were crude compared to today's standard, but the idea was to get youngsters off the streets and into an environment that would keep them out of trouble. The centerpiece of the PAL gym was a boxing ring and the cops taught everyone the fundamentals of the sport. The place smelled of sweat and liniment, and I was taken by the grit and toughness expected of the boys admitted to the gym. Everyone had been in some type of trouble that was brought to the attention of the local police. Knocking over fruit stands and ripping off a few apples and oranges was common, as was street fighting and hub cap theft. Many of the guys took well to the gym and the lessons the police were teaching. Many of them entered the military after graduation from high school. Not surprisingly, a lot of guys went on to fight in the New York State Golden Gloves. These were tough guys—Italian, Puerto Rican, Irish, black—and I took a lot of hits in the ring from many of them who, in most cases, were older than I was. It was sport that brought us together and little was said about who we were, where we came from, or what color or ethnicity we were. It was a time when how good you were on the ball fields or in the ring was what counted. My adventures with the law did not end entirely and I was in trouble a few more times before graduating high school, but sports and the academics at Pelham Memorial High School in the mid to late sixties dominated my life and kept me focused on legitimate and noble pursuits.

By the early sixties, my family had moved to an apartment house in Pelham, New York; quite a change from the homes in which my brothers and I had lived. The highly diverse, ethnic neighborhoods to which I had grown accustomed gave way to a predominantly white, middle-class town, that various black organizations in the mid/late sixties referred to as a "white enclave," that bordered the towns of Mount Vernon and New Rochelle. Pop worked for the New York Central Railroad as a machinist; I was entitled to a pass that enabled me to ride the trains to New York City free of charge. I would often do so on Saturdays to work the corner of 42nd and 1st Street with my shoeshine kit. I was taken by the gentlemen whose shoes I shined, many of whom were "big shot" businessmen and government officials. The United Nations building dominates the area and once again the streets in my life were filled with foreign languages, strange-looking people, often in native garb, and the "hustle and bustle" of Gramatan Avenue I remembered so well from living in Mount Vernon. I managed in time to pick up some street Spanish which, coupled with four years of high school classes and physical training sessions at Westchester County's Rye Beach, where I played three-sided handball with my Puerto Rican friends, was actually pretty good. It would come in handy throughout my military career.

In retrospect, the entire experience growing up in the highly diverse, ethnic neighborhoods of the Bronx, Mount Vernon, and the streets of New York City was a significant prelude to what the Army and my multinational assignments in the Middle East held in store for a soldier who came of age in an environment that reflected the old world with many different peoples, languages, and cultures.

CHAPTER 2

United States Central Command and the Central Region

The Middle East is a tough neighborhood.

—General A. C. Zinni, USMC

I was very excited about my assignment to U.S. Central Command (USCENTCOM) in the summer of 1994. Naturally, I had hoped to be selected to command a brigade, but that was not in the cards so I was determined to make the most of any assignment and see where it led me. Our year in Carlisle, Pennsylvania, had been a rewarding and somewhat restful time for me and my family but, soon after my class graduated from the U.S. Army War College, Judie and I packed out the household goods, loaded what baggage we could in the car, secured our two daughters in the back seat, and headed for Lorton, Virginia, where we boarded the auto-train for an overnight ride to Sanford, Florida. Several hours later, we drove to our new, albeit rented, home in Valrico, Florida, a small town about 25 miles east of the city of Tampa. I had no way of knowing at the time that USCENTCOM would become a permanent fixture in my professional life or that Florida would become our adopted state of residence.

Other than being assigned to a tactical command, an assignment to the Central Command Staff meant being where the action was. I was not a stranger to serving at a geographical command headquarters. I had been assigned to the Operations Plans Staff (J3) of U.S. Pacific Command at Camp Smith, Hawaii, in 1986–88 following my graduation from the Armed Forces Staff College. I would hold a variety of command and staff assignments at Central Command Headquarters and in the Central Region over the next 10 years. I was not a foreign-area specialist, but I very quickly gained a rare appreciation for the region, its people and customs, their religion, the desert, and the key political and strategic issues confronting our country. I became very confident in my ability to operate effectively in its challenging environment, often described by the commanders of the day as "one tough neighborhood."

U.S. Central Command is located at MacDill Air Force Base in Tampa. It has never been an assignment for an officer looking to have an easy time. Central Command's mission is to command and control forces deployed to the Central Region and conduct exercises and combat operations when circumstances dictate. In 1994 it was one of five geographical combatant or war-fighting commands and is a premier assignment for a hard-charging officer in any of the four services seeking to make a difference in planning and executing America's commitments in a tough, challenging, and vitally important part of the world. USCENTCOM's vast area of responsibility in 2003 included 27 countries in the Middle East, East Africa, and Central and South Asia. Its service components (Army, Navy, Air Force, and Marine Corps) maintain bases throughout the Arabian Gulf and Central Asia. An assignment to USCENTCOM offers an officer an opportunity to expand his professional knowledge, travel widely, and gain the kind of military and cultural experiences that could never come from a book or a classroom.

In March 1980, President Carter decided any outside attempt to control the Central Region in the aftermath of the Iran hostage crisis and the Soviet invasion of Afghanistan would be taken as an assault on U.S. vital interests. An ad hoc Rapid Deployment Joint Task Force was established to enforce the new Carter Doctrine. It evolved into a regional unified command and was designated U.S. Central Command in 1983 under the command of General Robert C. Kingston, USA. General Kingston was one of the toughest combat commanders I had ever met. I had served as his aide-de-camp when he commanded the 2nd Infantry Division in Korea in 1979. He was a no-nonsense soldier; holder of the Distinguished Service Cross and multiple Silver and Bronze Stars for combat heroism in both the Korean and Vietnam Wars, he was a superb choice to lead this vitally important command.

Central Command had essentially been on a wartime footing since the late 1980s. It was severely tested during the Iran–Iraq War. Iranian mining of the Arabian Gulf and the near sinking of USS *Stark* in 1987 resulted in the president's direction to plan and carry out a retaliatory response codenamed Operation *Praying Mantis*. USCENTCOM forces destroyed Iranian oil platforms and severely damaged or neutralized several Iranian naval vessels. Iraq invaded Kuwait in August 1990. Coalition forces under USCENTCOM initiated Operation *Desert Storm* in January 1991 and by late February a cease-fire was declared. The Iraqi military was badly defeated, having lost over twenty-five hundred tanks, nearly twenty-two hundred artillery pieces, three hundred aircraft, and many personnel. No-fly zones imposed by the U.S. were established to prevent Saddam from attacking his own people or threatening Kuwait. The no-fly zone established south of the 32nd Parallel was enforced by USCENTCOM utilizing the naval and air forces of its subordinate Joint Task Force Southwest Asia for over fifteen years.

In addition to containing Iraq, USCENTCOM conducted Operation *Provide Relief,* an airlift in August 1992 to address widespread starvation in Somalia. USCENTCOM later led the Multinational Coalition in Operation *Restore Hope* to secure transport and distribution centers, secure relief convoys, and assist humanitarian relief organizations. It also commanded operations to withdraw all United Nations forces from Somalia in 1995.

USCENTCOM's near-continuous presence strategy in the Central Region emphasized deterrence through forward presence, combined exercises, and security assistance programs, assisted by the power projection and combat readiness of forward-deployed forces. It was an effective, long-range approach to maintaining peace and stability. Saddam's threats to the region between 1994 and 1998 tested American resolve and resulted in major troop deployments. USCENTCOM conducted Operation *Infinite Reach*, launching missile strikes against suspected terrorist targets in Afghanistan and Sudan in August 1998. During Operation *Desert Fox* the following December, missile strikes over three days were conducted against Iraqi WMD (weapons of mass destruction) program installations and major command-and-control facilities.[1]

I was assigned to USCENTCOM as a war planner in the Plans and Policy Directorate (CCJ5). It was an exciting and challenging time during which I participated in the development of the Two Major Theater of War Strategy. As the chief of the War Plans Division during the third and final year of my tour, I led the continued development of Central Command's plans to support the strategy. Prior to my departure in the spring of 1997, the plans team submitted the Iraq war plan for Joint Staff approval. The War Plans Division benefited from the leadership and professional acumen of General Binnie Peay, USA, who personally guided Central Command's planning efforts and took a personal interest in every detail. Three years of planning for war in the Central Region was as educational as it was demanding and professionally satisfying. I served a year-long tour of peacekeeping duty as Senior Observer and United States Contingent Commander with United Nations Forces along the Iraq–Kuwait Demilitarized Zone in 1997–98 before returning for a second tour at USCENTCOM as the executive assistant to the commander, General Anthony C. Zinni, USMC, from 1998 to 2000. I accompanied him on numerous trips to nearly every country in the Central Region, including the Central Asian States of the former Soviet Union, Pakistan, and the Gulf Cooperation Council (GCC) States. It was a fascinating time during which I was encouraged to converse with members of national military and diplomatic staffs and learn as much as I could about their immediate and long-range concerns. I also gained an appreciation for the terrain in Pakistan and Afghanistan that would serve me well during America's long war in Afghanistan (Operation *Enduring Freedom*). Long discussions with General Zinni concerning the Central Region's issues, and my exposure to numerous diplomats, military leaders, and heads of state—including President Mubarak of Egypt, King Abdullah of Jordan, and President Musharraf of Pakistan—provided me the equivalent of a PhD-level education in Middle Eastern studies, strategy, and military diplomacy that could not have been acquired elsewhere. The general's genius for military diplomacy ensured our nation's good relations throughout the region. His honest and objective discussions with Egyptian and GCC leaders made him an immensely popular figure with the Arabs and his efforts to provide security assistance and training to the militaries of the Central Asian States were a key factor in securing basing to support our operations in Afghanistan during Operation *Enduring Freedom.*

In the spring of 2000, I departed USCENTCOM to assume the responsibilities of the Chief of Staff of the Multinational Force & Observers (MFO) and Commander, United States Task Force Sinai. This task force is the American contribution to the MFO that monitors compliance of the peace treaty between Israel and Egypt and ensures the demilitarization of the Sinai. I had orders to coordinate and organize the separate American units and staffs in the Sinai under a single Task Force Command and assume command of it shortly after my arrival. I was confident in my ability to meet the challenge of this dual-hatted position. I had been most fortunate to have held multiple command and staff assignments at the tactical level, and the exceptional education and mentorship I had received from Generals Peay and Zinni, coupled with a tour in Iraq with the United Nations, and six continuous years focused on the critical issues confronting operations and planning in the Central Region, more than prepared me for this undertaking. I enthusiastically looked forward to senior-level command in a demanding multinational military environment and simultaneously serving as the chief of staff. It would be my second multinational assignment in what would be a series of such assignments that would follow in the challenging Middle East and provide a huge appreciation for the intricacies of multinational command.

CHAPTER 3

Leading U.S. and Multinational Forces in the Sinai

A true leader has the confidence to stand alone, the courage to make tough decisions, and the compassion to listen to the needs of others.

—General Douglas MacArthur

I had wanted an assignment in the Sinai since I was a company commander at Fort Campbell, Kentucky. The 1982 deployment of the 1st Battalion, 502nd Infantry—the first battalion of the 101st Airborne Division to support the mission—was a major event in the division's history and I could not help being envious as I watched the unit prepare to go. In 1997, I was serving with the United Nations Iraq–Kuwait Observation Mission (UNIKOM) as the senior logistics officer and commander of the U.S. Observer Contingent. During a force build-up in Kuwait in response to Saddam's non-compliance with United Nations inspections, Colonel Larry Casper, the commander of the United States Military Observation Group–Washington (USMOG–W), met with me in Kuwait and introduced me to a new concept he was staffing that would streamline command and control of American units assigned to the Multinational Force and Observers (MFO) in the Sinai Peninsula under a single commander. He asked me if I was interested in going to the Sinai when I completed my tour with UNIKOM to serve as the MFO chief of staff and lay the groundwork for the proposed command. I liked the idea but, after serving a year in Iraq, I thought it would be best to return to a stateside assignment. In December 1997, General Zinni offered me an opportunity to return to Central Command to serve on his personal staff. I reported for duty as his executive assistant in July 1998. By the fall, however, recognizing my assignment would only be for two years, I met with several officers assigned to USMOG–W during one of the general's numerous visits to the Pentagon and asked them to submit my name to fill the MFO chief of staff position as a follow-on assignment in the summer of 2000.

The MOG's staff officers occupy office space in the bowels of the Pentagon and work for the Army Deputy Chief of Staff for Operations (DCSOPS). By the end of 1998, I had met with these officers on several occasions to coordinate my assignment in the Sinai. My persistence paid off and I was on the docket to take the position in

June 2000. I had all but forgotten the changes in the MFO staffing Colonel Casper had introduced to me in Kuwait but, by November 1999, the Army had decided the MFO chief of staff would be dual-hatted and assume command of the three separate Army commands that served in the Sinai. The separate units included an infantry battalion, a forward support battalion, and the United States Army Element to which American officers, noncommissioned officers, and administrative support personnel who worked on the MFO staff were assigned. Lieutenant General Dick Cody, USA, the DCSOPS and my War College and seminar classmate, told me I would be first commander of the U.S. Task Force (TF) and I would have the challenge of developing it in its first year as an active operational organization. I attended the Commander's Courses at Fort Benning and Fort Leavenworth that are designed to orient prospective battalion and brigade-level commanders for the rigors of command and to refamiliarize them with up-to-date training techniques, fundamental tactics, techniques, procedures, and relevant Army policies. I also attended the Commander's Legal Course in Charlottesville, Virginia, before reporting for duty in the Sinai at the end of June 2000.

The MFO had been deployed as a part of the agreements made by the Camp David Accords in 1982. The treaty that brought peace between Israel and Egypt called for an international peacekeeping force to oversee a demilitarized Sinai after the Israelis withdrew and returned the land to the Egyptians. Both the Israelis and the Egyptians avidly support this force and insist on its continued deployment as well as the continued involvement of the United States. The number of countries that comprise the peacekeeping force, as well as its overall strength, has varied over the years. When I arrived, there were 11 nations that contributed troops or staff members to the multinational force. The official MFO observers are U.S. State Department or other, contracted, American civilian employees and are designated the Civilian Observer Unit. The civilian hires are normally former military personnel with a wide variety of experience. The mission of the MFO is to observe and report any discrepancies or violations of the peace treaty. Its essential tasks include operating 30 remote checkpoints and observation posts, within a designated area known as Zone C, and conducting reconnaissance patrols. The bulk of these duties are accomplished by infantry battalions provided by Fiji, Colombia, and the United States. The duties of the soldiers on these remote sites are arduous, at times hazardous, and more often boring. Long days and few sources of entertainment provide time for extensive individual combat and physical-training sessions and educational opportunities that noncommissioned officers, particularly from the United States, conduct and closely monitor. In addition to the desert operation, an Italian naval contingent ensures freedom of navigation through the Strait of Tiran in the Gulf of Aqaba. The environment is truly international; I immediately took to it given my previous experiences with the United Nations in Iraq and Somalia and my almost continuous service in the Gulf region since 1994.

Over the years, the Civilian Observer Unit and members of the Force have observed and reported minor violations of the treaty by both sides. There have been no serious challenges to the peace accord or significant violations of the Sinai, however, by either side since the MFO's deployment. As a result, there was a tendency to be somewhat complacent about duty there in all the assigned national contingents, something that bothered me almost from the beginning of my assignment. It has always been my experience that complacency leads to shoddy staff work, poor morale, breaches of discipline and, worse, unnecessary accidents, injuries, and fatalities.

I was welcomed to the Sinai as the chief of staff, but no one, particularly the Norwegian force commander, wanted anyone to "make waves." Change is not something with which multinational organizations are comfortable and though MFO Director General Ambassador Arthur Hughes and Major General Tellefsen publicly welcomed the reorganization of the American units into a single command, it was apparent the force commander viewed it as unnecessary and an effort to gain the United States a greater role in commanding the MFO. Another concern of his was that a dual-hatted chief of staff would focus more on his duties as a commander than as his chief of staff and second senior officer in the MFO. Convincing him otherwise would prove to be an uphill climb.

XVIII Airborne Corps was designated Task Force Sinai's next higher command. The team of American officers we assembled from the MFO staff built Task Force Sinai by thoroughly examining the documents that governed XVIII Airborne Corps and ensured everything we did was in accordance with the unit's training guidance and command orders, policies, and directives. Despite the extensive staff work accomplished by the Pentagon-based MOG staff, including briefings to the Corps staff, the Corps headquarters and commander appeared to be taken almost completely unaware of Task Force Sinai's imminent activation in October 2000. Nearly every detail—from the TF's organization to its official heraldic colors and the publication of its official orders—had been coordinated. USMOG–W and the American staff officers in the Sinai were never out of contact with the Corps on the issues pertaining to the unit's activation. The Army did not change its decision to activate the command and plans to proceed with it continued.

Major General John Ryneska, Deputy Commanding General, XVIII Airborne Corps, arrived at MFO's headquarters on 10 October to preside over the command's activation ceremony. In our first meeting, I was informed the TF would not include command of the infantry battalion. All I could expect was a coordination linkage with the battalion for force-protection issues. I thought it best to just get on with it, thinking the Army could sort it out later. General Ryneska had spent a lot of time prior to our meeting with General Tellefsen. He told me the key point for the Task Force Sinai commander to understand was that anything the TF did was to be transparent to the MFO. I understood that and assured him the command's actions would be no different from any of the other national contingents. Our principal mission was to enhance the overall efficiency of the American effort. I felt efficiency could be enhanced through superior training, improved safety policies, discipline, fiscal responsibility, and professional development of our officers and noncommissioned officers. There were several issues in the 1st Support Battalion that only a senior commander on the ground and in that battalion commander's direct chain of command could address. I suspected the command issue with the infantry battalion would be modified at some point and fully brought under TF command.

The activation of Task Force Sinai on 11 October was a magnificent event. Participating in the ceremony was the 2nd Battalion, 505th Parachute Infantry Regiment, the 1st United States Army Support Battalion, and the TF staff led by the MFO's chief of logistics who was dual hatted as the TF deputy commander. The entire MFO seemed in good spirits. The troops were rightfully pleased with their performance, and I was satisfied I had said the right things to defuse any suspicion about the command's purpose or mission. I emphasized the "transparency" of the reorganization of the American contingent, but added that its improved efficiency, morale, and overall performance would make it a better national asset in support of the MFO's mission. It was an historic day for the U.S. Army and the MFO, and I was hopeful both the U.S. and multinational leadership accepted the change. I was sadly mistaken and tough days were ahead for all of us associated with the new command.

A professional American military officer understands, appreciates, and accepts the reality of change. The officer corps places a high degree of professional importance on an officer's ability to adapt to his environment. An officer's loyalty to the command is essential to every aspect of unit effectiveness and morale. My challenge was getting the young American officers to adapt and excel and simultaneously convince the multinational command the change in the American command structure would enhance American support to the mission and benefit the entire force. In other words, I had to convince leaders of all ranks and nationalities that change was good and that, in time, all would benefit both personally, professionally, and organizationally.

It was a tough time in the Sinai. The Al-Aqsa or second Intifada had begun in late September. This wave of violence between Palestinian Arabs and the Israelis, that resulted from the failure of the 2000 Camp David summit to reach a final agreement on the Israeli–Palestinian peace process, significantly raised the risk to our transporters and other personnel who routinely left the compounds to execute their duties. The TF and MFO operations and logistics staff managed the risk superbly and it was exciting to interact with its principal members about force-protection measures, route selection, and increased reconnaissance efforts. As the MFO chief of staff and the American contingent commander, I was able to work with significant authority through both the MFO and the American chain of command to fine tune force-protection and safety procedures. Never was the need for a streamlined and coordinated chain of command in the Sinai more important as we dealt with the reality of the Israeli–Palestinian conflict and the specter of terrorism. During this critical point in the conflict, Mr. Doug Kent, the chief of the Civilian Observer Unit, informed me of his concerns with continuing observation flights over the critical area designated Zone D on our maps due to the large Arab and Palestinian presence in the Israeli urban areas and the Gaza Strip. Mr. Kent told me his observers and our helicopter pilots had noted the presence of small-arms weapons, including rocket-propelled grenade launchers, among pockets of civilians in and around the marketplaces. Observation of Zone D was critical to maintaining situational awareness of any military activity along the border with Israel and there had to be a way we could do it while mitigating risk to our aircraft and observers. I discussed the concerns with both Mr. Kent and the commander of the aviation company. I thought we could change the usual flight route to avoid directly flying over the built-up areas and maintain enough standoff to still observe any significant military activity. We drew a new route on our maps with several "dog legs" or deviations in the flight and agreed to fly the proposed route the next day. I was very pleased both our pilots and the observers were satisfied the mission could still be accomplished without any degradation in reporting after we completed the flight. As simple as it was to make this adjustment, it took both the authority of the American contingent commander, in coordination with his aviation company and the Force chief of staff, to actually propose, plan, and institute the change in the flight route. Mr. Kent was particularly happy; his kind remarks were personally very rewarding.

After assessing the readiness of the 1st Support Battalion, I was amazed to learn its soldiers were not provided a basic issue of combat equipment: there was only 50 helmets in the entire battalion; there was not enough weapons to issue every soldier; there was only a handful of pistol belts, rucksacks, or any other fundamental items of issue; and bottled water was a substitute for canteens. I was astounded! Could this have possibly been the case for nearly twenty years? Had anyone bothered to report it? Did anyone care? The TF deputy commander and I worked with the battalion's S-4 and his logistics staff members, and the commander of the 1st Corps Support Command, to get these vital items to outfit and protect our soldiers.

Shortly after the command's activation, I was informed XVIII Airborne Corps had decided to place Task Force Sinai under the command of the 1st Corps Support Command. I welcomed this development, but I was alarmed when its commander, only one month later, informed me I was in trouble with the MFO chain of command for not concentrating on my duties as chief of staff. Those closest to me in the Office of the MFO Chief of Staff, including my British civilian secretary and deputy chief of staff, an Australian lieutenant colonel, shook their heads in disbelief. You did not have to be a genius to understand that the MFO chain of command was uncomfortable with a dual-hatted chief of staff, sought to discourage the arrangement, and return to what had been the status quo.

I enjoyed working with the international members of the staff who were always cooperative and friendly. I was totally engaged in the MFO's vital staff work and focused on American TF issues only after MFO matters were put to bed for the day. The American chief of logistics held the systems critical to our sustainment and budget in check and worked closely with me and the 1st Support Battalion to get our equipment on order and delivered. Our focus was squarely on operations, communications, long-range planning, contingent maintenance requirements, safety, and general administration. Twenty-hour days were common for me. Saturday afternoons were devoted to TF planning and writing annual and quarterly training guidance and other documents designed to focus the command, clarify policy, and improve training, and safety procedures. I captured fundamental thoughts on my philosophy of leadership and command in 10 points which I placed on a 3 × 5 index card and issued to every leader in the TF. My intent was to highlight the primacy of our MFO mission, then point out what was important to our success as an American command in a multinational setting. The points were as follows:

1. The MFO mission coupled with personal and unit readiness to respond to any contingency is our focus.
2. The fundamental elements of a military unit's success are leadership, discipline, and training.
3. An elite unit executes the fundamentals, fundamentally well.
4. Discipline is evident in personal and unit conduct, military bearing, and appearance, attention to detail in training and safety, maintenance, and property accountability.
5. A leader is first and foremost a soldier of character who is approachable and readily available.
6. A decision dictates a full-out effort. There are no shortcuts to excellence.
7. Essential elements of training include personal fitness, individual combat skills, weapons proficiency, and squad and platoon live-fire exercises.
8. Quiet, confident competence is the mark of the professional.
9. We are in the business of finding ways, not excuses.
10. Always do your best. Excellence is the standard.

There was not an officer or soldier in the Sinai who disagreed with the fundamental significance of these points, but there was resentment nonetheless as many complacent leaders came to grips with the changes in training and operations these points led them to make. I had learned long before this assignment that change under most circumstances is best accomplished gradually. Soldiers tend to resent changes thrust upon them too quickly. I believed we had the time to avoid making radical changes, but some of our officers were reluctant to accept a more dynamic environment and training regimen regardless of how slowly changes were made. Only attrition could solve that problem. The re-orientation of the Task Force to a true readiness and mission-oriented posture only became a reality three or four months before the end of my tour.

As the chief of staff, I interacted with all the national contingents on a daily basis to improve the lot of every individual soldier and enhance the general efficiency of the force. I was particularly determined to improve conditions on the desolate outposts where Fijian, Colombian, and American infantrymen sweated it out every day. It was the Colombians, however, for whom I felt the most empathy. They were solid combat veterans of the drug war in their country. Coming to the Sinai on a true, stable, peacekeeping mission was considered good duty for all ranks. They never complained and were content to occupy their outposts, do their jobs, and not be in daily life-threatening situations that defined their combat service in Colombia. Many of these tough men had been wounded and the ugly scars of bullet and shrapnel wounds on their legs and arms were evident when they were in the gym and on the playing fields in athletic clothing. My street and classroom Spanish was a good basis to develop good speaking skills, but I was out of practice and did not speak it particularly well. I could hold a conversation but only with a great deal of effort. The language had been very useful to me in UNIKOM where I had worked closely with Argentinean engineers and Uruguayan transporters. In the Sinai, the language helped me to develop a better working relationship with the Colombian chain of command. I frequently visited their outposts, reporting their facilities' deficiencies to our engineers and logisticians; we were able to improve the maintenance of the outposts and the general welfare of the individual soldier. The battalion commander appreciated our efforts and decorated the force commander and me with the Colombian Commendation Medal during a quarterly medals parade in November 2000. It was a wonderful gesture that I immensely appreciated and humbly accepted along with the steady recognition I received from the other contingents. The mementos they presented in appreciation of our close relationships filled the shelves in my office.

A former commandant of cadets at the Virginia Military Institute once advised me and several of my classmates to "Avoid being the first into any action and the last to leave." I reflected on that guidance quite a bit as I contemplated the subtle disdain from many officers in Task Force Sinai and the MFO front office for our new training programs. I was advised by Fort Bragg and the force commander that conducting live-fire training at squad and platoon level in the 1st Support Battalion was dangerous and would detract from the MFO mission. The poor attitude toward meaningful training, coupled with the shameful lack of individual combat equipment, was totally alien to me. I was not at all surprised when the Jessica Lynch affair became public knowledge in April 2003. Private Lynch and the 507th Maintenance Company were ambushed in An Nāṣirīyah, a city in southern Iraq, in the early days of the invasion. The soldiers' readiness for battle was highly suspect. The poor readiness of these soldiers highlighted the sorry state of realistic combat training the vast bulk of Army support troops received at that time. Army Deputy Chief of Staff for Force Development Lieutenant General Stephen Speakes would later state, "We found to our horror that this was a logistics unit that had no major weapons, no night vision, none of the modern enablers of war." He added, "Well, they were never supposed to fight."[2] My efforts to upgrade the status of training and readiness of all soldiers, including women, were opposed "tooth and nail" by the MFO commander and the commander of the 1st Support Battalion. Under pressure from the MFO, the commander of the 1st Corps Support Command directed me to stop planning live-fire exercises. We nonetheless made considerable headway in other areas of defensive training and fundamental marksmanship. The soldiers loved it.

The officer corps is entrusted with the readiness of the Army and its soldiers. I was deeply concerned many of our junior leaders did not understand what was expected of them regardless of the branch in which they were commissioned. Our history has shown time after time that, on any given battlefield, all soldiers, be they front-line combat or support troops, inevitably will fight. I remained steadfast to providing the training our young soldiers and officers so desperately needed to survive and win in combat and ensure the unit's peacekeeping efficiency.

My close association with the other national contingents in the Sinai was a great professional joy. Foreign nationals have a certain fascination and respect for American soldiers. Soldiers of nearly every nation view the Americans as top-notch fighting men who know how to win wars. Our total dismemberment of the Iraqi Army in Operation *Desert Storm* had impressed our friends and allies in ways few could imagine in the war's aftermath. As a battalion commander in Panama, I had many conversations with Argentinean, Uruguayan, and Honduran officers about maneuver

Reviewing officers at the activation ceremony of TF Sinai: Major General Ryneska, Colonel Tiso, and Major General Tellefsen. (SFC Terry Webster)

Assuming command of U.S. Task Force Sinai, 11 October 2000.

warfare, our use of fire support, and logistics issues. I used these opportunities to conduct mini professional-development classes, albeit in a conversational manner, seeking to discuss their approach to operational warfare to avoid a one-sided, professorial-like environment. The Colombians loved to talk about their combat experiences. We would gather in their Officers Club, get a beer, and discuss military subjects sitting in chairs arranged in a circle. Once again, my rough Spanish was appreciated, but I kept an English speaker close by my side. I always left these sessions with an appreciation that Americans do not have a monopoly on military expertise and professionalism and a lot can be learned from allies.

I enjoyed my relationship with the fun-loving Fijians. They are superb soldiers and excellent athletes. Many of them were combat veterans of service in Lebanon. Many had been wounded in action. My greatest joy came from watching them on the drill field. The Fijians have an outstanding military heritage as a member nation of the British Commonwealth. They executed the Queen's drill in a manner the finest British regiments would no doubt admire, or even envy. The Fijians provided an honor guard for all visiting officials to the command. The MFO was justifiably big on military honors for visiting dignitaries and the Fijians never failed to put on a great show.

As the Intifada continued into the spring, Canadian Major General Meating, the force commander who assumed command of the MFO in March 2001, asked me to tour the observation posts he established overlooking the Gaza Strip and report on the activities of the Fijian soldiers who manned them. The conditions on these temporary, but important posts were lousy. The mosquito-infested evenings would have discouraged the most disciplined soldiers, but the Fijians took every assignment in stride. They maintained an around-the-clock watch, rendered accurate reports, and never lost their sense of humor. They, like all soldiers, appreciated an officer that would endure the difficult conditions in which they lived and would always offer me whatever food and drink they had available. I made recommendations to the commander to improve their situation materially; the chief of logistics and the supporting staff came through with what was needed. You do not have to do much to gain the respect and appreciation of allies but providing fundamental mission equipment and general welfare is paramount to any organization's success and morale. Ultimately, soldiers of all nations want a competent chain of command that cares about them. I was honored with numerous invitations to their parties and national observances where I was often asked to speak. Attempts to use a few national expressions were always appreciated. The Fijians are famous for their food and appetite. They encouraged their American friends to wear Fijian native dress to their lavish pig roasts and I enjoyed wearing the colorful island shirts that reminded me of my tour in Hawaii in the late 1980s.

The social atmosphere in the Sinai was as wonderful as it was potentially dangerous. There were 13 officially recognized clubs in North Camp that housed the MFO headquarters. I made it a point to tour the clubs every evening, remaining in uniform to avoid innumerable offers of beers and hard drinks. Everyone knew that, when I was in uniform, I would not partake, but they appreciated my company, and it was a rare party I did not attend. My greatest concerns with these affairs were alcohol related—fighting and driving under the influence. These were concerns more closely associated with the Americans than with our European and Latin friends. Their discipline about alcohol was far more mature, an observation I have made just about everywhere I have been posted. Every country did something different: the Uruguayans had huge barbeques, as did the Aussies; the French loved their champagne parties, and the Hungarians had several traditional events serving their wonderful goulash. National or Independence Days were always observed, and official events followed by parties were the norm. The 1st Support Battalion also had a club and, in the absence of General Order Number One that banned alcohol consumption by service members in Saudi Arabia and Kuwait, I insisted the TF and battalion chain of command looked in frequently to monitor events and act as required to avoid any problems. The International Globetrotters Club was particularly enjoyable. The favorite haunt of the civilian contractors and British expatriates, the atmosphere was always friendly, and the welcome mat was always out for their "Yank" chief of staff. The guys and gals in this club were older and more mature and they understood the real issues that drove the MFO. You can learn a lot at a bar if you take the time to talk to folks in a friendly way and get to know them. I held a great deal of respect for the expats, and I attended their dances, dart board competitions, and other special events whenever I could.

In June 2001, the expats and citizens of British Commonwealth nations held a wonderful black tie birthday celebration in honor of Her Majesty the Queen. I was delighted to be invited as the American representative of the original "rogue" 13 colonies and asked to give a short speech in which I outlined my admiration and respect for all things "British." It was yet another event that demonstrated the need for a senior American officer to always be ready to speak in an intelligent, diplomatic, and charming manner.

I visited the Italian contingent on duty in the southern area of the Sinai as time would permit. The American infantry battalion is the predominant element at South Camp on the outskirts of Sharm El-Sheik, the Egyptian resort city often referred to by Egyptian President Mubarak as "Peace City." The Italians provided the naval piece of the multinational force, and their highly disciplined, well-trained crews operated three patrol craft built specifically for patrolling the Straits of Tiran. They maintained a separate headquarters where their patrol craft were moored and seemed to enjoy a good life on the beach. The Italians were well liked by locals and tourists alike. They seemed to enjoy my company, something I attributed in part to my Italian heritage. I spoke only a few words of Italian, but that didn't seem to matter. I have never been comfortable aboard ships. I never developed my "sea legs" and always tended to get seasick. My duty with General Zinni had often placed me on ships at sea. An avid fisherman, he had often engaged with high-ranking governmental and military officials while fishing and, when I had to be there, I did my utmost to persevere. The Italians frequently offered to take me on patrol in the Straits and I jumped at the chance. Besides, the ship's chef always prepared a special meal at sea when visitors were aboard. On the day I chose to sail with them, the water was very calm and smooth. It was a bright and sunny day; I thought I had it made. It was not long, however, before I started getting that nauseous feeling that inevitably leads to the sweats and vomiting. I tried to cover it up but to no avail. I was feeling poorly when Commander Chionna, the Italian contingent commander, offered me the ship's cabin to lie down. I fell asleep and awoke to an invitation to a lasagna dinner with the ship's officers. I could not do it justice, but I complimented the chef profusely for a beautiful Italian meal that reminded me of my mother's cooking, the ultimate Italian compliment. I learned my lesson though; the next time I got on board I had a regimen of Dramamine that kept me straight. It was important to me to get back to sea with the Italians as soon as possible and make up for my previous failure.

The manning document for the MFO did not include a billet for a deputy commander so, in the absence of the commander, the MFO chief of staff is the highest-ranking officer in the command. Our force commander was on leave in the fall of 2000; I was asked to preside over the change of command of the Italian contingent. It was an official duty and I loved it. I lauded the exceptional command qualities of Commander Chionna in my remarks, pointing particularly to his strength and abilities at sea while quickly referring to my own "inadequacies" as a sailor. The sailors with whom I had gone on patrol stood in the ranks with broad smiles on their faces. Later, the Italians presented me a framed photo of their ships on patrol in the Red Sea acknowledging that I was a "Skilled soldier who had become a sailor" serving with the Italian Navy. Events like these reminded me that you do not have to be the best at everything there is to do, but you do need to participate and do your best. It also reminded me a little self-deprecating humor can go a long way in international relations. I truly appreciated the Italians; they returned that appreciation many times over.

I reveled in this wonderful, multinational environment. There were countless opportunities to meet dignitaries from the contributing nations and they were quick to show their appreciation for any additional effort that may have been expended to support their national contingent. This was particularly true of the Hungarians. The Hungarian contingent provided the military police to the international force. Service in the MFO had been a bold step for them and visitors from various ministries of the Hungarian Government were frequent. The visits inevitably involved official dinners and other events that allowed us to get to know one another and engage socially as well as officially. I had the distinct pleasure of meeting Colonel Janos

Isaszegi, the director of the Hungarian Joint Operations Center. Janos attended the Hungarian National Day parade in the Sinai. He was a brilliant officer with degrees in electrical engineering and a doctorate in economics. Janos surprised me with his ability to speak English, Russian, German, and Ukrainian, even as he studied French and Italian. We became excellent friends. In May 2001, I was in Rome with the chief of logistics and the force finance officer to present an annual budget briefing to the director general of the MFO. I took the opportunity to visit Janos at the NATO Defense College where he was a student. He had just been notified he had been selected for promotion to brigadier general; we celebrated his good fortune by having dinner. He was particularly appreciative of my close association with the Hungarian contingent in the Sinai and I was honored when he specifically mentioned my assistance in dispatches to General Lajos Urban, vice chief of the Hungarian Defense Staff. Janos would later serve as Coalition Chief of Liaison on the Combined Joint Task Force-7 staff at Camp Victory in Iraq in 2003 and would make numerous visits to the Polish-led multinational division during my assignment as senior American liaison officer and adviser to the commanding general.

Duty in the MFO was not unlike that on any number of Army posts in the continental United States when it came to social events and holidays. In overseas posts, the importance of such things as Thanksgiving and Christmas observances, unit functions such as traditional, dress-uniform affairs, and informal "get togethers" take on even greater importance. The opportunity to speak at various events brought me closer to the officers and soldiers of the TF and the international staffs at both North and South Camps. I was particularly proud to serve as the principal speaker at the 1st Support Battalion's Winter Formal in December 2000, an invitation I never thought would be offered given the battalion commander's reluctance to accept the Army's directed change of command that had so significantly changed the battalion's standards, culture, and overall military environment. I was encouraged by the opportunity to speak to the battalion's leaders in a relaxed, social setting and thoroughly enjoyed the evening.

In the spring of 2001, the commander of the 1st Battalion, 21st Infantry, asked me to serve as the unit's guest speaker for an Expert Infantryman's Badge Ceremony at the MFO base at South Camp, which was located on the outskirts of Sharm El-Sheikh. The Expert Infantryman's Badge is a prestigious award presented to those infantry soldiers who pass a series of rigorous examinations that test their physical endurance, marksmanship, fundamental combat skills, and overall professional acumen. The ceremony was held one evening immediately following the completion of the last qualifying event, a grueling three-hour, 12-mile march. I was thrilled to do this. The loose linkage of the infantry battalion to Task Force Sinai without a formal command arrangement made opportunities like this invaluable to me as the senior American commander in the Sinai. Opportunities to be visible in large events like this ensured the troops knew a higher-level American commander in the Sinai could be called upon if the situation merited to serve their needs and represent them on all matters impacting their lives so far from MFO headquarters.

The best opportunity to speak to the infantry battalion and the international staff at South Camp came on 12 December 2000. This date marked the 15th anniversary of the tragic loss of 248 soldiers, primarily from the 3rd Battalion, 502nd Infantry, who, after the successful completion of their peacekeeping assignment in the Sinai, crashed on take-off from a refueling stop at Gander, Newfoundland, on 12 December 1985. The commander of the ill-fated battalion had been both a mentor and a close friend of mine. Knowing this, Lieutenant Colonel Rich Hooker, commander of the 2nd Battalion, 505th Parachute Infantry Regiment (PIR), asked me to speak at the dedication of a memorial to the "Gander Battalion" that was placed in front of the South Camp Headquarters. The loss of Lieutenant Colonel Marvin Jeffcoat in 1985 had made me even more determined to serve in the Sinai. He had been an exceptional officer who I first met in 1976. Then Major Jeffcoat had been assigned to the 1st Battalion, 506th Infantry, as the Battalion S-3 (Operations) and I was assigned as his assistant operations officer. We worked for a great commander named Lieutenant Colonel (later Lieutenant General) James W. Crysel and our brigade commander was the now famous General, and former Secretary of State, Colin Powell. The years I served under these men remain among the finest and most memorable of my entire career. "Jeff" was a colorful and handsome officer who had fought in Vietnam with the famed 173rd Airborne Brigade. His distinguished combat record included award of the Silver Star, seven Bronze Stars, and two Purple Hearts. He was unmarried, wore a mustache (quite the exception for an airborne officer), and was quite a hit with the ladies. He was a superb tactician and an exceptional leader. He loved the company of soldiers and we loved him. His loss at Gander highlighted the huge magnitude of the loss of so many American peacekeepers on that fateful day in 1985. All of us were very touched by the magnificent memorial to their memory. Shortly after this ceremony, the paratroopers of the 505th PIR completed their mission and returned to Fort Bragg.

On 1 March 2001, after commanding the MFO for four years, Major General Tellefsen relinquished command to Major General Robert G. Meating of Canada. I welcomed the chance to serve with a commander who was not encumbered by the ways things were before October 2000. By March 2001, many people assigned to the TF and the international staff who had not dealt well with change had moved on to other assignments and the training, logistics, force protection, and safety programs we had initiated the previous October were viewed positively by nearly all who replaced them. General Meating was a major supporter of all the national contingents' activities, and he valued his chief of staff. Our relationship was positive from the beginning. An armor officer who had served as Canada's Joint Intelligence Chief (J-2) in his previous assignment, General Meating had a distinguished record as a commander through brigade level and had served multiple tours with the United Nations in the Middle East. He had served with Americans before and held an American decoration of which he was immensely proud. The command atmosphere changed almost immediately with the arrival of this great gentleman. His presence served to reinforce the understanding a confident, competent, and caring leader can make a huge difference in any organization. General Meating's broad smile, willingness to listen to and discuss issues, and get out and see soldiers, significantly contributed to the overall morale and enthusiasm of the entire command.

The French contingent in the Sinai is primarily responsible for providing fixed-wing aircraft support to the MFO. The French aviators were competent, dedicated to the MFO mission, and always a pleasure to be with. Several members of the civilian staff were French, and one husband and wife team was particularly colorful. Colonel (Retired) Gerard David and his wife Micheline had been with the MFO for over ten years. Gerard had served the bulk of his military career in the French Foreign Legion, a fact of which he was immensely proud. As the chief of staff, I tried to stay cognizant of anything noteworthy in the national history of our contributing nations or their respective militaries. There was no better way to honor Gerard and the French contingent than to pay tribute to the French Foreign Legion on Cameroon Day, 30 April. On that day in 1863, a company of legionnaires under the command of Captain Danjou fought a legendary battle against the Mexican Army, during which nearly every one of its men was killed in action, but only after they had exacted a large toll on the Mexican force of over two thousand men. Their achievement has long been recognized as a symbol of self-sacrifice and gallantry that characterizes the true spirit and discipline of the Legion. My office staff, in coordination with British expat employees in the MFO mess hall, managed to coordinate a wonderful coat and tie and service dress-uniform affair at the Officers Club that included a cake-cutting ceremony in the finest traditions of the Legion. The appreciation of the French officers was overwhelming. The goodwill and friendship gained by recognizing our friends and allies on special occasions such as this one was always worth the effort and cost.

The last several months of my command tour were among the most satisfying of my career. The challenges we had faced in forming Task Force Sinai were nearly behind us with the arrival of young officers anxious to train and serve in a tough, disciplined environment. Our efforts to attain situational awareness and intelligence through the classified nets we had established were producing excellent information that we shared with the American infantry battalion and the other national contingents as classification of the material allowed. The relationship between the TF staff and the infantry battalion at South Camp grew stronger as a result. A new 1st Support Battalion commander also made a world of difference in the relationship between the battalion and the TF staff. We became a team and the efficiency and effectiveness the Army had sought by forming U.S. Task Force Sinai had taken root.

As slow as the positive trend had been to develop, it was a welcome transition that bolstered morale and efficiency. These were dangerous times and, as we approached the month of July, we were all increasingly aware of the trouble our nation faced in the Middle East. The Intifada continued unabated and Palestinian and Israeli casualties mounted. Violent incidents in the Gaza Strip were a daily occurrence. MFO personnel were barred from vacationing in Israel as the security risks increased. We enhanced force-protection measures for all MFO convoys operating throughout the Sinai and in Israel. There were alerts regarding possible attacks by the Saudi Arabian terrorist Osama bin Laden against American forces, a reality check for us since the suicide bombing of USS *Cole* by al-Qaeda in October 2000. Underlying all of this was the rumor of a partial withdrawal or reduction of U.S. forces in the Sinai. The Defense Department's intent at the time was to contract logistics and aviation support to civilian companies and cut the U.S. military contribution to the MFO by one third. Shortly after I assumed command of Task Force Sinai, the MFO director general asked me to study how the U.S. Task Force could be streamlined given the efficiencies of improved command and control. I offered that contract support to some of the services provided by the 1st Support Battalion was a viable way to lower the uniform profile in the Sinai, but that the military command and staff structure should not change. The activities of the 1st Support Battalion and the contributions to the international staff that Americans made daily were critical to the MFO's effectiveness. Neither Israeli Prime Minister Ariel Sharon nor Egyptian President Hosni Mubarak supported a full U.S. withdrawal. Withdrawal rumors permeated the entire command and I frequently spoke to soldiers of all the contingents to minimize false rumors and inform them about what we were hearing through official channels about the future of the MFO. The director general was appropriately concerned newspaper articles about an "American withdrawal" from the Sinai, like one that appeared in the *Army Times* in July 2001, could cause considerable stress to both the Egyptians and the Israelis.[3] Change was inevitable, but any change in this environment seemed to always create a discouraging sense of stress and disapproval. There was considerable discussion that the aging, Vietnam-vintage UH-1H "Huey" helicopter fleet would have to be replaced at some point in the near future. Many international staffers believed this would significantly change the MFO's operational appearance and lead some to think a withdrawal was planned as the aircraft were switched out. I was amused and amazed by this short-sightedness and false assumption. I could only imagine the heartache and disapproval that occurred in the Army when horses were eventually replaced by tanks. My sense was little would change for our aviation unit for at least 3–4 years and that proved to be accurate.

In the wake of these and other concerns, the MFO athletic and physical training coordinators from Australia stepped up the athletic programs and competitions in both major camps. Soldiers love to see their officers and commanders participate in athletic competition. The Aussies coordinated master's competitions to get the over-forty crowd more athletically involved and compete for medals and recognition. I know of no better distracter from the challenges and stress of military concerns than athletic competition. Commanders and unit leaders have to lead the way, just as they do in combat and field training, to encourage the large participation necessary to any program's success. When time allowed, I participated in running, swimming, bicycling, and weightlifting competitions, and was encouraged by the enthusiasm my participation, as well as other senior officers, appeared to generate in American and multinational soldiers.

As difficult as life in the Sinai had become compared to previous years, I was beginning to see the fruits of an increasingly successful and efficient MFO and its U.S. contingent. I was particularly pleased not one soldier in the MFO had died in an accident in over a year. It was an unprecedented safety achievement and a tribute in large measure to the reorganization and policies of a single U.S. command structure, our safety and force-protection programs, our involved chain of command, and the MFO staff's close coordination and communication with all national contingents.

It had been an exceptional year in the Sinai. The standup of U.S. Task Force Sinai, the arrival of a new MFO commander, the Intifada, unprecedented force-protection initiatives, new construction requirements, significant personnel changes to the MFO international staff, multiple external budget audits and inspections, significant logistical adjustments, and new and professional training programs, had made what was once described as the "Army's best kept secret" into a professionally satisfying and relatively grueling assignment for all ranks. As much as I loved it, I knew further refinements to the U.S. Task Force and the MFO staff would have to be made by my successor, Colonel Robert G. Fix Sr., USA, to whom I passed the TF and U.S. contingent colors on 26 July 2001.

The TF change-of-command ceremony was the single largest event in recent memory in the Sinai. It appeared that anyone who could take time away from their duties that morning was present on the parade field at Memorial Square. I was touched by the presence of nearly the entire Colombian battalion and the Fijian chorus that sang a traditional farewell at the completion of the parade. The recently arrived 2nd Battalion, 87th Infantry, 10th Mountain Division, had replaced the 1st Battalion, 21st Infantry, from Hawaii and enthusiastically participated in the review with the 1st Support Battalion. In a few years, the command linkage between Task Force Sinai and the infantry battalion would be formalized in accordance with the original TF organizational plan. I suspect everyone eventually saw the value and reasoning of the original plan to create the TF, but the National Guard's assumption of the infantry mission in the MFO from the Regular Army undoubtedly helped to make that decision a reality.

Considering the unhealthy start that characterized the first several months of its existence, I was proud of how the TF had evolved. Our team in the Sinai had developed it with minimal senior-level guidance. The assignment had provided me the opportunity to better appreciate how a multinational, military environment functions given my unique perspective as both a national contingent commander and multinational chief of staff. It is important to understand multinational organizations tend to be operationally lock-step. Dynamic situations and the dynamic actions they require are not their forté. An American commander operating in a multinational environment must be far more patient than he would in a homogenous situation if the organization must change its established routine. Dynamic leadership may not always provide desired results. The force commander was not prepared for an organizational change in October 2000. Change in the multinational environment requires a great deal of coordination and explanation to ensure the cooperation and mission execution of senior commanders. Operations in long-term peacekeeping missions like the MFO or United Nations missions, though inherently dangerous, often become routine and potentially result in a sense of complacency. Discipline may be adversely impacted and attention to detail may slacken. Leadership at the noncommissioned and junior-officer levels is as important in these situations as they are in actual combat. It was very clear to me that multinational organizations seek approval at all levels up to and including the national level before they execute most tasks beyond the norm. National contingents in these organizations are therefore slow to respond to orders or react to change. In most cases, knowledge of the commander's intent is not good enough in the multinational environment to ensure appropriate tactical actions will be taken. Orders are best when they are written in very precise language. Expending energy with frustration and anger is worthless and a waste of time. People are reluctant to assume responsibility in a multinational environment. Energy is better utilized by carefully explaining why things are the way they are, maximizing coordination, and co-opting as many people as possible with close staff coordination and command presence.

As negative as some of these observations may sound, I appreciated the difficulties a multinational force commander has commanding a unit like the MFO or a United Nations organization. The commander must be sensitive to the perceptions and requirements of all the units and nations represented in his command. He must avoid excessive criticism that could lead to the possible withdrawal of national units from the mission. However, there was something else as I reflected on my relationship with the force commanders with whom I had worked—my perception was that an American officer must work exceptionally hard to develop a good and trusted relationship with his commander and the various nationalities with whom he interacts. The need for cultural sensitivity I had come to appreciate during my tour with UNIKOM in 1997 was reinforced by my experiences in the MFO. The credibility one gains from speaking another nation's language, working beside the troops, and participating in their national events and sports activities cannot be measured. These efforts are valuable, force-multiplying actions that will determine the difference between true operational success and "just getting by." The American military is looked upon with tremendous admiration and even envy by many of its foreign comrades. In many cases, an American officer with extensive command assignments, staff and war college training, a strong academic background, and combat experience, may be prejudged as arrogant and difficult to get along with. It is a challenge that can only be overcome with positive personal engagement and a genuine effort to assist in every mission endeavor wherever and whenever he can. This would never be more true than when serving in the assignments I would have with multinational forces during Operation *Iraqi Freedom*.

I regret I could not make the MFO force commander more comfortable with the changes to the U.S. contingent command structure in the last five months of his nearly four-year tour of duty. His actions were typical of numerous military commanders who are slow to accept change, and often find themselves using yesterday's tactics to fight today's wars. As difficult as it made Task Force Sinai's transition, I nonetheless benefited from the experience. My experience complemented my experiences with the United Nations in Somalia and Iraq in the 1990s. They were lessons that would prove invaluable to me in Iraq during Operation *Iraqi Freedom*.

I completed my 13-month tour of duty as Chief of Staff of the Multinational Force and Observers, and Commander, United States Task Force Sinai, in late July 2001. I had been a commissioned officer for 28 years and logically sought another assignment at U.S. Central Command for both personal and professional reasons. Professionally, I thought my background and experience in the Middle East would allow me to have an immediate impact staffing the important issues of the day. The Army insisted I go elsewhere after my change of command. Negotiating with the Army's Personnel Command via telephone and email was frustrating, stressful, time-consuming, and distracting. I looked for a better way and reluctantly turned to Lieutenant General Lawson W. Magruder, III, USA, for assistance; he was an old friend who was serving as the deputy commander of United States Forces Command at Fort McPherson, Georgia. I had had the good fortune of serving with him in the Hawaii-based 25th Infantry "Tropic Lightning" Division when he commanded the 2nd "Warrior" Brigade from 1988 to 1990. A gentleman and an outstanding leader, he was disappointed the Army would not allow a "twilight tour" of my choosing after the tough assignments I had had. He made several calls on my behalf, and I received orders to U.S. Central Command before I relinquished command. I was elated my final years in uniform would be meaningful, relevant, and well spent. I could not have been prouder of U.S. Task Force Sinai, my personal contributions to its establishment as a unified command, and its numerous accomplishments and enhanced value to the Multinational Force & Observers, but little did I know the next several years would be the most challenging of my career.

CHAPTER 4

Fighting the Force-Protection Battle in Saudi Arabia and Afghanistan

To expect the unexpected shows a thoroughly modern intellect.
—Oscar Wilde

I reported for my third tour of duty on the staff of U.S. Central Command (USCENTCOM) in August 2001. Many of my fellow officers and friends thought I was a "glutton for punishment." Staff work in its stressed environment, coupled with long hours and never-ending reports and high-profile briefings, gave cause for many to refer to it by its unofficial name, "SADCOM." The events of September 2001, and the planning for what became decisive campaigns in both Afghanistan and Iraq, placed the staff on a wartime footing. Twelve-hour days or longer were not uncommon. I was quickly deployed to Egypt to participate in Exercise *Bright Star*, a large land, sea, and air exercise with Egyptian forces that had been in existence since 1980. I deployed to Saudi Arabia and Afghanistan in 2002 and, in March 2003, I was given a special assignment in Kuwait. Another war with Iraq to finish off Saddam Hussein was imminent, and I was going to have a front seat for the anticipated invasion of Iraq.

I was initially assigned to the Joint Security Directorate (JSD) of USCENTCOM in an excess billet. I was told no one in the command group was happy about my assignment, including the commander, an old friend named General Tommy Franks, USA. I guessed I was considered "old team," particularly when I learned that pictures of the previous commander had been removed from the headquarters' hallways almost immediately after the change-of-command ceremony in July 2000. Someone suggested I was not considered a high-enough quality senior field-grade officer to serve on the new USCENTCOM staff. I was surprised by the comment as a former battalion commander, just returned from brigade-equivalent command in the Sinai, who had previously served as the executive assistant to the USCENTCOM commander. The deputy commanding general, Lieutenant General Mike DeLong, USMC, and the JSD director, Brigadier General Gary Harrell, USA, quickly assigned me as the deputy director over the incoming designated deputy who was a military police colonel coming from tactical brigade command in Hawaii, the operations officer who was an Air Force colonel with an extensive security police background, and the incumbent who had announced his plans to retire. I was happy to have the position and when General Harrell deployed to Afghanistan to coordinate and command USCENTCOM's newly formed Joint Interagency Coordination Group, I became the de facto director.

The JSD was formed because of the Downing Commission report in 1996 that strongly recommended USCENTCOM establish an organization with the specific mission of assessing security procedures and the security posture of American and other key installations throughout its area of responsibility. The Khobar Towers tragedy in June 1996 had caused considerable alarm that not enough was being done to prevent or mitigate the effects of terrorist attacks. The JSD was staffed with military security professionals; a forward element led by a colonel in Saudi Arabia was quickly established. JSD-Forward physically conducted vulnerability assessments of sites including U.S. embassies, military installations, and key industrial and governmental sites in all the countries to which we had access. JSD-Forward's assessments were designed to identify security weaknesses to installation and unit commanders and recommend how to fix them. When significant resources were required to achieve desirable results, the JSD would make recommendations to allocate specific security related funds to purchase materials, provide equipment, or provide additional security personnel as required to address the identified shortfalls. The JSD was an exciting organization in which to work, with a cutting-edge mission. I thought I was a good fit for the mission and the position to which I was assigned.

The operational tempo increased significantly during the post-September 11 period and the spin-up to fight the Afghanistan campaign. The directorate worked hard to support General Harrell's efforts in Afghanistan, respond to General Franks's regional base security requirements, and support and facilitate vulnerability assessments of installations conducted by our Saudi Arabia-based staff and security personnel. The command group appreciated the professional staffing conducted by the directorate during this period; General DeLong voiced his personal appreciation on several occasions. I was pleased when he told me General Franks was happy with the directorate's work, particularly the operations and security assessment briefings my team prepared and I reviewed and presented every morning at the command update.

In May 2002, the incumbent JSD-Forward director in Saudi Arabia, an Army special forces colonel, left the assignment several months before the end of his normal tour of duty due to a medical emergency in his family. This was a critically important billet. The director provided the leadership and overall management of the directorate's assessment teams tasked to evaluate and report the force-protection status of American and Coalition bases and facilities throughout the commander's area of responsibility. General Harrell temporarily assigned me as the director of JSD-Forward. He fully recognized senior leadership and supervision of this piece of his directorate was critical to the success of the overall force-protection mission. I appreciated his confidence in my abilities to direct and lead this vital organization.

I arrived at Eskan Village on the outskirts of Riyadh early in June 2002, excited about my newfound independence and opportunity to "command" again. Our people lived in comfortable villas built by the Saudis prior to the Gulf War to house the Bedouins. Fortunately for us, the Bedouins thought better of occupying them. Eskan Village provided housing for our troops both during and after the war. I was greeted at the airport by Lieutenant Colonels J. C. Abney and Steve Rathbun, the outgoing and incoming deputies. Both were military police officers with superb records. My in-briefings began as soon as I got in the car; it was very clear I had my hands full. The schedule of vulnerability assessments, personnel, equipment, and coordination issues, and a host of other details that should have been addressed before I arrived were all seemingly on hold for the new director, but our mission was critical to USCENTCOM and things had to change quickly to get our mission back on course. We energized the staff, worked long hours to get our administration and reports updated, our training scheduled and executed, and our headquarters cleaned and decorated. We also closely coordinated our planning efforts with the Joint Counterintelligence Support Element (JCISE), a JSD asset responsible for providing intelligence support for force protection. It served as the Theater Counterintelligence Coordination Authority, an intelligence fusion center that gathered and collated the reports of all counterintelligence assets in the Central Region and ensured they were widely disseminated. The JCISE was led by Lieutenant Colonel Rob Dukat, an Air Force intelligence officer, and, together, we ensured the JCISE and JSD were one team focused on the business of force protection.

I was very concerned about our requirement to execute a comprehensive vulnerability assessment of Afghanistan. There had been little contact with two JSD personnel deployed to Bagram Air Base on a semi-permanent basis by my predecessor early in the war to assist with security efforts there and at other bases throughout the country. There were no reports of their activities or assessments and my sense was they were not fully employed. Scheduling and coordinating vulnerability assessments of our vital facilities in the Bagram–Kabul complex, including the U.S. Embassy, was very important to USCENTCOM's overall force-protection posture. It was a huge challenge that required meticulous planning and a lot of convincing to gain access to the various facilities. With a solid deputy in Steve Rathbun covering Eskan Village, and the directorate well on its way to good health, the team coordinated a series of Pre-Deployment Site Surveys into Afghanistan for the express purpose of developing the scope of the assessment mission, scheduling it in accordance with the desires of the commanders on the ground and, most importantly, explaining to often edgy commanders, who "Do not need any more help," that our mission was to conduct true assistance visits designed to provide force-protection assistance, including materials and funding. I emphasized our reports were intended for their use and the information we gathered provided a database for general situation awareness. Our efforts, in this regard, were enthusiastically supported by the JSD director at USCENTCOM, and my new boss, Colonel James H. Schwitters, USA, who had been selected for promotion to brigadier general. He recognized the need to develop relationships on the ground and was wary of how we would be initially received. He approved of our multiple trips to Afghanistan, and I kept him abreast of our activities.

We pored over the maps of Afghanistan to gain an appreciation for its road complex and the ruggedness of the terrain. I was not a total stranger to the South and Central Asian portion of the USCENTCOM area of responsibility. I had first seen Afghanistan during a fascinating trip to Pakistan on my first mission as General Zinni's executive assistant in July 1998. Our country orientation included a trip to the Siechen Glacier in the Himalayan Mountains near the disputed India–Pakistan border. We were briefed by the commander of the 323rd Infantry Brigade on his soldiers' high-altitude and cold-weather training, and the conduct of his unit's operations on one of the toughest battlefields in the world. We later toured the Special Services Group Headquarters in Cherat, a little over thirty miles southeast of Peshawar, the capital of Khyber Pakhtunkua Province in the Federally Administered Tribal Areas of Pakistan. A former British cantonment and health station in the early 1860s, it is literally carved out of the rock and steep slopes that characterize the area. We observed tough Pakistani special forces soldiers conduct martial arts and counterterrorism demonstrations before moving by helicopter to a military base at Landi Kotal on the western edge of the Khyber Pass, then by vehicle to the forward-most observation post—known as Michni Post—for an orientation on the Khyber Pass. One of the most famous mountain passes in the world, the Khyber Pass is the most important thoroughfare between Afghanistan and Pakistan. It had been the setting for countless invasions, including those of Alexander the Great, the Persians, the Mongols, and the Muslim armies. The British had fought three Afghan Wars and countless battles using the Khyber Pass as its gateway to Afghanistan. The pass had served the great caravans of traders from the Orient and the Middle East for hundreds of years. The steep and treacherous terrain would have been obvious to the most casual tourist. I was struck by the immensity of this difficult border Pakistan shared with Afghanistan and the difficulty any army would encounter sustaining combat forces on this ground for any period. The Pakistanis manned the border with Afghanistan with their Frontier Corps and, before our departure, we had lunch with the officers of the famed Khyber Rifles in their mess hall and toured their barracks facilities. The officers and men of the unit were proud of their heritage and stood tall in their dress khaki uniforms. It was one of several paramilitary organizations serving under the regular British Army when it was stood up in 1896. Its members had been Afridi tribesmen led by British officers provided by regular Indian regiments. Disbanded during the Third Afghan War in 1919, it had been reconstituted in 1946 and eventually transferred to Pakistan in 1947. Many distinguished diplomatic and military figures had visited the facilities in the past and on display was a wall filled with photos of distinguished dignitaries that included the familiar face of General Douglas MacArthur, who had been there in the late 1940s. I left Pakistan not only with an appreciation for the rugged terrain, but with a deep respect for the Pakistani Army and the tough Mujahadin fighters of Afghanistan.

Bagram Air Base was a very busy place when our C-130 Hercules landed late one evening in June 2002. It was the largest American base in Afghanistan, located 40 kilometers north of Kabul. At that time, all aircraft landed at night; on our final approach I could plainly see from the cockpit the tracers of either a local firefight or the celebratory fire for which the Afghans are famous. I was accompanied by Captain Jack Ewell, USMCR, a marine reservist and a good man by any standard. A policeman and SWAT team commander in civilian life, Jack had rugged good looks and a country and western way about him that reminded me of Clint Eastwood. He was older than most captains and I enjoyed his company and friendship; I called him "Clint." We were greeted by our Bagram-based two-man JSD team and quickly moved to their encampment, the headquarters of the 3rd Special Forces Group (SFG), known as Camp Able.

The 3d SFG was commanded by Colonel Joe Celeski, USA, who provided me a cot and living space in his tent. Joe had been a Special Operations Command war planner in 1996 and we had worked together at Scott Air Force Base during numerous planning conferences to develop the deployment data for the Iraq war plan. Joe had a great reputation as a special forces commander. His insights regarding what was going on in Afghanistan, where I should go, and which commanders I should meet were invaluable to me.

The Bagram Air Base garrison at that time was under the overall command of Colonel Scott Pritchett, USA, a tough airborne commander unfamiliar with the USCENTCOM security assessment program and understandably wary of our mission. Scott was the key to any success we could achieve at Bagram; I carefully explained our mission, solicited his input, and discussed scheduling an assessment in accordance with his unit's convenience. He assigned his force-protection officer, Major Jarnot, USA, to show us around the base. The major impressed us with his enthusiasm, work ethic, and general knowledge of the base.

Bagram was a force-protection challenge that merited a lot of attention and engineer support. Most significantly, the large number of mines in and around the complex dictated an immediate reinforcement of mine-clearing equipment. Civilian housing in some cases was within rock-throwing range of the base perimeter and Jarnot told us, "We were cased regularly." Efforts to link the base perimeter to a single operations center were still underway and Jarnot was concerned about unreliable communications with all elements, but particularly the non-U.S. forces on the base. He helped arrange a meeting for us with the Bagram counterintelligence team who addressed local issues outside the perimeter and voiced their concern about the effectiveness of the warlords who supposedly patrolled designated sectors outside of the base. The warlords had told them most of the locals were pro-U.S. and strongly feared the Taliban's return should the Americans withdraw. Other meetings held with Air Force security personnel went extremely well; our assessment was highly encouraged by nearly everyone with whom we spoke.

Our team moved on to Kabul where Brigadier General Jack Kern, USA, an old friend of mine serving as the Office of Military Cooperation (OMC) chief at the U.S. Embassy, received me with a smile and gave me an Afghan hat and scarf as a welcome gift. Jack had graduated from the Virginia Military Institute with the class of 1970; I had known him during my first or "Rat" year as a cadet. He was very enthusiastic about our mission and introduced us to several key members of the embassy staff. There was considerable construction scheduled on the embassy grounds and the regional security officer was convinced our assessment would have a positive impact on the final building plans of what would eventually become one of the largest embassy complexes in the world. Construction was scheduled to begin in January 2003. I assured him we would have the right people to look over the grounds and the proposed construction. Overall, General Kern and the embassy staff were very cooperative and appreciated our visit.

General Kern highly recommended we assess the Afghan National Academy. We made a thorough survey of the camp and determined our requirements for the assessment after meeting with camp commander Lieutenant Colonel "Mac" McDonnell, USA, who commanded the 1st Battalion (Airborne), 3rd Special Forces Group. Mac was another old friend of mine and very receptive to our mission. I also got my first look at the Afghan National Army. The Army's 2nd Battalion was in training and the 3rd Battalion was being formed on the academy's grounds. I got a huge appreciation for the training task as I looked at the rugged recruits standing in formation looking for their first meal. Starting an army from scratch is no small undertaking and I watched with a grin of disbelief as I observed another formation taking physical training in various forms of dress and sandals. Fundamental military training always begins with orienting the recruit; how to carry himself, march, speak respectfully, and good old physical training. I thought there were no better ways to establish baseline discipline and a proper orientation for more technical and tactical training, not to mention a shower, a haircut, and a proper uniform. These were hard men and I thought about the seriousness of the undertaking and the resources it would take. Our special forces trainers had a big job ahead of them.

Our efforts during the pre-deployment site surveys succeeded in gaining the confidence of the commanders on the ground and convinced them our team was truly assistance oriented. Encouraged by the endorsement of Combined Joint Task Force-180 Chief of Staff Brigadier General Stanley A. McChrystal, USA, with whom I had an outcall at Bagram before our return to Saudi Arabia, we went about the business of putting together an assessment plan and identifying a team of people with the requisite training and experience to address the vulnerability assessments of our key facilities in Afghanistan.

We returned to Afghanistan in August with a formidable team including expertise in explosive ordnance, physical security, engineering and construction management, food handling and preparation, and communications. We accompanied day and night security patrols along the base perimeter and observed security forces personnel surveilling the perimeter using scopes from within the security operations center. We looked for dead (unobserved) space along the perimeter that could be more easily accessed by infiltrators. Our assessments were detailed and our recommendations called for enhanced night-vision capability and tactical communications to reinforce our security police and their overall ability to maintain 24-hour surveillance of the base. Our recommendations also called for additional construction to reinforce barriers and improve selected defensive measures throughout the base and its long perimeter.

The briefings and "hot wash" initial findings we presented were well received. The out-brief to the chief of staff of XVIII Airborne Corps and director of the staff of Combined Joint Task Force-180 (CJTF-180) at Bagram was initially strained; it was clear he was not happy we had "run around in his back yard." I assumed he had not been advised of our assessment visit since we had not seen him during the survey in August. I knew Brigadier General Benjamin R. Mixon and he grilled me about a briefing point that criticized a unit's inability to attain mutually supporting fires in its current base-defense and force-protection posture. He looked hard at me and said, "Any infantryman would have seen that is not realistic," making reference to the impossible task of attaining mutually supporting fires from various outposts along Bagram's extensive perimeter. Having only reviewed the slides during our drive from Kabul to Bagram, I calmly acknowledged his comment and stated the point should have been written to suggest additional effort be taken to attain mutually supporting fires where it was possible to do so. I directed my team chief to make the necessary correction on the final report and pushed on with the briefing. Upon completion of the briefing, General Mixon thanked our team for its efforts, smiled at me and said, "Okay, Roland, don't misconstrue what I said," shook my hand, and walked out. All the assembled CJTF-180 officers congratulated us and thanked us for our professional efforts, just as the Air Force security personnel responsible for Bagram and the embassy staff had done earlier that morning. I left Bagram Air Base satisfied we had been immensely successful.

Our mission to conduct a vulnerability assessment of Kabul Airport was one of the better experiences we had in Afghanistan. The airport was under the command of the Turks. Tough and professional, these guys were very wary of our team and, I suspect, any other foreign group seeking information about their facilities or operations. I sensed our mission at the airfield would be very "touch and go."

This was not my first experience with the Turks. I had served with Turkish officers when I was assigned to the United Nations Iraq–Kuwait Observation Mission in 1997–98. In addition to their toughness and professionalism, I found them slow to befriend and bordering on aloof. I had taken the time, however, to get to know them, exchange professional thoughts on warfare and regional issues, assist (when asked) with their staff work and reporting, and otherwise demonstrate a sincere concern and respect for their perspective on Iraq and the peacekeeping mission. I frequently stopped by the UN Officers Club in the evenings to engage socially with them and gain a better appreciation for their views. My experience reinforced my belief a sincere and honest approach to officers of any nationality develops trust and respect. It was no different in Afghanistan.

The Turkish commander, Colonel Kazim Ondul, was an exceptional Air Force officer who was friendly and personable but skeptical of our Vulnerability Assessment Team and its true mission. It was understandable. Like any American commander's fear of the old Inspector General Inspection teams that conducted the organizational maintenance and readiness inspections and made or broke a unit's reputation for a year or more, Colonel Ondul was initially reluctant to accept our team and provide access to his facilities. The initial coordination for this visit had taken place a month earlier so I was very uncomfortable when Colonel Ondul informed me of the requirement to secure yet another "Okay" from his boss to allow us to proceed. I covered my discomfort with a broad smile and told him I understood. Patience was never one of my finer points, but I controlled myself from squirming in my chair. Out of the blue, Ondul then invited me and several of my officers to a Turkish-hosted BBQ and social that evening. I saw the invitation as an opportunity to get better acquainted and press the importance of our assistance visit to both his command and the coalition effort in Afghanistan. It turned out to be exactly what we needed.

I was amazed at the spread of food and activities the Turks had arranged. I had expected a short evening carefully choreographed with appropriate formal remarks. There was some of that, but I did not realize entertainment would also be provided. National contingents were expected to provide native entertainment. I was totally unaware of this requirement but, before I could even think about getting nervous, Major Moses Perez, USA, an ordnance officer and explosives expert, reached over to me and said, "No sweat, boss, I got it covered. Trust me; all I need is a guitar."

It turned out Moses was an accomplished musician and country music singer. I introduced "Mo" when it was our turn in the barrel and he blew everyone away with several country songs including one of my favorites, Merle Haggard's perfect *I was drunk the night my Mama got out of prison*. Mo brought down the house and, after a brief sigh of relief, I calmly accepted Colonel Ondul's compliments and told him rather nonchalantly, "We regularly do this kind of thing." He slapped me on the back, shook my hand again, and quietly told me he was certain his commanding general would approve our mission to conduct a vulnerability assessment of the airport. Approval came the next day and the team chief, Commander Bob Olson, USN, and our experts enthusiastically pored over the airport and related facilities with their Turkish escorts with virtually no restrictions. My job, as it turned out, was to maintain our hard-earned good relationship with the Turkish commander. Colonel Ondul insisted on my participation in a favorite Turkish officer's game, soccer volleyball. It is literally a volleyball game played soccer style with no hands. An old running back still proud of my athletic prowess, I had ignored soccer in high school as a game for those guys who could not measure up to football. It came back to haunt me as I once again found myself on the chopping block to uphold our nation's honor and my athletic pride. Clumsy and not delicate enough with the ball initially, I eventually got the hang of it and the officers enjoyed my efforts. Like all team sports, it brought us together in a friendly endeavor and reinforced the camaraderie of the previous evening's BBQ. We had a great time, but the game was mercifully cut short when the French airport contingent claimed the net and the ball and sent us packing. The assessment came off without a hitch and we out-briefed Colonel Ondul and his staff the next day. The written report was completed several weeks later, after I had left Saudi Arabia. At my insistence, Commander Olson returned to Afghanistan to personally hand the report to the Turks and brief its specifics. He also delivered a small gift—a red, white, and blue regulation soccer ball we purchased at the Eskan Village PX. Bob told me the soccer ball was a "real winner" and was very enthusiastically accepted.

Our mission in Afghanistan was a huge success, a tribute to over two months of planning, coordination, predeployment on-site briefings and surveys, and a whole lot of military diplomacy and friendly "arm twisting." We had established excellent relations with the tough troopers of the 3rd Special Forces Group at the Afghan National Academy, the U.S. Embassy staff, the Civil Affairs personnel at the Joint Civil Military Operations Task Force Headquarters in Kabul, the skeptical staff officers and commanders of Task Force Dragon and CJTF-180 at Bagram, and even the suspicious and reluctant Turks at Kabul Airport. Our Bagram team was withdrawn and returned to Saudi Arabia, and we programmed Afghanistan into the annual vulnerability assessment cycle, making more efficient use of an officer and noncommissioned officer that, for nearly a year, had languished in Afghanistan with few responsibilities. I recorded a note in my journal that captured my feelings about the entire experience:

> Professional behavior, a sincere approach, a willingness to listen, and a strong, evident desire to assist commanders, wins every time.

My temporary assignment as the director of JSD-Forward ended in late September 2002 when my replacement arrived at Eskan Village. I left Saudi Arabia on a "cloud" with a 19th-century Afghan sword my officers purchased at an antique shop in Kabul and presented at a party held in my honor the night before my departure.

I returned to Tampa and reported to my new boss, Brigadier General Designee James H. Schwitters who had replaced General Harrell shortly after I had departed for Saudi Arabia. We had gotten acquainted over the phone as I religiously reported our activities to him and sought his guidance. General Schwitters is a good man, and I liked his quiet, competent style. Unnerving to some, he left me alone and seemed to appreciate my relationship with the staff that freed him to perform his other duties. Like General Harrell, his previous job had been commander of the vaunted Delta Force at Fort Bragg. It was not unusual to see him assigned to special duties away from USCENTCOM and his directorate. I enjoyed our relationship but, with an invasion of Iraq looking imminent, I sought an extension to my mandatory retirement date of 31 May 2003 and an immediate assignment to Kuwait. I told General Schwitters what I wanted to do and requested his permission to see General Franks to secure an extension and orders to the theater. He respected my position and agreed.

General Franks was a formidable commander who was feared by many of his officers. My perspective on the general was significantly different. I first met him in Kuwait during Operation *Desert Thunder* in 1997. He was the Third U.S. Army and U.S. Army Central commander at the time and had deployed his headquarters to the American base at Camp Doha in anticipation of yet another strike against Saddam's defiance of UN protocols regarding weapons inspections. As Senior U.S. Observer with the United Nations Iraq–Kuwait Observation Mission (UNIKOM) in the demilitarized zone (DMZ) separating Iraq and Kuwait, I represented another set of "eyes" for his use inside Iraq. United Nations Commander Major General Esa Tarvainen, of Finland, directed me to serve as the UN liaison officer to all American forces in Kuwait. The relationship between UN and U.S. forces was a particularly sensitive issue for both commanders. General Tarvainen was strongly opposed to any meeting with American officers in the DMZ. He was also reluctant to discuss any plans with U.S. planners to withdraw the UN force. In mid-February 1998, however, I accompanied him to the U.S. Embassy where he met with then Lieutenant General Franks and U.S. Ambassador to Kuwait James LaRocco to get acquainted, discuss possible military options that would impact UNIKOM's mission, and exchange information about the current situation in the DMZ. There was considerable concern on both sides of the possibility of a significant refugee challenge in the DMZ in the event of hostilities. UNIKOM was in an excellent position to provide early warning of any massive refugee movement toward the Kuwaiti border and everyone understood the Kuwaiti Government and UN agencies, such as the High Commissioner for Refugees, would have a considerable role with managing refugee requirements. During this cordial session, it was agreed I would make frequent trips to the American base at Camp Doha and report UN and Iraqi activity, as well as any other relevant information, directly to General Franks. The weeks that followed were particularly intense and a show down with Saddam appeared likely. The flow of forces into the region was consistent with the war plans USCENTCOM had developed in 1996. I sensed we were serious this time as carrier task forces entered the Persian Gulf, but, more importantly, as Army infantry and Marine units started coming ashore. This was no bluff. Over the next couple of months, I frequently met with General Franks in his quarters and I sensed he appreciated my efforts and observations. He never failed to welcome me with his broad smile, a handshake, and a huge slap on the back.

Operation *Desert Thunder* concluded without combat action when UN Secretary General Kofi Annan signed an agreement with Iraqi officials to defuse the weapons-inspections crisis in February 1998. There was a tremendous sigh of relief at UNIKOM Headquarters with the secretary general's successful effort to preserve the "peace," but the feelings at Camp Doha were mixed. By this time, the forces available were capable of initiating operations toward ending our anguish with Saddam, and there were many guys who just wanted to "get it on." The United States would repeat the process in December with another strike against Saddam's military forces, in an operation dubbed *Desert Fox*, but, for now at least, the crisis had been averted and many units began to pack up and redeploy. By the end of May, there were still over twenty-eight thousand personnel, 13 warships, and 195 aircraft in the region as a deterrent to Saddam's regime. Regardless, the dangerous game Saddam insisted on playing continued; no one doubted we would hit him again at some point.

Before General Franks left Kuwait in the spring of 1998, I gave him a paperweight I had crafted using a vision block from a destroyed Iraqi mechanized vehicle in the DMZ. He, in turn, gave me a Third Army commander's coin. Our relationship improved over the following two years when I served at USCENTCOM as the executive assistant to General Zinni. General Franks occasionally traveled in the region with General Zinni, and we engaged both professionally and socially. I genuinely liked General Franks and certainly was not afraid of him.

I arranged an office call with the commander's staff and reported to him on a Saturday morning in late January 2003. It was customary to work in civilian clothing on the weekends and I was not surprised to see the general wearing a comfortable pair of jeans, a button-down shirt, and loafers when I entered his office. He greeted me with his characteristic smile and made me feel welcome. We spoke for only a few minutes. It had not occurred to him that I was close to my mandatory retirement date; he quickly concluded a senior colonel with nine continuous years in Central Command and the Central Region was too valuable a commodity to be sent packing at such a critical point in time. He not only granted the extension I needed but told me I would deploy to Kuwait within a month. Two weeks later, General Delong approached me in the Main Conference Room after the morning battle update and informed me I had an assignment waiting for me in Kuwait. Finally, I was going to war!

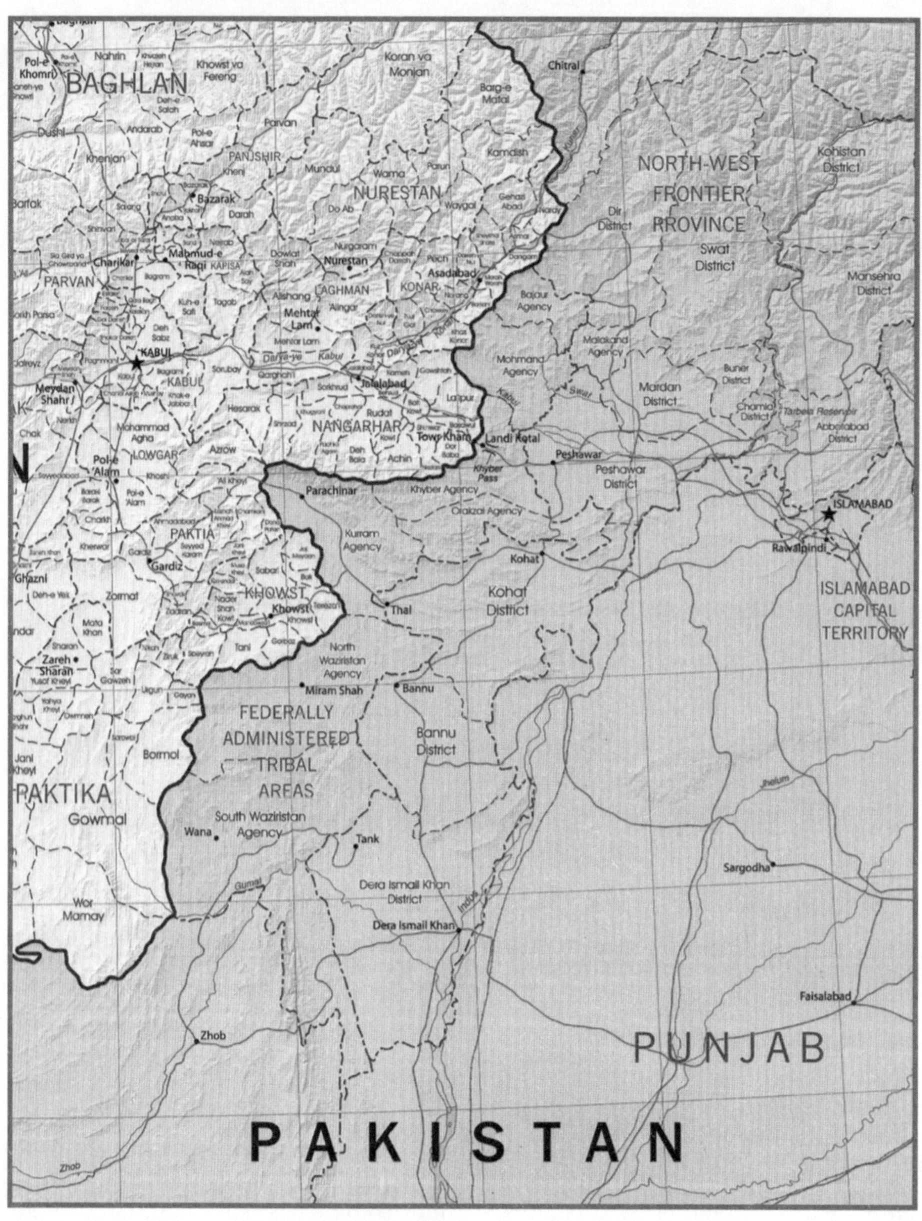

Afghanistan–Pakistan Border. (U.S. Central Intelligence Agency)

CHAPTER 5

Planning the Inevitable War

In preparing for battle I have always found that plans are useless, but planning is indispensable.

—General Dwight D. Eisenhower, USA

The great debate in the aftermath of the Gulf War in 1991 was whether the Coalition should have taken the war to Baghdad and removed Saddam Hussein. The decision to leave him in power led many to believe that at some point Saddam would do something that would result in another war. The inevitable war, as planners came to see the situation in Iraq, all but consumed the Pentagon and the plans community throughout the remainder of the decade and beyond.

I was assigned to U.S. Central Command (USCENTCOM), Plans and Policy Directorate (CCJ5), War Plans Division, in July 1994 following my graduation from the U.S. Army War College. Colonel Rich Stouder, USA, led the War Plans Division. We became very good friends but only after a rough start. Rich was disappointed to receive an infantry lieutenant colonel with limited mechanized experience. I was schooled in maneuver warfare at Fort Benning and had attended the maintenance course at the Armor School at Fort Knox, but I had not had the opportunity to command a mechanized unit. I had a good planning background, but Rich firmly believed mechanized and armored experience was essential for success in his plans shop and never failed to remind me. I initially worked in the "Lesser Contingency Branch" of the division and was specifically assigned responsibility to overwatch the ongoing United Nations peacekeeping effort in Somalia. I was well suited for this "break-in" assignment and deployed to Somalia on two occasions to assist planning the withdrawal of United Nations Operation in Somalia Second Phase forces. It was an exciting assignment. In addition to coordinating and addressing UN and USCENTCOM issues and concerns, I worked closely in the field with both the Indian and Pakistani brigade staffs to plan and conduct a withdrawal of their units by both sea and air lift. The withdrawal was completed in February 1995. By that time, Rich was either satisfied I knew something about planning or had given up trying to get another officer with mechanized experience. In March 1995, he placed me in charge of his Major Regional Contingency Branch and this meant working the major plan of the day—Operations Plan (OPLAN) 1002/1003, the Iraq war plan.

Colonel Stouder was one of the most competent and respected strategic planners in the plans community of the mid-1990s. He had graduated from the National War College in June 1992 and was assigned to USCENTCOM's War Plans Division as the lead planner for OPLAN 1002-92. The plan was already in development and had both Joint Staff (JS) and secretary of defense approval. Rich had commanded a mechanized infantry battalion during Operation *Desert Shield* and was assigned to the XVIII Airborne Corps Operations Staff (G-3) where he served during Operation *Desert Storm*. He was highly qualified, tactically and operationally, to lead the development of this plan.

The new plan was an extension of OPLAN 1002-90 which was executed during *Desert Storm*. Its mission statement called for the defense of Saudi Arabia and Kuwait from Iraqi aggression. The forces envisioned for OPLAN 1002-92 were almost exactly those deployed during Operations *Desert Shield/Storm*. The planning process was accelerated when Operation *Vigilant Warrior* was undertaken in August 1994 to defend Kuwait against a Saddam Hussein threat to attack across the border with ground forces. Rich deployed to Kuwait with General Peay, the USCENTCOM commander, to establish a forward headquarters and coordinate the forces and actions necessary to defeat an invasion. As our forces began to deploy and build up, Saddam backed down and withdrew the forces that threatened Kuwait. General Peay did not have an approved operations plan to base the actions necessary to defeat an Iraqi invasion, or deploy and employ the forces to do it, but *Vigilant Warrior* convinced the JS and senior defense officials that a plan was needed; work began in earnest to finalize OPLAN 1002-92.

The Joint Planning Process is on a formal two-year cycle. Each of these cycles starts with the issue of the Joint Strategic Capabilities Plan (JSCP). This is a top-secret document that is the bedrock of joint planning. It is a subset of the National Military Strategy which supports the National Security Strategy. These three documents are, at least in theory, tied together and represent the will of the president and acceptance by the administration. The JSCP assigns all the geographical or unified commands their missions and tasks and allocates forces for the execution of the plans their respective staffs must develop to accomplish them. The planning cycle is in phases with different portions of the plans developed by the commanders of the geographical commands and reviewed by the JS for comment and approval. At each one of the phases, the Services, and the Office of the Secretary of Defense (OSD) can also comment. At the end of the planning cycle, the final version of the plan is sent to the JS and, after a short comment period, the commander and his staff brief the substance of the plan to the chairman of the Joint Chiefs of Staff and then the secretary of defense.

General Joseph Hoar, USMC, was the commander of USCENTCOM during OPLAN 1002-92's development. Rich Stouder accompanied him to the Pentagon to brief the plan for final approval by the secretary of defense. The briefing was attended by Secretary of Defense Dick Cheney, Chairman of the Joint Chiefs of Staff General Colin Powell, and Under Secretary for Policy Paul Wolfowitz. The briefing went well until the operational-execution phase of the plan and the force levels of the ground forces were presented. The plan called for two Army Corps and one Marine Expeditionary Force (MEF), an Army Corps equivalent. Secretary Wolfowitz questioned why the large levels of ground forces were needed. His question centered on two points: the Iraqi forces were significantly reduced in capability and, with the continued advance of precision munitions, we could reduce the number and size of ground forces while increasing the number of Air Force wings dedicated to the plan. General Hoar took the position that the intelligence assessment of Iraqi capability merited the large American ground forces and that most of Saddam's Republican Guard had escaped with minimal damage during *Desert Storm*. General Powell sided with Hoar as he was advocating his doctrine of overwhelming force. The plan was ultimately approved when Secretary Cheney intervened and effectively ended the discussion.

The JSCP for 1994 reflected the new administration's focus on the Pacific and introduced the Two Major Regional Contingency (2MRC) concept that focused America's defense strategy on how to fight a war in Southwest Asia and Korea near simultaneously. During the writing of the new JSCP, the geographical combatant commanders were allowed to comment on the missions, tasks, and force allocations. In the summer of 1993, Colonel Stouder represented the USCENTCOM commander in the 2MRC and force-allocations discussions, which were led by the Joint Staff Plans Directorate. At the same time, an initiative by the OSD Policy Directorate to degrade the 1002 OPLAN to a minor regional contingency, designating the OPLAN for war in Korea as the only major regional contingency, was under consideration. A heated debate ensued between USCENTCOM, the JS, and OSD. The USCENTCOM Intelligence Directorate produced a detailed intelligence assessment for 1002-94 that said Iraq could attack Kuwait and Saudi Arabia with 30–40 divisions with 10–12 days' notice. The JSCP directs commanders to use the current National Intelligence Estimate (NIE) as the foundation intelligence document to base war planning. The NIE vastly understated the number of Iraq divisions, overstated the warning time, and assumed "The Coalition" would consist of some five Egyptian divisions, two Syrian divisions, two British divisions, a French division, and an Arabian Peninsula Force of up to two division equivalents. The NIE stated the number of American ground forces could be drastically reduced from the *Desert Storm* force given the contributions of "The Coalition." The NIE talked about "The Coalition" like it was a NATO-like entity when, in reality, the coalition that had fought in *Desert Storm* evaporated quickly after the completion of the 100-hour ground offensive. The Defense Intelligence Agency was sold on the NIE as written and had the backing of the Department of State and the Central Intelligence Agency.

USCENTCOM disagreed with the draft NIE and it was published with some of its concerns as footnotes. In August 1994, General J. H. Binford Peay, USA, assumed command of USCENTCOM. He had been briefed of the disconnect between the USCENTCOM Intelligence Assessment and the NIE and had signed off on the nonconcurrence. USCENTCOM asked for an exception to JSCP policy to base its OPLAN for Iraq on its intelligence assessment versus the Iraq NIE. Chairman of the Joint Chiefs General John Shalikasvilli, after a series of additional briefings and discussions on the subject, approved the exception to policy.

The 2MRC concept was heavily debated in the Clinton Administration before it appeared in the National Security Strategy. Colonel Stouder led the discussions for retaining Southwest Asia as a major regional contingency using the USCENTCOM Intelligence Assessment as a primary argument and the importance of oil as a secondary argument. The United States had national interests in the Arabian Gulf region and the Iraqi regime remained a credible threat to those interests. America had tacit agreements to defend Saudi Arabia dating from the Franklin D. Roosevelt Administration. Since the end of Operation *Desert Storm*, U.S. stated policy was that it would defend Kuwait. If Saddam Hussein threatened these two countries and had a military capability to attack them, then the United States had vital national interests in their security. The free access to oil from the region was another vital national interest. America was getting over fifty percent of its oil from Saudi Arabia and Western Europe was getting over seventy percent from the region; Japan and South Korea were getting over eighty percent from the region. The world's economy was essentially based on free and open access to oil from the Arabian Gulf. Saddam Hussein could not be allowed to take over the oil fields of Kuwait and Saudi Arabia and then dictate terms to the Western world. The OSD took the position that the West did not need oil from Southwest Asia as all the oil demands could come from the former Soviet Union. The USCENTCOM Intelligence Directorate had a section with experts in oil production and reserves in the Arabian Gulf. They produced numerous reports on the importance of oil in Southwest Asia and the data to make the requisite arguments to that affect. One of the statements that had the most impact was that when all the oil in Russia had been used, there would be 100 years of oil remaining in the ground in Saudi Arabia. The final decision was that Southwest Asia would remain a major regional contingency for planning.

The next planning debate focused on the force allocations for the two respective MRCs. Each of the two MRC commanders argued for the forces required in their respective war plans. In one of the initial meetings, the planners tallied the forces required. These forces exceeded the total force structure of the American military. There was significant pressure from the administration to dramatically reduce the size of the military since, with the fall of the Soviet Union, there was no peer competitor. The drawdown of forces was started by the George H. W. Bush Administration. The primary architect of the drawdown was Secretary of Defense Dick Cheney. The reduction in the size of the military was interrupted by Operations *Desert Shield* and *Desert Storm*. After the conflict, Cheney proceeded with the reduction despite objection by the Services and the warfighting commanders. The experienced professionals across the military knew human history has had few periods of peace and that when one foe is vanquished another seems to take its place. The world of post-Soviet Union was still sorting itself out and many senior military leaders felt it was too soon to reduce America's military forces. All the Services and the commanders opposed a precipitous drawdown, knowing it would be done with imperfect knowledge of the future and reducing too much capability too quickly. The force reductions that occurred would haunt efforts during Operation *Iraqi Freedom*.

As USCENTCOM, Pacific Command, and U.S. Forces Korea debated the requirements for forces, their respective planners, and the JS planners, developed the concepts for OPLANs when either was the first MRC or the second MRC. The National Military Strategy had the requirement to "win" in the first MRC, "hold" in the second MRC, and then shift forces as the first MRC was won. There were several wargames to determine forces required in the first MRC and the "hold" MRC, and then shifting forces as needed. Out of these wargames came the terminology "near simultaneous MRCs." There was considerable debate about the warning required to execute the MRC in Korea and Southwest Asia as well as the timing for movement of forces to the "hold" MRC and shifting of forces from the first to the second ("hold") MRC. An underlying assumption was that if either the North Koreans or the Iraqis initiated hostilities then the other would sense vulnerability, take advantage of the focus on the first MRC, and attack. The planning community finally agreed there would be, for planning purposes, a 45-day separation between the first and second MRCs. This scenario posed a dilemma when it came to force allocation and ability to "hold" in either theater.

The planners from U.S. Forces Korea and USCENTCOM developed a very good relationship during this process and attempted to find ways to solve the many problems this strategy presented. There were several Army, Marine, Air Force and Navy formations that were absolutely required in each theater. The compromise with the concurrence of the JS and OSD was that these key formations would be "dual apportioned." This meant an air-assault division and a cavalry division would be apportioned to each theater when they were the first MRC. Where the force drawdown took its biggest toll was in the combat service support force structure. The second MRC, or the "hold" MRC would not have the required combat service support to effectively sustain combat operations. A second part of this concept was that when the first MRC was completed, there would be a strategic shift of forces from the first theater to the second. The numbers of strategic lift availability and capability made the planners realize there was not enough available considering the stability and logistic demands in the first theater, the lift already engaged in support of the second MRC, and the very demanding requirement to shift forces from one theater to the other. The prevailing wisdom was the second MRC would have a significantly hard time sustaining operations.

The planning staffs at USCENTCOM and U.S. Forces Korea began planning for two major war plans for each of their respective theaters—one OPLAN for when they were the first MRC and one if they were the second MRC. It was apparent, however, that the 2MRC concept was not doable. The USCENTCOM planners continued with the OPLAN development but decided to assign the plan a "high risk" designation. The JSCP allows the commanders to assign risk to OPLANs but not to accept more than moderate risk. General Peay agreed with the high-risk assessment and OPLAN 1003 (the first MRC plan) was submitted to the JS with the high-risk designation in April 1997. The plan was neither approved nor rejected but remained on the shelf somewhere in the JS and OSD as planning continued.

The JSCP in 1994 directed the USCENTCOM commander to defend the territorial integrity of Saudi Arabia and Kuwait, defeat the Iraqi military, maintain Iraq as a nation-state capable of defending itself, and act as a counterbalance to Iran. These tasks were very challenging given Iraq's ability to attack with only 8–10 days' notice, and the distance the American military had to deploy to accomplish these mission tasks. These tasks caused USCENTCOM to go from a primarily defensive OPLAN to a multi-phased plan that included offensive actions into Iraq. Due to the proximity of Iraq to Kuwait, the lack of defensive forces in theater, and the capabilities of the Iraqi military, it was not possible to keep Kuwait from falling into Iraqi hands. The plan was initially to deploy a defensive force to protect Saudi Arabia, build up forces, attack to restore Kuwait, and then attack into Iraq to defeat the Iraqi military.

A huge challenge the planners needed to address was defeating the Iraqi military and having enough of it left that could defend the country and act as a counterbalance to Iran. The decision was to destroy Iraq's Republican Guard, which was loyal to Saddam and better equipped, while minimizing destruction to the Regular Army. There was general agreement the Iraqis could be convinced to not have the Iraqi Army fight with the promise it would not be destroyed, that it would be the force that would support the post-Saddam government. This last point was essential to accomplish the missions USCENTCOM had been given; covert actions were initiated that gave credence to this assumption. The intent was to have special operators meet with the Army generals, convince them to "stand down" when the attack was initiated, and ensure them they and their men would form the Army of Iraq once Saddam and the Republican Guard were eliminated. The Iraqi Army was deemed a critical factor in the eventual postmaneuver phase of a campaign to occupy Iraq, secure its borders, and prevent sectarian violence.

OPLAN 1002-94 was submitted to the JS for approval, but discussions continued with the Services, the JS, and OSD on the warning timelines and the forces in the plan. Discussions with OSD focused on the number of ground force battalions and the number of Air Force fighter squadrons to execute the plan. OSD insisted USCENTCOM could reduce the number of ground battalions by employing more fighter squadrons capable of employing precision munitions. The Joint Operations Planning and Execution System, which is the "Bible" for how to conduct joint planning, requires the commanders to wargame their OPLANs prior to submission for approval. USCENTCOM had employed a rigorous process for wargaming OPLAN 1002-94. Its discussions with OSD used the data from the wargaming to defend its force recommendations. The data overwhelmingly validated USCENTCOM's argument for forces, but Secretary Perry did not accept the rationale for the number of ground forces which were not for defeating the Iraqi military as much for securing critical terrain, facilities, and lines of communication, and controlling large population centers throughout Iraq. The justification for the size of the ground forces was doctrinally sound. Secretary Perry was less concerned with the facts, data, or doctrine and focused on the large number of ground forces in the plan. He argued we could do with less ground forces while increasing the number of Air Force fighter and bomber wings. Underlying this was a desire by the Clinton Administration to cut military force structure. Once forces were in an approved OPLAN, they became part of the requirement that had to be supported. Air Force fighter wings were cheaper than Army or Marine divisions. Additional briefings and discussions with Deputy Secretary of Defense White at USCENTCOM Headquarters apparently convinced him the plan was solid; OSD approved the plan.

OPLAN 1002-94 included an offensive phase, a significant difference from its predecessors. This phase was planned to occur after the restoration of the territorial integrity of Saudi Arabia and Kuwait. The force required for this phase was two Army Corps and one Marine MEF. It culminated with the defeat of the Iraqi military. The OPLAN was defensive only as long as it took to build up the forces to then go on the offensive, first restoring the borders and then destroying Iraqi forces. The planners discussed a postconflict phase and agreed one had to be planned, but the depth of discussions about it were far less comprehensive than the counteroffensive phase.

The publication of the next JSCP did not change USCENTCOM's missions. The planning for OPLAN 1002-96 continued to engage the planners at U.S. Pacific Command, U.S. Forces Korea, and USCENTCOM on matters regarding apportionment of forces between USCENTCOM and Korea, as well as the development of the strategy, operational tactics for offensive operations, and significant thinking regarding postconflict operations. The single biggest issue that confronted the planners was the concept of dual apportionment of forces by the JS to satisfy the requirements of both theaters of war. The commanders of the unified geographical commands were not happy with the concept, but the reality of the forces available dictated there was no alternative to satisfy the requirements of both theaters. Dual apportionment was a planner's nightmare at the strategic, operational, and tactical levels of war.

The planners from the three major geographical commands, the JS, the Services, and OSD had numerous meetings regarding dual apportionment and divided up the military forces between the commands to accomplish their respective missions and minimize risk given a first MRC and a second 45 days later. Forces were apportioned to support each of the respective war plans. These detailed discussions confirmed what the planners already knew or suspected—the military was critically short of: strategic air and sea lift; combat forces that could meet the deployment timelines; combat and combat service support forces; high-demand, low-density forces in the Air Force and Navy; and carrier battle groups. Though "high risk" at best for both plans, the respective commanders and, eventually, the chairman of the Joint Chiefs of Staff approved the apportionment plan.

Colonel Stouder and his planners spent a considerable amount of time working with the Army Component Headquarters, Third U. S. Army/Army Forces Central Command (ARCENT), and the Marine Component Headquarters (Marine Forces Pacific, which was dual hatted as Marine Forces Central Command) in defining the strategic and operational tasks and synchronizing ground and air maneuver and timing of operations. What differed in OPLAN 1002-96 was the level of detail involved in offensive operations. Planners met with the force component and the corps-level headquarters to work out the details of ground maneuver and how air forces would support an integrated air–ground operation, seamlessly moving from restoration of the borders of Saudi and Kuwait and into counteroffensive operations in Iraq. The planners expected to defeat opposing Iraqi forces, but it would take time and the required number of forces. The forces on the ground included seven Army divisions in two U.S. Corps and two Marine divisions, and a Marine Air Wing under a Marine Expeditionary Force headquarters. This ground force exceeded 300,000 and was necessary to accomplish all strategic and operational tasks, secure the lines of communications, and transition to postconflict operations. War gaming for this plan was conducted at the same level of detail as the previous planning cycle and produced the same result. These force levels were required to accomplish the assigned tasks with moderate risk.

Postconflict operations were a complex proposition with numerous assumptions. Proper planning for postconflict required an understanding of Iraq, Arab, and Middle East culture, politics, and, most importantly, religion. Iraq's most dominant cultural feature was clans, the impact of which was deep and wide; clans dictated total allegiance. Iraq was not only a country of clans, it was a country of mixed Arabs and races all linked, and fractured, by the religion of Islam. There were the Kurds in the north, the Sunnis, and the Shi'ites. There were centuries of animosity between these groups. Saddam was the glue that held these groups together and he did this through force. Removing Saddam would unleash the same type of ethnic and religious violence that was evidenced in Bosnia and Kosovo.

The Kurds wanted an independent Kurdistan and Saddam stationed many of his divisions in the north to keep them in check. The Turks also opposed Kurdish autonomy and conducted combat operations against the Kurdish Workers Party, an armed guerrilla movement seeking increased rights for Kurds in northern Iraq and southern Turkey. The split between the Sunnis and the Shi'ites was a dominating issue. The ruling Baath Party was Sunni despite being in the minority in Iraq. Saddam repressed the Shi'ites throughout his reign, gassing and killing thousands who received moral and material support from the Iranians. Lastly, the planners knew, once Saddam was eliminated, there had to be a quick transition to a new Iraqi government because, no matter how good American intentions were, Westerners would be viewed as occupiers. The requirement was to rapidly transition to postconflict operations with support from the other Arab countries in the Gulf.

The planners decided detailed postconflict operations planning was not practical given the directed Joint Strategic Capabilities Plan requirements and the realities and unpredictability of dealing with a post-Saddam Iraq. The assumptions were too long and the unpredictability too much to plan for. It was more prudent to list the assumptions and have a very general concept of operations. General Peay understood this and accepted the broad outline in the OPLAN of how we might conduct postconflict operations. A detailed plan would have to be developed once the operation commenced and more concrete information was available. Other matters of vital importance to plan development focused on command and control and doctrinal fire-control issues that were calmly and intelligently agreed upon under the superb leadership of General Peay and later under General Zinni, who succeeded Peay as the commander of USCENTCOM.

Regarding the critical matter of command and control, General Peay decided he would retain the title of Joint Force Land Component Commander (JFLCC) while making the ARCENT commander the deputy JFLCC, with the responsibilities of the everyday functions of the JFLCC. This mollified the Air Force and Marines somewhat and it was written into the OPLAN.

Throughout the decisive period of war planning between 1995–96, I had a front-row seat, in my position as the branch chief for Major Contingencies, and wrote or reviewed a significant portion of the operational language in OPLAN 1002-96. Rich had carefully guided my introduction to the region and the planning issues. In March 1995, he sent me to Saudi Arabia, Kuwait, and several other countries in the Central Region to acquaint me with the operational area, talk to regional commanders, key staff members at ARCENT Headquarters-Forward, and port officials in Saudi Arabia and Kuwait, and get a fundamental base of knowledge on the terrain and available facilities. I was assigned an Arabic speaker who was thrilled to travel throughout Kuwait and Saudi Arabia. This unique opportunity allowed me to track the OPLAN campaign on tactical maps and get a "birds-eye" view on how we could deploy and sequence forces into theater and then employ them in the defense of Kuwait and the attack into Iraq. My orientation included visiting an American destroyer on patrol in the Arabian Gulf. Upon my return to headquarters, I was ready to take charge of completing OPLAN 1002 and transitioning it to what was to become OPLAN 1003. I participated in many of the forces and operational discussions at both the Pentagon and various headquarters, as well as the various conferences at Scott Air Force Base, to plan the sequencing of apportioned forces to the theater at execution. The battle over forces, fire-support coordination, and command and control had been largely fought, and decisions made by the plans community and the warfighting commanders, when I assumed leadership of War Plans Division in April 1996. The highly respected Rich Stouder went to U.S. Army Alaska as the garrison commander. His mentorship was invaluable. Our turnover was seamless and the USCENTCOM Plans Team proudly continued the mission.

In the summer of 1995, Lieutenant Colonel Steve Kidder, USA, reported to the division, having graduated from the U.S. Army War College in June, and assumed the responsibility of developing the vital "lesser contingency plans" of the day. The principal mission at that point was to complete the writing of OPLAN 1003 and, as importantly, fully develop its force sequencing or Time Phased Force Deployment Data (TPFDD). This process took place in a series of conferences involving USCENTCOM and service planners at Scott Air Force Base in Illinois. In April 1996, we worked to develop the TPFDD with continued input and guidance from General Peay. In the fall of 1996, I was directed to begin planning for a contingency with Iran. This effort required considerable work and time, but it did not deter our effort to complete OPLAN 1003 or the second MRC plan, OPLAN 1015. In April 1997, OPLAN 1003 was submitted to the JS for approval, though the plan would continue to evolve through 1999. Its submission in 1997 was a huge achievement for those officers who had diligently worked the issues of its development for over four years.

I was proud to have led the effort in my third and last year as War Plans Division chief before my tour of duty at USCENTCOM came to a close. OPLAN 1002-92, and its successors, OPLANs 1002-94 and -96, were developed and coordinated by USCENTCOM war planners, but every Service, every geographical command commander, the JS, and the OSD had been involved, and had reviewed, commented, and concurred. Colonel Stouder personally briefed Secretaries of Defense Cheney, Perry, and Cohen; all of them and their staffs had approved these planning efforts. Those efforts translated well in the development of OPLAN 1003. In sum, there was nearly a decade worth of military and civilian intellectual capital in the OPLAN, a great deal of which would essentially be ignored when the decision to invade Iraq was taken in 2003.

Steve Kidder became the division chief upon my departure and submitted OPLAN 1015 to the JS for approval in July 1997. No sooner was the plan submitted than work began to develop the operational concept for OPLAN 1003 and OPLAN 1015 as tasked in the 1998 JSCP. The USCENTCOM planners wargamed five courses of action over the summer, one of which considered an insurgency by Iraqi forces. The strategic concept was developed and refined with General Zinni's guidance. Throughout this period, USCENTCOM was criticized by the OSD for requiring too many ground forces in its plans. The Air Force argued that much of what we were trying to do could be accomplished by air operations. USCENTCOM maintained its need for four heavy (armor or mechanized) divisions, one light division, one armored cavalry regiment, two Army Corps, and one Marine Expeditionary Force since the analysis clearly showed it would take much more force to occupy and tame Iraq in a posthostility environment than it would to simply remove the regime.

The indomitable Rich Stouder returned from Alaska in the summer of 1998 and assumed the duties of G-3 (Chief of Operations) at ARCENT Headquarters. The Third Army was commanded by the colorful, then Lieutenant General Tommy Franks. General Zinni commanded USCENTCOM and had designated the commander of ARCENT as the JFLCC. General Zinni felt that not only was it right for ARCENT to be the JFLCC, but, since he was a marine, his decision would not be opposed by senior Marine Corps leadership.

The theater had changed by 1998. There was a much larger presence of ground forces. In the years after Operation *Desert Storm*, there had been a growing presence of air and naval forces to enforce the United Nations sanctions against Iraq. There were now three ARCENT forward headquarters located in Saudi Arabia, Qatar, and Kuwait. Additionally, there were Patriot air-defense units in Saudi Arabia and a rotating infantry battalion task force in Kuwait which was in country for 180 days.

The changes for war planning were also significant. First and foremost was the concept of Flexible Deterrent Options (FDOs). The FDOs were flexible force packages that would allow American forces to build rapidly during periods of tension. These packages signaled American resolve to deter aggressive actions by Saddam. They could be quickly deployed to achieve deterrence or as the front end of the entire sequenced OPLAN force deployment. The FDOs included increased air, naval, and land forces. Some of these FDO forces would reposition from within the theater, some came by air, and some came by ship.

Another aspect of change was the presence of prepositioned stocks of Army and Marine equipment. The Army had decided to leave an armored heavy brigade's equipment in Kuwait. It had also committed to create another brigade and selected division equipment in Qatar. Lastly, there was another Army and Marine brigade equipment set stored on maritime afloat prepositioned ships in Diego Garcia, the largest of 60 islands of the Chagos Archipelago in the central Indian Ocean. These equipment stocks allowed the USCENTCOM commander to quickly move troops by air from bases in the United States, link up with the prepositioned equipment, and have forces available much faster than having to move troops and equipment from the continental United States. The movement of these troops and ships was a significant part of the FDOs available to the commander.

The Army had recognized the importance of the Third Army and provided its headquarters with more personnel, the quality of whom, based upon their previous assignments and schooling, was significantly enhanced. Additionally, ARCENT had become a joint headquarters with Marine, Air Force, and Navy personnel assigned and totally immersed into the staff.

General Franks knew that, as the JFLCC, it was his responsibility to quickly establish a functional forward headquarters in theater when required. In late November 1998, Saddam ordered the UN weapons inspectors out of Iraq, and it looked like the U.S. was going to strike in response. ARCENT staff quickly moved to stand up a forward headquarters in Kuwait; Saddam backed down and agreed to allow the inspectors back into Iraq about an hour after a strike force of B-52 bombers had taken off from Diego Garcia.

In mid-December, the U.S. decided to strike Iraq in response to Saddam again ordering the UN inspectors to leave. General Franks quickly deployed members of his staff to Kuwait, arriving there some four hours before the first strikes. This was Operation *Desert Fox* and the U.S. hit targets in Iraq for three days. There was little damage to the Iraqi military and Saddam did not allow the UN inspectors back into Iraq. The general feeling in both USCENTCOM and ARCENT Headquarters was the United States should have more aggressively pursued its decision to strike Iraq until Saddam agreed to let the UN inspections continue. Many felt little had been accomplished and that Saddam had gotten away with thumbing his nose at the world with little resulting pain to him or his regime.

Further decisions were taken to address the growing possibility of another war with Iraq. American ground forces in Kuwait were increased from a six-month presence to a full year. The composition of this force was also increased to include Apache attack helicopters, utility helicopters, and a multiple-launch rocket system. ARCENT moved a Patriot battery from Saudi Arabia to Kuwait and another battery to Qatar. These unit movements meant the U.S. had ground battalion rotations into Kuwait, and Patriot battalion rotations in theater, twice a year.

USCENTCOM had assumed, since *Desert Storm* in 1991, that America would have access to the two large ports in the Eastern Province of Saudi Arabia. There was increasing agitation by the Saudis against U.S. presence in their country, especially by Saudis in this province. The questionable use of these ports for force generation meant USCENTCOM had to depend on the ports in Kuwait. This presented several challenges, including the proximity to the Kuwait–Iraq border. Since USCENTCOM did not have the requisite forces stationed in the region, it depended on adequate warning to deploy them as required. Previous war plans had ceded the invasion of

Kuwait to the Iraqis with the intent of building up forces in Saudi Arabia to defend Saudi from attack and then retake Kuwait in the first phase of the counterattack. These plans assumed the use of the ports in Saudi Arabia. Not having these ports added another degree of complexity and increased risk. During this same time, America pledged to Kuwait it would not allow them to be invaded again. Having to rely on only the two ports in Kuwait required more warning time for the U.S. to deploy forces. This was the genesis of the concept of FDOs, which allowed the U.S. to mitigate that risk.

The issue of warning time was again at the forefront of an ongoing debate between USCENTCOM, the bureaucracies in the Pentagon, and the intelligence community. USCENTCOM put a lot of demands on the intelligence community and national intelligence collection assets to ensure it had the requisite warning it required. ARCENT and USCENTCOM reviewed the indicators and warnings every day to ensure Iraq did not cheat on the no-fly zone restrictions imposed after the First Gulf War and a no-drive zone later adopted by the United Nations to further limit the proximity of Iraqi ground forces to Kuwait. These restrictions contained Iraqi air and ground forces north of two lines, 33- and 32-degrees N latitude respectively, and began a long-term erosion of Iraq's combat forces.

Postconflict operations still lacked sufficient detail for execution in the latest version of OPLANs 1002 and 1003. General Zinni was confident Saddam's military could be defeated but what kept him awake at night was a concern about someone assassinating Saddam or "Saddam just dies in his sleep." General Zinni knew that would unleash sectarian violence and America would be called upon to intervene. USCENTCOM and ARCENT planners then started a compartmentalized or separate planning effort designed to address this contingency. This plan was eventually named *Desert Crossing*. As the JFLCC, the ARCENT commander was charged with the major portion of this plan, including all actions by the ground forces. A plan was developed that assumed the Iraqi Regular Army could be turned and convinced not to fight, with the understanding they would be the main military force for the new Iraq. There was some intelligence that indicated this was a feasible assumption. Destruction efforts would be focused on the Republican Guard and Saddam's personal security forces during the counteroffensive. Planners divided Iraq into regions with a division commander (two star) responsible for each with two corps-level (three star) area commanders. ARCENT planned to rapidly transition to postconflict operations as it secured territory and moved north to Baghdad and beyond. The Marines were responsible for securing Baṣrah, a city in southern Iraq on the Shatt-Al-Arab waterway, which could be accomplished in two days. The Marines' reasoning was they could transition to postconflict operations while the two Army corps were still intensely involved in the counteroffensive. There was no need to wait for weeks until the completion of the counteroffensive before they transitioned to postconflict operations. Therefore, closely following the combat forces were the forces necessary for the many tasks associated with postconflict operations. ARCENT planners defined the tasks associated with postconflict planning and the number and type of forces necessary for this mission. This also required the planners to re-examine the force-deployment data and force-deployment timeline. The TPFDD sequenced the forces into theater to meet the missions and timelines associated with the campaign plan. The traditional OPLAN 1002/1003 TPFDD was front loaded with combat and logistics forces while the forces associated with postconflict deployed later in the force flow. The planners now had to ensure the TPFDD had the right force mix necessary for a simultaneous counteroffensive and rapid transition to postconflict stability operations.

When the planning for *Desert Crossing* was completed, General Zinni coordinated an interagency meeting and wargame in Washington to obtain concurrence of all the governmental agencies necessary for postconflict operations. He was able to get very high-level attendance, including the actual heads or the immediate deputies of the major governmental agencies. Military attendance was limited to the Service Component Commanders (three stars) and selected USCENTCOM and JS, to include the chairman of the Joint Chiefs of Staff. The meetings and wargame were held in Washington and coordinated by Booz Allen Hamilton Inc, a defense contractor tasked with organizing the facilities, facilitating the discussions, and compiling an after-action report. The meetings occurred over nearly two days, but no decisions or commitments were made by the various governmental agencies.

I accompanied General Zinni as his executive assistant throughout the wargame and attended all the meetings. He was interested in my thoughts and insisted on my honest evaluation. My sense was the attendees were somewhat overcome with the complexity of the issues. I suggested that, at the very least if any of the scenarios occurred, the Washington crowd could not claim to be unaware or ignorant of the issues. I told General Zinni I thought I observed a great deal of enthusiasm by many of the attending Washington staffers, but I doubted many of them would present their thoughts and observations to their seniors. I did not think anyone really wanted to think about the possibility of another ground war in Iraq. General Franks later told Colonel Stouder that "Zinni was very frustrated" and "the problem was too large for the Administration to grasp."[1] The silver lining to this effort was that USCENTCOM had a plan that was understood by its staff and the Service Component Commands. There was no formal submission of the plan to the JS, but they had cognizance of the level of magnitude of the challenges of such a scenario and at least one way to address them.

Planners at both USCENTCOM and ARCENT watched the events unfolding in the run up to war with Iraq with utter fascination in 2003. The number of units being mentioned in the press as preparing to deploy, or, more accurately, the lack of units being activated, was particularly surprising. Colonel Stouder, retired from the Army in the late summer of 2001, was both curious and concerned about these developments. He thought the press was missing the exact number of units given the secretive reporting of units being committed to Operation *Iraqi Freedom*. As it became clear only a fraction of those forces were being deployed, that years of planning had determined were required for this operation, his and other planners' concerns grew. I watched it develop from my desk in the Joint Security Directorate and thought more forces were being prepared for a later deployment. General Franks, now the USCENTCOM commander, knew the total and type of units required for success from when he was the ARCENT commander. At the end of the maneuver phase of combat operations in Iraq, it became known that the decisions to restrict force deployments in 2003 were made in the OSD. In all the OPLAN 1002 and 1003 development cycles, the one thing that remained constant was the requirement for four Army heavy divisions, an air assault division and two Marine divisions. These numbers represented a decade's worth of thinking, planning, and war fighting analysis. The small number of ground troops committed to this war was the first of several fatal decisions. The under-resourced ground forces did not allow the lines of communications to be secured, did not allow quick transition to postconflict, did not allow the policing required when the Iraqi military was defeated, did not provide the operational flexibility that would allow the field commanders to respond to developing events, and did not allow the commanders to crush a nascent insurgency.

The next two fatal errors occurred in quick succession. Ambassador Paul Bremer, within hours of taking over the Coalition Provisional Authority, decided to disband the Iraqi Regular Army and ensure de-Baathification of the new Iraqi Government. These decisions doomed long-held U.S. goals for Iraq in the aftermath of the fall of Baghdad. In the mid-1990s, when the JSCP gave USCENTCOM the mission of retaining Iraq as a nation-state, with the capability of self-defense and able to act as a counterbalance to Iran, the commanders and planners understood they had to retain the integrity and capability of the Iraqi Regular Army. Additionally, as they learned in the planning for *Desert Crossing*, the Iraqi Regular Army was key to successful postconflict operations. Not only did the U.S. need these forces to help secure and govern Iraq, but the decision to disband them put tens of thousands of trained, angry men on the street ready to sell their services to anyone who would pay them.

OPLAN 1002/1003's occupation forces were never fully discussed but the assumption was that USCENTCOM would have no less than ten Iraqi divisions in addition to the large American ground force so badly needed to secure its lines of communication. These forces were envisioned to play a large role in securing Iraq and discourage any guerrilla or terrorist activity that could follow the maneuver phase of the campaign. A large U.S. force was not expected to stay in Iraq for more than a year before being relieved by forces under the leadership of a multinational organization.

Ambassador Bremer issued an edict barring former Baath Party members from serving a new Iraqi government. Under Saddam, a man could not hold any governmental position unless he joined the Baath Party. Many of these officials had no loyalty to Saddam Hussein but were forced to be Baathists just to have a job in government. This meant that those Iraqis with governing experience were eliminated from any possibility of being in the new government, forcing the employment of a greater proportion of inexperienced personnel and placing more angry and influential Iraqis out of work.

The combination of these decisions, not enough troops on the ground, disbanding the Iraqi Regular Army, and de-Baathification of the new Iraqi Government, significantly limited the chances of American success in postwar Iraq. Ambassador Bremer alone cannot be held accountable for these decisions as he clearly had guidance from the OSD, if not directly from the White House. These decisions indicated an ignorance of the nature of the Iraqi state and Arab culture and ignored a decade's worth of military planning for war in Iraq. In May 2003, having, not surprisingly, achieved Operation *Iraqi Freedom*'s maneuver goals with the seizure of Baghdad with essentially two divisions, it quickly became clear available forces were too thin to ensure a viable occupation once the Iraqi Army was disbanded. The Arab formations originally thought to be available for occupation service never deployed into Iraq. The Peninsula Shield Force, an Arab organization comprised of combat units from all the nations of the Gulf Cooperation States, deployed specifically for the defense of Kuwait, and redeployed to their home countries shortly after Baghdad was taken.

I was sent to Baghdad early in May 2003 as a part of the vanguard of the Coalition Military Assistance Training Team that was tasked to recruit, train, equip, and field a "New Iraqi Army." This vitally important organization was grossly under-resourced. It would be expanded and more adequately resourced to become the Multi-National Security Transition Command–Iraq in 2004, but before the first battalion of this new Army was fielded in the fall of 2003, the insurgency had already begun, and it would be several years before large and capable Iraqi forces could enter the battle in large combat formations. It would become increasingly apparent, throughout the summer of 2003, that the entire stabilization phase of the Coalition's operations was under-resourced and critically short of "boots on the ground."

PART II

OPERATION *IRAQI FREEDOM* SPECIAL MISSIONS

CHAPTER 6

Staffing Posthostilities Operations

Never ask for guidance, you might get it!
—Lieutenant General Melvin Zais, USA

Judie and our daughters CJ and Allie stood in front of our Tampa home while our friend and neighbor Joe Liquori helped me load my gear into his van. Unlike my father, who had made his World War II transit to Europe by sea with his unit, I would fly as a passenger to Kuwait courtesy of American Airlines. I had always traveled light, but this time my load included a Swedish-made, SIG SAUR 552 Commando model assault rifle, a 9-mm pistol, and a host of other special items of combat-related equipment.

The weapons and equipment were courtesy of the Joint Security Directorate's equivalent to "Q" in "James Bond" movies—Master Sergeant Carl Gingola, USAF—an amazing man who had attained near legendary status as a weapons trainer and personal security expert at U.S. Central Command (USCENTCOM). A big man with a wide, friendly smile and a perfectly shaved head, Carl had been in the Joint Security Directorate (JSD) since 1999. I had quickly befriended him when I was assigned as the deputy director and often stopped by to visit him in his office near the main entrance to the headquarters. Carl is one of those guys who knows a lot about just about everything and, when I needed an opinion on any issue or sought a little relief from the ordinary, I could always count on him for some friendly conversation and valuable advice. When Carl thought my frustration level had peaked, he would take me to the firing range and allow me to shoot an assortment of weapons to my heart's content. I was never a particularly good shot, but Carl ensured I was a true expert with the rifle and reasonably proficient with the pistol. Carl managed the JSD warehouse in which he stocked many unusual gadgets he received from various gun and special weapons and equipment dealers throughout the state of Florida. His administration and supply discipline were impeccable and he took great pleasure in preparing JSD personnel for every conceivable mission. I was never lacking for infrared marking lights (chemical light sticks that glow in the dark), medical supplies, knives, special tools, the latest body armor, and even mission-related civilian clothing. The consummate professional, he was "Carl" to officers and enlisted alike. To my daughters, he was "Q." The JSD could not have had a better, more professional, and caring trainer and security manager.

Joe completed loading the van and I took a few more minutes with my girls for final hugs and goodbyes. As Joe began to drive off, I looked back long enough to wave a final goodbye. It was not the first time I had left them huddled together and wondering when I would be back. It would be another long year before I would see my wonderful and supportive family again.

I landed at Kuwait International Airport late in the evening. It was clear by March 2003 that the United States intended to invade Iraq. By this time, over one hundred twenty thousand Coalition troops were in Kuwait. The U.S. Congress had passed a Joint Resolution to authorize the use of U.S. Armed Forces against Iraq in October 2002. Preparations were well underway for the invasion. I was comfortable I was in the right place at the right time. The Kuwaitis, on the other hand, were uncomfortable that I was carrying guns and threatened to confiscate them. Finding the right guy from the Ministry of the Interior to stamp the innumerable documents necessary to register and transport weapons would have been difficult during regular work hours, but at midnight it was next to impossible. Somehow, it all came together and I was allowed to proceed through the airport. War may have been imminent, but in the airport and Kuwait City it was all "business as usual." I managed to get a lift to the U.S. headquarters at Camp Doha with a group of late-arriving soldiers and by 3 am I was processed, given a room number, and on my way to a warehouse that had been converted into officer and NCO billets. I did not enamor myself to any of my sacked-out buddies as I struggled through the hallway with all my gear, occasionally banging the walls en route to the properly numbered room. Accommodations were tight and, unknown to me, my room was already occupied by an Army air-defense major. A flick of the light switch brought a startled look and the usual expletives you would expect from a rudely awakened soldier. One of the great unwritten rules of the Army is never unnecessarily disturb a sleeping soldier. I quickly and quietly apologized, turned the light off, and felt my way into the unoccupied bunk. My gear could wait until later; I had caused enough trouble for one night.

My roommate was up in a couple of hours. His duties as a watch officer with the morning shift in the Combined Forces Land Component Commander's Tactical Operations Center ensured we would not see much of each other and, given the size of the room, it was just as well. I took stock of my surroundings. A large double-wall locker easily accommodated my uniforms and combat equipment. There was a face basin, running water, a TV, a refrigerator, and a small desk. It wasn't the "Ritz" but, from my perspective, I was in "Fat City." It really did not matter. My intent was to get out of there and into the field as soon as I could.

My orders assigned me to a new organization designated Task Force IV. This outfit's unique designation supposedly came from a reference to Phase IV of the proposed Iraq campaign plan that specifically dealt with posthostilities operations. Task Force IV had deployed to Kuwait between January and February 2003 as a separate and distinct command with the specific mission of planning the posthostilities effort in Iraq. Planning for operations after the fighting was over was not exactly what I had in mind to do in this war, but it was the only "ticket" I had at the time. I had no idea what position I would be given or what my responsibilities would entail. I didn't even have the foggiest idea where the unit was located or to whom I should report. Several hours after I arrived, I turned my weapons into the armory, slipped into the mess hall for some chow, and began to search for the strange and exotic sounding unit to which I was assigned. I did not have to go very far. Task Force IV was located one street over from my quarters, practically next door to the headquarters of the Combined Forces Land Component Commander (CFLCC). I walked by its entrance several times thinking it was a doorway to a maintenance facility. Unlike the almost pristine look of CFLCC Headquarters, a finished building with superb facilities, Task Force IV was housed in a hovel. Still, the structure had an expeditionary appearance that I hoped meant the Task Force would be moved early and quickly committed in Iraq. Carpenters literally erected walls around people as they worked and the sound of hammers and saws in action provided a continuous din throughout the building. Making my way past a platoon of carpenters, computer installers, and furniture haulers, I surveyed the main floor of the building to spot anyone who might be in charge. A young Air Force major named Scout Kinnan asked if he could be of some assistance and, shaking my head in continued amazement, I mumbled something about needing to see someone about reporting for duty. Kinnan introduced me to Colonel Jim Rabon, the deputy Task Force IV commander. Jim was an outstanding officer who I had met at USCENTCOM just before he deployed the organization to Kuwait. He had a great reputation as an aviation commander and was temporarily assigned to Task Force IV from his assignment at Fort Leavenworth to stand up the organization and facilitate its initial planning efforts. Jim was the "sanity check" in what otherwise appeared to be a poorly led, ill-conceived, last-minute, no doubt "cover your ass" organization that, except for a select few, was a conglomeration of misfits from all services, flung together as an afterthought to think about the posthostilities battlefield. I admired Jim's professionalism as he quietly and competently went about his business and provided what little leadership one could find in this organization.

The international debate whether to attack Iraq and remove Saddam Hussein's regime did not concern me as much as how quickly our planners thought we could drive to Baghdad and end the war. I understood the Iraqi war machine we planned to fight in the mid-1990s was significantly less potent now. Weapons embargoes, sanctions, and aging Soviet-built equipment had taken a serious toll on Iraq's overall military readiness. Planners are taught to never underestimate the enemy but, though I never doubted the outcome of a conventional, symmetrical battle with Iraqi forces, I was far less certain about how long it would take to defeat them. More than that, I was very uncertain of what the aftermath of the initial campaign would look like. My pessimism was based primarily on the long discussions I had had on this subject with Generals Peay and Zinni and the former War Plans Division chief, Colonel Rich Stouder, during our long hours of Iraq planning sessions at USCENTCOM in 1995–97. The plan provided a force like the one we had employed in the First Gulf War. We were convinced such a force was needed to engage the enemy on multiple axes of advance with overwhelming force and destroy the Iraqis in detail. But it was General Peay who made the comment most relevant to what would soon come to haunt us in Iraq: "Even if I could destroy Saddam's armies in short order with a smaller force, I will still need several Corps to establish law and order throughout a country that vast."[1]

General Peay and his successor General Zinni appreciated what it would take to secure and rebuild Iraq. Both of these great commanders thought the decisive battle would come after we removed Saddam. An "infidel" army as an occupation force in Iraq would go over like a lead balloon in the Middle East. It was evident to both generals that we needed to quickly outfit and deploy a 10 division Iraqi Army to secure the country's borders, contribute to its overall occupation and stability, oppose any Iranian designs on Iraqi territory, and eventually facilitate an American withdrawal. This is what the seminar wargame named *Desert Crossing* in June 1999 was all about. General Zinni and all the players in this hauntingly predictive seminar left the building with the harsh reality of what a coalition occupation force would face in a defeated Iraq. It verified the need for a large ground force to establish security and stabilize the large, tribal, religiously divisive, and otherwise broken country. General Franks had attended the *Desert Crossing* seminar wargame and had the benefit of having Colonel Stouder as his operations officer (G-3). He had personally briefed him on the specifics of OPLAN 1003, including its troop requirements of some 350,000 personnel.[2] It included two Army Corps, with the equivalent of nearly six divisions, a Marine Expeditionary Force with two divisions, and a division equivalent of Marine air and special operations forces. General Franks was as well versed as anyone on the plan and the reasoning behind the forces required. The modified plan for the invasion of Iraq in 2003 did not have nearly enough ground troops to address post-invasion contingencies. It was clear to anyone who had a hand in planning the Iraq war that the complexities of the Iraqi state and the absence of Saddam Hussein could lead to chaos.

One is left to draw their own conclusions about any discussions Secretary Rumsfeld and General Franks may have had about this subject. General Franks did not like OPLAN 1003-98, but reluctantly signed the document when he became the USCENTCOM commander and stated there would be changes to it during his command tour. He strongly believed operations would not require the time, or the troops, outlined in the plan. His focus was clearly on the kinetics of the maneuver battle and not on stability operations.[3] Secretary Rumsfeld certainly challenged the Joint Chiefs of Staff and the conventional military approach to military planning. It has been suggested he failed to understand the complexities of Iraq and simultaneously criticized the Joint Chiefs for failing to understand modern warfare as he knew it. General Franks is often accused of having been too accommodating to Secretary Rumsfeld. General Jack Keane, the Army's vice-chief of staff, even suggested General Franks thought that the posthostilities portion of the war plan was not his responsibility to plan or execute.[4] The USCENTCOM war planners were told it was not.[5] There was significant posthostilities planning conducted at the action officer level in the fall of 2002, but there was little or no senior leadership attention paid to it and it was never a major topic of discussion before the invasion. The failure of senior military officers to insist on the doctrine of overwhelming force ultimately produced an operations plan in 2003 that failed to muster the strength to secure and stabilize a fractious Iraq after the fall of Baghdad. It was, in retrospect, a fatal blunder. It was clear to everyone in 1999, that operations in Iraq after the maneuver phase of the campaign would not be easy. Time would prove General Franks's predecessors correct in their assessment of a need for a considerably larger force than the United States ultimately deployed in Iraq.

I reflected on the seriousness of those invaluable conversations and experiences as I gazed upon the pitiful organization to which I was assigned. Task Force IV was supposed to be the nucleus of a military organization that would lead the reconstruction of postwar Iraq. The organization resulted from a series of discussions initiated by USCENTCOM planners with the Pentagon's Joint Staff regarding the complexity of posthostilities operations and the unique policy and funding decisions that would have to be made. The USCENTCOM planners suggested a Three-Star General Headquarters with an ambassador and staff was required in the late summer of 2002 to plan and coordinate these efforts. Two organizations resulted from these discussions—the military element (Task Force IV) and the Office of Reconstruction and Humanitarian Assistance (ORHA)—which would initially oversee the political/military effort in Baghdad. Task Force IV included a section of engineers and an assortment of lawyers, communicators, military policemen, civil affairs officers, and administrative and logistics personnel. It was strictly a planning organization with no assigned units and, like the ORHA, it lacked specific guidance, a clear understanding of its chain of command, and proper resourcing. I assumed the Army's fighting commands would be anxious to leave Iraq as quickly as they had in the First Gulf War, and that a reinforced Task Force IV bolstered with appropriate service and support units would perform the inglorious task of putting the "Iraqi Humpty Dumpty" back together again. The USCENTCOM planners gave considerable thought to the posthostilities battle, but readily admitted it had no impact.[6] Task Force IV was never really taken seriously by USCENTCOM or the CFLCC and was destined to be left in CFLCC's wake. By June 2003, it had all but ceased to exist. While some of its assigned engineers would play a major role in establishing services in Baghdad, the bulk of its diverse, but talented, "misfits" were used as fillers for more viable formations in Kuwait and Iraq or sent home.

Jim Rabon informed me I would be the chief of the Civil–Military Operations Branch and introduced me to my division chief and immediate boss, Colonel Tony Puckett, USA. Tony, in turn, introduced me to the officers in my branch and briefly described what they were doing. It essentially amounted to situational awareness. All these officers were bright guys and gals, but it was very apparent to me that no one had a clue as to what they should be doing. They had not received any guidance. Any senior officer knows that bright people with no leadership and direction ultimately accomplish nothing. Lieutenant General Joe Kinzer, USA, an old friend and mentor of mine, often said, "When you don't know where you're going, any road will get you there." It was certainly the case here. I did not know enough to blame anyone and chose to keep my mouth shut. Tony Puckett was a good soldier and I sensed his frustration. I was impressed by how computer literate everyone seemed to be. The fascination of staring at the "one-eyed monster," as I often referred to the computer screen, could easily divorce a man from what was going on around him. People can look busy and get totally immersed in their business without sharing their observations or thoughts. Everyone looked forward to the daily Information Work Space (IWS) conference call—the morning information dump and staff-guidance session under the overall direction of irascible Task Force Chief of Staff Colonel Mike Williams, USMC, and monitored by Brigadier General Steve Hawkins, USA, the Task Force commander. I laughed as I watched everyone scramble to program their computers, with the characteristic battle cry of "Beat the rush," to log in. This was a new experience for me and I struggled with it until one of my officers helped me out with the procedure. I never particularly liked this leadership technique, though I saw the value of the technology in an environment where a staff or units were separated in multiple facilities or by significant distance. My concern with computers is that leaders often become prisoners of a never-ending flow of information, fail to get up, make a decision, or lead at all. I do not doubt many officers think sending an email that directs something be accomplished is all that's required to make it happen. They are ultimately doomed to fail.

"Big Mike" Williams conducted the IWS like he undoubtedly commanded a platoon of Force Recon marines. A former recon battalion commander, Mike had come out of retirement to become Task Force IV's chief of staff. I had first met him when he was assigned to the Marine Chemical Biological Incident Response Force (CBIRF) at Camp Lejeune in 1999. I accompanied General Zinni when he visited this elite special operations unit formed specifically to address chemical and biological accidents or terrorist incidents. He was respectful and friendly toward me, and we talked from time to time about non-business matters. He was tough as nails, an action figure, totally miscast for his role as a planner and staff coordinator.

His bully like approach struck fear in most of the young officers and more than a few of the older ones. I concluded it was best to stay clear of him. I may have admired his toughness but, like me, I thought Mike needed to be someplace else. How Jim Rabon and Mike Williams ever hung their hats under the same roof speaks volumes about military professionalism and restraint.

I took stock of my assets and thought about what my branch could do for the upcoming campaign that could be valuable. I had not received any guidance and did not think any would be forthcoming. It did not concern me. I remembered attending an officer call as a young captain in 1980 at Fort Campbell, Kentucky, and listening to the great Lieutenant General Melvin Zais, USA, former commander of the 101st Airborne Division in Vietnam and XVIII Airborne Corps who, when asked by an officer when he should ask for guidance, quickly replied, "Never ask for guidance, you might get it!" The implication in that grand soldier's words was very evident to me—never go out of your way to limit your maneuver space, do things your way, and get the job done. I met with the officers in my branch to seek their input. By this time, though we did not know it, we were less than three weeks from the date our forces would invade Iraq and the branch had essentially done nothing to prepare for our mission. The officers thought the branch could focus its efforts to develop a comprehensive intelligence preparation of the battlefield (IPB) by capturing what we knew or could find out about everything—from the Iraqi road network to demographics, to communications nodes and governmental facilities, to medical, legal, and military infrastructure, and anything else that could be valuable to commanders in the reconstruction effort—on a single compact disc (CD). We had the requisite expertise given our assortment of communicators, logisticians, political/military officers, civil affairs, information operations, and psychological-warfare planners. We even had a lawyer who doubled as an accountant; he was placed in the branch because no one knew what else to do with him. I outlined our plan of action to our division chief, requested the temporary assignment of two engineers to the branch, and went about the business of leading the development of a product that the civil–military staff would consider valuable for planners in the posthostilities phase of the campaign.

Our portion of the headquarters suddenly came alive. I provided guidance to my computer guys regarding how to organize the CD and left them to collate the data. The computer screens were now active with efforts to locate information from various intelligence sources instead of card games and other nonsense. We conducted "face-to-face" meetings every evening in a plush conference room across the street in the Civil–Military Affairs (C-9) staff warehouse to discuss our progress, answer questions, secure additional assets, and otherwise provide a "sanity check" on our activities in the quiet of a peaceful and controlled setting. I was amazed by the nature of the issues. I found myself involved in discussions concerning electrical power grids, water supply, sewage, agriculture, tribal relationships, civil administration, and the various duties of the Iraqi ministries of government. The exceptional talent of this group, now harnessed to a specific effort, had us well on our way to producing the CD in a little over a week. I was satisfied the data and general information we were producing could prove valuable to a commander and staff who took the time to review it. On 9 March, we were informed an organization led by retired Lieutenant General Jay Garner, USA, would be responsible for leading the stabilization and postwar recovery effort in Iraq. If nothing else, our officers were doing something that would get them smart on their piece of the Iraq reconstruction effort. Task Force IV would likely provide the initial manpower for a variety of organizations in direct support of the stabilization effort. Overall, I was feeling pretty good about what our team was doing to prepare for this challenging mission.

I was several days in the unit before I was allowed to pay a call on Brigadier General Hawkins. I had not met him before, but he was an engineer and I had never met a combat engineer I did not like. Our meeting reminded me there are first times for just about everything and while I suspected some of the challenges with Task Force IV had to do with the front office, my office call convinced me. General Hawkins had a solid reputation as a commander in the First Gulf War, but the man who sat before me as I enthusiastically entered his office was sullen, seemingly uninterested, and downright boring. Our "get to know each other" session had hardly begun when he received a brief phone call, hung up, and quickly informed me he had to see General McKiernan, the CFLCC commander. He never looked at me, wished me well, and ran out of the building without inviting me back. The British teach that an officer should never run for fear he will be viewed as silly or, worse, provoke panic among the troops. It is excellent advice. I was as disappointed as I was amused by the general's quick exit. I walked out of his office convinced this outfit under his command was not going anywhere and went back to work in my branch. Except for informing me sometime later that the font on a particular data page we were developing for the IPB project was too small, I never spoke to or heard from him again. General Hawkins later entered Baghdad in command of Task Force Fajr, a group of some 60 engineers and operations personnel, some of whom came from Task Force IV, and did a magnificent job leading the effort to restore the city's power, water, sewer, and hospital services.

In 12 days the Civil–Military Operations Team produced a CD that I proudly delivered to my division chief. I also provided a copy of the CD to British Major General Albert Whitley who occupied a small office in the Task Force IV warehouse. General Whitley had been given command and operational control of Task Force IV, something that undoubtedly irked General Hawkins to no end. He was a short, feisty, and brilliant officer of engineers, and an absolute pleasure to be around; he was calm, good-natured, and genuinely liked soldiers. He called me and said, as only a British officer with his pronounced British accent could, that he was, "Positively thrilled with your team's magnificent product." I believe it was the only product Task

Force IV ever produced in Kuwait. He asked me to provide him additional copies and thanked me and my team for our great service. I appreciated his kind words and passed them to my team. I was quite proud of this staff achievement but, with less than a week to the invasion, I wondered what else I could do in an outfit that desperately needed to be wanted. And then I got a break.

CHAPTER 7

Duty with the United Nations

Peacekeeping is not a job for soldiers, but only soldiers can do it.
—Dag Hammarskjöld

I knew a lot of people on the Combined Forces Land Component Command (CFLCC) staff, but the chief of the Civil–Military Affairs Directorate (C-9) was one of my best friends. Colonel Marty Stanton was an old Middle East warrior who had worked for me when I was chief of the War Plans Division at Central Command (USCENTCOM) in 1996–97. Marty's service in the Central Region pre-dated the First Gulf War, when he served as an adviser to the Saudi Arabian National Guard. He had chosen to vacation in Kuwait City early in August 1990 and was present when Iraqi forces entered the city. His exceptional conduct and gallantry shortly after Saddam's invasion and during his tenure as a detainee had earned him the Silver Star, America's third highest award for valor. A veteran of Somalia with the 10th Mountain Division, he had seen 15 years of continuous service in USCENTCOM and the Central Region, including six months in Pakistan and Afghanistan in 2001.

Marty had a mission that was made to order for me. Before we could invade Iraq, the United Nations Iraq–Kuwait Observation Mission (UNIKOM) had to withdraw from the demilitarized zone (DMZ) that separated the two countries. Marty's directorate was given the responsibility to oversee the withdrawal and who better to coordinate the action than an old UNIKOM veteran who knew the terrain and the general layout of Kuwaiti border police and United Nations facilities? Marty asked General Whitley if I could be temporarily assigned to his staff to oversee and report the withdrawal of the UN force and coordinate with Coalition forces in the area as required. General Whitley agreed and I quickly moved across the street to the C-9's office spaces to get better acquainted with the staff and prepare for the mission. Considering UNIKOM had been deployed for nearly twelve years, pulling it out of the DMZ would be no small task.

The United Nations Security Council approved a plan to create and deploy the UNIKOM to monitor the DMZ on both sides of the border, and the Khawr Abd Allah waterway, in April 1991. Fully deployed by May of that year, its mandate was to monitor the 40-kilometer-long waterway and a DMZ some two hundred kilometers long, extending 10 kilometers into Iraq and 5 kilometers into Kuwait, deter violations of the boundary through its presence and surveillance of the DMZ, and observe and report any hostile action between the two former warring nations.[1] The organization and strength of the force had varied somewhat since its inception but, during my tour in 1997–98, the force consisted of approximately 1,100 personnel (including 197 unarmed observers), a mechanized infantry battalion from Bangladesh, an engineer unit from Argentina, an aviation unit from Bangladesh with two UH-212 twin-engine helicopters, a logistics unit from Austria, and numerous UN civilian administrative, logistics, and maintenance staff. Thirty-three countries contributed troops or observers to the mission, an interesting mix of people, equipment, standards of conduct, and values and ethics that never ceased to amaze me. Success in this environment required a lot of patience. The direct approach on any issue, either with the UN civilians or the military staff, usually met with failure. It was an entirely new working environment for me, but an excellent training ground for dealing with the complexities of the multinational or coalition environment I would encounter later in Egypt and Iraq. As the chief logistics officer, or U-4, I was posted to the main headquarters at Umm Qasr, a former Iraqi naval base and one of Iraq's principal ports. The UN force commander divided the DMZ into a northern and southern sector, and exercised command and control through his two sector commanders.

During my tour of duty in UNIKOM, I frequently visited our observers who served on isolated posts throughout the DMZ. I was able to learn firsthand what their maintenance and logistical shortcomings were and quickly acted to correct them. There were seven observers on each of 17 patrol observation bases between the Khawr Abd Allah waterway in the north, to where the borders of Kuwait, Iraq, and Saudi Arabia converge in the south. It was a huge expanse of desolate desert to recon and observe. I always had a vehicle available, but the preferred method of travel was by helicopter. During my 12-month tour of duty, I logged over one hundred fifty flying hours spread over 100 separate reconnaissance missions with our gallant Bangladeshi airmen. Between the air-reconnaissance missions and my long daily drives, I got to know the DMZ very well. It aided my ability to render more accurate reporting during Operation *Desert Thunder* in 1997–98, significantly improved my situational awareness, and provided me the opportunity to engage with all the Mission's assigned officers. The DMZ was a dangerous place and, while the threat of combat action had abated considerably since the last foray of Iraqi units in 1993 to retrieve property left in Umm Qasr during the First Gulf War, banditry, drug and alcohol smuggling, sporadic weapons firing, and the ever-present threat of mines often disturbed the "calm and quiet" usually reported by our observers. In November 1997, one of our patrol observation bases on the Iraqi side of the DMZ came under fire and an observer from Ghana was seriously wounded. Another incident in February 1998 involved the hijacking at gunpoint of one of our patrol vehicles that was found, stripped of its vital parts and equipment, a month later. The observers were not injured. In both cases, the identity of the attackers was unknown, but we strongly suspected these incidents and most other illegal or terrorist-like acts in the DMZ were perpetrated by Iraqi soldiers.

The DMZ was littered with the refuse of a defeated Iraqi Army, including the hulks of numerous tanks and other armored vehicles. Saddam had constructed several concrete underground command centers and hospitals in the DMZ during his occupation of Kuwait; I explored these structures to find recent evidence of unauthorized Iraqi entry into the DMZ. The Iraqis frequently entered the DMZ in small numbers to scrounge parts from the rusting hulks. Road wheels were particularly valued, and I thought the embargo of military weapons and spare parts imposed on Iraq was likely very effective. I also thought these structures were used as way stations for smuggled goods. Alcohol, including everything from Johnny Walker to Jim Beam to fine wines and champagnes, was a heavily smuggled commodity. In addition to mines, the DMZ was littered with unexploded ordnance. I was surprised by the extent of this problem when I reviewed the monthly statistics of destroyed unexploded ordnance recorded by our outstanding Argentinean combat engineers. The Argentineans were garrisoned at Camp Khor, a large installation that also housed the troops from Bangladesh, Austria, and Uruguay. Having served in Panama and trained and parachuted with both the "Argies" and the Uruguayans, I was very comfortable accompanying them on patrol as they very systematically went about their dangerous business of finding, marking, and destroying unexploded ordnance. I spoke enough Spanish to understand and converse with them, something they appreciated immensely. Regardless of how dedicated they were to the task, however, the removal of mines and other ordnance from the southern Iraqi desert was expected to continue for years.

On one of my frequent air-reconnaissance missions in March 1998, I monitored a radio call from one of our observers requesting immediate medical evacuation (medevac) of three Iraqi civilian men who had been injured by a mine. The rainy season had heavily watered the desert since it had begun to rain in late October, and highly prized, protein-rich, mushroom delicacies known as truffles grew in abundance throughout the DMZ. Unfortunately for these three men, one of the truffles they harvested turned out to be an antipersonnel mine. The blast caused all three to lose a leg each and they all suffered numerous fragmentation wounds. Their only hope was to be medevaced to Umm Qasr for treatment by our outstanding German paramilitary medical unit (GERMED), whose medical professionals were provided by a humanitarian organization known as Malteser International. Our pilots quickly located the scene of the incident, and we joined our other aircraft already on the landing zone. I threw myself into the rescue effort helping to load the Iraqis onto the aircraft even as the medics attempted to stabilize them. It was a long ride back to UNIKOM's headquarters and I stared at these poor guys almost in awe. They did not as much as moan. They were strong, ruggedly handsome men, but thin and wiry and covered in filth and blood. My uniform was heavily blood stained as well. The GERMED doctors and nurses were standing by to receive their patients when we arrived at the helicopter pad at Umm Qasr and quickly wheeled them into the medical clinic. The head surgeon was an exceptional man. Dr Michael Paulus was an experienced surgeon who had served on several UN missions. No stranger to traumatic wounds, he assessed each patient, organized his team for surgery, expertly tended to their wounds and cleaned and prepared their stumps to accommodate a prosthesis. He and his team of nurses and doctors worked for over six hours before their three patients were out of danger and resting in the recovery room. It was an amazing display of medical professionalism by a brave and exceptionally talented team that merited everyone's utmost respect.

Doctor Paulus was very concerned about me and his staff as the entire affair had been like a scene from a horror movie. Later that evening, he tended to the psychological needs of his nurses and assistants, and he asked me to join them for a German home-cooked dinner. I was very grateful; though this gathering was a bit subdued compared to other events with my German friends, the food was fantastic and I enjoyed their company. A little time with good-looking German nurses and traditional German food was a real treat after the day I had had and I suspected Dr. Paulus knew that. He was several years older than me and I once asked him if he was related to Field Marshal Von Paulus of the ill-fated German Sixth Army that had surrendered to the Russians at Stalingrad in 1943. He winked at me and whispered that Field Marshal Von Paulus had been his uncle and that it had been better in postwar Germany to drop the "Von." Dr Paulus lived an exciting and selfless life, perhaps in his own way making up for the ills of Germany's militaristic past.

General Esa Tarvainen, Finnish Army, commanded UNIKOM in December 1997. We would become very good friends within a few months, but there was little time to get acquainted in December. He had convened his staff to prepare for a total withdrawal almost immediately after assuming command during the American *Desert Thunder* force build up. I took it upon myself to conduct a reconnaissance of our withdrawal route, our assembly area in Kuwait, and the designated holding position at the UN Logistics Center in Kuwait City. The thought of abandoning the mission under wartime conditions had been frightful to many on the civilian staff who had grown used to its permanence and somewhat comfortable lifestyle. UN duty on a deployed mission is always expeditionary like when the peacekeeping forces and the UN staffers are initially deployed, but conditions in an established mission improve over time and life at UNIKOM headquarters was very good. Assignments to such missions can be very profitable and even comfortable for some, and it was not unusual for people to serve multiple tours of duty in Iraq and other seemingly inhospitable places where peacekeeping forces were deployed. I thought about the chemical warfare defense classes we had conducted for the civilians in 1997. The physical condition of some of the civilians was not the best and the thought of some of the portlier individuals donning protective gear would have been funny had the situation not been so real. The possibility of having to function for even a short period of time in a "dirty" environment was truly unacceptable. The bulk of the civilian staff was not fit for even a short period of time in protective masks and chemical suits let alone the stress of a combat environment. I suspected these same kinds of issues were burdening the military staff at Umm Qasr again as they prepared for another, imminent withdrawal to Kuwait.

UNIKOM, unlike many UN missions that were, at worst, failures or, at best, disappointments, had executed its mission well since 1991. But now, as American units began the process of cutting holes in the Kuwaiti fence that ran the length of the DMZ, and with its mission essentially about to end with an American-led Coalition invasion of Iraq, the issue was not if the force should withdraw, but when. It was 14 March and time was running out.

The CFLCC C-9 office space was in a well-developed warehouse. Colonel Stanton had been there since October 2002 and his office was spacious and well equipped with bookshelves, a computer, and comfortable furniture. He and his staff had worked diligently on a myriad of tasks that dealt with the politically sensitive issues of host-nation relations, Coalition coordination, and humanitarian assistance. The Coalition piece of his kingdom would only grow in importance as more nations signed on to participate in the war effort. Stanton's staff was actively engaged in getting Coalition contingents transported and positioned in Kuwait from where they would ultimately move into Iraq. The officers, noncommissioned officers (NCOs), and soldiers in the C-9 were good people. The experienced special forces senior NCOs on his staff were particularly impressive. The C-9 mission was never adequately staffed and I was pleased when the entire Civil–Military Branch from Task Force IV was eventually reassigned to reinforce Colonel Stanton's team. Its movement to C-9 was the first indication of Task Force IV's dismantlement. It was good to know the people with whom I had worked would be gainfully employed and, as importantly, well led and appreciated.

Colonel Stanton lost no time in explaining my mission. I was excited to learn I was to coordinate the withdrawal of the UNIKOM force from the Iraq–Kuwait border. The mission's implied tasks included reporting activity in the border area near Umm Qasr, providing American forces in the area with any information pertaining to the UN headquarters and Camp Khor, and providing any information on the disposition of Iraqi forces in the area. He introduced me to two great soldiers who were to accompany me: Sergeant Major DeGroff, a tough special forces soldier who was Stanton's senior enlisted adviser; and Major Adrian T. "Bogie" Bogart III, USA, a special forces officer who had graduated from the Virginia Military Institute with the Class of '81. Both men had been with the C-9 at Camp Doha for several months and were happy with the opportunity to do something exciting and meaningful in the field.

Marty and I closely reviewed the information he had gathered at this point from UN representatives in his meetings at the Logistics Center in Kuwait City, and we did a quick map reconnaissance. All the major features and installations were still very clear to me. I had driven the Coastal Road to Umm Qasr on more occasions than I could count in 1997–98 and I was anxious to get going. Final coordination for the mission with the UN was necessary, however, and we departed for the UN Logistics Center on the afternoon of 14 March to meet with British Colonel Peter Verge, UNIKOM military assistant to the force commander.

The Logistics Center sat in a section of Kuwait City known as Khaitan. During my UNIKOM tour, I had occasionally gone there on business. The buildup of American forces in the region for Operation *Desert Thunder* had all but eliminated any rooms or trailers for my officers at Camp Doha so, by late 1997, we would use the PX and other facilities, do our laundry, and then relocate to the UN Logistics Center to occupy a room for the night. I did not allow the officers of the American contingent to travel on the Coastal Road to Umm Qasr after nightfall, a safety precaution I strictly enforced. The road was dangerous for several reasons, not the least of which was the Kuwaiti habit of driving without the benefit of headlights. Accidents were common and they were normally catastrophic. The road was also frequently crossed by camel herds and hapless vehicles frequently met equally hapless camels in the darkness. Inevitably, both came out second best with disastrous results. The camel herds were a fascinating sight; we would stop to watch them from time to time while traveling or patrolling during the day. The sheep and camel herders were excellent sources of information if we had an Arabic speaker with us. The Logistics Center was within walking distance of several shops and "schwarma" (Arabic-style chicken sandwich) stands and, after checking in and securing a room, we would wander down to the shops and gorge ourselves on schwarmas while we listened to the evening call for prayer. I smiled, reflecting on those times nearly five years before. As Colonel Stanton and I pulled into the walled Logistics Center, it occurred to me nothing had really changed. Piles of unused equipment, including boxes of chemical-protection suits, were everywhere and I noted the section of smashed vehicles, a legacy of the danger of patrolling and working in the DMZ and driving the ever-dangerous Coastal Road.

Colonel Verge greeted us as we approached a series of offices along one of the center's long corridors. He had set up a map and a few briefing charts. Several other members of the UNIKOM operations staff were present. Marty introduced me and I was immediately welcomed as a former UNIKOM observer. It was clear to all of them that UNIKOM's withdrawal was now inevitable, hostilities were imminent, and that we better get on with final planning. Colonel Verge's briefing was informative and professional; I pressed him on various issues pertaining to various locations on the map. I left nothing to chance. Five years can dull the memory and I did not want to screw anything up due to a navigation error. Colonel Verge informed us UNIKOM was already withdrawing from its patrol observation bases on the Iraqi side of the DMZ and all land, air, and sea patrols on the Iraqi side had ceased or were scheduled to cease shortly. Patrols on the Kuwaiti side were increased but the entire northern portion of the DMZ was essentially unmonitored. He opined that this withdrawal may be the warning of hostilities Saddam's regime was looking for, and that the lack of patrols on the Iraqi side of the DMZ created the possibility for Iraqi ground forces to move into the DMZ and conduct further defensive preparations. There had been reports of Iraqis laying mines in the DMZ, but he dismissed these as less than credible. Reports of mines beyond the DMZ and along main roads and lines of communication were more likely to be true. He added that groups of armed Iraqi soldiers had been seen in the DMZ by the Kuwaiti Ministry of Interior troops who manned their border observation posts and anxiously followed the new developments in the DMZ.

The UNIKOM plan called for a withdrawal of the peacekeeping force to Camp Khor, the large troop garrison on the Kuwaiti side of the DMZ, where the force would establish an assembly area, then serial vehicles and equipment down the Coastal Road, and eventually close at the Logistics Center in Kuwait City. Some vehicles were scheduled to depart on the 17th, but the bulk of the force was expected to move the following day. We discussed communications, and it was agreed I would coordinate any business with UNIKOM from the final Kuwaiti checkpoint on the Coastal Road before entering the DMZ. It was a good meeting and Marty and I drove back to Camp Doha to make final preparations for the mission. After meeting with Major Bogart and Sergeant Major DeGroff, we agreed we would depart for the border the next day. I was anxious to move out but thought better of driving the Coastal Road during hours of low visibility. We used the afternoon and evening to check our equipment and vehicles and got a good night's sleep.

We arrived at the UN checkpoint by mid-morning on the 15th and checked in with the Kuwaiti Ministry of Interior border guards manning the position. It did not amount to much—two small shelters on each side of the road and a crossbar they manually operated to allow vehicles to pass. We positioned our vehicle off the side of the road. I intended to coordinate with Colonel Verge from this position and seek his permission to enter the DMZ. Our Kuwaiti friends in the meantime reported our presence to their commander who drove down from his headquarters for a look. I could not have been luckier; the commander was none other than Captain Hassan, a mountain of a man, a sportsman easily weighing 250 pounds, immaculately attired in a starched desert camouflage uniform and Fidel Castro-like utility cap. We had been good friends during my UNIKOM tour and I had frequently called on him at his comfortable headquarters. Unlike the Iraqi police headquarters and checkpoints in the DMZ that were hastily constructed hovels with minimal furniture and no power, the Kuwaiti Ministry of the Interior troops enjoyed first-rate facilities and were well fed and cared for. The Iraqis on the other hand, would often go days without a resupply of food and water, and it was not uncommon for them to beg patrolling UN observers for a bottle of water or a field ration. Hassan and I would exchange information, drink tea, and adjourn to the bench press to impress each other with our strength. It has never ceased to amaze me how physical strength, conditioning, and general health impress our Arab friends. I could not compete with Hassan given his enormous mass and natural strength, but I worked hard to improve throughout my tour, and he never failed to take notice. Always hospitable, he had introduced me to many senior government and military Kuwaiti officials and, during the closing days of my tour, had insisted I make a series of farewell office calls in Kuwait City so my service in Kuwait would be appropriately recognized. Hassan was a real piece of work, a real character. When he saw me, he smiled from ear to ear and yelled at the top of his lungs, "The King of the DMZ has returned!" It made a great impression on Bogie and I could not believe my good fortune. Hassan was a good man and I was confident he would help me if I needed him. But, for now, we simply talked about the current situation, and he confirmed Iraqi activity in the DMZ had increased. I suspected UN officials would protect their bureaucratic ideals and protocols to the very end and not allow us to enter the DMZ. Hassan, I thought, would be my "entrance ticket" when the time was right, as I reminded him of humorous incidents from our past and various personalities that had touched his life.

We continued to talk and joke, to the amusement of everyone around us, while Bogie and Sergeant Major DeGroff contacted Colonel Verge who joined us a few hours later at the checkpoint and updated us on UNIKOM's activities. The UN force was struggling with the realities of leaving a "house" in which it had grown far too comfortable. We listened to him describe the difficulties of the move; I tried to look concerned while thinking, "You've got three days to make it happen, Colonel." I suspected he would ask for additional time before too long. When I asked him if he would allow us to have a look at the DMZ and Camp Khor, he promptly said he could not. Colonel Verge was a good soldier, but he had his orders. I understood his position and was not resentful, but I resolved to have a look and I had already begun to think about how I would do it. After assuring us he would keep us up to date to facilitate our reporting to CFLCC headquarters, he sped off for Camp Khor, leaving us to locate nearby units and coordinate our presence in the area. Captain Hassan told me he would stop by the next morning and bring us a hot breakfast. I thanked him and he gave me his characteristic bear hug and drove off. I would put our friendship to the test the next day.

There were two units in our immediate vicinity. The closest was a Kuwaiti armored battalion that was within a few hundred meters of the DMZ checkpoint. There was very little activity there that we could see. The battalion's tanks and support vehicles were tactically parked, and, except for several security patrols, it appeared the bulk of the battalion was doing everything it could to lay low and stay out of the sun. Not surprisingly, the Arabs are smart about life in the desert. They normally move after sunset when things cool down a bit. The Bedouins I had observed in Southern Iraq always broke camp around nightfall and would settle into their tentage early the next day. It made a lot of sense and, not expecting to see or speak with anyone of significance, we set our sights for the 15th Marine Expeditionary Unit (MEU) which was located several kilometers southeast of the UN checkpoint and well into the desert.

Activity at the Marine encampment was more intense and, not surprisingly, many marines were engaged in some form of physical training, staying sharp for the combat that lay in front of them. They exercised with sandbags, pipes, and anything else they could lay their hands on. One officer referred to it as "jailhouse P.T." Unknown to us, the marine running along a desert path when we drove in was the MEU commander, Colonel Tom Waldhauser. I have always admired the Marine Corps' physical-training ethic. Even support troops maintain a hard PT regimen and a respect for their personal weapons and equipment, something I wish Army support units did. The failure to exercise these fundamental disciplines in Army service and support units would cost us in blood during the next several weeks.

We made our way to the MEU Tactical Operations Center where we introduced ourselves to several staff officers and explained why we were there. They were happy to see us once we explained our mission was to monitor and report UNIKOM's withdrawal from Umm Qasr and the DMZ. Several Coalition teams had already cut huge lanes through a border-long fence the Kuwaitis had erected to prevent Iraqi infiltration and to control the movement of refugees. Our presence was convincing evidence that combat operations were imminent since UNIKOM's withdrawal was a critical last step before Coalition forces could attack into Iraq. The marines quickly oriented us on their maps. Their initial mission was to seize the city of Umm Qasr and its vital port facilities. These facilities were particularly important to support Coalition logistics and humanitarian operations and I talked at great length about what I knew of the facilities and the general layout of the port.

The UN Oil for Food Program had brought many ships to the port since the end of the First Gulf War. As logistics chief (U-4), I had become very familiar with the port since UNIKOM monitored the offloading of these ships and accounted for their cargoes. The type and number of offloaded stores were routinely briefed to the UNIKOM commander during his daily morning update. I often observed operations in the port, boarded offloading ships, and conversed with local and port officials. Umm Qasr was an interesting place, and its marketplace was particularly active. Despite the rumors and headlines of starving Iraqi kids in southern Iraq, the market appeared to be well stocked with fish and other foodstuffs. The Iraqis had always struck me as a very innovative people, perhaps made that way due to the absence or scarcity of many goods and services since before the First Gulf War and the embargoes that came later. I frequently observed mechanics working on cars that easily would have been targeted for the junk yard in the United States. They engineered and rebuilt parts and kept equipment of all kinds running. I was impressed by their ingenuity and remember thinking what these guys may have been capable of doing with modern tools and machines.

The evidence of the massive buildup of Iraqi forces in the vicinity of Umm Qasr during Saddam's ill-fated war with Iran in the 1980s was everywhere. Rusted hulks of damaged and destroyed military vehicles and equipment littered the port and the littoral areas of the waterway. Not far to the east was the World War I-like landscape of the al-Faw Peninsula. During the Iran–Iraq War, it had been the scene of horrific combat that had included massive artillery duels, chemical warfare, and Iranian human-wave assaults. On at least two occasions in 1997–98, UNIKOM patrols found near whole skeletal remains of Iraqi soldiers in the long trench lines that cut through the vast, pot-marked, moon-like desert surface.

Colonel Waldhauser and his staff were interested in my insights and descriptions of the objective area, so I stayed with the intelligence and operations officers for several hours reviewing every detail I could recall. They were also interested in the UN headquarters. Prior to the First Gulf War, it had served as an Iraqi naval headquarters and hospital. Anchors and other trappings of naval culture were on the building's grounds. The headquarters had served as the centerpiece of the UNIKOM command group and staff for nearly twelve years. Other smaller buildings on the grounds were former medical storage sites, including a former morgue that had been converted into the deputy UNIKOM commander's quarters. The Marines assumed the Iraqis would reoccupy the headquarters as soon as it was abandoned, and listened carefully as I described its long, wide corridors and twisting passageways. This and other sessions with the Marines were particularly satisfying to me. I wanted to contribute to the war effort in a special way and, for the moment, this seemed like an excellent way to do it.

They allowed us to bed down at their camp for the night; I settled for the passenger seat of our Humvee for sleeping quarters while Bogie sent our report to CFLCC via a secure phone. I was anxious to see Hassan in the morning, so I asked Sergeant Major DeGroff to drop me off at the DMZ checkpoint. Hassan arrived at the checkpoint with several covered paper plates and a big smile, and loudly exclaimed, "King, I have brought you a wonderful breakfast!" You had to love Hassan. He had always been very good to me and, as we sat by the shelter and ate our chow, I asked him if he would take me into the DMZ for a quick look at the border area. It was, of course, illegal, but, after a short delay, he said very nonchalantly, "Okay, when do you want to go?" I said, "Dusk, just before nightfall," thinking I would most likely see movement after the temperature cooled off a bit. He agreed.

I was primarily interested in the area near the UNIKOM headquarters at Umm Qasr. There were several vantage points along the berm from where I could use my binoculars to observe Iraqi police stations and checkpoints and scan the areas near them for vehicles and personnel. Captain Hassan and I linked up at 6 pm, giving me about three hours of good reconnaissance time. It was more than enough. As long as I was with Hassan and maintained a low profile, I did not consider myself in a particularly dangerous situation as long as we stayed on the Kuwaiti side of the ditch that separated Iraq from Kuwait. My biggest concern was being seen by UN officials or observers still on patrol. But I was in luck and for the next several hours we didn't see another vehicle on the DMZ border road. It appeared the DMZ mission was at an end and the UN force was totally committed to packing up Camp Khor. It was a nightmare scenario that required the help of every observer, soldier, and civilian assigned to the command.

In addition to their fence, the Kuwaitis had dug and maintained a ditch and berm along the entire length of its border with Iraq since the end of the First Gulf War and the establishment of the DMZ. During the buildup for Operation *Desert Thunder* in 1997, I had coordinated several link-up points along the ditch to facilitate an emergency withdrawal of the U.S. contingent with special forces elements that worked for the Special Operations Central commander, Brigadier General Frank Toney, USA. The epitome of a "soldier's soldier," Frank Toney was a great commander and the most combat-oriented warrior at his rank I have ever known. Fearless and physically imposing, he took his mission to extract the American contingent from Iraq seriously. He personally infiltrated the DMZ on several nights to recon locations along the ditch that would facilitate our ground extraction, and he coordinated helicopter extraction points in Iraq with us if the situation dictated our withdrawal by air. I never doubted his sincerity. Our coordinated meetings in and along the ditch during the crisis of 1997 were exciting and professionally stimulating. It was good to know our general officer-selection process still managed to secure a few pure warriors like Frank Toney.

I looked for the area where General Toney and I had met over five years ago, remaining careful not to position our vehicle in direct line of sight of an Iraqi police checkpoint. Captain Hassan drove slowly as I reconned the Iraqi police stations and looked for indications of Iraqi activity. We saw several Iraqi trucks but there was no evidence of armored vehicles or large formations. Still, there was far more vehicular activity than I remembered from my observer days. Hassan and I covered about fifty kilometers from our entry point near Umm Qasr, west along the ditch and back. Hassan was normally very talkative and funny, but he had been very quiet and sullen throughout our near three-hour recon. He knew my return to the DMZ meant things were about to happen that would significantly change his world. He dropped me off and, happy to be done with me for the night, recovered his huge smile and said, "I'll see you in the morning, King."

"Will you bring breakfast?"

"For a king," he replied, as he drove off with a screech.

Colonel Verge joined me at the checkpoint a half hour later and discussed the status of the withdrawal. As I suspected, the situation at Camp Khor was frantic. I strongly recommended UNIKOM consider leaving its station property that could not easily be transported and focus its efforts on the withdrawal of personnel, personal baggage, and administrative and operational files. I very matter of factly reminded him UNIKOM's withdrawal timeline would not be extended beyond the 18th, a point Colonel Stanton had clearly articulated during our meeting at the UN Logistics Center. Our conversation was friendly enough, but I could see the stress in his face. UN missions rely heavily on the military professionalism and education of officers from the United States, the United Kingdom, and other Western powers. As the military assistant to the force commander, Peter Verge had a very difficult job and I do not doubt the vast bulk of the planning for this withdrawal had fallen squarely on his shoulders. He told me there had been more reports of Iraqi activity around UNIKOM's headquarters. It would be totally abandoned by 17 March and he fully expected the Iraqis would quickly occupy it. I made a mental note to include this information in our evening report to CFLCC and to share it with Colonel Waldhauser and the MEU staff.

We spent the bulk of the next day with the Marines. Bogie and Sergeant Major DeGroff spoke with a Coalition Support Team consisting of two special forces noncommissioned officers who were assigned to a Kuwaiti armor battalion. We typically assigned such teams to Coalition forces to advise, monitor, and assist them as required. Their insights and observations of Iraqi activity, that they had observed, verified my earlier conclusions and the information Colonel Verge had provided. It was clear the Marines would have a fight on their hands shortly after they crossed the border and entered the former UNIKOM compound and Umm Qasr. I had violated many of the rules and guidance I had been given by going on my reconnaissance, but I was satisfied I had seen enough to ensure our reporting was accurate. Colonel Verge reported that UNIKOM would withdraw from the DMZ by mid-morning on the 18th and the bulk of its station property would be left behind. Captain Hassan was also aware of this when we linked up at the DMZ checkpoint after nightfall. I positioned our team at the checkpoint that evening to ensure we did not miss anything, and to count all UNIKOM vehicles and personnel that withdrew through there the next morning. It was a cool evening and we settled down for the night in the guard shelter after Bogie rendered our evening report to CFLCC headquarters.

Several UN vehicles of various types passed through the checkpoint early the next morning. By mid-morning, the traffic picked up, but what I thought would be disciplined serials of 6–10 vehicles separated by 10–20 minutes of driving time, were one or two vehicles that appeared to have loaded their respective cargo and simply departed Camp Khor on their own accord. It was not until 10 am that a major convoy took shape. UNIKOM was essentially moving in a single serial and it appeared to be more of a rout than a disciplined and orderly march. Sedans were mixed in with heavy transport trucks and tactical vehicles, including the wheeled armored personnel carriers of the Bangladeshi infantry battalion. Soldiers stood up in the cargo compartments of the trucks and mingled with equipment that had been manhandled on board. Heavy equipment was loaded on the heavy transporters and, to the drivers' credit, was tied down and seemingly secure. It was not the most orderly road march I had ever seen, but I assumed there was a method to it all.

I was standing by the checkpoint making a mental note of the number and type of vehicles passing, when I was hailed by several folks who looked very familiar to me. I was amazed to see two UN workers who had been a very important part of the logistics team during my UNIKOM tour. Fernando, a Malaysian who ran the Officers Club and managed the bar, and Nixon, a Filipino who had been my loyal and efficient logistics office manager, were in a sedan and pulled off the road to converse with me and shake hands. I had very fond memories of our time together. Recognizing how each of them had relied on the UN system for years to sustain their families in their respective countries, I thought briefly about their future and felt sorry for them. Sometime tomorrow, the United States would initiate major combat operations with the aim to overthrow Saddam Hussein. Their lives, like so many others in 24 hours, would be forever changed. They were happy to see me, however, and we had a good laugh reminiscing about old times in the mission together. They suggested we get together in Kuwait City for dinner sometime; while I really did not think it was possible, I told them it was a great idea. They drove off and I rejoined Bogie and DeGroff, who were dutifully counting vehicles. Colonel Verge joined us and he appeared happy the withdrawal had finally begun. He told me the force commander and members of his personal staff would be in the last vehicles to leave the DMZ and I nodded an acknowledgement. I really did not have much to say at that point. My team had performed our mission well. Our reports were well received and the withdrawal of the UN force, however disorganized in appearance, was occurring on schedule. If no one got hurt on the way to Kuwait City, I thought, it would be a major achievement.

Captain Hassan drove up to our little group and dramatically announced, as only he could, that UNIKOM was very close to clearing out of Camp Khor and that we could expect to see the last group of vehicles passing through the checkpoint very soon. We waited another 30 minutes before a serial of seven or eight sedans and pickup trucks approached the checkpoint. In the first vehicle, sitting in the front passenger seat, was the great Dr. Michael Paulus. Upon seeing me, he directed his driver to pull off the road. He approached me and managed a smile. He was visibly upset at what was happening and, as he shook my hand, told me he hoped peace would result from yet another war with Iraq. He wished me luck and, after peering into my face with the saddest of looks and a slight delay, turned and got back into his sedan. I would never see him again.

Lastly, a sedan with UN flags and carrying the force commander passed into view. Major General Franciszek Gagor of the Polish Army had assumed command of UNIKOM only two months earlier in January. He directed his driver to pull over and, stepping out of the rear of the vehicle, pulled himself up to his full height, assumed the position of attention, faced me, and rendered the two-fingered hand salute of the Polish Army. I returned his salute and complimented him on behalf of the Coalition Land Forces Commander for the successful completion of his mission in Iraq. He seemed satisfied with that, dropped his salute and, without a word, got back into his vehicle and departed. General Gagor would remain in Kuwait as the UNIKOM commander "in exile," and operate from his new headquarters at the Logistics Center in Kuwait City until July 2003. I did not realize it, but it would not be the last time I would be in the company of Polish generals.

CHAPTER 8

Stability Operations in Iraq

The military needs to refine its capability to anticipate and stockpile the materiel likely to be required in a stability operation, so that the resources can be made available in a timely way.

—Dr. Lawrence A. Yates

I tried to convince Combined Forces Land Component Command (CFLCC) headquarters to allow my team to stay with the Marines who would attack Umm Qasr. Colonel Waldhauser recognized our value and was amenable to having us during the initial assault, but my disappointing orders were to return to Camp Doha. I went to Task Force IV to pick up a few items, then to the Civil–Military Affairs Directorate (C-9) staff area to find out what my next assignment would be after thanking Bogie and Sergeant Major DeGroff for their efforts. Colonel Stanton greeted me with a handshake and congratulated me on the successful completion of the UN withdrawal mission. General Whitley complimented me as well. Colonel Stanton told me that shortly after Umm Qasr was taken, elements of General Jack Kern's 352nd Civil Affairs Command would enter the city to assist the local government to restore services. It was assumed Umm Qasr would be a permissive environment by the second day of the invasion and we would immediately begin the process of rebuilding Iraq. He asked me how I would feel about being attached to a Civil Affairs Brigade to assist them during their initial operations in Umm Qasr. It seemed like a good idea at the time. I really had no other option. I had paid a short office call on General Kern on 6 March; we discussed our experiences in Kabul the previous September and the upcoming challenge in Iraq. Stanton had already discussed attaching me to the 352nd with General Kern and he was very amenable to my assignment. General Kern wanted me to accompany members of the media once the brigade was committed in Umm Qasr and orient the brigade on the terrain and the populace as required. I agreed, thinking it afforded me a lot of latitude and that eventually I could find a more productive and permanent assignment on his staff or elsewhere in southern Iraq.

The 352nd Civil Affairs Command is one of four Army Reserve formations that help to transition a campaign from war to peace. Its most valuable asset is its people, a diverse, professional group of experts with skills in law, government, engineering, sanitation, business, and just about anything else it takes to run a community. Many of the great Americans that comprise these units perform the same job or function in civilian life. Since *Desert Storm*, they had been called to active duty almost continuously and many of them were veterans of Bosnia, Kosovo, Haiti, Somalia, Afghanistan, and the First Gulf War. The 352nd consisted at that time of two brigades, each of which had three battalions.

I was ordered to pack up and move to Camp Arifjan, an American base well south of Camp Doha and Kuwait City where the 354th Civil Affairs Brigade was assembling. The brigade was under the command of Colonel David Blackledge, USAR, and its mission was to conduct operations in the port city of Umm Qasr. I did not know a lot about the civil affairs business when I arrived at Camp Arifjan, so I was surprised by how top heavy with high-ranking officers these organizations are. There were several colonels in the brigade and many other field-grade officers in the rank of lieutenant colonel and major. I did not doubt there was a pecking order. Everyone seemed to know everyone else and there was a clannish atmosphere that would make any "outsider" feel uncomfortable. The headquarters where the 352nd Civil Affairs Command and the 354th Brigade had set up was a hot bed of activity when I arrived on the 19th. It was very apparent General Kern had not told anyone I was coming, but the chief of staff welcomed me when I told him why I was there and arranged to get a bunk for me in the warehouse barracks. He introduced me to the staff that evening and, having talked to General Kern by then, announced I would assist with the media and help with reconnaissance once we got to Umm Qasr. I did not have much to do and simply used my newfound time to get to know people and help wherever I could. I also secured a basic load of ammunition. The barracks warehouse was my first real indication I had entered a world far different from my disciplined orientation in the infantry. The chain of command did not think it was necessary to separate the ranks and, in some areas of the building, the genders weren't separated either. It was not unusual for reserve units' discipline and the chain of command to be secondary to informal friendships. It concerned me when I thought about the detrimental effect such an arrangement could have on operational effectiveness in combat. I talked with several junior officers who were interested in my unusual assault rifle. These young officers were good men, full of enthusiasm and anxious to get into the fight. It was clear, however, that the more senior guys were standoffish. I was determined to do everything I could to help them and become an accepted member of their organization. It's important that a soldier "close ranks" quickly with their assigned unit regardless of where they would rather be or what they'd rather be doing. It is also one of those unwritten rules of professionalism in the Army. I felt certain things would get better in Iraq.

The United States went to war that night and my thoughts were with the 15th Marine Expeditionary Unit as I watched some of the action on the TV monitors in the headquarters. I should have been with them and silently cursed the decision that had prevented it. The next several days were taken up by Iraqi Scud missile attacks and a variety of alerts. I found myself increasingly amused by the reaction of some of the troops during the chemical attack alerts, all of which, as I suspected, were false. Every Scud was assumed to carry a chemical warhead and, while this was prudent, I sensed an almost desperate attempt on the part of some leaders to play everything by the book and not apply a modicum of common sense to the situation. During one Scud attack that occurred somewhere in Kuwait, the alert was sounded and the doors to the warehouse instantly locked. The rules were that anyone caught outside would have to find some other shelter to prevent them from contaminating everyone else in the building. I suppose that would have been logical if a chemically tipped Scud had scored a hit on our base, but I was dismayed one afternoon when a young female soldier missed the door closing by less than a minute. Her feverish knocking on the door and pitiful cries for help were all I could stand as she pleaded, "Please, please let me in!" I calmly went to the door, while several officers stood by and watched, directed the guard, a young private first class, to let her in, and ended it. The worse thing a soldier can be is a "lock step" fool, but I did not blame or scold him. Somewhere behind almost every stupid event is an officer that faithfully and blindly carries out his orders while failing to understand the commander's intent, apply a sense of logic to his orders, or encourage younger soldiers and junior leaders to act accordingly. The value of leadership should never be underestimated.

The 354th moved out several days later and commenced a long convoy movement, closely monitored by Kuwaiti Ministry of Interior troops, that ultimately took us to the Coastal Road, through the former DMZ checkpoint, through the berm, over the ditch, past the former United Nations Iraq–Kuwait Observation Mission (UNIKOM) headquarters currently occupied by elements of the British 16 Air Assault Brigade and the Royal Marines of 42 Commando, and finally to the port of Umm Qasr. I suggested to the convoy commander that he consider using the Port Authority building as the brigade command post. It was badly beaten up by our Marines who were well on their way to Baghdad by this time. Smashed windows and evidence of a fight were everywhere but, with a little cleaning up, we had a good structure from which to operate. Eventually, a British mess hall opened for business not 300 meters from us in an abandoned maintenance shop. In fact, British support troops were all around us as 16 Air Assault Brigade and various armored units were engaged in combat outside the major city of Baṣrah, not too far north of us, and as far south as the outskirts of Umm Qasr where "mopping up" operations were still underway. The British 1st Armoured Division commanded a force of three Army brigades: 16 Air Assault Brigade, the 7th Armoured Brigade, and the 102nd Logistics Brigade. The Royal Marines' 3 Commando Brigade was also under the operational command of the division. These were the forces we would encounter as the 354th Civil Affairs Brigade entered the port city and began to initiate its operations.

Not surprisingly, the British had supported the Coalition effort in Iraq in a relatively large way. Aside from the United States, the United Kingdom contributed more resources and troops to the Iraq mission than any other Coalition partner. The Brits had committed about forty-six thousand troops to Operation *Telic*, the codename of all British operations in Iraq, from the March invasion through the end of major combat operations in June 2003. During this phase of the campaign, some twenty-six thousand British Army soldiers, 4,000 Royal Marines, 5,000 Royal Navy and Royal Fleet Auxiliary sailors, and 8,100 Royal Air Force airmen were actively involved in the operation.[1]

The land offensive began on 20 March 2003, less than twenty-four hours after the air campaign started. The British 1st Armored Division's initial objective was to seize the al-Faw Peninsula and secure the vitally important port of Umm Qasr. Simultaneously, 40 Commando (Royal Marines) and other Coalition forces launched an amphibious helicopter assault to seize key Iraqi oil infrastructure on the al-Faw Peninsula. The assault was supported by the British Joint Helicopter Command, a variety of landing craft, and three Royal Navy frigates providing fire support. Securing the peninsula and the Rumaylah Oil Field in southeast Iraq by British and American forces allowed Coalition personnel to quickly move north. The United Kingdom's attention then turned to securing Baṣrah, Iraq's second-largest city, to prevent Iraqi forces from staging attacks on Coalition logistical lines of communications. Despite encountering significant Iraqi resistance, British forces seized Baṣrah's airport in four days and began expanding their area of control in the surrounding region. After several days, they took the town of Az Zubayr, southwest of Baṣrah, and entered Baṣrah on 6 April. The British commanders, in coordination with local leaders, assisted in restoring a functioning police force and the first joint British–Iraqi police patrols took place just one week after the city had been liberated. British success in southeast Iraq enabled American troops to advance swiftly toward Baghdad and take control of most of that city by 9 April.

Unit rotations began shortly after the declared end of major combat operations. The 19th Mechanized Brigade relieved the 7th Armoured Brigade in June 2003, and the 3rd Division replaced the 1st Armoured Division in July 2003. The 3rd Division controlled numerous other Coalition forces in southeast Iraq, including contingents from Italy, the Netherlands, Denmark, the Czech Republic, Lithuania, Norway, and New Zealand. The British-led force was designated Multinational Division (South East). During their nearly six-year involvement in Operation *Telic*, British forces helped the Iraqis secure and rebuild the country at the end of major combat operations, supported reconstruction in southeast Iraq, and assisted the Iraqis build their economy. They contributed to training the New Iraqi Army and participated in combat operations.

Entering the Port Authority brought back old memories of calmer times with UNIKOM. The building was a total mess. I picked my way through the officials' office spaces while the staff established its living quarters in a spacious bay. I had had numerous dealings with the port officials in 1997–98 when I accompanied UN civilians to review ship cargo lists associated with the Oil for Food Program. I briefly wondered if it had been necessary to "rough up" the building this badly, but I suspected the Marines did what had to be done. I picked up a few small office items as souvenirs and quickly concluded the vast bulk of the files strewn over the floors were of little or no intelligence value. It would not be the last time I would see the records and facilities of the Iraqi regime's ministries and Army in such disarray. I would be sickened by the destruction of the Iraqi Army training centers and garrisons I would later inspect for use by the New Iraqi Army throughout northern, central, and southern Iraq. I dropped my bags by an empty cot, walked outside, and hitched a ride to the port. Several rusting ships were tied up and several Iraqi coastal patrol boats that I remembered so well were still there. This port was vitally important to any humanitarian assistance effort the Coalition planned to undertake, so I took note of some of the obvious repairs that were required. It was a mess, but I suspected the heavy cranes critical to the port's operation were either tenuously functional or, at worst, repairable. I gave my report to the brigade's S-3 and encouraged him to, "Press whatever buttons necessary to expedite repair and salvage teams to Umm Qasr."

One of the more colorful individuals I met during this period was Lieutenant Colonel (Doctor) Chuck Fisher, USAR. "Doc" Fisher was a reservist on assignment to Special Operations Command and, like me, had been attached to the 354th Civil Affairs Brigade. A highly credentialed medical professional, Chuck Fisher was also a hard-core soldier who carried his weapons as competently as his medical bag. As a fellow "outcast," we got along very well. Doc enjoyed weapons and insisted I take a few photos of him holding my rifle while standing next to a mural of Saddam at the entry to the Port Authority. Doc Fisher was a good guy to know and the next couple of days would reveal he was the only friend I had. The Civil Affairs folks seemed to grow increasingly "clannish." I had seen evidence of this at Camp Arifjan, but I thought it would disappear once we entered Iraq. I grew increasingly frustrated by the unit's lack of activity. Vehicles were in short supply and, in a unit with more officers than enlisted personnel, everyone seemed to think their mission was the most critical. I accompanied two female journalists who were embedded with the unit into Umm Qasr on a couple of occasions. We found several food and water points and they "snapped away" with their cameras and conducted interviews while I concerned myself with security and what other humanitarian-related requirements I could note and report. Like the GIs of World War II and every war, I handed out candy or chocolate to the kids. I also carried cigarettes which are particularly useful for getting information or developing relationships with men and local officials. The Iraqis were very appreciative of the services, but the situation was desperate. Long lines of women, children, and old men beside the water tankers and food lines were a common sight. Control and security at these sites are critical to avoid a "survival of the fittest scenario." If a mob moves on a site, only the strongest will get to the water spigots or the food. Older women and children will end up on the short end of the bargain. In Umm Qasr and elsewhere, water trucks with multiple spigots were badly needed. The answer to the challenge was eventually answered by extending the Kuwaiti water pipeline into southern Iraq. In civil affairs operations, you can never have enough engineers and medical personnel. Restoring and maintaining infrastructure and fundamental social services are critical to operational success. You could not help feeling sorry for these people. The living areas in Umm Qasr were cramped and the streets were trashed. Services were lacking and the smell throughout the town was generally odorous, a combination of trash, unwashed bodies, animal feces and cooking smells. It reminded me at times of the old Bronx and Mount Vernon neighborhoods of my youth, only a lot worse.

The amazing Doc Fisher managed to get a vehicle one morning. He had undoubtedly stolen it. He picked me up at the Port Authority and we headed downtown to visit local medical facilities. Finding the hospital was no easy task, but a U.S. Army ambulance outside the building gave it away. We were welcomed by the Iraqi hospital staff and invited to tour the facility by the chief administrator. The Iraqi patients we saw were in terrible shape. The ambulance provided some medical supplies, but Doc took stock of what supplies were available and assessed the hospital to be in worse shape than its patients. He was primarily concerned with infection and general cleanliness. "This ain't Johns Hopkins, Colonel," he said with a smile as he continued his assessments. It was clear we could not get aid to this place soon enough. The chief administrator handed a letter to me as we departed that included a long list of critical medical supplies. We scoured the area to fill the list from units in the area and took whatever we could get to the hospital. But Doc's days in Umm Qasr were numbered. His efforts were largely unappreciated by our adopted unit and he was soon detached and returned to Camp Arifjan. It was yet another disappointing decision by officers who appeared to be desperately afraid of "outsiders" and were seemingly threatened by our very presence.

My hopes of working in the brigade's operations shop never had much of a chance. The S-3 was an experienced civil affairs officer with the rank of major, but his shop was clearly undermanned and, from what I could see, he was desperate for assistance. He operated out of the cargo pocket of his trousers. There was no schedule of events or daily operations briefings to the staff, no allocation of available vehicles by mission, and no posted maps and operational overlays. My offers to help were politely refused and I knew my days in Umm Qasr were also numbered.

In retrospect, it is understandable that many of these guys would not accept someone who was not a regular member of their club-like organizations. Job security meant more to these reservists than any professional assistance or expertise that someone from outside the organization had to offer. As the 354th Civil Affairs Brigade grew more comfortable with its surroundings, the likelihood of meaningful employment grew even more remote and I found less and less to do of value to the unit or the war effort. I took stock of my situation—I was in Iraq and had taken on a few exciting missions. Compared to the hapless staffers at CFLCC, I was at least in the field and away from meaningless staff work and assorted paperwork. Without transportation and an assigned billet, limited responsibilities, and little hope of securing a better assignment from the brigade commander, however, I figured my time was about over. I called Colonel Stanton on a cell phone one of the journalists let me borrow, told him my mission with the 354th Civil Affairs Brigade was completed, and asked to be reassigned to contribute to the war effort in a more positive manner. I would later learn my efforts in Umm Qasr were commended. Fortunately for me, my call could not have been timelier. I was needed elsewhere and I was recalled to Camp Doha for another mission.

CHAPTER 9

Advising the Peninsula Shield Force

The Business of business is relationships; the business of life is human connection.
—Robin S. Sharma, Canadian author and speaker

My new orders were to serve as the Combined Forces Land Component Command (CFLCC) Senior Liaison Officer and Military Adviser to the Peninsula Shield Force (PSF). The PSF is an Arab combat formation that roughly equated to a mechanized infantry division in ground combat power during its deployment in Kuwait. It was formed in 1984 as a two-brigade force of 10,000 men by direction of the defense ministers of the Gulf Cooperation Council (GCC). The GCC is an organization designed to confront security challenges collectively, and includes the United Arab Emirates, Saudi Arabia, Kuwait, Oman, Qatar, and Bahrain. The possibility of another desert war with Iraq convinced the Kuwaitis to ask the GCC to deploy the PSF in the defense of Kuwait. Elements of the PSF had deployed on exercises before, but this was its first wartime deployment. The PSF's headquarters and its Saudi units are garrisoned at King Khalid Military City in northeastern Saudi Arabia. The force is commanded by a Saudi major general. The national elements of the force had arrived in Kuwait by both ground convoy and sealift in late February 2003. The PSF moved into the western Kuwaiti desert and established a static defense in coordination with CFLCC Headquarters. The PSF proved to be particularly useful during the period that preceded the invasion of Iraq. It occupied a division front on the border with Iraq where it was deployed by national unit. The 10,000-man PSF had significantly reinforced the Kuwaiti Army that barely numbered 20,000 men. It assisted with security missions in Kuwait, including the protection of Coalition base camps, airfields, and fuel farms when American and other Coalition forces entered Iraq.

I never doubted the usefulness of the PSF if for no other reason than the political statement its presence in Kuwait meant to the Coalition and, more importantly, to Saddam Hussein. Its presence was a clear indication Saddam was totally isolated. The PSF's orders, however, were to defend Kuwait and, by the time I arrived at PSF Headquarters, it was clear it was in the backwater of the war. Its commanding general had described a typical day for his troops as, "Moving left to right and front to back." Any offensive operations by the PSF would require orders from the Kuwaiti Minister of Defense.[1] I would have preferred an advisory mission in Iraq, but I was excited about the assignment and there was still a chance portions of the PSF would be deployed in southern Iraq. Recalling that original OPLAN 1002 planning assumed a ground force that would include several Arab divisions, I thought the PSF was the vanguard of a larger Arab force to assist in the occupation of Iraq. I had to be patient, develop good relationships with the unit commanders, report unit activities as required, and mentally prepare myself for any mission possibilities.

I was accompanied by Major Dave Wilson, USA, an artilleryman and Middle East foreign-area officer. Dave spoke Arabic and had been assigned to CFLCC C-9 for several months. This assignment was exactly what he wanted—an opportunity to serve with Arab units in the field, improve his Arabic, and gain a better appreciation for their customs and lifestyle. He would prove to not only be a fine officer, but a good friend to me as well. On 2 April, with Dave at the wheel of an SUV, we struck out on our long haul from Camp Doha, west to Ali Al Salem Air Base, and 60 kilometers further west across the seemingly endless desert on a highway filled with wheeled and armored vehicles belonging to the U.S. 4th Infantry Division. I was relieved to finally turn north onto a desert road where we passed several checkpoints before arriving at the PSF desert encampment.

Compared to how an American Division Command Post might look, the PSF's was incredibly spartan. There was a mess tent, a series of small and medium general-purpose tents for billeting purposes, several tents for social gatherings or diwaniya sessions (during which officers of all ranks discuss everything from politics to business to world events and cultural issues), and a row of trailers that housed senior officers, normally colonels and generals. Two large, well-furnished trailers comprised the commanding general's quarters. Conditions were austere, but not particularly uncomfortable. In fact, our Arab comrades were quite comfortable in the desert. As youngsters, all of them had frequently camped in the desert with their families, an attempt to return to their "roots." During my United Nations Iraq–Kuwait Observation Mission (UNIKOM) tour, I had frequently driven the Coastal Road en route to Umm Qasr and enjoyed watching the Kuwaitis camp out with their SUVs, generators, carpeted tents, and huge satellite dishes that undoubtedly provided unlimited television channels. It was not exactly what their ancestors had experienced in earlier and leaner times.

Dave and I found the designated trailer for the "American Liaison Team" and unloaded our gear. The trailer wasn't exactly the "Ritz"; it was not air conditioned, nor did it have a shower. I hooked up an Australian shower, an outdoor canvas bag with an adjustable shower head that filled with water and provided an excellent field expedient to wash up. It was beginning to get hot in the desert, and temperatures would soon exceed 120 degrees. Our only furniture consisted of our Army cots and a single chair. On the positive side, the trailer had a bathroom complete with a Western-style commode and ice-cold running water.

We moved to the Operations Center where we hoped to meet members of the staff and arrange an office call with the PSF commander. The Tactical Operations Center was underground in a tunneled labyrinth of staff sections, planning spaces, and conference rooms. Unlike the bustling activity of an American headquarters, the place was practically deserted. An infantryman guarded the entrance but allowed us to enter after Dave spoke to him. This underground bunker was probably built by the Iraqis during their occupation of Kuwait. I had seen Iraqi construction of this type in the demilitarized zone (DMZ) during my UNIKOM days when I stumbled upon underground command posts and hospitals of concrete construction during routine patrols. The desert in this area was filled with the remnants of Saddam's defeated Army from the First Gulf War; helmets, uniforms, boots, wire, trash, chemical equipment, and various repair parts, tires, and assorted rusting hulks dotted the vast, sandy landscape. Dave and I walked downward into a darkened passageway that turned sharply to the right into a tunnel with small spaces for various staff sections on both sides before it emptied into a well-lit conference and briefing room. There were no computers or other fancy devices of any kind. A butcher pad of paper, an overhead projector, and maps depicting the area of operations took me back to simpler and more austere times as an infantry battalion operations officer (S-3) in 1982–83. Our staffs were less compartmented back then and staff officers often knew more about the operation than some of the operations staffs I had seen in the nineties that were almost totally focused on computers, digital maps, and information specific to their staff area of concern. Enlisted soldiers from several countries lingered about, but it did not appear that anything significant was occurring. The operational pace or "OPTEMPO," as Americans would say, was slow, but it was not too long before several staff principals entered the conference room to prepare, I assumed, for the evening command briefing.

The staff was nationally diverse. It did not appear to me that staff procedures or written standard operating procedures existed and we wondered how they coordinated their operations and patrol plans, tracked unit activities, or presented briefings to the commander.

The PSF operations officer (G-3) was an Omani colonel named Said al Hosni. Said was a good-looking officer with a broad smile and a wonderful sense of humor. He spoke briefly and seemed very pleased to have a senior American liaison officer with the staff. CFLCC had provided a major early in the PSF's deployment. He had been very popular with the staff, but the demands of the CFLCC staff, the growing number of national contingents in the Coalition, and their requirements at Camp Doha, had dictated his recall. Rank is important in multinational settings. I had been told before I left Camp Doha that the CFLCC staff wanted to have a colonel with the PSF who might have greater influence with its senior officers, particularly the commanding general. Said introduced me to the personnel officer (G-1), an Emirati colonel who was both friendly and courteous. He offered to secure an appointment for Dave and me to call on the commanding general. I thanked him and, with little else to do, we moved back to our trailer to finish unpacking and get something to eat at the mess tent.

I assumed field rations were the order of the day out here, but the PSF enjoyed good food and normally ate prepared meals. The PSF officers mess was housed in a medium general-purpose tent. Food was prepared by two older, civilian men of unknown origin who spoke a rough Arabic dialect and cooked the meals in a series of pots and grills near the entrance to the tent. It was not unusual to have grilled meats of various types, though chicken and lamb were particularly popular. They curried the vegetables and just about everything else. Breakfast consisted of eggs, beans, hummus, and yogurt. The commanding general frequently dined at the mess tent where he enjoyed talking to his officers and seeing who was present for duty. It was no secret that more than a few officers took any opportunity they could to slip off to Kuwait City for the more comfortable environs of its numerous hotels and night life.

The commanding general of the PSF was Saudi Arabian Major General Omar Ben Hassan BaBa'eer, a short, bearded, calm, and courteous gentleman who had served his country for well over thirty years. He received me and Dave with a broad smile after his aide-de-camp ushered us into the living area of his quarters. The general looked very familiar and after a few minutes it occurred to me I had met him during a Central Command-sponsored command-post exercise in Kuwait in 1995. I briefed him and a room full of other Arab senior officers on the notional disposition of Coalition forces in the Kuwaiti desert preparing for an offensive against an unnamed aggressor force that was obviously Iraq. The Syrian senior representative, a major general, had a great deal of difficulty following my briefing that was translated by a young and very intelligent Kuwaiti draftee. The general spoke no English, had little, if any, computerized wargaming experience, and failed to understand the concept of operations and the assumptions the planners had made to facilitate the exercise. He was abusive toward the Kuwaiti translator and discourteous to everyone. General BaBa'eer moderated the discussion and eventually succeeded in calming the Syrian. He later pulled me off to the side and told me he thought the Syrian was ignorant and I should not be upset. It was all quite clear to me and I reminded the general of our previous encounter. Eight years had passed since that exercise, but we laughed about it and conversed like two old friends.

The Arabs are among the most hospitable people in the world, a fact often lost in a world racked with terrorism and the challenges of the Middle East. A general or a commander at any level will almost always call for tea and sweets served by enlisted aides when he has visitors. Guests are obliged to accept this hospitality. As a rule, relationships are developed over time and guests should be careful not to engage in business too quickly, allowing the host to establish the agenda. A "get to know each other session" normally focuses on health and family and, in this case, old times, Central Command exercises, and the war in Iraq. I was perfectly content with this. I had no idea how long the war would go on and I had no desire to return to a staff assignment at Camp Doha. I suspected there would be many meetings in which we would have serious discussions. General BaBa'eer encouraged me in his rough, but understandable English to work closely with his staff, brief him on the Coalition's progress in Iraq, and visit his units in the field. The meeting could not have gone better. The general was delighted Dave spoke Arabic. We spoke for over an hour before his duties demanded a recess. He warmly shook our hands, welcomed us to the PSF, and encouraged us to stop by often. It was a genuine invitation. As we walked to the mess tent, Dave, like Major Bogart after my reunion with Captain Hassan in the DMZ less than three weeks before, expressed surprise at my numerous Arab connections and particularly my relationship with General BaBa'eer. I was thrilled my luck was holding.

Equally fortuitous was the relationship we quickly established with two Kuwaiti officers also serving in liaison positions to the PSF: Lieutenant Colonel Salem and Major Ali who was nicknamed "Ali al Sahaf" for his tall tales reminiscent of Muhammad Saeed al Sahaf's (better known as "Baghdad Bob") bogus interviews with CNN while serving as Saddam's Minister of Information. We had no sooner emerged from the mess tent when we were invited to a cookout at the Kuwaiti trailer. Salem and "Sahaf" had somehow managed to buy fresh fish and arranged a barbeque. In keeping with characteristic Arab hospitality, they invited the newly arrived Americans to their trailer. This provided an opportunity to meet and talk with several other members of the staff including the PSF intelligence officer (G-2) from Qatar, and Colonel Nasser, the personnel officer (G-1) from the United Arab Emirates. The camaraderie was great, but I was anxious to get deeper into the desert and introduce myself to the brigade and battalion commanders. I was quickly coming to appreciate the genuine hospitality we were experiencing in the PSF encampment was a one-way ticket to the Army's overweight or "fat boy" program. Clearly, Dave and I would have to maintain a strict physical-training regimen.

The briefings I had received at CFLCC had alluded to the possibility of a deployment of an Arab formation to southern Iraq and the most likely unit to do it was the Emirati brigade. Having reported to the commanding general, my next priority was to meet the Emirati commander and quickly establish a good relationship. I had assumed that when, or if, the brigade moved into Iraq in the postmaneuver phase of the campaign, Dave and I would go with it in an advisory capacity. We drove nearly forty minutes before we saw the Emirati national flag fluttering in a light breeze. We were surprised once again by the spartan-like Brigade Command Post. A series of tents outlined the encampment along with a variety of armored and commercial vehicles. The Emirati Tactical Operations Center was also underground in a well-prepared bunker complex with a tunnel-like passageway. The guard allowed us to pass, and we walked along the dark passageway to a briefing and conference area that had a big screen television. Several junior members of the staff greeted us and immediately offered us tea, a variety of sweets, nuts, and dates. "I won't be able to train hard enough to keep from getting fat at this rate," I thought as I patiently waited for the arrival of Colonel Mohammad, the brigade's commanding officer.

The Emirati brigade consisted of two infantry battalions equipped with Russian armored personnel carriers, an armor battalion with French LeClerc tanks, and an artillery battalion of South African G6 155-mm self-propelled howitzers. A variety of smaller combat and support units, including a reconnaissance company and several armed helicopters, brought the brigade's strength to roughly 2,500 men. Colonel Mohammad was a strong, calm, and cautious man who spoke in a low, very deliberate tone of voice. He rarely smiled and carefully weighed everything he said. I recognized very quickly that establishing a positive relationship with him would take time and work. He appreciated our visit to his command, however, and I asked him how he was getting along, and about the health and welfare of his family. He did not appear to be happy, but his reserved manner exuded the strength of a commander in firm control of his brigade. He was ably assisted by his deputy, Colonel Abdullah. Another large, strong-looking man, Abdullah was an accomplished athlete who had once played volleyball on the Emirati national team. Reluctant to talk at first, he nonetheless was very friendly and never failed to smile. Both men were very pleasant and courteous. I offered to assist their efforts in any way I could and request any resources they may need. Mohammad thanked me and though he was quick to point out there was no need for assistance or material requirements at the present time, he would not hesitate to ask in the future (the Emirati brigade would require our assistance in a big way the following month when the decision was made to redeploy the entire brigade to the United Arab Emirates). Colonel Mohammad gave us a tour of his command post and provided an extensive and detailed briefing of the location, readiness, training, and mission of his battalions. I did not doubt his brigade was a good outfit. During my tour as General Zinni's executive assistant, we traveled several times to the United Arab Emirates to meet with its colorful Army chief of staff, Mohammad bin Zaid. Better known as "MBZ," he was the crown prince of the Emirate of Abu Dhabi. In May 2022, he was elected to the presidency of the United Arab Emirates. He was determined to modernize his nation's military. Discussions often focused on equipping and training special operations forces and the Air Force, but the equipment and overall capability of his conventional ground forces were also very important to MBZ, and he was determined to have the best possible armed forces his nation could muster.

The PSF staff battle rhythm or schedule of events and activities included a briefing to the commander every evening at 6 pm. I prepared a briefing from the situational update we had received before we departed Camp Doha in accordance with General

BaBa'eer's wishes and guidance to me earlier that day. The staff meeting that evening was a command and staff meeting; the brigade and separate battalion commanders also attended. General Baba'eer formally introduced me to his commanders and principal staff officers and was delighted when I offered to present an update on the situation in Iraq. Dave provided the translation, with some assistance from Colonel Said, the PSF G-3. I used charts and maps to depict the movement of our soldiers and marines on two axes of advance oriented on Baghdad. I spoke freely but carefully, ensuring the bulk of my comments were not too unlike those of the retired colonels and generals on FOX and CNN television. General BaBa'eer was very pleased and again welcomed us to the PSF. Over the course of our short but eventful tour with the PSF, Dave and I provided many of these situational awareness briefings to the general and his staff. Their curiosity concerning the location of Saddam Hussein was profound. They all agreed his death or capture was vitally important to Iraq and the region. The briefings gave us a great deal of credibility; our popularity and familiarity throughout the command grew substantially.

I was determined to visit every unit in the field and evaluate their combat readiness. The PSF was deployed along a wide front that we would drive for miles across the desert relying almost entirely on our GPS. Long hours in the SUV, coupled with increasing temperatures, and the quick closing darkness of the desert evenings, made for stressful and tiresome days. Happiness was seeing the national flag of the brigade or battalion headquarters we wanted to visit as I scanned the distance through my binoculars. Our travels often took us over former Iraqi command posts and logistics bases. The desert was awash with Iraqi refuse, and we often picked up helmets or other items of military equipment we thought could be used as trade bait with American units in the future.

Our visits to the Saudi brigade were as rewarding as they were challenging. The brigade was commanded by Brigadier General Mozan, a quiet and capable commander who was never particularly comfortable with our company. His brigade was task organized with two battalions of mechanized infantry mounted on the venerable American M113 armored personnel carrier and a battalion of American M60A3 tanks. The Saudis also had an artillery battalion with American M109 self-propelled howitzers. It was a formidable brigade task force. General Mozan lived comfortably in a large trailer that included a queen-sized bed. He understood English but preferred to speak Arabic; he employed a lieutenant colonel to translate. This is a common technique used by many Arab leaders who use the translation time to formulate a measured and effective response. It made perfectly good sense to me. General Mozan enjoyed the company of his officers and, whenever we paid a call on him, several of them were normally present watching television. Colonel Said al Hosni accompanied us on several of our visits to conduct business while simultaneously, I suppose, keeping an eye on us. Our conversations with the Saudis quickly moved from readiness and training issues to regional political issues. Mozan was particularly keen on hearing my views pertaining to the Israeli–Palestinian issue. I had a "ring-side seat" to watch the Israeli–Palestinian problem with the second Intifada in 2000 during my command tour in the Sinai and I had a good understanding of the emotions the issues generated among the Arabs. I always emphasized the American desire for peace in the region and a solution that was ultimately fair to both parties. I was careful to ensure General Mozan understood my views did not necessarily represent official American policy. I suggested an international response to the Israeli–Palestinian issue was necessary to achieve a lasting peace. I also shared my long-held belief that Jerusalem should be an international city. It was a comfortable, measured, and somewhat neutral position to take, considering the company, and one that General Mozan accepted rather well.

These sessions could be stressful, but they were also enjoyable. We almost always talked about our families and the tea and sweets his aides served us eased the tension considerably. There is no substitute for honest and objective conversation and responses to questions, however cautious and measured, to develop a strong relationship and gain respect from an Arab counterpart.

Our visits to the smaller, separate battalions were equally challenging. Bahrain's tank battalion was equipped with American-built M60A3 tanks. It was commanded by the colorful Lieutenant Colonel Rashid, a graduate of the American Armor Officer Advanced Course at Fort Knox, Kentucky, and our prestigious Command and General Staff College at Fort Leavenworth, Kansas. We would later learn Colonel Rashid is a member of the royal family. Rashid's command post was a dug-in American M577 command tracked vehicle and his staff was trained, efficient, and impressive. In this environment, Colonel Rashid focused our discussions on tactical and operational matters. His questions were those of a student of warfare and a true professional soldier. He reserved any political discourse of his interest for the diwaniya officer gatherings normally conducted in the evenings. His battalion clearly reflected his professional military education, training, and leadership.

The Kuwaitis contributed a company of M-84 tanks to the PSF. The M-84 is a variant of the Russian front-line T-72; it is manufactured in Yugoslavia. The Kuwaitis maintain several types of fighting vehicles, tanks, and artillery in their inventory of weaponry and some of it is of questionable value. A former seminar and Army War College classmate of mine, and now a highly respected Kuwaiti general, told me his nation's military purchases were often a method to curry favor with major countries in the United Nations. He told me that, "Small countries like Kuwait require favorable votes from the Security Council." He recognized that maintaining a variety of complex systems was inefficient and costly, but it made a lot of sense on the political level. Their front-line systems, however, were American-made Abrams tanks, Paladin self-propelled howitzers, and F/A-18 fighter aircraft. The Kuwaiti company commander was a major who was very uncomfortable with our visits, perhaps thinking we were inspecting his operation. I was conscious of this, having commanded two infantry companies earlier in my career. Young commanders in all armies are wary of senior officer visits that too often detract from training or maintenance activities. The Kuwaitis pulled their maintenance early in the morning and, like the others, laid low in the afternoon to escape the heat and discomfort of the day. He was generally available when we showed up to talk to him, but his low-key, seemingly uninterested, manner was an indicator he wanted me to make it fast and move on. It would take more time to convince him and several other commanders that my assignment to the PSF was to advise and assist. Patience is a true virtue when attempting to cultivate an effective and trustworthy relationship with Arab commanders.

The Omani motorized reconnaissance battalion was equipped with a British-built, Swiss-designed wheeled armored personnel carrier known as the Piranha. It is a very capable vehicle the Omanis had purchased in large quantities in the late 1990s. The vehicle mounts a 7.62-mm or 12.7-mm machine gun. The Omanis had long been considered the best trained of the GCC armies. Their equipment was new and well maintained, and the Omani soldiers impressed us with their enthusiasm and training. I was not surprised by this given the significant British influence and advisory effort that continues in Oman to this day. The battalion's young commander, Lieutenant Colonel Mohammad, was a handsome and pleasant soldier who enjoyed our company and proudly showed off his command. The Omanis patrolled a large portion of the PSF front along the Iraqi border and Mohammad invited us to participate in these patrols as often as we liked. Our discussions were less politically oriented, focusing more on military training and readiness. He never asked for any material assistance and when it came time for his unit to return to Oman, he did so overland in a disciplined convoy movement he coordinated and executed to perfection.

Our activities during our first several days with the PSF were extremely demanding. The long hours, heat, long desert drives, self-imposed stress from visitations, and preparation of staff briefings took a toll on me; I developed a fever and a severe headache. I should have been smart enough to slow down and get some rest, but a visit to the PSF and Emirati brigade headquarters by Brigadier General Said, chief of Emirates Land Forces, was too important to miss and not hear what he had to say. General Said was in Kuwait to inspect the Emirati brigade and discuss its employment in southern Iraq. I was excited about the possibility of a new mission in Iraq that would get at least a portion of the PSF into the war. Dave and I were invited to have lunch with the brigade, and we arrived at the command post at around noon on the 5th. We were warmly greeted by members of the brigade staff and invited to indulge in tea, dates, and chocolates while we waited for General Said and Colonel Mohammad.

General Said's visit called for a special meal prepared in his honor. A special guest to an Arab unit is normally feted with a slaughtered goat, the featured centerpiece of the meal. A rug is spread on the ground and the invited officers and guests assume a yoga-like position around the rug. After nearly ten years in the Central Region, I had never acquired a taste for lamb. The thought of another "goat grab"—as we sarcastically called these meals since you reached at the goat with your right hand, pulled the meat you wanted, and placed it on your plate—made me a bit more nauseous, but I was duty bound and felt the responsibility to perform and fake my way through the meal. I sat opposite General Said at his invitation and, feigning enthusiasm and my "love" of goat, I dug into it and expertly mashed the meat with yogurt in my right hand, rolled it into a ball, and "popped" it into my mouth. This is the preferred and traditional technique and, when practiced by a Westerner, is much appreciated by our Arab hosts. My "Oscar-winning" performance was convincing, but lamb brings out the worst in me, and I fought my fever and bouts of nausea with huge quantities of water.

General Said was a very handsome man. Short in stature, he appeared very fit and youthful, and spoke excellent English. We discussed the possibility of the brigade's deployment to Iraq. It was a commitment he favored, calling it a very positive action. I agreed with him and suggested an Arab commitment in Iraq would be viewed positively throughout the world and that it would probably accelerate a peaceful transition to a new government and the ultimate withdrawal of foreign troops. After lunch, he quietly mentioned to me he would recommend a deployment of some size and shook my hand.

We drove to Ali Al Salem Air Base where I reported General Said's comments to the CFLCC staff. The adrenalin and general excitement I had felt earlier in the day had begun to wear off and, when we returned to the PSF encampment, I was burning with fever and hurting from head and body aches. I could not remember feeling so bad. I stripped down and threw myself on my cot. Dave got some aspirin for me, but I could tell it was going to be a long night. Salem and Ali, the Kuwaiti liaison officers stopped by to talk and drink tea and were visibly upset by my condition and left. I awoke the next morning to the sounds of saws and hammers. Our Kuwaiti friends had all but threatened to kill the maintenance people if they did not install an air conditioner and a shower in the trailer so my health would improve. I fell back to sleep, awoke just before noon, and sitting at the foot of my cot were Salem, Ali, and Dave on newly acquired chairs and a cooler filled with ice-cold drinks close by.

"Colonel, we hope you will enjoy the improvements to your trailer. How about a Coca Cola?"

I could not believe it! I was bathed in sweat, but my fever had broken. I drank several cans of soda and thanked our friends profusely. Life was looking good again and, after taking my first, albeit ice-cold, shower, and with all my systems back in the "green," we were off to the Emirati brigade at Colonel Mohammad's invitation to discuss his possible mission in Iraq.

Colonel Mohammad appeared despondent and quieter than usual. It was clear there had been serious discussions concerning his brigade's move to southern Iraq before General Said had departed. A planning conference at CFLCC Headquarters was scheduled for 7 April, and I had been directed to determine the number of vehicles the Emiratis would take into Iraq. The intent was to order the requisite number of VS-17 signaling panels necessary to appropriately mark the Emirati vehicles to mitigate the chance of fratricide. This seemed simple enough, but Mohammad would not give me a number, nor would he provide the name of an officer to attend the planning conference. I took it all in stride and avoided making any "faces" or sounding emotional one way or the other about the issue. I thought it best to let Mohammad set the agenda. He questioned me extensively about southern Iraq, particularly the cities of Umm Qasr and Safwan. I had not driven the streets of Safwan or flown over it since my UNIKOM tour, but I managed to recall quite a bit, and I briefed him about Umm Qasr in detail. He was very grateful, but clearly deep in thought about a mission I suspected he preferred not to execute. We left Mohammad to render our evening report at PSF's headquarters and, during the long drive, I estimated the number of panels the brigade would need. It all seemed a bit strange to me. If I was commanding a brigade task force, I would be chomping at the bit for an operational mission in Iraq. I just could not understand Mohammad's reluctance. On the other hand, he was a fine man and it occurred to me he was probably trying to keep his emotions to himself and not let me know his feelings one way or the other.

Dave and I attended the two-hour planning conference at Camp Doha on 7 April. The conference was chaired by Lieutenant Colonel Steve Holmes, USMC, an operations officer from C-3 Operations Plans. There were many British officers present which did not surprise me given the large presence of British troops throughout southern Iraq. The faster an Arab formation, or any formation for that matter, could replace them, the better off they would be. I learned the Royal Marines securing the Rumaylah Oil Field were very keen to re-embark on their amphibious warship, HMS *Ocean*, for other missions, and Army units in the vicinity of Umm Qasr and Safwan wanted to consolidate with other British forces operating further north in Baṣrah. The conference concluded with an agreement for a proposed Emirati area of operations and I was provided with an operations overlay to brief Colonel Mohammad. On our way out, we ran into British General Albert Whitley who encouraged me to "pressure" the Emiratis to move to a tactical assembly area to facilitate a reconnaissance and as early an occupation of the designated area of operations as possible. It occurred to me everyone thought an Emirati deployment was a done deal, but I knew better. I was encouraged, however, by General Whitley's characteristic enthusiasm and positive manner. He seemed genuinely pleased to see me and he was a difficult man not to like.

We reached the Emirati command post at 6 pm. We had a long night move back to PSF Headquarters with limited visibility to look forward to as I settled down to brief a quiet, moody, and seemingly unenthusiastic Colonel Mohammad. Always courteous and introspective, he absorbed every word of my briefing, questioned me extensively about command-and-control issues, and asked my opinion regarding possible dispositions of his units once his brigade was deployed in his area of responsibility. He informed me he would fly to Dubai in the morning for briefings with the Emirati general staff, and that he absolutely needed to know the exact location of the British 16 Air Assault Brigade's command post, the number of helicopters the British had at their disposal, and the size and principal locations of the indigenous population in the proposed Emirati area of responsibility. We pored over the map and overlay at great length, essentially doing a detailed intelligence preparation of the battlefield. Mohammad was shrewd; he pumped me for every bit of information I could provide. I made suggestions based solely on our map reconnaissance as to where I would place his forces, his headquarters, and fire-support assets. He thanked me and escorted me to my SUV, shook my hand, and returned to his command post for what I thought would be a very long night for him.

Dave had the engine running and we were off for another "hair-raising" adventure through the sea-like desert expanse, relying on dead-reckoning and periodic checks of our GPS. We drove through several PSF checkpoints, and the young Arab soldiers who manned them were armed, scared, and dangerous. The desert is particularly dark at night. I was always taken by how fast the darkness closes on you. It was "spooky" and I could not blame these young men for being a little edgy. The maneuver war may have passed them by, but gunfire and criminal activity was still a common occurrence along the border. The battalion and brigade patrols and static-position guards were always alert. Dave was quick to acknowledge any roving patrol with the characteristic Arab greeting, "As salaam alaikum," meaning "Peace be upon you." His smile and personality was a huge plus for us as he engaged in friendly conversation and put everyone at ease, but it was with a huge sigh of relief when we closed on PSF Headquarters and our last manned checkpoint.

I briefed a more spirited Colonel Mohammad at Ali Al Salem Air Base the following morning where he and several of his officers awaited the arrival of an Emirati transport aircraft. I answered his questions from the previous evening and we again reviewed in detail the map and operational overlay with proposed troop dispositions and unit command posts. He was grateful and thanked me in his characteristically subdued, but courteous manner. I felt pretty good about the effort we had made to prep Mohammad and his staff. We ate a good American lunch courtesy of the Air Force mess hall and prepared the evening's briefing to the PSF commander and staff. I had a lot to brief. Despite "Baghdad Bob's" denials, Baghdad had fallen, and the Emirati deployment into southern Iraq would be delayed pending approval by the Gulf Cooperation Council.

Planning for the Emirati deployment continued at CFLCC Headquarters, and we again drove to Ali Al Salem Air Base on the 9th for another planning session with Lieutenant Colonel Holmes and several other C-3 representatives. Colonel Stanton informed me there was a very good chance I would lead a reconnaissance of the proposed Emirati area of responsibility in southern Iraq, and that preparations were being made to form a special reconnaissance unit with available headquarters personnel, vehicles, and equipment. It was an exciting thought, but I did not have a lot of confidence the GCC would approve an Arab mission in Iraq. I assumed a negative decision would negate any reconnaissance mission.

Later that day, I met with Colonel Abdullah, the Emirati deputy commander. Abdullah always appeared happy, eager to talk, and appreciative of our company. He was the perfect deputy for Mohammad with his warm personality, loyalty to his commander, and readiness to execute his duties. He spent a lot of time with the brigade's subordinate units; I sensed in him a high level of enthusiasm for the brigade's mission in Kuwait. He had not heard from Mohammad and did not have anything new to share with us about the proposed Iraq mission. He invited us to have lunch with him the next day to honor a group of physical-training instructors who had come to Kuwait to improve the brigade's physical fitness programs during its desert deployment. I enthusiastically accepted. Abdullah would play a vital role in any Iraq-related mission and while I feared another "goat grab," I thought it best to attend.

Our dominant concern with the Emiratis during this period did not detract appreciably from our engagement with other national units and the PSF staff. I frequently attended the diwaniyas, the "bull sessions" that convened almost every evening in the PSF encampment. The PSF officers enjoyed these sessions a great deal. Many would wear traditional Arab garb, smoke "shisha" (a flavored tobacco), and talk and laugh until late into the evening. I enjoyed their company and the discussions immensely. The deputy commander of the PSF was a colorful Qatari paratrooper. Brigadier General Yousef frequently attended these sessions, resplendent in Arab dress, comfortably seated, and smoking shisha through a water pipe that we comically referred to as the "hubbly bubbly." The sound it makes as the smoker inhales is unmistakably that of bubbles moving through the pipe. Yousef never failed to offer me a smoke, but I always declined, more out of fear of failing a random drug sampling, or "piss test" as soldiers called it, than anything else. He was a very thoughtful man who freely spoke about various issues concerning politics and the challenges of the Central Region, but he preferred to talk about the subjects that brought everyone pleasure including family, travel, and, of course, women and sex. Our Kuwaiti friends often joined these "stargazing" sessions, and the tea drinking and smoking mixed with raucous laughter often continued until the late hours of the evening.

Challenging discussions were the norm with Colonel Rashid of Bahrain. Rashid frequently spoke about the importance of providing humanitarian assistance to the people of Iraq. It was, "Vitally important for the Iraqis and all Arab people," he opined, "to see America's humanitarian efforts on television." Rashid understood the importance of information operations and strongly recommended America focus the media's efforts to make the invasion of Iraq more palatable to the Arab street. The Americans, he said, "Should quickly produce evidence of Saddam's death." The insightful Rashid understood the power Saddam's image had on the Iraqis. He added that little or no progress could be made until he was killed or visibly removed from power. Like General Mozan, the Saudi brigade commander, Rashid talked about the importance of resolving the Palestinian issue. He said educated Arabs understood the complexity of the issue and America's concern with the Israelis, but that Arab emotions were fueled nonetheless by their belief we overwhelmingly favored the Israelis, to the detriment of the Palestinians and Arabs in general. These intense sessions reminded me that an American officer is best inclined to intently and patiently listen and, when the opportunity presents itself, very calmly provide an unemotional and informed response. Only then could you expect your words to have a positive impact, and in the process develop a meaningful, respectful, and trusting relationship with the Arab participants. I was fortunate for the experiences and study that had prepared me for these most interesting and challenging discussions.

My daily regimen in the isolated, spartan-like world in which we lived included a long run and a rigorous set of strength and aerobic drills that were the subject of great interest and private discussion among the officers of the PSF staff. Many Arab officers are not particularly interested in physical conditioning. Many think running and physical training in general are drills appropriate for the troops, young lieutenants in school, and commandos, but certainly not for them. One evening during a large diwaniya session, I was asked to comment about physical training in the American Army and, "Why do you do all of this running?" I had to be careful not to be condescending or to preach. I explained the importance of strength, endurance, and flexibility for combat leaders. I talked about the effects of stress on the body and the devastating impact it can have on one's health.

"In combat," I said, "Stress can wear down a healthy and fit man and, combined with fatigue, could break his will to fight."

The Arabs love to smoke, and they frequently asked me why I chose not to smoke. "After all, Tiso, you are too old to be a sportsman; certainly, you can smoke."

They listened intently and respectfully, however, as I suggested a soldier of any age is a "sportsman" who must train throughout the year. "Leaders get older, but soldiers only get younger, and yet we officers are expected to lead from the front, set high standards, and serve as an example of discipline and personal excellence. And besides, my dear brothers, a man is better in bed if he is fit and strong."

The last point brought laughter and nods of approval. References to hearty sex are always a big hit with Arab men. I could speak for hours about the ill-effects of smoking on night vision and physical endurance, but comments about sex would be the ones they would remember. It was, after all, a man's world out there and we were free to speak freely, a welcome relief from the "PC world" of American society and its associated social graces. I did not expect to change any attitudes, but I enjoyed the opportunity to speak. You never know when words backed by personal example can have a positive impact. Dave and I noticed several members of the staff exercising by their trailers and running around the encampment during the next several weeks. Colorful athletic garments and running shoes were visible around the command post and I smiled as more and more soldiers honked their horns and waved to me as they drove along my running route. Even General BaBa'eer waved in approval. In the final analysis, the only things that ever count are the things that work; if hearty references to sexual performance could sell physical training, better leadership, and combat readiness, then I was all for it.

In Umm Qasr, Iraq, outside Civil Affairs Headquarters.

CHAPTER 10

Reconnaissance of the Rumaylah Oil Field

NCOs provide the leadership which is most apparent to soldiers on a day-to-day basis.
—NCOPD Study, 1986

I could not believe it: "Return to Camp Doha to complete planning for a reconnaissance of the Rumaylah Oil Fields. Details to follow; reconnaissance to commence on 12 April." Marty Stanton's uplifting phone call changed our itinerary considerably. We had less than a day to get the reconnaissance and survey plan together. I advised Colonel Said, the Peninsula Shield Force (PSF) G-3 (Operations), that Dave and I would be gone for several days to conduct another mission and asked him to inform General BaBa'eer. We then drove to the Emirati command post to inform Colonel Abdullah. Our navigation to the headquarters was complicated by a severe sandstorm. I was relieved to finally clear the desert after our meeting, turn onto an asphalt road, and drive to Camp Doha.

Marty and several selected officers and noncommissioned officers (NCOs) were standing by for our arrival. Planning had already commenced; we worked late into the evening to finalize and coordinate details. The reconnaissance unit I was to lead was an ad hoc organization consisting of seven highly skilled, combat arms NCOs assigned to the Civil–Military Affairs Directorate (C-9) and three officers including myself, Dave, and Captain Gandy, an artillery officer and Arabic speaker. Tired of staff work and anxious to get into the war, these exceptional combat soldiers were both individually and collectively the most impressive soldiers I had seen since my battalion command tour ended nearly ten years before. Master Sergeant Williams, a special forces sergeant major selectee, was a superbly conditioned, calm, confident, and experienced professional soldier. An Arabic-speaking, combat veteran of the Gulf War, he had amassed a lot of experience in the Central Region working with many different national armies. He exuded a level of professional confidence that would ease the stress of any commander. Master Sergeant Sean Collins was a reservist and served as the unit's operations officer. A combat veteran of the First Gulf War and Somalia, he was a qualified combat medic who had seen service with the famed Delta Force. In civilian life, he was a highly successful, self-employed, pharmaceutical distributor. He was accustomed to being in charge and his manner was curt and occasionally disrespectful. He preferred to be addressed by his first name, a common occurrence in the special operations community that I did not accept. He was, by any measure, an impressive, highly knowledgeable, professional soldier. If our initial meeting was a little rocky, we nonetheless got along rather well during the mission. I was fortunate and happy to have him on the team. All the other NCOs had solid, combat arms backgrounds. One had served in the airborne battalion I had commanded in Panama; all were battle-tested veterans.

Our departure the next morning was delayed after I looked over our three vehicles and insisted the men perform a series of pre-combat checks on the vehicles, weapons, and radios. The absence of several pieces of equipment, failed radio checks, improper frequency settings, and no preventive maintenance checks performed on the vehicles were shortfalls I had not expected to find in the company of such outstanding men. The individual readiness of these hardened professionals was never in doubt, but their rush to get into Iraq left a few things to be desired. After securing the missing items of equipment and conducting the pre-combat checks on all weapons, vehicles, radios, and personal equipment, I directed Sergeant Collins to get everyone together to allow me to review the mission and concept of operations. It was clear to me a lot had been assumed and key elements of operational information had not been disseminated to everyone. These fundamental planning procedures were my responsibility and I was not about to assume anything regardless of the experience and individual professionalism of this elite group. Operations that start according to plan generally end that way. Having missed our self-determined start time to correct our deficiencies, we were in excellent shape when we rolled out of Camp Doha with our three Hummers properly tied down with all required equipment, machine guns manned, and radios working. I could not help thinking we looked like a modern rendition of the 1960s TV show *The Rat Patrol*, which was about a reconnaissance unit operating in the North African desert during World War II. I also knew I had not made any friends with the senior NCOs who were somewhat embarrassed by our faulty start, but the shortfalls I noted that morning reminded me command is not about popularity and that respected leaders insist on doing things right. They are the kind of leaders with whom you ultimately want to go to war. Everyone was properly oriented and there were no other shortfalls during what was to be a near perfectly executed mission.

Our route initially took us up the famed Coastal Road now cleared of all Kuwaiti civilian traffic, but just as dangerous as ever. It was the Coalition's main supply route and was heavily traveled now by all sorts of transport and combat vehicles headed to and from Iraq. Our first stop was Camp Commando, a small encampment where we coordinated with civilian contractors who were scheduled to enter Iraq to repair and eventually operate the Rumaylah oil facilities. Everyone understood the success of the postwar reconstruction of Iraq was dependent on the revenues generated by the Rumaylah Oil Field as well as other oil fields in northern Iraq. We met with representatives from Kellogg Brown and Root Inc (KB&R) who reviewed our reconnaissance plan and provided additional details of what we could expect to find at designated locations. We then proceeded to Umm Qasr, passed the ruins of the former United Nations Iraq–Kuwait Observation Mission (UNIKOM) Headquarters, and made our way to the headquarters of the British 1st Division. Our route took us through a few populated areas and all of us were amused by the large number of children who lined the streets armed with Iraqi paper money that featured a picture of our old nemesis Saddam Hussein. This was the closest we came to a World War II-like liberation experience. We drove slowly through these places, careful not to hit anyone, but I told Sergeant Collins to keep moving, and ensured our gunners were ready for action. Baghdad may have fallen, but I remembered the small arms and mortar fire we had encountered in Umm Qasr in late March and I never doubted our need for caution and strict security measures. Coordinating with the 1st Division staff was a smart move on our part. We verified that responsibility for securing the oil fields had passed from the British 16 Air Assault Brigade to the Royal Marines. We adjusted our plan accordingly and Sergeant Collins and I agreed our next destination should be the headquarters of 42 Commando, Royal Marines, which was in the northernmost portion of the oil field. This would be a long movement and we would not close on 42 Commando until just before sunset.

Her Majesty's Royal Marines are the United Kingdom's amphibious force and generally regarded as some of its best trained infantry. Royal Marine training, coupled with its unique capabilities, gives it a special forces flavor. The Marines are trained as commando forces and can operate in all types of terrain. During my tour of duty on General Zinni's personal staff, I had accompanied him to the Royal Marine Headquarters in Plymouth, England, where he had received several briefings on the organization and capabilities of this magnificent force and its colorful history.

The Royal Marines trace their heraldry back to 1664. Two data points that stayed with me were that recruits undergo 32 weeks of basic training, the longest of any infantry force in the world, and that their battle honors are so diverse and numerous that the globe is the centerpiece of their symbol. The main organization for the Royal Marines is 3 Commando Brigade. The unit we were visiting, 42 Commando, was one of three battalion-sized formations that comprise the brigade. These commandos are further organized into six companies and total approximately 600 men. The Royal Marines had been deployed to Afghanistan in 2002 but had not seen any action. It had been 42 and 40 Commandos' good fortune to participate in the United Kingdom's first amphibious assault in over two decades to capture the al-Faw Peninsula in March 2003. Their mission was to secure the port of Umm Qasr to allow humanitarian goods to flow into the port and to secure key oil installations located in the area before they could be sabotaged by retreating Iraqi forces. They would later conduct combat operations with the U.S. Marines of the 15th Marine

Expeditionary Unit and the 1st Marine Division. Both Commandos received the U.S. Presidential Unit Citation for their heroic actions during that period.

The Royal Marine commander was hard at work in his headquarters, a large building among a series of various structures and storage facilities that had undoubtedly served as a maintenance support site. Lieutenant Colonel F. H. R. "Buster" Howes, RM, was one tough, all-business, professional soldier of the sea who both welcomed and invited us to stay for the night within the security of his encampment. He had previously established his headquarters in a useable portion of the heavily damaged, former UNIKOM Headquarters, and we had met there shortly after I had completed my mission in Umm Qasr with the 354th Civil Affairs Brigade. He remembered me and provided a lengthy and detailed briefing of his area of responsibility and the disposition of his forces. He had nearly 800 men and 110 vehicles of various types under his command, including a company of security troops from the Royal Air Force. They were stretched thin, but Colonel Howes' assessment was that the area was "Somewhat benign," and he felt no need for additional reinforcement or assistance. He was, however, very interested in our mission because the arrival of the Emirati brigade, or any other troops for that matter, would allow his Marines to withdraw to their ship, HMS *Ocean*, and allow it to continue its "Worldwide mission." There was no doubt in my mind Colonel Howes wanted us to succeed and would help us anyway he could.

There were still a few hours of daylight available and Colonel Howes offered to have Major Kevin Oliver escort us to the northern limit of the fields before nightfall to give us the opportunity to look over two Gas Oil Separation Plants (GOSPs) that elements of his unit secured there. Considering our late start and route change, I jumped at the chance to accomplish a few reconnaissance tasks before the end of the day. Major Oliver explained that each major facility was secured by a platoon that numbered 25–40 men. Sergeant Collins and several others of our unit looked over the facilities in detail while Oliver and I talked about his unit's operations over the past month. They had had "A good go of it," he said, but were, "Truly anxious to get out of here." He said there was occasional rifle and mortar fire in the fields, but nothing that had posed a serious threat. He further opined that any enemy activity appeared to be criminally motivated. The Royal Marines at each position were in full battle dress and combat ready. Sergeant Collins carefully photographed the facilities. If these facilities were any indication of the state of maintenance throughout the fields, then truly our contractor friends at KB&R had their work cut out for them. There was considerable evidence of looting that provided some credibility to Oliver's comments about criminal activity that I carefully noted.

I woke up early on 13 April and remembered it was my daughter's 15th birthday. It was the first time I had really thought about my family, having been totally consumed by my activities since I had left our home in Florida six weeks earlier. In the past nine years, I had spent four months in Somalia, another four months in Saudi Arabia and Afghanistan, two peacekeeping tours of a year or more in Iraq and the Sinai, two years traveling almost continuously as the executive assistant to the U.S. Central Command commander, and now this. Fortunately, I am married to a saint and our two daughters understood their "soldier dad," who "Always worked hard for our country." It occurred to me how lucky I was to have such a wonderful family.

Colonel Howes proposed an air reconnaissance of the vast western portion of his area of operations; I quickly accepted his invitation and asked Sergeant Collins to accompany us. There was a small oil field out there consisting of some 29 wells and a GOSP. Portions of the desert were believed to be mined. Howes pointed out that, while the vast western area of his area of operations (AO) was of little value, he did occasionally conduct some ground reconnaissance, or "recces," of the terrain. The helicopter, though, was the best platform to get the job done quickly and efficiently. Our aircraft arrived a little before 7 am courtesy of the Royal Navy. We flew to the far western edge of the AO and landed at Viper Base, the desert home of an American Marine Air Wing, where we spoke with Lieutenant Colonel D. J. Barham, and the wing's commander, Colonel Kevin Donahue. This was an excellent opportunity for Colonel Howes to coordinate his unit's dispositions and activities with the U.S. Marine commanders, and I took the opportunity to talk about the possibility of 42 Commando's relief in place by the Emirati brigade. The Marines were very interested in this development and were particularly concerned about the types of vehicles and equipment the Emiratis would bring and how they would be marked to avoid fratricide. Our discussions were short but focused. I answered their questions as best as I could and assured them additional coordination would be conducted by the Emirati command group when it was deployed.

We flew a reconnaissance pattern over the western AO on the way back to 42 Commando Headquarters. Sergeant Collins and I agreed with Colonel Howes's assessment that there was little out there of any concern. The 29 oil wells in the Luhais Field near the western edge of the AO paled in comparison to the nearly 500 wells between the northern and southern Rumaylah fields. There was a large airstrip with many destroyed vehicles and other assorted debris on it from one end to the other that effectively denied its use to anyone. It was close enough to the Rumaylah fields to mark it as potentially useful for future operations once it was cleared off.

We wasted no time getting ready for our ground reconnaissance of the day. We surveyed five GOSPs, spending over eight hours climbing in and out of our vehicles, walking in and around the facilities, and talking with several contractors and their armed Iraqi security personnel. There were even a few unarmed Iraqis who were formerly employed by the Iraqi Oil Ministry. They had remained on site to prevent looting and safeguard their future employment. My officers spoke with many of these men and all of them hoped the Americans would soon have them back in business. One look at these facilities, however, told us it would take a lot of work and money to get things running again. Sergeant Collins carefully documented everything on film, most of which I would use in my final report to Combined Forces Land Component Command. He was an invaluable member of our team and I appreciated his advice and assistance throughout the mission.

Our original plan was to make camp at nightfall at the last GOSP we surveyed and continue south in the morning, but my NCOs suggested it would be smarter, from a security perspective, to return to 42 Commando Headquarters for the evening. They were right; we could easily cover the straight-line road distance to the GOSP in the morning and pick up where we left off. We got back to 42 Commando just in time to attend Palm Sunday Anglican mass. I had forgotten it was Easter, but 42 Commando had a chaplain and he held mass under a large awning where we parked our vehicles. A good number of men attended, many of whom were veterans of Northern Ireland and now Iraq. I noted several campaign medals on the chaplain's vestments. It was not the first time he had served mass from the hood of a vehicle. The chaplain had somehow managed to acquire a large amount of palm fronds from one of Saddam's palaces, and had weaved them into small, 6 × 4-inch crosses that he presented to everyone who attended. It was a wonderful souvenir that I tucked away along with the program he provided. The service included the impressive Royal Marines prayer by which I was particularly moved:

> O Eternal Lord God, who through many generations has united and inspired the members of our Corps, grant your blessing, we beseech you, on Royal Marines serving all round the globe. Bestow your crown of righteousness upon all our efforts and endeavors, and may our laurels be those of gallantry and honor, loyalty, and courage. We ask these things in the name of him whose courage never failed, our Redeemer, Jesus Christ. Amen.

The values imbued in these Royal Marines place them among the world's finest fighting men; I was proud to be with them. The service was a pleasant departure from the war, a touch of Western civilization that has always made a difference for us. It was all too short as I gathered my notes and prepared for another round of discussions with Colonel Howes and Major Oliver.

I asked them for any overlays of minefields and oil facilities they could provide, and we again discussed how their units were currently deployed and the nature of the threat in the area. Colonel Howes offered to write an assessment of his AO in the form of a hard-hitting memorandum he referred to as a "Loose minute." It was a gracious offer I readily accepted and promised to add it to my report. I did not completely agree with his concise and, in many ways, brilliant assessment, particularly his description of the AO as "benign/permissive," downplaying almost totally the possibility of an insurgent threat. Our discussions with the contractors and several of the Marines at the GOSPs led us to think the area and its infrastructure were at greater risk than "benign/permissive" would imply. He did, however, have a genuine concern for the criminal threat. Civil authority in the area, including a police force, needed to be restored. In my view, the situation required a considerable amount of security considering the looting that had occurred and the abject poverty in the area. Howes aptly pointed out that the locals, "Lacking faith in the future, seek short term gain by stripping infrastructure that represents their near-term livelihood." Getting people back to work was paramount, a point on which we totally agreed. Until that could be achieved, I considered the area to be at moderate risk. Significantly, Howes thought that, due to its proximity to the oil fields, "The security and stability of Rumaylah Village is therefore key and should represent 'ME' (main effort) rather than point defense of infrastructure per se."[1] If the Emiratis deployed in force, they could not only provide a more adequate defense of the infrastructure, but additional security for the neighboring villages as well. I was very impressed with Colonel Howes and his overall assessment of the situation and had every intention of submitting a balanced report that included his thoughts; I was very appreciative of his views and comments.

We settled in for the evening and I sacked out under an awning. It was a wise choice as it rained very hard with thunder and lightning not normally characteristic of mid-April throughout the night. It reminded me of the fall/winter of 1997–98 during my tour with the UN when the southern Iraqi desert turned a shade of green from huge rainstorms. It would not be much longer, however, before the rains would dissipate and the oppressive heat of summer would return. I wondered if the truffles were in bloom in the former demilitarized zone and how many people would mistake them for mines. Iraq, I thought, is a deadly place for soldiers and civilians alike.

The senior NCOs and I reviewed our program and made final map checks for the day as the men loaded our vehicles and completed their pre-combat checks and services. We then briefed everyone and I conferred with the officers. This would be our last day in Iraq and I was determined to complete our patrol without a mishap. We had been lucky up to this point and I directed the officers to check our equipment and vehicles closely to ensure everything was accounted for.

There was a lot of activity in the area as the Royal Marines prepared for their tasks and missions as well. The Royal Marines are a tough breed of men who pride themselves on their physical conditioning. Many of them had just completed what had to be a grueling run.

"After all," one Royal Marine sergeant said, "A war is hardly an excuse for not maintaining one's fighting condition."

They were without a doubt the most tattooed group of men I had ever seen; we laughed at their bawdy humor and raucous manner. Their reputation as an elite fighting force was no doubt well deserved. I entered the headquarters building to pay my respects to Colonel Howes and his staff before departing. Colonel Howes was still in his running shorts and sweating from a hard run as he typed out the final thoughts of his "Loose Minute" and placed it in an envelope. I thanked him again for his assistance, wished him luck, and moved to our vehicles already lined up and ready to move.

We quickly covered the distance to where we had left off the previous day and commenced our reconnaissance and survey of the southernmost facilities. Sergeant Collins's navigation was flawless as we efficiently made our way from one facility to the next. In almost every case, the buildings and complex workings of the pipelines were intact but badly in need of spare parts and general maintenance. The buildings had been looted of furniture and broken glass was everywhere. We occasionally found a poster of Saddam or other small items of interest that we happily passed around as souvenirs. Several containers revealed spare parts with the markings of several different countries in the region and Europe. It was clear Saddam was never short of what he required to pad his pockets and ruin Iraq. It would undoubtedly take a lot of resources and money to rebuild the infrastructure of this country; much like I had seen in Somalia and Afghanistan, I marveled at the waste.

Our procedures at each site were automatic by this point: post security, conduct a general reconnaissance, then a detailed survey of each facility with photos. Our officers and Sergeant Williams questioned anyone on site. In nearly every case, the Iraqis were oil field workers anxious to get back to work and were cleared to be there by the Royal Marines or Royal Air Force security troops. By mid-afternoon we cleared a Kuwaiti checkpoint and entered Kuwait with plenty of daylight to spare. We surveyed several tactical assembly areas (TAA), the boundaries of which I carefully recorded to propose to Colonel Mohammad, in keeping with General Whitley's desires to have the Emiratis in a TAA as soon as possible. Sergeant Williams rarely spoke to me during the patrol, but he kindly offered that we did not need to over-do our reconnaissance of the TAAs.

"Sir, the Arabs are very good at this sort of thing; they'll road march, occupy their TAA, and recon key locations and facilities in Iraq with the best of them."

Sergeant Williams had worked extensively with the Arabs over the past 10 years; I accepted his sage advice. He calmly and effectively reminded me I was not the brigade commander and that Colonel Mohammad would eventually do things his way. It was also his way of telling me I had "beaten everyone up enough." It had been a long day and a long patrol. We had what we needed; it was time to head for "home" and prepare a detailed after-action report.

We took the better part of the evening and the next day to piece together our findings and data. We produced a first-rate document that I insisted everyone in our unit review for details and correctness. Sergeant Collins expertly integrated the photographs he had taken. General Whitley commended the report, describing it as "Most helpful." Several days after Dave and I returned to the Peninsula Shield Force, however, we learned the mission to deploy an Arab force in southern Iraq had been cancelled. Our report was passed to the Brits and then to the civilian contractors who eventually provided the security and maintenance personnel to operate the vital facilities in the Rumaylah Oil Field.

Sergeant Monroe, Colonel Tiso, and Master Sergeant Collins in Rumaylah oil fields.

CHAPTER 11

Redeployment of the Peninsula Shield Force

There is but one straight course, and that is to seek truth and pursue it steadily.
—GEORGE WASHINGTON

By the time Dave and I returned to Peninsula Shield Force (PSF) Headquarters on 15 April, it was clear things were changing. The PSF had been deployed barely three months and personnel changes to the staff were already occurring. There were rumors the mission was nearing completion. The PSF had been deployed to defend Kuwait. The fall of Baghdad, the apparent demobilization of the Iraqi Army, and the immediate threat to Kuwait essentially eliminated meant the PSF's days in the Kuwaiti desert were numbered, assuming it would not enter Iraq as an occupying force. Several details came to light on the 16th after we dug ourselves out of yet another huge sandstorm that had raged throughout the evening. The encampment was even more desolate than usual and the headquarters was deathly quiet.

Colonel Ali of Kuwait introduced himself as the new G-3 (Operations); our good friend Colonel Said al Hosni had returned to Oman. We had said our "goodbyes" before the Rumaylah mission and I was glad he was now with his family in Oman. We were surprised, however, by the departure of the deputy commander, Brigadier General Yousef of Qatar. He left without notice and was replaced by Brigadier General Mohammad of Oman, a combat veteran with 33 years of service who quickly impressed us with his competence and professionalism. Unfortunately, he arrived too late to significantly influence the seemingly disjointed, uncoordinated "stand down" of the force he had been sent to lead. The PSF G-1 (personnel officer), Colonel Nasser of the United Arab Emirates, and Major Ali al "Sahaf" Fahad, the Kuwaiti liaison officer, informed us the PSF mission was winding down and would probably end by the first week of May. This didn't surprise me, but Colonel Mohammad, who had recently returned from the United Arab Emirates, "dropped the bomb" the next day when he informed us there would be no mission requirement for his brigade in Iraq, though a mission could still be given to another unit. A significant Arab deployment in Rumaylah or elsewhere was very unlikely in view of the imminent PSF stand down. Lieutenant Colonel Rashid of Bahrain informed me he would "load out" his battalion within the next several days. During one of our conversations, I learned Colonel Rashid is a member of the royal "al Khalifa" family. He had never said a word about it during our frequent visits to his unit, preferring to be viewed as a hard-working battalion commander and professional soldier, all the while addressing me as "sir." A visit to the Omani battalion and Lieutenant Colonel Mohammad began with tea and dates and ended with the presentation of commemorative plaques to me and Dave. If that was not convincing enough that "end game" was fast approaching, General BaBa'eer announced on the evening of the 19th that the PSF Mission would conclude on 3 May with a formal ceremony on the parade field at the headquarters of the 35th Kuwaiti Brigade.

We kept the Combined Forces Land Component Command (CFLCC) staff aware of these developments and continued our regimen of unit-assistance visits, patrolling, and briefings to the staff. Special requests kept us busy; Colonel Abdullah asked us to provide the Emirati brigade the exclusive use of a "Wretch" (RTCH, rough terrain container handler), a large piece of equipment designed to pick up and load containers on heavy equipment transporters. The Saudis requested maintenance and road-clearance assistance to move by convoy to PSF Headquarters at King Khalid Military City in Saudi Arabia. I recommended to the PSF G-3, Colonel Ali, that he schedule and coordinate the PSF's activities and record them in a single program or itinerary of events, establish times for movement and road priority, and establish and coordinate security requirements for the command post. It all seemed so basic, but the only reaction I got was the "1,000-yard stare" by a man who clearly had little idea or experience of coordinating the operational requirements for a major unit movement. Everyone was motivated to leave and it looked to me the movement was a "free for all." I reported the requests we had received from his units to General BaBa'eer, who nodded his approval. He seemed satisfied with the decisions being made by his commanders at brigade and battalion level and it struck me he just might be the most effective "hands off" commander I had ever seen, content that his operational intent was being carried out in good order.

It was not chaos, but it was a vastly different approach than an American unit would take. The redeployment was decentralized to the point of almost totally removing the PSF staff and command group from the decision-making process and mission execution. But the intent was clear—"Get out of Dodge and do it quickly." We reported the Arab troop movements to CFLCC Headquarters. We also recognized and thanked every major unit commander for their service in the defense of Kuwait. Gift exchanges are important to our Arab counterparts; I thought it wise to present something meaningful to every unit commander and principal staff officer. I failed to convince the CFLCC protocol staffers to provide a few appropriate gifts that I could present on behalf of the CFLCC commander, but I was able to "con" the CFLCC deputy chief of staff into giving me a handful of the commanding general's coins for excellence. Colonel DellaJacano was a Military Police Corps officer with

30 years of service and a lot of time in the Central Region. He knew my request was reasonable and helped me out. Naturally, a few Iraqi war souvenirs we picked up along the way helped to sweeten the deal. The bureaucrats in protocol may not have appreciated it, but the CFLCC was well served as we presented the coins with the compliments of its commander. In every case, the commanders and other recipients were very appreciative.

In the meantime, the redeployment continued as the units moved their tanks and heavy equipment to various staging areas along the main supply route (MSR) south of PSF Headquarters and the garrison of the Kuwaiti 35th Brigade. We coordinated the use of the highly valued Wretch for the Emiratis with the help of the "mayor" of Camp Victory. Lieutenant Colonel Landris was another one of those unique characters who somehow find themselves in the U.S. Army. A Greek foreign-area officer, he was a reservist who had previously served in the Air Force as a fighter pilot. Camp Victory was one of many American staging areas where units marshalled and soldiers acclimated before moving into Iraq. The camp was an endless sea of tents and motor parks set in a swirling maelstrom of dust and soldiers going about their duties in various forms of dress. It was conveniently located about thirty kilometers west of Ali Al Salem Air Base astride the MSR. Colonel Landris managed the camp with a small staff. If you needed anything, he was the guy who could provide it. While we sat and waited for him in his command post, I took note of several packages of candies and dates he had received in the mail. You never know when a small bit of information can be helpful. Landris was a friendly person with a very difficult and demanding job. When I introduced myself and Dave and told him about our assignment and our unusual requirement for a Wretch, he suggested we talk about it over a pizza. It was one of those offers you just could not refuse. We were in luck. As a foreign-area officer, Colonel Landris was sensitive to our mission and understood the importance of Coalition relations, cooperation, and assistance. Carefully checking his notes, schedules, and a list of available assets, he offered to provide a Wretch and an operator on 25 April, precisely the day the Emirati brigade needed it. I promised to provide him a supply of what turned out to be his passion, Middle Eastern dates. It was a great trade, reminiscent of my earliest days in the Army when a fifth of a supply sergeant's favorite liquor produced the items your company could not account for. Later, I told Colonel Abdullah a "Wretch" could be made available on the 25th for a box of fancy dates. Abdullah was no fool; he knew the "system" well and, with his characteristic smile, produced two large boxes of dates and sweets and said, "Tell the good Mayor to enjoy them."

Moving the Emirati containers, including tons of ammunition, was an all-day affair. The Kuwaitis provided the heavy equipment transporters on which the containers would be loaded. Two Wretch operators from Camp Victory, Sergeant Becklam and Specialist Douglas, began the Herculean task of lifting the containers at 9 am. The number of containers they moved over the course of the next 10 hours without so much as a single complaint was absolutely astounding. We were in awe of these two great soldiers who worked non-stop to finish the job before nightfall. Abdullah was present the entire time and Mohammad checked in regularly as he tended to other command-related affairs. They could not have been more appreciative. Abdullah insisted the two operators join the officers for a fish dinner served Arab style on the floor of a nearby building they had occupied. He also presented each of the operators with a commemorative watch.

General BaBa'eer was a difficult man to contact during the redeployment period. Office calls and other diplomatic duties of his position dictated his presence in Kuwait City nearly every day. When we finally caught up to him, he greeted me in his quarters barefoot and wearing pajamas. He appeared tired, but in good spirits. Colonels Ali and Nasser had just briefed him on the status of the redeployment, and he thanked me and David for our efforts to out load the Emirati brigade. I took this opportunity to present him with one of the CFLCC coins, "On behalf of the commanding general with his compliments." The general was scheduled to retire soon so he appreciated these little trinkets of service like all soldiers do. He told us he planned to take a three-month cruise of the Caribbean after his last parade. He was a real character. I honestly thought he enjoyed our company, and he moved our conversation from the business of the mission and redeployment to family, life after the Army, and, of course, the joys of sex. We parted with a great deal of laughter.

Our other calls on the PSF generals were equally interesting. General Hamad of Qatar, the PSF logistics officer (G-4), was hilarious. Hamad could always be found in the diwaniya tent in the evenings where he watched television, shared his wisdom concerning the problems of the Middle East, told outrageous jokes, and described in detail the wonders of exotic sex. I declined his kind offers to fix me up with Western women in Kuwait City. The good general could also be very introspective. He was very interested in Coalition operations in Iraq and the status of Saddam Hussein.

Saddam, he opined, was a household word throughout the Middle East, and his death or capture was critical to the campaign. His very name struck fear in the mind of every Iraqi. For all his jokes, Hamad spoke passionately of his family and looked forward to returning to Qatar.

General Mohammad of Oman, the newly arrived deputy commander, continued to impress us with his quiet, competent professionalism. The only operation he would plan and coordinate was the PSF farewell parade. The consummate professional insisted on rehearsals that eventually ensured a superb ceremony, but undoubtedly angered every unit commander focused on going home. General Mohammad was very appreciative of the coin we gave him given our short time together, but he was certainly deserving of recognition. He had "fired up" the PSF staff to get involved in the redeployment of the national units, and established movement tables, start point times, priority of movement, and fundamental coordination between the

PSF staff and the staffs and commanders of the national contingents. He had also restored and enhanced the security posture around the PSF encampment. He was frustrated by the turn of events that were ending his mission almost as soon as it had started. He questioned me about my views of the PSF and insisted I be candid.

"I am conscious, Colonel, of American courtesy and desire not to offend us. You can tell me the truth." I gave him an earful.

The PSF was not capable of providing command and control of its national units. It was fundamentally lacking in communications equipment, mobility, and staff. It was incapable of conducting 24-hour combat operations beyond the static defense in which it was deployed. Furthermore, the PSF was almost totally lacking in the combat support and combat service support units it required to conduct maneuver warfare. Though deployed as a division, it had no effective support command so key to overall combat effectiveness and logistical sustainment. The senior staff officers, normally in the rank of lieutenant colonel and above, appeared to be more concerned with creature comforts and privileges than the challenges facing the command, and appeared to lack sufficient training or even an appreciation for the complexities of modern warfare. The PSF was a solid security concept and the national contingents seemed to be well trained. Their equipment was excellent and selected leaders were capable and trained. The younger officers, particularly those who had training opportunities in the West, were generally solid. The PSF had provided an invaluable contribution to Kuwait and the Coalition with the physical presence of its military power, but its capability with regard to both training and assets to coordinate that power in offensive combat or in a mobile defense was weak at best. General Mohammad looked at me about as hard as anyone ever has and for a moment I thought, "Well, Tiso, so much for honesty, now you've offended everyone, and it's going to get back to CFLCC, and you've had it man." You can imagine my relief, therefore, when he extended his hand and thanked me for my comments.

"We Arabs aren't accustomed to getting the real truth from our military advisers, but you, Colonel, are absolutely correct."

General Mohammad had already discussed several of these issues with General BaBa'eer. He was determined to address the PSF's organization for combat, command-and-control and communications issues, logistical support, and combat power requirements including military police, air defense, engineers, and aviation shortly after getting back to King Khalid Military City. I wished him luck. He had a lot of work ahead of him if he was going to make the PSF a combat-ready force.

My war was amounting to a series of office calls, diwaniyas, redeployment status reports, and dreaded "goat grabs." Everyone was happy about leaving the desert. Not unlike our soldiers, Arab troops were amazingly fast and efficient with packing up and going home. The summer was quickly approaching and the characteristic oppressive heat of the region was beginning to kick in. The ice-cold showers we took in the Coalition liaison trailer were lukewarm now; an ominous sign of the coming

120 degree or more temperatures. The long drives to the desert encampments, Camp Victory, Ali Al Salem Air Base, Camp Doha, and back to PSF Headquarters provided periods for reflection about the war, the possibility of losing the peace, the war's cost, its effects on our economy, and our presence in the region. A long-term presence in Iraq of an "infidel army" was bound to breed discontent throughout the region. Recognizing that, in 1995, our war planners at Central Command under the brilliant Colonel Stouder had briefed the importance of standing up a 10-division Iraqi force that could quickly establish internal security, keep Iran at bay, and allow Coalition forces to withdraw within a reasonable period. It was reasonable to think the commanders and planners in Baghdad were of the same mind. They were not and, unknown to me at the time, the impending decision to dissolve the Iraqi Army altogether would seriously impact my immediate future and, more significantly, the future of Iraq.

Dave and I were proud of our short, but meaningful tour with the PSF. Several small gifts and honors were heaped upon us as we drew closer to the final ceremony now scheduled for 5 May. Salem and Ali, our Kuwaiti counterparts, gave us traditional Kuwaiti sleeping shirts. Small regimental mementos were presented by the Omanis and the Emiratis, and General BaBa'eer gave us each a wristwatch featuring the PSF logo. The general praised us at length for our contributions to the PSF, and he signed a letter of commendation that he presented to each of us with a kiss on each cheek. Initially embarrassed, it reminded me of Gary Cooper, in his Oscar-winning role as Sergeant York, getting kissed by French Marshal Foch after receiving the *Medaille Militaire* for his exceptional heroism during the Argonne offensive in World War I.

The closing ceremony ending the PSF mission in Kuwait was attended by many generals and Kuwaiti officials, including the minister of defense. General BaBa'eer directed me to stand with the PSF staff and proudly introduced me to the minister as his "American adviser and LNO." Major General J. D. Thurman, USA, the CFLCC C-3, represented the CFLCC commander. A big man with a friendly "good ole country boy" approach to business, he warmly shook my hand and, with his characteristic broad smile, said, "Tiso, I'd been told you were keeping strange company."

I had to smile; "Yes, sir, you might say that."

CHAPTER 12

Assignment to the Coalition Military Assistance Team

If you don't know where you're going, any road will get you there!
—General Joe Kinzer, USA

The festive end to the Peninsula Shield Force's (PSF) deployment in Kuwait was a lot like the good feeling that characterized Camp Doha and the Combined Forces Land Component Command (CFLCC) staff. The occupation of Iraq had barely begun, but many people had already packed up and left for home or were preparing to go. I was happy for my roommate Major Chris Mitchell. His Patriot unit was ready to go, having successfully completed its air-defense mission to protect our forces and Kuwait from enemy missile and air attack. His departure on 9 May, and the lack of "hustle" on Camp Doha that had been so evident in March and April, gave the appearance of a successfully concluded war. I was okay with that for the moment. I had played an interesting and diverse role, there had not been too many of our guys killed or hurt, and, by all accounts, Baghdad had fallen in grand and classic style. It all seemed like a grand victory with more honors for our colors and perhaps another grand parade in New York City. Underlying all of this, however, was the reality of the stabilization effort in Baghdad and other parts of Iraq. My work at U.S. Central Command (USCENTCOM) in the years before the invasion suggested to me a lot of grief was yet to come.

I did not know much beyond what I saw on TV and I had plenty of time to watch. I was a man without a job after I completed my report on the operations and observations I had made of the PSF. I had been very careful to provide a detailed after-action report on my activities during the Umm Qasr and Rumaylah Oil Field missions and I spent nearly two days collecting and recording my thoughts, obser-vations, and recommendations on the deployment, operations, and readiness of the PSF. I honestly felt this politically important, but tactically unwieldy and logistically unsustainable, force was something that deserved our attention. Ultimately the Gulf States would have to defend themselves from any number of possible threats, not the least of which was the specter of Iranian hegemony in the region. I appreciated that a large American presence in the region was not in anyone's best interest. Our presence was undoubtedly necessary to protect our sea lines of communication and maintain access to the Gulf States, but a large, prolific, ground force would eventually provoke the ire of the Arab world, a land and people long on memories of the crusades and colonialism. The PSF was a logical place to start building an indigenous, defensive, regional capability. I focused my comments on command and control and logistics. The Emirati and Saudi brigades could conduct maneuver warfare. Likewise, the individual national battalions were well led and capable. The ad hoc nature by which the PSF staff had been formed, combined with its lack of modern, secure, and redundant communications, and wholly inadequate combat support structure, made it nearly impossible to engage as a major combat force beyond the security and defensive role it had played in the western Kuwaiti desert. My comments about the tactical capabilities of the individual contingents were very positive and I was certain that, had the Emiratis accepted the Rumaylah Oil Field security mission, they would have been successful. I emphasized the need for training exercises at the tactical and operational levels, the need to "flesh out" the PSF staff with competent and trained planners, operators, communicators, and logisticians, and the need for aviation assets to address tactical lift, logistical support, and reconnaissance. I was convinced that improving the combat readiness and capability of the PSF was an excellent way for the Gulf Cooperation Council to address its defensive shortfalls and that the United States should play a significant role by providing training and material assistance. With the war seemingly behind us, however, I doubted my report ever got beyond the office of the CFLCC chief of staff. I was pleased to learn from General McKiernan's executive officer that the reports we had submitted throughout our mission with the PSF had been briefed daily to the command group. In fact, General McKiernan had directed him to present Dave Wilson and me with his commander's coin for excellence. It was nice to know he had considered his liaison officers a relevant piece of his staff and that we had made a positive difference after all.

My future was on hold as the CFLCC staff dwindled in size and went about the business of deploying selected personnel to Iraq and moving units long deployed in Kuwait and elsewhere back to the United States. I was told I was being considered for several positions and a decision would ultimately be made by Major General Blackman, USMC, the CFLCC chief of staff. General Blackman had been director of Budget and Finance (CCJ8) when I was assigned to the USCENTCOM staff in August 2001. I had gotten to know him quite well and talked to him about the possibility of an assignment to the CFLCC staff after I learned of his new assignment. I thought highly of General Blackman who was later selected for a third star and command of the III Marine Expeditionary Force on Okinawa. He was destined to lead the tsunami-relief effort in southern Asia in 2005. I felt I would get a "fair shake" from him.

I whiled away the next few days, following the news, consuming rations, reading old westerns, and working out. A week passed before I received word to report to the deputy chief of staff, my old friend Colonel DellaJacano. "DJ" said General Blackman had approved an assignment for me to a project that would ultimately become one of the most important aspects of restoring a sovereign Iraq—the formation of the "New Iraqi Corps." I assumed the "NIC" would be the foundation of the Iraqi Army that had been envisioned in the original Iraq war plan. I was excited about the project, but "DJ" had no idea what my specific duties would be. He simply said I would be assigned as a staff planner in a new command designated to build an Iraqi security force. He directed me to report to Colonel Kevin Benson, CFLCC's War Plans (C-5) chief, for further instructions.

"And if I don't see you again, Tiso, it'll be too soon," he said smiling as I headed for the door.

"DJ" was a good guy, but he was no doubt happy to be rid of me. I was another officer looking for a job or a way home. Chances were that if something lousy needed to be done it came across his desk. I understood his situation quite well.

I waved to him as I hit the door. "Okay, DJ," I said, "I got the word, and thanks."

Colonel Kevin Benson, USA, was a brilliant officer and a highly skilled and experienced war planner. We had first met and worked together in 1995, when he was an Army Central planner assigned to the Third U.S. Army staff at Fort McPherson and I was the lead Iraq planner and later chief of War Plans Division at USCENTCOM. The projects that had dominated our lives during that period were USCENTCOM's original Iraq family of war plans and their transition to the national strategy's Two Major Theaters of War concept of plans. Kevin had been a significant contributor to the effort and I was not surprised he had returned to Headquarters, Third U.S. Army, and now the CFLCC staff, during this crucial period in our history, as its chief planner. A cavalryman, he had commanded a squadron before the war that had participated in Operation *Uphold Democracy* in Haiti. He had graduated from the War College and was promoted to full colonel. I considered him one of the Army's great gentlemen, a gentle giant, and, by all accounts, an outstanding leader. Always respectful, Kevin addressed me as "sir", acknowledging my seniority and our previous relationship. Good officers do that. Having been extended beyond my mandatory retirement date, I guessed I was one of the most senior colonels in the entire theater at that point. But none of that mattered. Kevin was glad to see me; we took a few minutes to swap old stories. There was very little, however, that he could tell me about the NIC project. He mentioned a team of officers and Department of Defense civilians assembling in Baghdad under the leadership of former Undersecretary of Defense Walter Slocombe. His job was to assist the development of the Iraqi Ministry of Defense and lay the groundwork for a New Iraqi Army.

"And somehow, sir, you are to be a part of it all. I suspect you'll find your niche."

My initial thought made me laugh. "Kevin, what have I got myself into this time?"

He shook his head and smiled; "Well, it can't be worse than the Major Theater of War Plans project we worked." He could not have been more wrong!

Both Kevin and his deputy, Lieutenant Colonel Mike Hendricks, thought it was a good idea for me to go to Baghdad as soon as possible. Arrangements would be made and, in the meantime, they would let me know about anything that came up. I trusted Kevin; "Alright," I said, "I'll lay low, check in daily, and wait and see what you get." I left wondering where this was going and headed for my room to pack and think. I decided to keep the room, leave any civilian clothing and non-essential gear in my wall locker, and mail a couple of packages containing assorted war trophies and mementos of the past two eventful months to my home in Florida. I accompanied Colonel Benson that afternoon to a video teleconference (VTC) concerning the New Iraqi Corps at CFLCC Headquarters. The VTC was with the Army's deputy chief of staff for operations, my War College seminar mate Lieutenant General Dick Cody, USA. The CFLCC staff group included several generals, including General Thurman. As usual, General Cody was humorous. He spoke calmly and appeared somewhat "laid back" about the mission. I do not recall the specifics of the discussions, but the uneasiness of the CFLCC staff with the possibility of having to support the program was clear. The last thing anyone wanted at this juncture was another tough challenge. There was friendly banter and laughter between Cody and Thurman, but there was not a great amount of guidance or information provided about the Iraqi Army and I remember walking away thinking not a whole lot had been accomplished, or any decisions made, during the VTC. I sensed there were more than a few officers on the CFLCC staff who thought they had accomplished their mission to win the war and the job of reconstructing an Iraqi military, or anything having to do with postwar Iraq, was someone else's job. I could not blame them, but the sense of angst in the room was thick enough to cut with a knife. They had been a liberating force alright, but what they failed to recognize or acknowledge is that only a military force can occupy a conquered country. Still not knowing what was expected of me, I nonetheless was beginning to feel that whatever I was called upon to do was going to consume me. But there was no time to dwell on it. No sooner had I walked out of the room than Colonel Benson informed me I would fly to Baghdad on the next available flight. I had the rest of the day and evening to get "squared away" before flying out the next morning.

Iraq's security forces in a post-Saddam regime scenario had been discussed for many years by war planners who understood Iraq's strategic geographical position with regard to the threat to its east. Iraq had long been regarded as the Arab bulwark against Iran. It had fought a devastating war for nearly eight years against its Persian neighbor and been supported financially to one degree or another by many other Arab nations. The consensus of two former USCENTCOM commanders and their war planners had been that reconstituting 10 Iraqi divisions in the aftermath of a campaign that brought down Saddam's regime was critical to securing Iraq's borders while simultaneously providing a secure environment from which an orderly withdrawal of Coalition forces could take place. This consensus was consistent with the planning guidance provided by the Defense Department and the Joint Chiefs of Staff that charged USCENTCOM with developing a plan that defeated the Saddam regime, maintained Iraq as a nation state, and insured it remained a counterbalance to Iran with the assets required to conduct a credible defense of its national borders. These same planners had estimated the initial assets required to occupy Iraq and secure its borders included more than 350,000 troops and three corps-level ground organizations. It was clearly spelled out in the war plan that continued to evolve over the years since its approval by the joint chiefs in 1996.[1] By every war-fighting analysis conducted from 1992–98, it was clear defeating the Iraqi military was never an issue. The forces and capabilities given in the plan, coupled with the training level of Iraqi forces, and the effects of sanctions, made the tactical and operational defeat of Iraq inevitable. The questions that concerned us focused on postconflict operations. We had no real feel for how things would go. We knew postconflict operations would be a fractious situation with Saddam out of the picture. Like it or not, Saddam was the glue that held Iraq together. If he was removed, there was always a chance Iraq would come apart at the seams. Violence was anticipated. The plan's intent, therefore, was to adjust to the postconflict situation as it developed. General Peay appreciated the need to refit Iraqi forces to address the longer-range Iranian threat. His successor, General Zinni, often referred to a post-Saddam Iraq as his "Worst nightmare." His attempt to focus on the postconflict environment in the USCENTCOM-sponsored *Desert Crossing* exercise in June 1999 addressed both his humanitarian and security concerns. While the objectives of this interagency exercise were not fully realized given the complexity of the issues, it nonetheless provided USCENTCOM and Washington's interagency with a better grasp of the problem. The exercise validated the troop list the planners had developed to prosecute the campaign, occupy the country, and reconstitute the Iraqi Army to assume its lawful responsibilities to defend Iraq.

Reflecting on these issues in my Camp Doha warehouse quarters, I understood the complexity and the urgency of the Slocombe mission. I assumed the fundamental infrastructure and trained Iraqi formations, minus blatant war criminals, would form the basis of the new corps or army we would develop. There were several discussions prior to the invasion about dropping leaflets to Iraqi garrisons encouraging them to hold in place and not oppose Coalition forces. The intent was to employ them in a security role given that General Franks had nowhere near the 350,000 troops the original war plan projected he would need to conduct successful stabilization operations. I learned from several CFLCC staff officers before the invasion that Generals Franks and McKiernan were counting on intact Iraqi formations to assume several missions, including border control, after the war. I did not know if the leaflet drops had occurred though I later learned several thousand leaflets had been dropped late in 2002 to discourage Iraqi units from fighting. Some, most notably the Army's 51st Division, had surrendered early in the war after choosing to cooperate with

British requests not to fight.[2] Recalling the CNN footage of Iraqi troops from the northern Iraqi garrisons near Mosul abandoning their posts, donning civilian clothes, and calmly walking south toward Baghdad, I wondered just how much of the Army still existed. Most regular military units emerged from the invasion fully intact and without having been engaged by Coalition forces, particularly in southern Iraq. It was not long, however, before the reality of what was left of the Iraqi Army, and the decision to formally disband it, hit me square in the face.

I walked into the Baghdad international military reception building after collecting my bags from the C-12 passenger and cargo aircraft that provided a comfortable flight from Kuwait. I hauled my bags into the makeshift terminal that was under the management of noncommissioned officers from the 101st Airborne Division's transportation office. It was already hot; sweating, hassled-looking troops contributed to the seemingly chaotic movement of passengers moving to and from the building. Water and ration packs were stacked in a corner; I grabbed a bottle and a meal as I waited for a lift to Saddam's former palace, now headquarters of the Office of Reconstruction and Humanitarian Assistance (ORHA). After a 4:30 am wake-up, a 6 am take-off, and a more than two-hour flight, I was more than ready to eat something. I dragged my bags outdoors, found a shaded place off the beaten path, and tore into a main course of cheese tortellini. Not exactly like Mom's, and certainly not my idea of breakfast food, but a good way to fuel up and pass the time. It was a couple of hours before I was picked up by a vehicle the CFLCC staff had coordinated the day before. I had lost some time, but I appreciated the ride. I thanked the driver for coming. There was not only a shortage of people in Iraq, but transportation as well. I put on my best smile along with my combat gear, threw my bags in the Humvee, and took off happy to be on my way.

I had anticipated seeing the remnants of the "Battle of Baghdad" but neither my observations from the flight or the drive to the headquarters indicated any more than the trash and junk heaps that characterized many Arab landscapes throughout the Central Region. There was no obvious evidence that spoke of a fight. In fact, I didn't sense any danger, though I remained alert and curious along the entire route. My uneventful arrival at ORHA Headquarters was quickly followed by a general orientation of the massive palace by two CFLCC officers who I never saw again, and a stop by the Kellogg Brown & Root Inc contractor trailer where I was issued bedding. I navigated the marbled hallways of the palace and eventually found my way to a large, ornate room with seven or eight Army cots arrayed between several lounge chairs and sofas. They were first-class accommodations considering I was the only guy in the room. I suspected that wouldn't last. I was lucky to have a functional bathroom; for all the talk about Saddam's opulent palaces, it was quite apparent by the "out of order" signs in nearly all the latrine and bathroom facilities that our Iraqi predecessors did not quite get the plumbing right. I had experienced shoddy plumbing and improper pipe sizing in latrines in other Arab countries that were attributable as much to graft as poor workmanship. The tendency of our Arab friends to cut corners on construction projects has never ceased to amaze me.

The Republican Palace was a sight to behold. I was awed by its size. Adorning the roof of this massive structure were four gigantic bronze busts of Saddam himself, resplendent in military uniform and a ceremonial helmet. These would ultimately be removed, but for now the heroic busts were the least of ORHA's concerns. As beautiful and awe inspiring as this and other palaces may have been, it was less than adequate to house and facilitate a modern staff poised to execute the occupation and reconstruction of a large and broken country. Work had already begun to generate the power required for a modern headquarters. There were wires everywhere. Bundles of cables were veritable trip wires that traversed the palace's long hallways. Construction of office space was needed to accommodate and separate the various staff elements. Piles of plywood and other building materials were stacked everywhere. Eventually, the large ballrooms would be sectioned off and the palace converted into a modern office building complete with all the governmental ministries of the future Iraqi Government. There was no air conditioning, and it would not be too much longer before the grueling summer heat would exact its toll on the efficiency and energy of everyone who worked there. The civilian contract engineers and construction crews worked feverishly to build the infrastructure required to support this now professional office building, but it was several months before it was a comfortable place to work. Like everything else, or so it seemed about the Saddam regime, the palaces simply indicated the "emperor had no clothes." The infrastructure I saw in Iraq throughout my tour of duty reflected nothing short of shoddy, sorry workmanship, often camouflaged by ornate appearances of marble and gold-colored fixtures. Iraq was a mess!

What may have been one of the world's largest hotels did not lend itself well to a comfortable, sleep-filled night. After exploring the palace grounds and much of the neighboring areas and buildings, I returned to my room in the evening only to find the lights did not work. I kept my flashlight handy to avoid the furniture as I made my way to the cave-like entrance of the bathroom in the middle of the night. The absence of windows made the heat even more oppressive. I managed to nod off, only to wake up several hours later soaked in sweat. At times like these, a soldier's sense of humor is one of his most valuable "weapons." Compared to the thousands of guys on the line, sacked out in tank hulls, on Humvee hoods, or on the desert floor, I figured I had it pretty good.

I finally met some people connected to the NIC program on 16 May. Major Jim Torglar and Lieutenant Colonel Laura Shally were happy to see me. They were part of an advance team, a quartering party for Slocombe's staff. Colonel Shally was a communications officer responsible for establishing phone lines and administrative equipment to support the front office. Torglar was a "jack of all trades," a reservist who seemed to have his hands into everything. I never really understood what his job or title was. I was welcomed and introduced to other members of the team, including Walt Slocombe who immediately impressed me as a dedicated public servant. I suspected his duties and responsibilities as the defense adviser in Baghdad, coupled with his task to build a New Iraqi Army, would be one of the biggest challenges of his already illustrious career. Slocombe was Undersecretary of Defense for Policy in the Clinton Administration from 1994 to 2001. That he was selected by a tough Republican Administration for his current position spoke volumes about his desire to work for the good of the nation and stand above partisan politics.

Mr. Slocombe was ably assisted by Colonel Greg Gardner, an exceptional infantry officer and combat veteran who had previously served as the 25th Infantry Division's operations officer (G-3) in Hawaii, and had commanded the Army's prestigious "Old Guard," the 3rd Infantry Regiment in Washington, D.C. This regiment is a showcase unit to the nation's citizens and the world; its mission includes conducting ceremonies, upholding the traditions of the Army, and protecting the National Capital Region. He had held several demanding positions in the Pentagon and was by any measure a tough, high energy, "take charge," kind of officer who was dedicated to his boss and the mission. Greg would have a lot to say as to who did what on this team and I thought it best to speak carefully, mind my business, and wait to see what role I would be given.

Surprisingly, we were given orders to pack up and return to Kuwait. The decision made sense, though I was initially disappointed, having just arrived a few days before. Clearly the facilities at ORHA Headquarters were lousy and the people with whom the Slocombe team needed to plan and coordinate were at CFLCC Headquarters at Camp Doha. It was the right decision. The C-130 flight to Kuwait provided a period of reflection, beginning with the loading of the aircraft. We were delayed pending the arrival of the remains of an American soldier who had been killed in action. Standing at attention, and later at rest during the flight, I remember staring at the flag-draped coffin and thinking how lucky I had been. Somehow it always comes down to that—luck. "There but for the grace of God," I thought. There was no real glory in any of this. There were no medals or personal honors that could talk to the heroism or personal sacrifice of this American soldier. It is good for a senior officer to be humbled in these ways, or else be guilty of taking himself too seriously or thinking he is far more important than he really is.

"Just do your job, Roland," I thought, "Whatever it is they want you do, make it all worth the cost."

The overflow of U.S. military personnel and contractors arriving in Kuwait were billeted at the Hilton Resort Hotel on the beach in Kuwait City and that's where we were ordered to live. I could not help feeling a little guilty about it—beach-house living, excellent restaurants, it just did not seem right. I even had dinner one night with R. Lee Ermey, the famous and popular marine gunnery sergeant and television host of *Mail Call* on the History Channel. My officers and I drove to Camp Doha every day over the next two weeks and worked according to the Army half-day program, at least twelve hours a day. We focused on developing a concept briefing and a statement of work for what was now officially known as the New Iraqi Army (NIA) project. We were amused to learn that the acronym "NIC" for the New Iraqi Corps had to be changed because when pronounced in Arabic it either meant, or sounded like, "fuck." In the company of soldiers, an occurrence like this always provokes laughter and jokes typical of fighting men. Mr. Slocombe needed these products to brief and gain approval in Washington to proceed with the project. Like most "start from scratch operations," the process was painful but, to his credit, Mr. Slocombe rolled up his sleeves and worked with us as though he was an action officer. There was no need to second guess what the boss wanted; he was never very far from us. His guidance was clear, and we engaged at length with Generals Blackman and Thurman to ensure CFLCC was aware of the direction of our planning. Their approval of the fundamental NIA concept of operations was vitally important since CFLCC, or whatever command succeeded it, would ultimately have to support the program. It was clear any thought I had about retooling 10 Iraqi divisions and quickly deploying them in the defense of Iraq was a non-starter when I was informed the Coalition Provisional Authority (CPA) had decided to officially demobilize the Iraqi Army, and the decision was final.

I had no idea of what remained of the defeated Iraqi Army. It had essentially dissolved itself during the Coalition's march to Baghdad. The CPA order formalized what appeared to be the reality on the ground. I thought the trained military manpower under Iraqi leadership and supervised by the Coalition could be recalled, reorganized, and allowed to function in a security role. My thoughts were based on the manpower requirements our war planning and exercises in the 1990s had determined were needed to keep a potentially explosive Iraq under control. The Iraqi Army had a sullied reputation in the world since its defeat in the First Gulf War and its brutal campaigns against its Kurd and Shia populations. Many Iraqis, however, saw it as a noble institution that had defended the nation from the Jews and the Persians first in the 1973 October War and then in the eight-year Iran–Iraq War. Iraq had been supported by many Gulf nations, including Kuwait, in its role as the Arab bulwark against Persian expansion and hegemony in the Middle East. An army of one million men in a country of twenty million people in the early 1990s had a significant impact on the political, economic, and cultural make-up of the country. Reduced in stature by the time of the invasion in 2003, its dissolution along with its associated intelligence services had placed 400,000 men out of work. There was general distaste for the Baath Party and Saddam's former security forces, but only the Kurds approved of the dissolution of the armed forces. Even the Shia, who had filled most the Army's enlisted ranks, viewed the Army as a significant part of Iraq's culture. They wanted change and more opportunity, but to dissolve it outright and replace it with the original NIA concept of a small, professional force of 40,000 men bereft of any significant fighting capability was not a satisfactory option. Former Sunni officers were not only out of work, but deeply resentful of their sense of lost honor. Adding insult to injury, General McKiernan, the CFLCC commander, ordered all groups in Iraq to disarm, but he exempted the "Peshmerga," the Kurdish branch of the Iraqi Armed Forces. This order led many former officers and Baathists to believe our aim was to dissolve the Iraqi state.[3] The CPA attempted to ease the strain on the unemployed military by paying a monthly stipend to some 250,000 former soldiers of various ranks. Struggling with the task of fielding 12,000 Iraqi soldiers by the end of 2003, it occurred to several of us in the newly formed Coalition Military Assistance Training Team (CMATT) that the stipend list could be used to recall and field a large organization that could be put to work cleaning up and securing military and government infrastructure. We could refit and rearm them over time, vetting and selecting the senior leadership of what could eventually be a powerful and respectable armed force. USCENTCOM planners were aware many former soldiers were standing ready to support us. Their use was supported by Generals McKiernan and Wallace, the Land Forces and V Corps commanders, but strongly opposed by Ambassador Bremer and Mr. Slocombe who were concerned such an effort would detract funding and energy from the development of a professional army. Unknown to me at the time, many former senior Iraqi leaders stood ready to assist us to put the military back together. As they were tainted by their association with the Baath Party and guilty of having attained senior rank under an evil regime, the U.S. chose not to deal with these men, choosing a politically correct approach that initially excluded all officers above the rank of major from returning to the Army. It was a doomed plan from the start. The formal dissolution of the Iraqi Army, coupled by an inflexible policy to recall large numbers of trained manpower under former senior Iraqi leadership, undoubtedly contributed to the insurgency that began to take shape in the summer/fall of 2003.

The decision to dissolve the Iraqi Armed Forces presented us with a monumental task. We did not have much of a staff to build a new army, but we were told the required personnel would soon arrive in Kuwait. A joint manning document had to be finalized and approved before the personnel we needed could be provided from stateside pools on a permanent basis. In the meantime, USCENTCOM, its service-component commands, and several Coalition countries would provide officers and noncommissioned officers on a temporary basis. It was not much to lean on, but I now understood how I got caught up in the project.

Our mission was to establish the facilities, the administrative structure, and the policies and standards that would facilitate the recruiting, organizing, equipping, and training of a force of three Iraqi motorized divisions—a total of 40,000 men. The force was to be lightly armed with rifles, machine guns, and light mortars. It was to be capable of conducting point, route, convoy, and border security, and disarm rogue militia groups. Administrative missions included battlefield clean-up and equipment consolidation. It would not be long, however, before we discovered there was little or no equipment from the Saddam regime to consolidate, let alone use, and that the former military facilities were mere skeletons of their former selves, stripped to the bone by local populations.

The New Iraqi Army's training program would focus on leadership, marksmanship, fundamental tactics, navigation, and patrolling. The Army was to be a source of national pride and serve as an example of ethnic integration. Our recruiting efforts had to ensure a healthy mix of Shi'ites, Kurds, and Sunnis, and this dictated we recruit from areas throughout the vast expanse of Iraq. The goals and objectives for this new Iraqi force would evolve over time but, in May 2003, as I looked about and considered the resources we had, the concept did not look very promising. It was clear from the comments we had heard during our briefings to Generals Blackman and Thurman that CFLCC expected and wanted a more robust Iraqi force. It was also clear CFLCC was very reluctant to provide resources for this project and careful to avoid playing a major role. It really did not want a role at all. I began to appreciate this project was going to be an uphill struggle by a small group of under-resourced guys from whom much would be expected, and little would be appreciated.

Somewhere in the process of developing the PowerPoint picture of this future Iraqi Army, I was designated the operations officer of what was to become the CMATT. I was encouraged by the arrival of a small "Corps of Marines" on temporary assignment to the project from the USCENTCOM staff—Lieutenant Colonels Mike Greer, Bob Sommers, and Joe Moore. My marines and I, together with several members of the CFLCC staff, developed the project's statement of work and a detailed reconnaissance plan of former Iraqi training bases and garrisons throughout the country. The statement of work and the concept briefing's approval in Washington was clearly the business of Mr. Slocombe and Colonel Gardner. I did not envy them. The execution of the reconnaissance plan was the responsibility of my operations team; we looked forward to it with excitement and enthusiasm.

CHAPTER 13

Building the Foundation of an Army

Never doubt that a small group of thoughtful, committed, citizens can change the world.
—Margaret Mead, American Anthropologist

On 1 June, my marines and I, along with two of the most colorful and unorthodox characters I have ever known—Lieutenant Sean McDougal, USN, and Major Randolph "Troll" Winge, USAF—returned to Baghdad to finalize coordination for helicopter support and prepare for the reconnaissance of Iraqi installations. Our objective was to locate suitable facilities and make recommendations for selected training and recruiting sites for the New Iraqi Army (NIA). McDougal and Winge had the unenviable job of preparing accommodations for the large and robust Coalition Military Assistance Training Team (CMATT) and Ministry of Defense (MOD) staffs we expected to eventually arrive in Baghdad.

I was not aware of the growing insurgency in Iraq when we settled back into our palatial bunk house at the Office of Reconstruction and Humanitarian Assistance (ORHA) Headquarters. The deteriorating situation in Baghdad, however, did not take long to become obvious to everyone. We went right to work, poring over maps of Iraq to discuss and finalize planning of our reconnaissance mission. The next day as I stood in the chow line, a young soldier informed me a large demonstration was in progress at the front gate of the palace grounds and that five former Iraqi generals wanted to speak to me. You can imagine my surprise, having been back in Baghdad for all of a day. "Why me?" I asked myself rather incredulously. "What do they want?" I could not believe it! Colonel Jim Frawley, USMCR, the designated MOD chief of staff could not be found and I was the only CMATT or MOD officer of any rank in the immediate vicinity. A Military Police (MP) officer who had been monitoring the demonstration informed me they wanted to speak to someone involved in the "Reconstitution of the Iraqi Army." I walked out to several parked vehicles where I was greeted by a colonel from the 354th Civil Affairs Brigade, the same outfit I had been attached to in April in Umm Qasr that had left me so cold. I could not resist asking, "Colonel, why the hell didn't you speak to these guys?" I let him babble on about what his responsibilities were before I cut him off and got in the lead vehicle. It was clear no one wanted to deal with these guys so why not grab the FNG (Army-speak for the "fucking new guy") and throw him into the ring? "Sure, right," I said, "Let's go."

Five Iraqi gentlemen, well dressed in Western suits, stood inside the gate in clear view of the demonstrating crowd. I directed the MPs to have them move under a tree on one side of the gate and far away from the view of the placard-carrying, ranting crowd. I then got out of the Hummer and approached them with a neutral, business-like expression on my face. I rendered the smartest salute I could muster to disarm them with a simple demonstration of respect for their former rank. I could tell they appreciated it. They returned the salute and introduced themselves. Their intent was to meet with representatives of the "American staff" and volunteer their services to reconstitute the Iraqi Army and secure retirement benefits and back pay for Iraqi soldiers. I listened carefully and advised them preparations were underway to address Iraqi security requirements and pay issues. I told them I would refer their desires and request to meet with higher authorities to my superiors and, to demonstrate good faith, I said someone would meet with them tomorrow at this same location and time with additional information. I then spoke directly to the general that appeared to be the senior officer of the group and quietly suggested he use his influence to calm the crowd and encourage them to disperse. He slowly nodded his head. The generals appeared to like my professional, but friendly, demeanor. We parted with handshakes and tight-lipped smiles. I was advised later the crowd quickly dissipated after our departure. I acknowledged the civil affairs colonel's compliments and made a mental note to inform Colonel Frawley of what had taken place and that he or someone on the MOD staff should meet with the generals the next day. "So much for lunch," I thought, as I walked by the now empty chow hall and back to our workspace.

My diplomatic mission completed, I met with Brigadier General Dan Hahn, USA, the V Corps, and now Combined Joint Task Force-7 (CJTF-7), chief of staff. V Corps had deployed from Germany and provided command and control of Army maneuver units during the invasion of Iraq. It and the First Marine Expeditionary Force had been under the overall command of the Coalition Force Land Component Commander (CFLCC). V Corps had transitioned to its post-invasion responsibilities in Baghdad and been redesignated CJTF-7. Hahn was a no-nonsense artilleryman who, like most senior members of the staff, appeared hassled, tired, and overworked. We knew each other and he addressed me by my first name. I liked General Hahn; he was very professional and appreciated the importance of the CMATT mission. We were a distraction to V Corps' overall scheme of operations, but he acknowledged that our reconnaissance mission and its aviation requirements had to be supported. Aviation support to our mission was significant to the resource-strapped V Corps staff, something I was reminded of almost every day by well-meaning officers. General Hahn referred to growing unrest and the possibility of an insurgency, the need for security, and the growing challenge we were facing to stabilize the country, and told me, "Roland, it's going to be a long, hot summer." I left his office with the impression some of our reconnaissance flights could very well turn into combat air assaults.

On 3 June, Mike Greer and I, accompanied by several communicators and Major Scott Redd, an Army engineer, took off from "Washington" helo pad near the palace headquarters in a lift of three UH-60 Black Hawk helicopters for the first of what would be many reconnaissance flights that would take us over much of northern and central Iraq and into countless former installations and training grounds of the Iraqi Army. Bob Sommers and Lieutenant Colonel Winston Mann, USAR, from C-5 (Plans) of the CFLCC staff, had remained at Camp Doha to coordinate and execute the southern portion of the reconnaissance, including sites as far south as Baṣrah and Umm Qasr.

Lieutenant Colonel Mike Greer was an immensely talented and unusual Marine officer. His academic pedigree was out of this world. As a student of American history at Columbia University, he was challenged by a professor to do something with the strength and vitality of his youth. Mike joined the Marine Corps and went on to secure several masters-level degrees from Harvard, Oxford, and Stanford Universities, eventually completing a Doctorate in Philosophy. Mike had seen action in the First Gulf War and in Bosnia and was trained as both an infantry and civil affairs officer. The senior of the three Marine lieutenant colonels, Mike served as the operations deputy and the challenges we faced over the next three months made us close friends. I appropriately addressed him as "P," a West Point term for "Professor" that had been the moniker of the great and scholarly Major General John "Tiger" Wood, USA, who commanded the 4th Armored Division in Patton's Third Army in 1944. I reveled in Mike's resentment of the name even though I used it respectfully. His talents would be severely tested during his short, but decisive tour in the CMATT.

Mr. Slocombe had outlined the initial requirements for our survey mission on 24 May in a briefing to the entire staff. We needed a training site, preferably in central Iraq, with the capability of supporting 4,000 recruits and a staff of 300 personnel. The facilities and infrastructure required water and sewage lines, messing facilities, parade and sports fields, small-arms ranges, a maintenance area, a motor pool, weapons-storage rooms, at least ten classrooms, a large warehouse, and other buildings for medical support, morale and welfare, and religious activities. Garrison sites with similar characteristics were required in northern, central, and southern Iraq. Additionally, we needed reception and processing centers in Mosul, Baghdad, and Baṣrah. These would serve as Military Entrance Processing Stations (MEPS) to support the recruiting effort. The sites were expected to provide overnight accommodation for up to three hundred recruits and fifty staff members, and include a 30-man classroom, rooms for medical examinations, an outdoor location suitable for daily parades and formations of recruits, and the potential to substantially increase in size as required. We did not have a clue as to what was out there that met these specifications. I simply took notes and acknowledged the requirements.

Executing the reconnaissance plan and meeting Mr. Slocombe's requirements required considerable effort. The importance of the mission, coupled with our ambitious timeline, the intense heat, the frustrating coordination process to ensure aviation support, and our poor findings in the field added to the difficulty of the task. Iraq's military and governmental facilities were almost totally trashed. The destruction we witnessed at such places as the large military depot and garrison at Taji, just 12 miles north of Baghdad, and training bases and garrisons near al-Ḥabbānīyah, Mosul, Al Asad Air Base, Tikrīt, and al-Fallūjah, was disheartening and demoralizing. The look on Lieutenant Colonel Greer's face as we flew from place to place, day after day, said it all. We were in trouble. The amount of work required to restore the barracks and other facilities to minimal occupation standards boggled the most liberal imagination. Our engineer shook his head in dismay. The destruction we saw at Taji did not surprise me as much as the rest of it. Taji had been targeted and bombed in countless strikes during and since the First Gulf War. The destruction of the other sites, however, had not been caused by our kinetic military action, but by the Iraqi people who had looted the facilities for everything they could put their hands on including tiles, pipes, plumbing fixtures, windows, and anything that could be carried away or loaded on a truck. Many of the looters were armed and Greer and I came under fire on several occasions as we approached these hard-working men stripping the bases for everything they could get. Military equipment and live ordnance littered the landscapes and facilities. Libraries of manuals and textbooks were strewn everywhere. In a base near al-Fallūjah, the motor pools were filled with trucks that had been stripped as efficiently and totally as any vehicle I had seen vandalized along the back streets and highways of the Bronx and Mount Vernon, New York, when I was a kid. An effort had been made by American combat units to move captured and abandoned military vehicles, tanks, and artillery pieces into assembly areas for possible use by a future Iraqi armed force, but the equipment and vehicles we saw at Taji were recoverable scrap metal at best. Taji reeked of death and defeat. Locomotives and container cars, victims of American airpower, lay in total ruin both off and on the railroad tracks that once served the Iraqi logistics system. Recoverable items of uniform and combat equipment had been looted by our boys as well as the Iraqis. One warehouse was filled with death shrouds, the bulk of which were strewn over the floor. I considered taking one as a souvenir until I noticed almost all of them were blood stained. I thought better of it and left them for the more morbid. Other warehouses still held Iraqi uniforms and individual issue items such as small rucksacks, pistol belts, and canteens, but we could not get the area secured fast enough before the bulk of these items were carried off as well. I assessed Taji as a possible training site requiring massive clean-up and reconstruction, but when I was asked by CJTF-7 Chief of Staff Brigadier General Hahn at a briefing several weeks later what I really thought of it, I didn't mince any words: "Taji, sir, is a shit hole!"

There was one location, however, that could work. Just as our mission appeared a hopeless failure, Mike Greer's face told a different story. We were about 100 kilometers east of Baghdad near the small village of Kirkush. During the Iran–Iraq War, Saddam had built many platoon, company, and battalion-sized posts to reinforce the Iranian border. Other garrisons far larger than those posts near the border were built to support them. Kirkush Barracks was one of several large garrisons Saddam had commissioned a Yugoslavian construction company to build. It was massive and appeared relatively intact from the air. Mike's voice over the intercom said it all, "Boss, I think we've found our training base." The sprawling garrison below us looked like Saddam's answer to Fort Benning, the U.S. Army's Infantry Center in Columbus, Georgia. It even had an airstrip. Kirkush Barracks had never been completed by its Yugoslavian builders. Their efforts were halted by a cash-strapped Saddam with the end of the Iran–Iraq War in 1988. Closer scrutiny indicated the infrastructure left a lot to be desired, but there was no denying the value of the location and the potential the site held for development and expansion. The buildings were sound and required far less clean up than other sites we had seen. A portion of the site was occupied by elements of the U.S. 10th Cavalry, 4th Infantry Division, that was tasked with reconnaissance and security responsibilities in an area that included a portion of the Iranian border. Its presence could assist our security requirements, assuming the decision was made to develop the site. Mike and I agreed it was without a doubt the best facility we had seen in over a week and our best bet to get the NIA project off the ground.

Our luck continued as we surveyed promising MEPS locations in Baghdad and Mosul. A tentative location in Baṣrah had been identified by the Brits as well and we arranged to survey the site at a later date. Assistance from CJTF-7, and particularly Deputy CJTF-7 Commander Major General Walt Wojdkowski, USA, was invaluable. I had first met him when he commanded the Office of Military Cooperation–Kuwait in 1998, while I was General Zinni's executive assistant. A highly decorated veteran of the First Gulf War, General Wojdkowski understood the importance of the NIA project and he was quick to make the necessary phone calls to get us the assets we needed. His office offered a rare avenue to a staff that was fully engaged with its occupation duties and did not want to be distracted by the project. Everyone was stressed, but "Wojo" knew the Iraqi Army was our ticket out of Iraq. Unfortunately, neither the senior leadership of the U.S. Army, the Office of the Secretary of Defense, nor the Joint Chiefs of Staff would understand that for almost another year.

In the meantime, Lieutenant McDougal and Major Winge had accomplished what, by any standard, was a veritable miracle. The CMATT had been allocated a set of quarters on the palace grounds to billet the members of its staff, assuming it could be brought up to an acceptable living standard. The palace itself was quickly being converted into a huge office building and the large rooms that once provided sleeping accommodations were badly needed for workspace. We had to get out. Armed with his personal toolbox, McDougal had rewired Uday Hussein's former home, repaired the air conditioning and the plumbing, and had hot and cold running water in the kitchen and bathrooms. McDougal was an outstanding naval engineer whose talents rivaled those of the American television character "MacGyver" who could get out of seemingly impossible situations by applying fundamental scientific principles and the simplest tools and materials. McDougal's talents were matched by the logistical genius of "Troll" Winge, who was always able to find, requisition, or mysteriously "acquire" the parts, tools, machines, fuel, and whatever else was needed to keep the house functional. We moved into the house on 12 June and in five days our mechanical and scrounging geniuses even had Uday's indoor pool up and running. Winge had procured the chlorine needed to service the water from a shop in Baghdad. How they took that putrid, mud-laden hole in the ground, and returned it to its previous glory as a first-class swimming pool was absolutely beyond us all. Their exceptional work exemplified the "can do" spirit of our organization in what was clearly a "shoestring" environment. Our lights, running water, air conditioning and, of course, the pool, eventually made the house a very popular place. I was amazed by the large number of visitors to our not-so-humble abode.

My principal concern, however, was to capture our data, observations, and photos of the installations we had surveyed into a comprehensive briefing for Mr. Slocombe, who had returned from Washington the same day we moved into Uday's former house. I wanted to brief him and Colonel Gardner on the 13th, and to seek approval to develop Kirkush Barracks and the MEPS facilities in Mosul and Baghdad. Greer and I decided to conduct the briefing in a room off the main lobby area of the house that served as a movie theater in the evenings for the staff. The briefing would also allow us to showcase the progress our team had made with our living quarters. Greer, Sommers, Redd, and I worked late into the evening to put it all together, but our efforts were worth it. The briefing was a resounding success. Mr. Slocombe knew we had a tough job on our hands; the extent of the destruction and overall state of the facilities we had surveyed shocked him. We also advised him of what had to be a sobering fact of life. We could forget about any thoughts we originally held to consolidate and refurbish large quantities of Iraqi equipment. Our photos spoke volumes about the status of the remains of Saddam's vaunted Army. He did not question our assessment. We got the decision we sought. Kirkush Barracks would serve as our principal training site during the first year of the NIA project. Mr. Slocombe directed us to provide the same briefing to Major General Eaton who would arrive that evening to assume the duties of the CMATT commander.

Major General Paul. D. Eaton, USA, was no stranger to military training. He had been called from his duties as the commandant of the United States Army

Infantry Center at Fort Benning, Georgia, to his new assignment in Iraq. He was eminently qualified to develop and train the NIA. A 1972 graduate of the United States Military Academy at West Point and a combat veteran of Somalia, he had had a wide variety of assignments in the infantry including command of a light infantry battalion in the 10th Mountain Division and a mechanized infantry brigade in Europe. I had known him since 1991 when we participated in a "United Forces" exercise as battalion commanders in Uruguay. His battalion later trained in Panama at the Jungle Operations Training Center and the battalion I commanded provided the opposing force for the three-day field training exercise that concluded the jungle-training program. We had also been classmates at the Army War College. Paul Eaton was a good friend and an exceptional officer. I was pleased he was our commander.

General Eaton looked understandably tired when he arrived at the house the next day. The time zones you pass through getting to the Middle East can tire the best of us and it typically requires a week to get a person's body clock back on track. He was genuinely happy to see me, and we gave him a quick tour of the house before delving into the briefing. He had received his orders to go to Iraq on 9 May and had spent three weeks at Fort Benning and Washington laying out the way ahead. I do not doubt he had been advised of the difficulty of his mission, but his concerns undoubtedly grew as he viewed our slides and gained an appreciation for the state of the Iraqi facilities. He was also concerned about the dearth of people he had to get the job done. Authorized a staff of 248 personnel, the organization never had more than fifty percent of its authorized strength during his command tour. General Eaton never questioned the 23 May decision by Ambassador Bremer to stand down the old Iraqi Army. In addition to the political factors involved in the decision, he accepted there was essentially nothing left of the old Iraqi Army. He had a huge job to do and, in his view, there was no sense in debating a decision the reality on the ground appeared to justify. He appreciated our briefing immensely and thanked us for the effort. He was quite genuine in his assessment of our work and marveled at what we had accomplished. But Paul Eaton was no fool. It was clear he had inherited what he later described as a "Disjointed fiasco," a mission that had been given only superficial planning.[1] Like any good commander, he wanted to put "eyes on the objective" and directed us to coordinate his personal reconnaissance of Kirkush Barracks as soon as possible.

As we labored to coordinate and plan the NIA project, I grew increasingly concerned with my personal situation. I was well into the fourth month of my 179-day orders from Central Command and the last thing I wanted to do was return to the headquarters in Tampa and the uncertain, no doubt dismal, fate of retirement that awaited me at a time when perhaps, in my own conceited mind, I never felt more needed or valuable to my country or the Army. During my period of inactivity at Camp Doha following the mission with the Peninsula Shield Force, I had heard about a Polish-led multinational division scheduled to enter Iraq sometime that summer. I began to explore what this multinational force was all about and determine whether advisers and liaison officers were needed to support its mission. I was committed to getting the CMATT mission "off the ground," but suspected it would not be long before the joint manning document would be filled with centrally selected officers, and I would be out of a job. I made my desires to serve with the multinational division known to the CJTF-7 personnel officer and I was pleasantly surprised when General Wojdkowski approached me at the Corps change-of-command ceremony at Camp Victory and told me the Polish job was mine if I wanted it. Timing was important, but I thought I could make it work. The first battalion of the NIA had to be recruited and on the ground at a renovated, functional Kirkush Barracks by mid-August, and the Multinational Division (Central-South) was supposed to be operational by the end of August when it was scheduled to assume responsibility for its operational area in central Iraq from the First Marine Expeditionary Force. It all seemed doable and when I informed General Eaton of my orders dilemma over dinner one night, he told me he would support my assignment in August. I trusted Paul Eaton and was encouraged by his support. I could not have been more motivated to facilitate the development of the organizational infrastructure we so badly needed to recruit and train the soldiers of the NIA.

Final approval to proceed with the development of Kirkush Barracks was given jointly by Mr. Slocombe and General Eaton following their personal reconnaissance of the complex on 16 June. We had assembled an impressive group of engineers to accompany them as well as representatives from the comptrollers and contracting offices of the former ORHA, now designated the Coalition Provisional Authority (CPA). We wanted everyone to understand the scope of the challenge. We were convinced Kirkush Barracks was the right place to start building the infrastructure for an Iraqi Army, but we had become more aware of the challenges it presented from the initial engineer assessments we had studied. Since the original Yugoslavian building project had not been completed, vital infrastructure, including water pipelines, had either not been constructed or completed. We knew power for the installation would be a huge challenge. It was all technically doable, of course, but ultimately it was a money issue and full support of the NIA project by both the CPA and CJTF-7 Headquarters, from CMATT's perspective, left much to be desired. I was very concerned the statement of work we had developed the previous month at Camp Doha was hopelessly inadequate, having never envisioned the demoralizing state of current Iraqi facilities we had found. The engineers were committed to the project and clearly wanted to manage it. The development of Kirkush Barracks was a task worthy of their professional education and training. They agreed to conduct follow-on technical surveys that commenced the next day. The magnitude of the challenge would grow substantially across the board from engineering and construction, to contracting services, to every conceivable aspect of building a complex training facility and an army over the next two months, but it was clear the future of the NIA hinged on this large, windswept, abandoned, Iraqi post.

Other parts of our plan had yet to come together. We still needed approval to renovate and establish the recruiting stations we had selected in Mosul and Baghdad. These sites had been government property but, not surprisingly, extended Iraqi families had occupied the Baghdad site and a banner across the entrance proudly proclaimed it as the headquarters of some unknown Iraqi humanitarian-assistance program. As unbelievable as it may have seemed, the pungent cooking smells, squawking chickens, barking dogs, assorted pets and animals, and young children playing on the grounds spoke the truth of the matter. I pondered the actions we had to take to evict them while simultaneously imagining myself on the front page of the local newspaper as the "Grinch of Baghdad" who kicked innocent, desolate families out into the street. "Nothing was easy," I thought as I made a note to inform the civil affairs staff of the problem. The same was true in Mosul. Arriving at the proposed recruiting site on 20 June, General Eaton and I were greeted by the "proprietor" of the complex who proudly showed us around his "home." Better to smile and let the civil affairs guys handle it. Ultimately, these situations and others like them that we encountered were managed by our civil affairs people, local Iraqi authorities, and Iraqi ministries slowly being reestablished at the Republican Palace. General Eaton was satisfied the recruiting sites filled our needs and directed me to go to Baṣrah at the earliest opportunity to survey the site the Brits had recommended to us.

General Eaton's trip to Mosul included a visit to the headquarters of the 101st Airborne Division (Air Assault), where we were briefed on its operations by Division Commander Major General Dave Petraeus. We knew each other from his tour as the executive assistant to Chairman of the Joint Chiefs of Staff General Shelton. In my position as General Zinni's executive assistant, we spoke frequently and saw each other often at the Pentagon. We had developed a friendly relationship. Assistant Division Commander Brigadier General Ben Freakley was a dear friend of mine from our lieutenant days together in the 506th Infantry at Fort Campbell, Kentucky. I also knew Ben's newly arrived replacement, Brigadier General Frank Helmick, who was undergoing his in-briefings and general orientation in Iraq. We had served together in 1992–93, when he was an operations officer on the U.S. Ranger Regiment's staff. The battalion I commanded had been attached to the regiment to participate in a series of exercises between the summer and spring of 1992–93, culminating in a Joint Readiness Training Center Rotation at Fort Chaffee, Arkansas. We enjoyed a very good friendship. These relationships were extremely valuable to me. The situation in Iraq during the summer of 2003 required mutual understanding and a sense of trust in the various organizations and units with which we dealt. A handshake had to mean something or we would go nowhere. I felt we could get the job done in Mosul with the "Screaming Eagles" of the 101st Airborne.

We concluded our visit to the 101st by flying to a large, division-size garrison complex near Al Kasik, about fifty kilometers northwest of Mosul. The site was the "spitting image" of Kirkush Barracks, only larger. The markings I saw on portions of the construction again pointed to the industrious Yugoslavians who were ordered to abandon the site before its completion as the Iran–Iraq War ended in 1988. During the visit, General Petraeus pulled me off to the side and told me he would welcome the opportunity to develop the site and train Iraqi forces with his division's assets. I was very sympathetic to this idea. It was consistent with how I thought the dissolved Iraqi Army could be recalled, rebuilt, trained, and redeployed in a more expeditious manner. I knew that ultimately the U.S. Army would have to get involved in the NIA's development and training. General Petraeus was convinced his division could execute the training mission and significantly accelerate the Army's development. I explained that the current concept called for contract civilian trainers to train the Iraqi Army and that funding currently only allowed the development of our first chosen site at Kirkush Barracks. His thoughts, however, were well intentioned and ahead of their time. I was in total agreement with him and told him I would share his thoughts with General Eaton, who subsequently thought well of the suggestion. Division assets were eventually used to develop local forces throughout Iraq. It seemed we could not move fast enough to satisfy anyone, but this division-sized site near Mosul held considerable potential for a northern garrison and was eventually refurbished as a major post for the NIA.

Underlying the infrastructure and construction challenges was the fundamental availability of weapons, uniforms, furniture, and items of personal issue to equip the force. We attempted to locate and assess any useable military equipment we could find. We started with absolutely nothing. American units in the field were directed by CJTF-7 to turn in any weapons they confiscated, but the number of AK-47 assault rifles our forces recovered was insignificant relative to the requirements of the project. We needed weapons and the solution, we were told, was located at the MEK bases at Camp Ashraf, some fifty miles northeast of Baghdad. The MEK, or Mojahedin-e-Khalq, had been disarmed by U.S. forces in May 2003 shortly after the fall of Baghdad. It was a highly disciplined Iranian force equipped in large measure by Saddam Hussein to free Iran of its Islamic regime. Some 3,000 MEK fighters and their families lived in a well-established community at Camp Ashraf where they held "protected person status" under the Geneva Convention. It appeared their fighting days were behind them.

Mike Greer and I picked a team of weapons experts including Captain Holland, a Marine infantry officer who knew Soviet small arms like the back of his hand. We flew to a small ball field near the headquarters of the U.S. 2nd Battalion, 8th Infantry Regiment, 4th Infantry Division, where we were greeted by its commander, Lieutenant Colonel John Miller, USA. He took us to a military storage site with numerous conex containers in a secured area a short driving distance from his headquarters. A young sergeant opened two conexes and what we saw provided an inkling of hope. Haphazardly stacked from floor to ceiling were rifles and light machine guns. Holland and his team went straight to work performing functional checks and assessments, but the sheer number of rifles limited us to a random sampling. Holland assessed that over ninety-five percent of the weapons were fundamentally sound. He personally field-stripped 22 AK-47s and pronounced all of them combat ready. I was not at all surprised by the ruggedness of these Russian-designed rifles. The virtues of the American M16 and the AK-47 are often compared, but the reliability of the Russian rifle, its 7.62-mm caliber round, 350-meter effective killing range, and near maintenance-free construction make it a formidable weapon. It is no wonder it has long been the weapon of choice of insurgents and many professional armies and has been found on nearly every battlefield around the globe since the end of World War II.

We drove a short distance to Camp Ashraf where the Iranian flag flew at the main entrance to the complex. We found the "mother lode." Stored in large, well-constructed bunkers with locked steel doors was the majority of the MEK's weapons stores. The weapons were superbly maintained, and large numbers of rifles and light machine guns were packed in their original packing crates and heavily coated in cosmoline. There were stores of heavy machine guns and mortars, a variety of anti-aircraft and anti-tank weapons, and grenades in large numbers. We assessed the bunkers contained enough light weapons to outfit at least two brigades. We documented our assessment with numerous photos and, having seen enough and noted several MEK recon parties watching our every move, I ordered everyone to pack up and return to the helicopters. It was time to write another report and build a briefing that would inform our senior leadership of the existence of these weapons and hopefully energize them to make the weapons available to the NIA project.

Colonel Greer and I returned to our new quarters on the Green Zone palace grounds to have my eyes opened to a new aspect of my experience in Iraq that, almost from the beginning, had been a very austere, spartan-like existence. As we approached the front door of the CMATT house, we heard loud music and saw several groups of people in various forms of dress standing in the courtyard inside the perimeter fence. Sweating profusely, still wearing our body armor and carrying our weapons, we found ourselves in the middle of a major house party—a "blowout" by any standard. I could not believe it! We were immediately welcomed by several members of the CMATT staff, glasses of beer were thrust into our hands, and a rather buxom young lady in a black mini skirt and three-inch heels asked me to dance. Imagine my amazement! I had been deployed for nearly four months and had lived the soldier's life in various camps, hovels and "shit holes" from the Iraq–Kuwait border to the western Kuwaiti desert, to the oil fields of southern Iraq. What I was experiencing at that moment had to be one of the most surreal moments of my life. I took the beer, took a raincheck on the dance, and grabbed a handful of hors d'oeuvres. I talked to several guys who were interested in our activities that day, but for the moment they were far more inclined to have a good time. I nearly passed out on a couch and quickly decided to break away from this seemingly impossible dream to get some sleep. Making my way up the marbled staircase, I laughed at the diversity of my lifestyle that had taken me from a dank weapons container and mildewed bunker in the middle of nowhere in 120-degree heat, to an air-conditioned party hall with good-looking babes and all the beer you could drink. "Hell," I thought, "My guys deserved anything they could get for now because tomorrow we're going back to work." Still dressed in my sweat-stained uniform, I quickly fell asleep to the loud reverb sound of "good ole rock and roll" and the surreal thoughts of the activities below.

The party was one of the many triumphs of the dynamic duo of McDougal and Winge. Uday's former house was a "pearl" in a sea of maintenance nightmares that Kellogg Brown & Root contract maintenance personnel labored over every day. In addition to the repairs our guys had managed to make and sustain, they had rummaged through bombed-out quarters and storage sites and found various pieces of art, weapons, silverware, and clothing. But, most importantly, they stumbled upon Uday's liquor cabinet among the rubble of an adjoining house that had been targeted by an air strike. They had also located various shops in Baghdad that provided everything from pastries to party favors, to various repair parts for every gadget in the house and the all-important chlorine that kept the pool in top condition. The residents of the CMATT house kicked in some money from time to time, but a lot of it came out of McDougal's and Winge's pockets. They amazed everyone with their ability to maintain the house, support the staff, and, when required, provide personal security for our senior leaders.

On 22 June, Bob Sommers and I hopped on a C-130 for a two-day excursion to Baṣrah to conduct a site survey of our proposed southern Iraq recruiting station. We met with British Army representatives led by Artificer Sergeant Major Dutton, a Royal Engineer. We were joined by a four-man American Forward Engineer Support Team that had already conducted a preliminary assessment of the proposed recruiting site. It met our fundamental needs despite the lack of standoff relative to public-accessible areas. The single most important site characteristic for force protection from truck bombs and the like is standoff, the distance from where a bomb can be detonated to the facilities the bomb is intended to destroy. The site was located well within the city in a heavily populated area, very close to a maritime employment office and the Iraqi River Front Patrol Headquarters. The traffic in and out of those buildings was almost continuous and long lines of people applying for jobs were not unusual. We figured, however, that if we did not occupy the buildings closest to the entrance gate, we could mitigate the risk to an acceptable level. The presence of a wall that surrounded the facilities was also helpful. I continuously called upon the lessons I had learned during my tour in the Joint Security Directorate at

Central Command. I carried a terrorist bomb-threat standoff card that provided threat descriptions, maximum explosive capacities, lethal air-blast ranges, and minimum building-evacuation distances. The minimum building-evacuation distance subject to a car or van stuffed with 1–4,000 pounds of explosives was upwards of 120 meters. I was always sobered by the data the card provided. The protection of the U.S. and Coalition military personnel, contractors, Iraqi recruits, and the civilian Iraqi personnel that would run these sites, not to mention our training site at Kirkush Barracks, was a major concern of mine. We always sought ways to reinforce our sites with additional force-protection and security measures. Bob and I stayed one night in Baṣrah and worked with the engineers well into the evening laying out our concept of operations for the site and what facility would house the various activities associated with the recruiting process. I told them I was confident they would be given the go-ahead order to begin the renovations; final instructions and approval came from General Eaton on 26 June.

Safely ensconced in Uday's former house, we endeavored now to develop a concept briefing to gain final approval for contracting the development of our surveyed recruiting stations and Kirkush Barracks. We were a desperate group of men. The magnitude of the effort required a professional team of business, contracting, finance, and engineering experts. The facilities were now just a small part of our concerns. A senior officer should never show he is stressed or worried, but my "never let them see you sweat" attitude was getting a little tough to maintain. We needed a decision regarding which organization would provide the civilian trainers, but we did not have a clue as to how we could accommodate them once they arrived in Iraq. The timeline for completing enough of Kirkush Barracks to house our recruits, the staff, and the trainers weighed heavily on everyone's mind. We needed transportation, a food contract, MWR (morale, welfare, and recreation) equipment, furniture, kitchen equipment, and a facilities and vehicle maintenance capability, and we still needed weapons. I was not the only one beginning to sweat. The seeming lack of concern for the NIA project by the CPA, even as it proclaimed that security was its number one priority, was disheartening. After our extensive reconnaissance of former Iraqi military facilities, we were perhaps more cognizant than most by just how broken Iraq was, and Mr. Bremer and his staff were literally up to their ears in the myriad of challenges they faced every day. The CJTF-7 staff could only do so much for us. Regardless of the good intentions of some of its senior leaders, the staff we dealt with daily viewed us as a sideshow looking for assets they desperately needed themselves. Everyone thought they were painfully understaffed. The joint manning document for the CMATT could not be filled by the services fast enough. The few people that began to arrive were almost immediately overwhelmed with administrative tasks and personnel issues; only a few were operators or planners. General Eaton did everything humanly possible to address our manpower concerns. His personal battles to address the needs of his vital organization were heroic.

He even relinquished his aide-de-camp to our operations shop and told me, without emotion, "You need him more than I do, Roland," and calmly walked away. I did not argue. Captain Geoffrey Fuller was a first-rate infantry officer, a Virginia Military Institute graduate, and a 10th Mountain Division Somalia veteran. Paul Eaton was magnificent during this desperate period as we battled against an unforgiving timeline to have a battalion in training by mid-August, a timeframe he adjusted from 31 July under great duress from several senior leaders in CPA Headquarters. We needed some help bad!

Relief came in the form of a team of operations and logistics officers from the 3rd Infantry Division led by Major Rick Monahan, an infantry battalion operations officer (S-3), and Major James Moore, an S-3 of a forward support battalion. These officers had been patiently waiting in staging areas to redeploy to their home base at Fort Stewart, Georgia, when they were "handpicked" by their chain of command to support the CMATT mission. They had participated in the initial battles in Iraq and had led the charge into Baghdad. They had been deployed to Kuwait long before the invasion in March and were not particularly happy to be taken from their troops to work for a renegade staff fighting yet another tough struggle; the sentiment was perfectly understandable. All of us knew how we would have felt if we were snatched from our units while preparing for a move. Who would want to be assigned to a nebulous, ad hoc, understaffed crew of desperate soldiers and marines with more questions than answers? After briefing them and focusing their efforts to a multitude of different projects in accordance with their military specialties and experience, I was impressed with how they threw themselves into the effort. It was characteristic of the way they had destroyed their Iraqi opponents in combat. We were manned to a point now that, as the operations officer of this august organization, I could delegate taskings, supervise the staff, focus my efforts, and coordinate with the developing Iraqi ministries, the CPA, and CJTF-7 staff.

The arrival of the C-5 (Plans) designee, Colonel Al Weh, a man often described by those who knew him as the "Meanest Marine in the Corps," enabled me to focus strictly on current operations while he took over responsibility for future developments and plans to support them. He was assisted by several Spanish officers including a Marine lieutenant colonel. At the not so tender age of 60, Al had fought to get recalled from retirement for Operation *Iraqi Freedom* and, despite his reputation, we got along great together. A Silver Star recipient from the Vietnam War, he was as "hard bitten" as any officer I ever knew, but we quickly acknowledged we were engaged in a hard fight that required cooperation and teamwork. Al would become the CMATT chief of staff after my departure in August and make a huge, positive difference for General Eaton and the entire staff.

The announcement on 26 June that Vinnell Corporation had won the contract to provide the training team and support staff for Kirkush Barracks was greeted with mixed emotions. As pleased as we were the contract had been awarded, we were nowhere close to being able to receive them. The contract was a one-year, 48-million-dollar deal scheduled to begin on 1 July and run through 30 June 2004.[2] Vinnell employed the services of several contractors to fulfill its responsibilities including Military Professional Resources Inc, Science Applications International Corporation, and Worldwide Language Resources Inc. Vinnell had a great reputation for training several foreign militaries, most notably the Saudis. It had been in Saudi Arabia since 1975, where it provided training and technical support to the Saudi Arabian National Guard. By 2003, it employed more than 1,300 employees under a five-year, 800-million-dollar contract to train Saudi air and land forces. Several friends of mine had served with Vinnell over the years and had enjoyed their association with the company. We certainly welcomed the announcement, but it further accentuated the need to make things happen. We fully realized we were far behind getting everything done in accordance with the timeline. The stress factor continued to build. It would not be long before a hundred trainers, a professional group of mostly retired officers and noncommissioned officers, would be on our doorstep. Questions regarding where they would be billeted and how we would transport them from Kuwait to Baghdad remained unanswered. The requirement to have the first battalion on the ground at Kirkush Barracks by mid-August had always been "a bridge too far" in my mind and, as we continued to engage and coordinate, it appeared even more so. I pushed our senior leadership to move the timeline to the right by a month. It would have made a huge difference for us. It was not to happen.

The efforts of the fledgling Iraqi ministries that operated in the palace were critical to developing the infrastructure we needed for the NIA. We made our presence felt as we engaged the Iraqis to gain their support, interest, and anything they felt they could contribute to our efforts. On 26 June, we coordinated a meeting of Iraqi representatives and their American mentors from the Ministries of Finance, Transportation and Communications, Housing and Construction, Industry and Minerals, Justice, Foreign Affairs, and Health during which our team briefed an overview of our plan for standing up the NIA and outlined the tasks they could be called upon to support. They listened politely, asked a few questions about our activities to date, and expressed their support. We never doubted the importance of these briefings and similar efforts to make the Iraqis and their American counterparts understand what we were doing and to "buy in" in whatever way they could. The NIA was Iraq's future defense force and General Eaton was determined to gain and maintain support wherever we could find it. The only formula for success was good staff work and persistence. Everyone was groping to succeed in whatever project they were engaged. We were not alone, but in a headquarters where security was the Coalition's top priority, it seemed odd we were not better resourced and so many people were uninformed about our efforts to develop an Iraqi Army.

The United States Army was as desperate to carry out its new responsibilities as an occupation force as we were to build an Iraqi Army. Our military leaders had never doubted the success of their maneuver campaign, but Iraq's postwar requirements were badly underestimated. Over thirty years of Saddam's tyrannical rule, coupled with the devastating losses of the war with Iran, the *Desert Storm* debacle, and 12 years of sanctions had left Iraqi society "flat on its back." Baghdad struggled with an electrical grid incapable of meeting the needs of the city. Nearly four years after the invasion, Baghdad would still be hard pressed to have more than six hours of power on any given day. Its sewers were inadequate and trash removal was a huge problem. Name any commodity (except guns and ammunition) that Americans take for granted and it was desperately short of supply. The 1st Armored Division, as the principal occupying force in Baghdad, struggled magnificently to deal with the multitude of challenges it faced. Our soldiers had their hands full as the reality of unemployed Iraqi men, vitriolic sermons in the mosques, and a growing resentment of our presence complicated their lives and the success of their mission in the aftermath of the triumphant capture of Baghdad. No one expected an insurgency, so the Army was not poised to fight one. Our military leaders had to build relationships with Iraqi leaders at all levels, develop a sense of confidence and trust, and gain an appreciation for the culture. It would take time and effort.

Our situation in the palace was no different. There had been little thought given to reestablishing the Iraqi Army, a vital piece of what was officially termed the Disarmament, Demobilization and Reintegration program. The officers assigned to CMATT assumed there had been little thought given to the need for a new Iraqi defense force given the "shoestring" manner in which the project had been initiated in Kuwait. Whatever plans existed to employ the former Iraqi Army to rebuild Iraq's infrastructure after the fall of the regime had been cast aside. Iraq was a time bomb without the gainful employment the Army represented for many disenchanted young men with military skills readily available to former regime elements and sectarian militias. Just as American division commanders struggled for trust, confidence, and reliable Iraqi relationships in the field, General Eaton and the CMATT staff worked the entire palace and the Iraqi ministries for all the support they could possibly muster to build the foundation of the nation's new Army. The Iraqi military's barracks, equipment, training areas, recruiting stations, administration, transportation, and its entire infrastructure, would ultimately fall on the backs of the Iraqi ministries and, we hoped, a democratically elected Iraqi government.

The immensity of our task was overpowering. Gone were the soldierly reconnaissance struggles of finding recruiting and training sites. In retrospect, those hot, sweaty, and physically exhausting days spent flying over the bulk of the Iraqi countryside and in the field dodging fire from looters, thugs, and God knows who else, had been fun, a continuation of my adventures in Umm Qasr, the western Kuwaiti Desert, and the Rumaylah Oil Field in March and April. Our efforts now were squarely on the difficult staff work any self-respecting combat officer seeks to avoid in favor of pursuing traditional duties with soldiers in the field. Engineers and contractors and their related projects dominated our time and focus. You can never have enough engineers in a postconflict scenario and the requirement to renovate, build, and maintain the infrastructure of the NIA was an immense engineering and logistical challenge.

The renovation of Kirkush Barracks began the last week of June and the work on the recruiting stations began on 1 July. We were besieged by several scenarios that always seemed to make our forward progress a "two steps forward, one step back" affair. Late on the evening of 29 June, we were advised an all-encompassing contract we had negotiated with Iraqi Airlines had failed. The airline's representatives informed us it was impossible for them to meet our requirements despite the Ministry of Transportation's assurances to the contrary. Our attempt to rejuvenate this industry's infrastructure and cashflow backfired on us in a major way. It was indicative of how little the Iraqis could produce at this point in time. I felt terrible and any warm feelings I had developed for our ability to feed and transport NIA recruits were gone. I dropped this "500-pound bomb" on General Eaton the next morning.

"Bottom-line," I said to him matter of factly, "the total logistics package for support to Kirkush Barracks is in the toilet."

In his usual calm manner, General Eaton sat, however red faced, as he thought through this setback. Clearly, CJTF-7 now had to support the CMATT's logistical requirements, something it was loathe to do. The developing insurgency and the affairs of a field army conducting an occupation of a conquered, but still hostile, country was its obvious focus. The CMATT was at best a sideshow for which CJTF-7 had little time and resources to devote.

With Colonel Greer over Kirkush Barracks, Iraq, June 2003.

After clearing his throat, the general said, "Roland, advise and coordinate with the CJTF-7 chief of staff. Ensure Colonel Brown [the CJTF-7 deputy chief of staff] knows he'll see a lot of CMATT taskings in the near term as we sort this thing out. I'll advise General Sanchez and Mr. Slocombe."

No general, but particularly a decent man like Paul Eaton, deserved the situation we were in. He thanked us as always for our briefing and hard work and walked out of his office.

CHAPTER 14

Making the Most of Scant Resources

The Line between disorder and order lies in logistics.

—Sun Tzu

I greeted the first day of July with the dread of a man on the edge of failure, but the workload left little time to feel sorry for myself or anyone else. Greer and I were machines at this point, going from one mission to the next with a fixed determination to make things happen. The hours got longer, but the news was not all bad. Work on the renovation of the Baghdad recruiting station began that day and Lieutenant Colonel Holt, the Combined Joint Task Force-7 (CJTF-7) engineer assigned to the Coalition Military Assistance Training Team (CMATT) project, provided encouraging reports about our progress at Kirkush Barracks. I informed Colonel Brown of the failed Iraqi Airlines contract and told him that, until we could work something out, we had no choice but to take our needs to CJTF-7.

"Dave," I said, "the needs of the CMATT and the New Iraqi Army are the U.S. Army's burden until we can work out another logistics plan."

Dave Brown was a fair and honest soldier and a good deputy chief of staff. Powerful and knowledgeable, I admired this mostly serious, but humorous, infantry officer who always seemed to take every crisis in stride. This time, however, Dave's smile quickly turned into a grim frown.

"Roland, you better prep a brief for General Sanchez and fast. He ain't gonna like this shit!"

We were already on tap to brief Mr. Slocombe that afternoon on our synchronization or "sync" matrix for the renovation of our facilities, the purchase of furniture and military equipment, and the reception and onward movement of the Vinnell contract trainers to Kirkush Barracks. We began to prepare a similar briefing for General Sanchez that included our logistics requirements in the wake of the Iraqi Airlines default. It was not until well into the following evening that we sat down with Generals Sanchez and Wojdkowski and the CJTF-7 staff at Camp Victory. This painful experience, a working session during which every point on our carefully crafted PowerPoint slides was questioned and discussed, ended at 10:30 pm. It was clear to me a number of guys in responsible positions had not taken any interest in the New Iraqi Army (NIA) project, or had not been adequately informed of its development, and I was irritated by the discourse that went so far as to question why Kirkush Barracks had been chosen as the training base in the first place. Surely, I thought, they knew the infrastructure to support the program was limited and the long line of communication (some one hundred kilometers) to Kirkush Barracks could not be avoided. General Sanchez was not unlike the rest of us. He carried a huge burden of responsibility, lacked the resources to meet those responsibilities adequately, worked long hours, and looked tired and hassled. He was a stickler for detail, and he grilled us as well as any general I had ever encountered. I admired his interest and focus and sensed that, despite the difficulty the project appeared to present, he would support it to the maximum extent he could. Everyone understood our Department of Defense-mandated program required assistance.

We walked away from CJTF-7 Headquarters feeling numb, tired, and satisfied we had made progress. CJTF-7 would meet its responsibility to support the CMATT and the NIA project. We, of course, were advised to do everything we could to ease the burden as much as possible. It was as much a grind for General Sanchez and the CJTF-7 staff as it was for us. Our combined sensing that evening was the project had a decent chance for success albeit with great pain along the way. We needed leadership, money, resources, logistics of all kinds, weapons, transportation, and more engineers; most of all, we needed time!

The arrival of Colonel Tony Bell, USA, the chief contracting officer for the Coalition Provisional Authority (CPA), was a huge boost to our efforts during these tough days in July. Tony was an artilleryman whose "can do" attitude and sense of humor were encouraging. My intent was to keep him happy. When Tony moved into our quarters, I told Sean McDougal to ensure he had all the beer he could drink. Tony was a serious guy who knew his business. He was familiar with the NIA program, having written the Vinnell contract; we sensed he was a supporter. As encouraged as we were by Tony's arrival, however, we were just as troubled by the continued paucity of personnel on the CMATT staff. We were scheduled to lose our hard-working 3rd Infantry Division guys in a few days and Lieutenant Colonels Greer and Sommers were scheduled to leave in two weeks. Bob Sommers had worked tirelessly to piece together the NIA recruiting program. He had teamed up with a former Ranger Course student of mine, Lieutenant Colonel Chad Buehring, USA, a special forces officer assigned to public affairs duties on the CPA staff. They had developed several advertising products to get the word out to the Iraqi public about the NIA; their efforts and briefings to Mr. Slocombe and the Ministry of Defense (MOD) staff were impressive. Mr. Slocombe was very satisfied with their work and had enthusiastically approved the recruiting program and the recruiting posters.

Neither Mike Greer nor Bob Sommers could be replaced; between the imminent departures of these two great marines and the 3rd Infantry Division planning team,

I sensed a queasy feeling in my gut even as Iraqi contractors worked diligently at the recruiting sites and Kirkush Barracks under the supervision of our engineer officers. Progress was evident. Underlying this anxiety for the program were my own selfish thoughts of what would happen to me. The orders that had gotten me to Kuwait in March were running out of time. I had no follow-on orders from Central Command, the CMATT, or CJTF-7. The overall personnel situation in the CMATT was so bad General Eaton directed me to employ his personal and special staff in Operations (C-3). As we prepared to transition the ones we thought would work out with their new duties, I reluctantly assumed I would see this effort through until October, at which time I would be required to return to Central Command Headquarters. Colonel Brown, in his usual joking manner, told me to be patient and laughingly said, "Roland, you'll be eating kielbasa with the Poles before you know it." It was a nice thought, but I had promised Paul Eaton the first Iraqi battalion and functioning facilities and systems before I did anything else. The August timeline to begin training the first NIA battalion was a huge "blip" on our collective screens. Getting there seemed impossible.

Our resource problems aside, all of us were impressed by the ability of the U.S. Army to provide for its soldiers on special occasions and holidays. As busy as the Army may have been, the Fourth of July was celebrated in a big way at CPA Headquarters. The renovation of the palace outdoor swimming pool demonstrated the CPA's efforts to improve the building and grounds. Amid the shorts and swimsuit crowd, as off-duty soldiers performed high dives into the beautifully clear blue water, was every kind of food one could imagine for such an occasion. Lobster tail, steak, hamburgers, shrimp, chicken, and all the usual salads, beans, and other accompanying dishes were laid out on the grassy garden area. Even the beleaguered CMATT staff took advantage of it. You would have thought we were attending a church picnic. We sat on the grass, ate our fill, and entertained ourselves watching State Department and contractor babes walk around in bikinis. Life would have been good if it was not for the desperate logistical situation we faced. We still needed a logistics contractor.

Looking at Mike Greer, I laughed and said, "Mike, how the hell are we going to get chow like this to our soldiers, Iraqi recruits, and contractors at Kirkush Barracks in a couple of weeks without CJTF-7 assets? How the hell are we going to move three meals a day, every day over 100 kilometers? We don't even have a mess hall yet!"

Mike shook his head. "Enjoy your meal, Colonel, we've got a lot of work to do."

The arrival of Colonel Tom O'Donnell, USA, to the CMATT was another encouraging development. Our personnel (C-1) section had told us help was on the way. Tom was assigned as the CMATT chief of staff. I was happy to relinquish those duties to him. General Eaton deserved a full-time chief of staff and with Colonel Al Weh now comfortably filling the C-5 (Plans) position, I placed all my efforts on current operations. The 3rd Infantry Division team left the next day even as the vanguard of the Vinnell contract trainers began to arrive. General Eaton approved our award recommendations for the members of the division team and we were very pleased when their efforts were officially recognized. He had us gather in one of the palace ballrooms that was decorated with murals of Iraqi missiles and other examples of lost Iraqi military might. After his sincere words of appreciation, he personally decorated each of them with the Joint Service Achievement Medal. It was a medal they could wear with a deep sense of pride. We would miss all of them.

Colonel O'Donnell had been at Fort Monroe as an executive assistant to a general when he volunteered for duty in Iraq. He sought the assignment to serve in combat before he ended his career. A West Point graduate, Tom was a fine officer, a gentleman who, like everyone else, had stepped into a literal "firestorm." He was utterly amazed by what we had accomplished under the circumstances and somewhat aghast at the magnitude of our mission. When he asked me what the best thing was he could do in the near term, I replied without hesitation, "Get us people, any people, and as fast as you can make it happen." I told him he was badly needed to facilitate coordination and staff relations with CJTF-7, and I encouraged him to get to know Dave Brown and other key players on the CJTF-7 staff as soon as possible. Tom O'Donnell was a good man and a good friend. He chose to leave the CMATT several months later to accept a field command stood up for the specific mission of protecting Iraq's vital oil pipelines, but not before he had substantially contributed to vastly improving the strength and overall effectiveness of the CMATT staff. The feisty and energetic Colonel Al Weh, USMC, replaced him.

Another welcome addition to the command in July was our deputy commander, Brigadier General Jonathan Riley of the British Army. He was the perfect complement to General Eaton and they got along famously. General Riley was commissioned in 1974 and had seen action and commanded troops on operations at every level during six tours of duty in Northern Ireland and five tours in the Balkans. Knowledgeable and competent, General Riley was a highly decorated combat veteran who had received the Distinguished Service Order for bravery and distinguished conduct in the Balkans. He never allowed the seriousness of our situation to interfere with a good opportunity to laugh. We got along very well together, and I knew I could count on his support. Generals more than occasionally fail to understand their very presence can be a painful burden for their subordinates. Our generals understood when to show up and when to leave, and they were quick to strip down to their t-shirts, lend a hand, and do whatever was required of them when the situation dictated. General Riley would stop by the operations shop to simply ask, "What do you need me to do?" It was no wonder he would receive a second star when he returned to England and command the British-led Multinational Division (South-East) on his second tour in Iraq.

Along with the arrival of key senior leaders and staff replacements were the Vinnell contractors. The "train" was moving fast and the pressure on General Eaton to get "boots on the ground" at Kirkush Barracks intensified. The senior commanders had acknowledged that getting a battalion of recruits there before August could not be done, but someone thought it was possible to recruit and train a smaller element consisting of former Iraqi Army junior officers who, once reoriented, would serve as a cadre for the first recruit battalion. We asked CJTF-7 to have the 1st Armored Division, the 4th Infantry Division, and the British force headquartered in Baṣrah in southern Iraq, to each find no less than twenty men to begin training at Kirkush Barracks by the third week of July. This was not anything the divisions wanted to do; their efforts produced mixed results. Clearly, the divisions were far too busy to support this requirement in the spirit it was intended. The division staffs were stretched to the limit and the effort to recruit a competent, trainable cadre failed miserably as barely enough men were recruited to make the project worthwhile and hardly any effort was made to train and orient those who were.

In the meantime, the CMATT staff was totally consumed by recruiting and related information operations, finding and coordinating equipment for the NIA, and the all-important effort to find a credible contractor to support logistical requirements at Kirkush Barracks. The Iraqi Ministry of Industry and Minerals was given the contract to produce barracks and office furniture. The ministry's leadership also assured us they could produce the individual equipment items needed to outfit a combat soldier in the Iraqi Army. The critical weapons issue was solved by Mr. Slocombe and the MOD staff led by the highly capable Colonel Gardner. Nearly 98,000 AK-47 rifles and a smaller number of light machine guns were miraculously coordinated for transfer from neighboring Jordan's excess stocks. The initial allocation to Kirkush Barracks was 1,000 rifles and enough machine guns to train and outfit the first battalion. The weapons we had stockpiled prior to this announcement had been captured by our divisions and provided to the CMATT at the direction of CJTF-7. There were less than one hundred rifles. The readiness of these weapons was fair at best and basic items of issue such as cleaning kits and sight-adjustment tools were non-existent. After the Vinnell contractors advised me of the sorry state of these weapons, I directed our own Lieutenant McDougal to personally assess the weapons and make whatever repairs he could. By mixing and cannibalizing parts and whatever else his mechanical genius allowed him to do, he was able to produce enough functional rifles to outfit two platoons of infantry. This was no way to outfit an army. We welcomed the arms deal with great joy, and I personally congratulated Greg Gardner for his efforts. Greg and I had clashed on occasion, but there was no denying his efficiency, hard work, and dedication to our mission.

The single biggest challenge we faced after the general logistics challenge was transportation. The availability of both rotary and fixed-wing aircraft in Iraq was problematic to say the least. Ground transport was growing increasingly difficult to coordinate as the developing CPA bureaucratic processes took root and the need for security increased. We often turned to the Kellogg Brown & Root (KB&R)

transportation coordinator with whom we maintained a good relationship. The contractor crowd enjoyed the CMATT parties at Uday's former digs and all we asked for in return was a little cooperation. The bus was the mass transportation system of choice and, until other contractual arrangements could be made, we relied heavily on our contacts at KB&R. The first wave of Vinnell contract trainers, having bunked in a ballroom in the CPA palace for several days, were ready to take on Kirkush Barracks and all its inadequacies to prepare to receive the first battalion of the NIA. They too would move by bus. Over the course of the next month, the CMATT operations officers would become the premier convoy coordination experts in Iraq.

On 14 July, Lieutenant General (Retired) George A. Crocker, USA, the senior Vinnell trainer, and the bulk of the Vinnell team boarded several buses we had staged at the former Iraqi parade ground known for its gigantic crossed Arabian swords. The swords were reputedly held by the equally gigantic hands of Saddam Hussein and were testimony to Iraq's "victory" over Iran in the bloody and disastrous war that ended in 1988. It was a good place to marshal people and equipment. Even a blind man could find this location unless, of course, you were an Iraqi driver on your own time schedule and driving a bus virtually running on empty. Given the importance we placed on our convoy movements to Kirkush Barracks, I personally supervised the staging and loading of bus convoys and made every effort to maintain communications with a designated officer-in-charge from start to finish. I personally briefed in detail the officers and noncommissioned officers in charge of supervising these movements. Hours of planning, coordination, and briefings had gone into this movement. General Crocker had a reputation for being a meticulous planner and stickler for detail. He had been the United States Army South commander in Panama during the last several months of my battalion command tour in 1993 and I wanted to show him and the other contractors that we had our act together.

Operations that start right normally end that way. This operation, however, had a comical start at best and neither General Crocker nor I found it particularly funny. The buses arrived late with nearly empty fuel tanks. Their maintenance and overall readiness were questionable. A broken bus was either repaired on site or we did without it. We noted the need to coordinate maintenance teams on station in the future for all contracted bus convoys. Long before we missed our departure time, every man on my team in the marshalling area was stripped to the waist, directing traffic, chasing people, restaging buses, securing more water as the mid-morning summer heat kicked in, or taking buses to any fuel point we could find. Just as things were beginning to look good, a young Vinnell subcontractor advised me 40 linguists were standing by to be picked up at one of the hotels downtown. There was no choice but to dispatch a bus with this young man to get them.

Before he left, I turned to him and asked, "Son, have you ever been in the service?"

"No, sir", he said, standing by the door of the bus with a broad, silly smile on his pink, pasty face.

"Okay, this is what I want you do. You take this bus down to the hotel, tell the driver to stay on board, go into the lobby, get your translators and stand them in formation by the bus where you can properly account for them and their gear before they load. Then individually load each man on the bus. I don't want anyone on this bus except your authorized translators. Do you understand?"

He acknowledged and with that same silly smile directed the driver to move out. Nearly an hour later, as General Crocker sat slowly but surely losing his patience, the bus finally returned. Captain Fuller, General Eaton's aide turned assistant operations officer, and I greeted the young man who did not appear very happy. I could not believe what he told me.

"Are we ready to go?" I asked.

"Not exactly, sir."

"What's wrong?"

"Well, sir, it's like this. I contracted 40 interpreters. Only 32 showed up but several guys not on my list jumped on the bus and now they won't get off."

I was beside myself. "Did you do what I told you to do?"

"Well, not exactly, sir. I thought we could just get on and go and make up for the lost time."

I was tired, hot, and angry. I felt surrounded by ignorance, apathy, and one very angry three-star general complaining about our lack of security and lost time. I did the only thing I thought the situation demanded of me.

"General, I'll take care of this. Young man, do you know who the unauthorized guys on the bus are?"

"Yes, sir," he said as he pointed out five guys sitting quietly in two rows of seats.

"Okay, you speak Arabic. You have two minutes to talk to those guys and have them dismount. If they fail to get off, I'll take over. Got it?"

"Sir, I didn't know you could speak Arabic."

"I don't, son, let's just hope they listen to you."

Standing outside with Captain Fuller and General Crocker, I contemplated my next move. There was no way those guys were getting off the bus. They were lean, hungry-looking, and desperate for work. They had obviously talked to the interpreters and figured they could get work at Kirkush Barracks. It was not long before my pasty-faced young contractor informed me our wayward Iraqi hitchhikers were not going to get off the bus. With nothing to lose and faced with yet another frustrating failure to make things happen, I boarded the bus, calmly made my way down the aisle to a position behind the row of our "hitchhikers," drew my unloaded 9-mm pistol, and pulled back the slide as if to chamber a round in full view for all to see. I then placed the weapon by the forehead of the guy on the end of the row and, in my best command voice, said, "Get the fuck off this bus now, or I'll blow your fucking head off!"

I have often taught young officers and sergeants there are times and places when desperate measures must be applied to accomplish a mission and while I would not have shot the poor fellow, he did not know that. I suppose, in retrospect, a less-dramatic technique could have been used in this case, but there was no denying the result. They likely did not understand one word I said but they certainly understood the tone and my "loaded pistol." Without hesitation, all five of our "hitchhikers" got up and ran down the aisle toward the door where Captain Fuller met them and lined them up in a single rank. Then, with everyone watching, I looked at Fuller and said, "Captain Fuller, you will load these men in your pickup truck and take them to the 14 July Bridge, where they will dismount and be free to return to wherever they came from. Do you understand?"

With a loud, "Yes, sir," Fuller saluted and took charge of our "hitchhikers," gave them a facing movement, marched them off in cadence, loaded them on his truck, and drove off. It was comical to watch them march off swinging their arms in the finest traditions of Her Majesty's Royal Guards. I wanted to laugh, but the ever-present General Crocker brought me quickly back to reality.

"General Crocker, sir, I think it's time you depart."

The general stared at me briefly, took note of my drawn pistol, turned, and moved to the lead bus. I was never happier to see a convoy move out. To this day I still shudder when I think of what my old boss thought of my actions that day. Several months later, however, several of the trainers at Kirkush Barracks told me that the "Old Man" frequently told the story and mentioned my name with a smile.

Episodes like these are as frustrating as they are humorous, albeit well after the incidents and normally over a beer. We were all tired, but I was happy for my teammates when I was told upon return to our headquarters that Mike Greer's and Bob Sommers's verbal orders to return to Central Command Headquarters were confirmed. General Eaton asked me to speak on his behalf at a hail and farewell party we held in their honor. Their achievements since May were unbelievable and yet relatively unknown and unappreciated by whoever had ordered them into the utter chaos that had characterized their existence for the past three months. Mike was primarily responsible for getting the logistics contract so critical to meeting our timeline to get Kirkush Barracks operational without further tasking the assets of a reluctant and stressed U.S. Army. "P" Greer never let me down. As men lined up in large numbers to enlist in the New Iraqi Army, I knew it was in large measure due to the efforts of Bob Sommers and Chad Buehring. Sadly, I would learn later that fall that Chad had been killed in action during a firefight and rocket attack on Baghdad's Al-Rashid Hotel on 26 October 2003. Chad was married and the father of two sons. He left a legacy of gallant combat service that included duty in Bosnia and Somalia with U.S. Special Forces. I am proud to have served with such an outstanding soldier.

CHAPTER 15

Recruiting, Organizing, and Training the New Iraqi Army

Nothing is Easy in the Middle East.

—UNKNOWN

The emergency repairs that kept Uday's former house functional were a never-ending project. Water and electrical outages were common occurrences. You learned to take it all in stride. I was thankful for the pool and I swam every night whether we had lights or not. My steady regimen of calisthenics and swimming was a huge relief from the stress and frustration of the day. These workouts were often conducted at midnight or after; I relied on the chlorinated pool to wash off the day's sweat and stink if the water in the house was not running. The pool time afforded me the opportunity to think and I used it to mentally prepare for the next day. The power of physical training goes beyond attaining physical strength and endurance. It undoubtedly sustained my general health and mental welfare throughout the grueling Coalition Military Assistance Training Team (CMATT) experience. The requirement of moving the Iraqi recruits to Kirkush Barracks in the weeks to come would prove to be the most challenging task of all.

By the third week of July, my operators were totally engaged with planning bus convoys to move Iraqi Army recruits. We had to move nearly 1,000 men to Kirkush Barracks from three major recruiting sites over the entire length of Iraq, the vast bulk of which was "Indian country," Army parlance for hostile territory. We were conscious of our security requirements, and we met frequently with the Combined Joint Task Force-7 (CJTF-7) staff and liaison officers to coordinate convoy escort responsibilities. The concept of operations called for the divisions to "hand off" responsibility for security as the convoy moved across their boundaries at specified coordination points. The details of these movements—to include coordination points, routes, and radio frequencies—were provided in writing and briefed to the liaison officers. Our initial effort had reeked of failure. We struggled on 19 July to move our 60 cadre recruits to Kirkush Barracks. Neither the 4th Infantry Division nor the 1st Armored Division escorts could get the security teams linked up with our convoys. The convoys from Mosul and Baṣrah were overdue and our recruits endured long hours moving or waiting, often without food. These men had been recruited by the divisions which clearly had not, or could not, devote the time, assets, or effort to find and recruit first-rate men for the cadre. The poor quality of the men, coupled with the poor movement and immature logistics infrastructure at Kirkush Barracks, undoubtedly contributed to them quitting en masse on 23 July. These men were privileged junior officers of Saddam's era and none of them had any stomach for the new Army we were developing. There was general agreement in the CMATT that it was just as well they had quit, but privately I thought about what the future held for the project. The incident certainly did not bode well for our overall success. The staff immediately planned and organized another convoy to bring the "quitters" to Baghdad where they were free to go home with the equivalent of some twenty U.S. dollars in their pockets.

The cadre recruit episode was a true indication of where we were in our preparation and general readiness. It did no good to think about the additional month we needed to pull this operation off professionally and efficiently. General Eaton was furious about the shortfall in the logistics infrastructure. The contractor had had difficulty delivering food and fuel and back hauling trash. Laudes Inc was the contractor we had chosen to do the job. The company was run by a competent, highly qualified American entrepreneur named Larry Underwood. He had competed, won the bid, and was optimistic he could accomplish the broad array of tasks expected of his company. The security and logistics situation in Iraq in the summer of 2003, however, made any effort to purchase and transport resources a major struggle. Nothing is easy in the Middle East and the increasingly complex situation in Iraq only compounded the usual difficulty of getting anything done. Like us, Laudes needed time it could not have. It was "full speed ahead" and, in retrospect, I do not believe any company could have delivered the goods with so short a timeline. General Eaton had to live with General Crocker who was not only dissatisfied with the food and logistics shortfalls in general, but with the living conditions and base security arrangements as well. Our hard-working engineers and building contractors struggled to get air conditioning and reliable power into the slowly improving, renovated barracks. Massive generators were required that had to be shipped to Iraq. The Vinnell trainers were living hard. Duty at Kirkush Barracks was nothing like the well-established facilities Vinnell enjoyed in Saudi Arabia; there was genuine concern many of the trainers would quit before our first recruits arrived. General Eaton would later comment that, "Soldiers were needed to train the Iraqi Army, not contracted civilians regardless of their competence and stellar prior military backgrounds."

By the end of July, General Eaton resided more at Kirkush Barracks than he did in Baghdad. What little sleep he allowed himself he took on the roof of one of the barracks where it was relatively cool compared to the power-starved offices and rooms. The stifling heat of an average day in July and August was over 120 degrees Fahrenheit. His intent was to handle the job site while General Riley ran the staff at the palace. My job was to deliver the troops.

Recruiting was going remarkably well. Driving to our Baghdad recruiting office, I was impressed by the long lines of potential recruits who patiently waited to get into the recruiting station compound. By the fourth day of the recruiting effort, we had recruited over fifty percent of our goal. It made sense; Iraq was poor and a soldier's salary was something any eligible Iraqi man would consider. Even before the invasion, a poor and demoralized Iraqi Army still gave its troops their only means of livelihood. We would have preferred a stronger sense of duty and patriotism, but we had to be realistic. Not unlike the U.S. military's all-volunteer force in the 1970s, money drove recruiting. It was the difference between our program's success and failure. Mr. Slocombe and General Eaton argued at length with the Coalition Provisional Authority (CPA) for higher wages. The original pay scale was below that offered by some of the militias, developing governmental agencies, and contractors. They emphasized that security was the CPA's highest priority, and the New Iraqi Army (NIA) was a key element of the security and future of Iraq. The pay scale had to be tempting enough to lure healthy young men to enlist. In a tough, competitive environment, they were able to negotiate an upward adjustment to the pay scale and keep the NIA program a viable option for Iraqi men.

Our recruiting stations were run by Science Applications International Corporation (SAIC) contractors who took their jobs seriously. The recruits were vetted to eliminate any former members of the Baath Party, former military officers above the rank of captain, members of the Republican Guard, and known criminals. These restrictions would later be modified or rescinded. The mental and physical standards of our recruits were high given the target end strength of the Army at that time of 40,000 men. The recruits filled out administrative forms and were examined by Iraqi medical teams. The process was slow as everything our recruiters did required translation. Linguists were in high demand, but I was impressed by how many Iraqis could speak English. I was reminded that before the Iran–Iraq War had nearly bankrupted the country, Iraq had a superb public education system. Iraq, I thought, could be great again, if the force we put together could secure and stabilize the nation to a point where matters like education could once again be a national priority. Until that could happen, you did not have to be a genius to see that political, economic, and social normalcy by any standard in Iraq was a long way off. The immediate challenge for us and Iraq was recruiting an army and it looked like it was happening.

The media would show up from time to time at the Baghdad recruiting station. Every soldier regardless of rank on the modern battlefield must be prepared to deal with a microphone thrust in his face. I frequently spoke with American and British reporters. The questions inevitably focused on what we expected to accomplish in terms of numbers of men, units, and training bases. There was particular interest in the program's intent to achieve an ethnically integrated force. At Central Command, General Zinni had emphasized the need to engage with the media to ensure they understood what we were doing. If we were courteous and receptive, we could get a positive message out to the public and the results could be overwhelmingly favorable to our operations. I passed this counsel on to all the officers and the contractors at the recruiting stations and we were generally successful in managing the media in a fair and professional manner.

The Mosul recruiting station was doing well, supported primarily by the Kurdish community further north. Encouraged by this, we opened a satellite office in Erbil to accommodate the Kurds and make joining the NIA more convenient to them. In the southern Iraqi city of Baṣrah, renovation of the recruiting facilities had begun later than in Baghdad or Mosul and conditions were less appealing to both potential recruits and our contractors. Our SAIC contractors understandably complained about the lack of power that prevented them from working a full day. Our engineers and the efforts of SAIC representatives, who purchased generators locally, eventually brought our power problem under reasonable control. Force protection was a greater issue. The Brits were responsible for securing the facilities, but they rarely provided enough manpower to adequately protect them. General Riley discussed the matter with the British division commander in Baṣrah and the guard was reinforced. We were always concerned with the lack of "standoff" we had from the street and other public facilities near the recruiting station. There was only so much we could do. Security challenges and the desires of our contractors were constantly monitored and I addressed the issues with their representatives at the palace every day. The last thing we needed was to be accused of a breach of contract. The possibility of a "walk out" or a temporary shutdown of operations always existed and all of us appreciated how ugly a situation like that could get. Fortunately, the contract leaders decided to stay with us. The security issue was real, but manageable. Regardless of how inadequate our facilities may have been, recruits continued to sign up and though we never got the healthy mix of Shia, Sunni, and Kurd for the fully integrated force our senior leaders desired, numbers of recruits overall were not a problem and very encouraging.

Our collective schedules were merciless with activity. There was much to do, and time remained our greatest enemy. On 27 July, Colonel Al Weh and I went to Camp Victory to participate in a future Iraqi Army basing conference and to present our future-basing concept briefing to Brigadier General Bob Williams, the C-3 (Operations) of CJTF-7. I had a good relationship with General Williams that dated back to 1997 when he commanded a tank brigade in Kuwait. I had met him during one of my many trips to Camp Doha when I was assigned to the United Nations Iraq–Kuwait Observation Mission. He was sincerely interested in our plans for the Iraqi Army and Al provided an excellent briefing that outlined our thoughts on basing, from Mosul in the north, to the former logistics base at Taji in central Iraq, to an-Nuʿmānīyah and Baṣrah in southern Iraq. Al also briefed our plans to develop and station a battalion of naval infantry at the port city of Umm Qasr to provide maritime security for both the port and the waterway.

Plans for the development of an Iraqi Air Force, though sketchy at that point, were also briefed and discussed.

Following the briefing, General Williams invited me into his office to discuss security requirements at Kirkush Barracks as well as the movement of Iraqi Army recruits from the recruiting stations to the training base. He was clearly concerned with the availability of units to get the job done; his concerns were totally understandable. There had already been considerable debate about whether the United States had enough troops in Iraq for the invasion and occupation of Iraq. It was clear to us on the ground that the size of the occupation force in the face of a growing insurgency was desperately inadequate. As the C-3, General Williams was in the business of allocating resources to tasks. When there are not enough resources to satisfy the number and magnitude of the tasks, the C-3 makes recommendations to the commander regarding priority of effort. Some tasks are more important than others; some tasks just have to wait. No military commander will ever say he has enough of anything to get a job done and really mean it. In August 2003, General Sanchez and the CJTF-7 staff was as desperate as we were to get the men and material necessary to successfully meet all of their mission requirements. During the 10 minutes we met privately, I talked about why the NIA program should be allocated the resources and security assets the CMATT had requested. The most significant reason, as I saw it, was the fundamental need for trained manpower to address the occupation duties and security requirements throughout Iraq as originally envisioned in the war plans. The situation demanded soldiers, and lots of them, if borders and towns were to be secured, lawlessness and sectarian violence minimized, and the growing possibility of an insurgency contained. I finished by stating emphatically, "Bob, if we fail to support this program, our Army will be stuck in Iraq indefinitely. The New Iraqi Army is our ticket out of here."

He listened, took a few notes, thanked me for my frank comments, and wished me luck. Before leaving, I asked him to favorably consider supporting the assignment of a Military Police (MP) company to secure Kirkush Barracks and allow our trainers and support personnel to focus on our training mission. I considered General Williams a good friend. Bob's tour of duty in Iraq was nearly over and I was happy to learn he would return to Germany to serve as the G-3 (Operations) for U.S. Army Europe and the Seventh Army, and later command the Armor Center at Fort Knox, Kentucky.

General Eaton had made every conceivable effort to get an MP company allocated to secure Kirkush Barracks. On 31 July, the advance element of a company arrived to establish the unit's command post. The decision to assign this unit could not have been timelier. General Crocker's biggest complaint about the conditions at Kirkush Barracks was its lack of security. The possibility of Vinnell declaring a breach of contract and "walking off the job" was a real one. The Vinnell contract trainers were unarmed and General Crocker's security concerns were justified to a considerable extent. During one of my visits to Kirkush Barracks, I asked General Crocker if he would feel more comfortable if I slipped him a box of rifles and ammunition to be opened if the circumstances dictated. I was perfectly serious and he knew it. He thanked me but, to my surprise, refused the offer.

On 3 August, the last wave of Vinnell contractors arrived in Baghdad and we scrambled to move them. Lieutenant Colonel Duncan Hayward of the Australian Army arrived at about the same time and was immediately assigned as my deputy. An armor officer, he would prove invaluable in the weeks and months ahead. He had a typically great Aussie sense of humor and was totally unflappable. In this regard, he was not unlike Lieutenant Colonels Mark Bornholdt and Ted Acutt who had, in turn, served as the deputy chief of staff during my tour in the Sinai with the Multinational Force and Observers. I told him his sense of humor would be severely tested in the days to come. We were lucky to have him.

The first week of August was one continuous blur as my new group of "desperate men" focused their efforts on moving the Iraqi Army recruits by air and bus from both ends of the country to our remote training base. Our experience with the failed Iraqi cadre effort had taught us a few lessons. Plans inevitably change at execution or "once the first shots are fired," as planners commonly are heard to say, but we worked hard to ensure our plan provided maximum flexibility, redundancy, and liaison. Communications were particularly emphasized as we developed the command-and-control architecture so vital to our success. Our plan included positioning an officer and a noncommissioned officer with every convoy. A small team would coordinate the operation from the CMATT Operations Center, and we positioned a young Marine captain named Glenn Seiffert as a liaison officer in CJTF-7 Headquarters to coordinate and accelerate operational requirements as they were needed. Our sole intent was to get our convoys through to Kirkush Barracks. Any failure on our part would have destroyed our credibility and, more importantly, that of the entire command.

Our buses were provided via a contract with the Iraqi al Dhilial Company that had negotiated with Colonel Tony Bell's contracting office. At my insistence, Tony arranged a meeting for me with the president of the company to coordinate the not-so-obvious things that might ordinarily be taken for granted. In addition to discussing assembly points, start times, and routes, I reviewed the requirement for him to provide well-maintained buses that were air conditioned and fully fueled. I was polite and spoke in a calm, unemotional voice, but my demeanor conveyed my message very emphatically. I constantly reminded our contractors and my officers what they already knew—nothing is easy in the Middle East—and we could ill afford to leave anything to chance. Nothing could be assumed or taken for granted.

The logistics requirements at Kirkush Barracks continued to burden us. The desperate pleas of Lieutenant Colonel Ray Combs (our communications forward coordinator) for medical teams, generators, water, more engineering support, and the timely delivery of food were a daily occurrence. The infrastructure and the communications available to us at the time did not provide clear voice communications. It was a struggle talking to Ray on the phone and I did not realize my efforts to talk to him were a source of jokes and hilarious laughter for my operations officers. As I literally screamed into the phone, the guys would stop working and start cracking up.

"Ray, can you hear me, Ray? Damn it, Ray, have the comms guys check your end. No damn it, I can't hear a damn word you're saying, Ray."

It was not uncommon to be somewhere in the headquarters and hear someone jokingly say in a loud voice, "Can you hear me, Ray?" Even Ray would get an occasional laugh out of it. I never doubted things were bad, but morale was high, at least in the operations shop. In the worst situations, soldiers always find something to grab on to for a good laugh.

Ray's report of our bat-, rat-, and insect-infested barracks was no laughing matter. Our besieged logistics contractor was responsible for pest control and something had to be done. The situation was serious, though it would later be the source of more jokes and laughter. Both General Eaton and I spoke with Mr. Underwood, the owner of Laudes Inc, and reviewed his contractual requirements. He calmly acknowledged them and ensured us everything would be accomplished. I assured Ray help was on the way and, after some hesitation, I said, "And so's Christmas, Ray!" Even Ray laughed as the shop exploded in laughter. Larry Underwood was as desperate as we were. By September, he had the systems, equipment, vehicles, and manpower in place to adequately execute the contract. Many vehicles and items of equipment had to be purchased in Jordan and then line-hauled across western Iraq. Larry reminded me nothing was easy in the Middle East. Like us, he needed another month to put it all together.

Our plan was good enough to survive the first day. Captain Geoff Fuller, General Eaton's former aide, moved to Mosul with the first convoy and, after a late start and a few challenges along the way, proudly entered Kirkush Barracks just before midnight. Geoff had picked up 123 recruits at Mosul, a disappointing figure considering we were expecting twice that number. When his convoy stopped for refueling, 12 recruits simply got up and left. It was hard to calm Geoff down as he voiced his frustration and anger over the incident via radio from Kirkush Barracks. We heard him loud and clear! It was the least of our concerns, however, as the week progressed. The number of "no show" recruits was a problem at every recruiting station. Only 199 recruits, again only half of what we expected, showed up at the Baghdad station. We directed the SAIC recruiters there to prepare a second lift of recruits later in the week and coordinated another convoy.

Our buses arrived a day late in Baṣrah where Major Trey Johnson, USA, took control. Trey, an Airborne Ranger artilleryman with service in the Ranger Regiment, was a "can do" self-starter to whom I had given the toughest mission. After 13 hours on the road, Trey led his convoy and 155 recruits into Kirkush Barracks late on the evening of 4 August. The situation at the satellite recruiting station in Erbil in northern Iraq was tenuous for Marine Sergeant McCaffery who arrived at the recruiting station late on the morning of 5 August. His departure was delayed while the senior leadership of the Kurdish Patriotic Union of Kurdistan, a political party desiring self-determination for the Kurdish people of Iraq, argued over which recruits could go. At one point, it appeared that none of the recruits would be allowed to leave but, late that afternoon, the convoy pulled out and arrived at Kirkush Barracks shortly after 1 am the following day with nearly 200 recruits.

Marine Captain Seiffert returned from his liaison duties at CJTF-7 where he had followed all the action. He was anxious to get into "the fight" and immediately volunteered to lead a team to Mosul and conduct a CH-47 helicopter movement of 25 more recruits we had recruited on 7 August. It was a critical and monumental day for the CMATT. The successful air movement that afternoon was encouraging; however, another convoy led by Captain Fuller with 28 recruits was ambushed by a huge improvised explosive device with the explosive power of a 155-mm artillery round. The incident occurred along our main supply route from Baghdad at 10:40 am. Two vehicles were damaged and one MP was slightly wounded. It was clear to everyone now we were not playing a game. There was a developing insurgency, and we were in it along with our deployed divisions and everyone else in Iraq. General Eaton received this report with anger and frustration. He genuinely liked Geoffrey Fuller and I quickly assured him he was unhurt. Geoff was angry he did not personally get a chance to engage the enemy, but we congratulated him anyway upon his return for having been "blooded" in his first combat with the enemy in Iraq and surviving the engagement.

The 500-plus recruits we delivered to Kirkush Barracks was a poor start from a pure numbers' perspective, but additional recruits were delivered the following week. Our attempt to recruit an integrated battalion of Shia, Sunni, and Kurdish troops was not a total failure. The reports indicated the numbers were not too bad at all. That we had accomplished anything close to the desired ethnic percentages was near miraculous. All of us who had worked to field this first element of the NIA were very proud of the achievement, but there was no time to "smell the roses." August 8 was my last day in the CMATT; I worked feverishly to clean up a multitude of staff actions and prepare various reports and briefings.

The CJTF-7 personnel "gurus" had secured permission from Central Command for my extension in theater and approval of my verbal orders to the Polish-led Multinational Division (Central-South). The Iraqi battalion was training at Kirkush Barracks and General Eaton, true to his word, had recommended approval of my orders. I had my first decent night's sleep in at least a week and the water at the house was working well enough to provide a hot shower that morning. I was thrilled to receive a call from Australian Colonel Colley who stopped by to present an Australian coin to me in recognition of my service in Iraq. Duncan Hayward had obviously put him up to it, but I was honored nonetheless. I closed out the day by dining with General Eaton and Tom O'Donnell, our chief of staff. After paying several courtesy calls on select members of the CJTF-7 staff, I made my way back to the house where "my boys" had arranged a farewell party in my honor including a hilarious roasting. Trey Johnson ensured a few good-looking State Department ladies were present to enhance the atmosphere. We all needed a good laugh and I had hoped to leave with everyone feeling pretty good about things. General Eaton offered a few kind remarks and I told the guys how proud I was of their gallant service and loyalty under the difficult circumstances of the past several months. I reached into my cargo pocket where I kept my "brain book," a small collection of laminated pages, containing information of various facts and figures to assist military planning, that I had carried for the better part of twenty years. The first page was a passage titled "All in the Day's Work" that tells the story of Thomas Atkins, the soldier from whom the name "Tommy" came to describe the average British soldier. Looking about the room, and doing my best to avoid getting emotional, I recited the passage:

> The Great Duke of Wellington stood on the path which runs around the ramparts of Walmer Castle on a sunny day in July 1843. Near him, standing at attention, was a young Staff Officer of the Adjutant-General's Department. He had just asked a question on a small matter of detail which the War Office thought should, as a courtesy, be referred to the Commander of the Forces. A name typical of the British private soldier was required, for use on the model sheet of the soldier's accounts to show where the men should sign.
>
> The Duke stood gazing out to sea while the young officer waited, searching in a long memory stored with recollections for a man who typified the character of Britain's soldiers. He thought back to his first campaign in the Low Countries where he had fought his first action with his old Regiment, the 33rd Foot.
>
> When the battle was over and won, Wellesley rode back to where little groups of wounded men were lying on the ground. At the place where the right of his line had been lay the right-hand man of the Grenadier Company, Thomas Atkins. He stood six foot three in his stockinged feet; he had served for twenty years; he could neither read nor write and he was the best man at arms in the Regiment. One of the bandsmen had bound up his head where a saber had slashed it; he had a bayonet wound in the chest, and a bullet through the lungs. He had begged the bearers not to move him, but to let him die in peace. Wellesley looked down on him and the man must have seen his concern. "It's all right Sir," he gasped. "It's all in the day's work." They were his last words.
>
> The Old Duke turned to the waiting Staff Officer. "Thomas Atkins," he said.

My team was credited with many things the CMATT accomplished, but none of us had given as much as Thomas Atkins or, for that matter, our brave soldiers and marines on the front lines throughout Iraq. I reminded everyone there was much more to be done and encouraged them to devote all their strength and loyalty to their commander and to their vitally important mission. I told them that moving on to my next assignment and leaving such a great group of guys was not particularly easy for me but, "After all," I said, "Nothing is easy in the Middle East." I loved those guys!

Making a farewell presentation to Major General Eaton, Baghdad, Iraq, August 2003.

PART III

SOLDIERING WITH THE MULTINATIONAL DIVISION (CENTRAL-SOUTH)

CHAPTER 16

Preparing for Duty with a Combat Division

You need fans in high places. I don't care how talented you are.
—Jaleel White (actor)

I had to get back to Camp Doha in Kuwait to pick up several items of equipment, including my assault rifle, before reporting to my new assignment. I had carried a pistol throughout the Coalition Military Assistance Training Team (CMATT) experience, but I my assignment with the "Polish Division" required more firepower. I could not resist stopping by CMATT Headquarters for a few final goodbyes before leaving for the Baghdad airport. I wished I had not immediately after stepping through the door. The team was still struggling to support the "foothold" we had established at Kirkush Barracks when I walked into the Operations Center. Everyone was engaged with some vitally important staff action and I left feeling a little guilty about not having done more to end the crisis management that kept the project alive. Only time and the honest realization by the highest levels of command that resourcing the New Iraqi Army project was in fact a top priority would ease the never-ending challenges the CMATT faced in the summer/fall of 2003.

General Eaton offered me a ride to the airport; it was not long before I was engulfed in the all-too-familiar smell of aviation fuel as I made my way to a C-130 Hercules transport with its propellers turning for what I hoped would be an uneventful and restful flight. There would be other missions and their accompanying challenges I thought, but it was as good a time as any to move on to my next assignment. We quickly gained altitude and turned toward Kuwait; having nothing to do at that point, I fell into a deep sleep.

I arrived at Camp Doha late that night after a long flight and a longer maintenance stop-over at the Kuwaiti Ahmed Al Jaber Air Base, 75 miles south of the Iraqi border. The next three days were as fast as they were restful. My warehouse room was still intact, and I was fortunate no one had moved in during my long absence. I went to the CFLCC (Coalition Force Land Component Commander) communications shop where I turned in several long-range iridium phones my team had been issued for our initial reconnaissance of Iraqi military sites in June. The guys in the communications shop were happy to have them back and I was very pleased to be rid of them. The phones had not worked as advertised and they had been a burden to carry. Sitting on the edge of my bunk, I realized how much of a toll the CMATT experience had taken on me. I had lost ten pounds and I was bone tired. In the privacy and comfort of my quiet room, I suddenly felt weak. I fooled myself into thinking I would pull some maintenance on my gear and identify items to exchange. The stench of the emptied contents of my duffel bag and rucksack could have easily gagged a maggot. It did not matter. I kicked off my boots, laid back on my bunk, and once again fell asleep.

I must have slept for more than twelve hours before my bladder cried for relief. I began to feel relaxed for the first time in nearly six months. The absence of responsibility and stress, the long uninterrupted sleep, air conditioning, a long, hot shower, and two huge double cheeseburgers at the mess hall made me feel energetic and strong again. Common chores—such as doing my laundry, writing letters, and going to the post office—never seemed more pleasant. It did not take long to see how Camp Doha had changed. Task Force IV had disbanded. Except for the engineers that had played a key role in restoring electrical services in Baghdad, the bulk of the other officers and enlisted personnel had gone home or were reassigned in theater. Originally thought to be the spearhead of the stabilization phase of the invasion of Iraq, Task Force IV had essentially become nothing more than a replacement depot. In retrospect, there were very few people at Camp Doha in March and April 2003 who were very serious about planning for posthostilities and the inevitable occupation of Iraq. Only a shell of the CFLCC staff was still present, and the energy generated by the large presence of personnel and equipment of the previous spring was long gone. I was fine with it all. There was no competition for hot water in the showers and I took advantage of the near-empty gym over the next couple of days to enhance my physical fitness and general wellbeing.

These three wonderful, near-carefree days did wonders for my health and general disposition, but the time had literally flown by as I stood on the tarmac with my rifle, rucksack, and duffel bag waiting for yet another C-130 flight to Iraq. Arriving in Baghdad at 1 am, I was advised by an Air Force noncommissioned officer (NCO) to wait until daylight at the distinguished visitors lounge just off the runway. It was nothing special—a conex with a couple of bunks, a table, and a collection of typically old magazines you normally find in a barber shop including *Newsweek*, *Time*, and *Field and Stream*. I dropped my bags and weapons and did what soldiers with time on their hands do best and fell asleep.

I awoke to a bright sun blazing through the open door of the conex and that same Air Force NCO, who told me to "Cool out, sir, ain't no helicopters going to Hillah today. All choppers are grounded for high winds."

I had expected to fly to al-Hillah, a city 100 kilometers south of Baghdad and about ten miles north of Camp Babylon. I was supposed to move by ground transportation to the headquarters of the Polish division. So much for that plan I thought, so I asked him for a lift to Combined Joint Task Force-7 (CJTF-7) Headquarters at Camp Victory. He very pleasantly surprised me. In 20 minutes, the sergeant had an SUV and driver available. He also had a tray with a hot breakfast of eggs, pancakes, bacon, a biscuit, some fruit, and a small carton of orange juice. I asked him, "Sergeant, what the hell did I do to deserve this?"

"Well, sir, one look at you and I said to myself this dude is going somewhere bad. You don't look like other colonels who come through here with that fancy rifle you have and all. I just figured I'd square you away before you left to go wherever you're going."

I did not know if I had just met a prophet or just another nice guy. His comments reminded me of the Swift Boat commander talking to Martin Sheen in the Vietnam War movie *Apocalypse Now*. I enjoyed the breakfast, thanked him for taking care of me, and headed out for Camp Victory in the SUV. The airport road was already notorious for vehicle ambushes, so I stayed alert as we made our way to the "Water Palace" at Camp Victory without incident.

The delay in my flight was a stroke of good luck. I went to the office of Major General Thomas Miller, USA, the recently arrived CJTF-7 Deputy Chief of Staff for Operations (C-3). We had first met as Ranger students in Ranger Class 501-72 in the summer of 1972. I considered him a good friend. Tom greeted me with a smile, apologized for having to attend a meeting, and kindly asked me to stop by to see him tomorrow. Turning to his aide as he headed toward the door, he directed him to get a room for me in the distinguished visitor quarters. I stopped by the billeting office and thankfully accepted the keys to a huge room in another ornate palace-like structure within five minutes walking distance of the headquarters. Once again, I was in awe of the marbled walls, ornate fixtures, and decorative furniture that characterized the opulence of the Saddam regime. I made my way down a sunny, well-lit hallway and opened the door to what had to have been the master bedroom of a royal couple. The king-size bed and gold-painted furniture were arranged in a huge room with pink-marble walls. The bathroom was large as well and I was glad to discover the shower worked. I couldn't believe it! I could not help but think General Miller had me intentionally billeted in the finest "cat house" in Iraq. I sat on the bed and thought that any minute a sexy Arabian princess was going to enter my room and offer me all the pleasures a dictator could handle. It was a nice thought quickly dissipated by the reality of a young corporal who knocked on the door and informed me I was to report to Major General Wojdkowski, the deputy CJTF-7 commander, in one hour and that the chief of Operations Branch wanted to see me as soon as I settled in.

I walked back to the headquarters to find Colonel Bob Radcliffe, whose position as the chief of Operations Branch was an 18–20-hour-a-day grind devoted to coordinating the daily operations of the Coalition Task Force. We exchanged greetings and sat down to discuss my assignment, but it was nearly impossible to have an intelligent conversation as Bob handled one crisis phone call after the other. He apologized and I slowly moved away to give him the space he required. One look at the Operations Center convinced me I was in the last place I would ever want to be assigned. It was a huge room filled with workstations, computers, and a lot of frustrated, angry people of all ranks trying to solve the critical challenges of corps-level staff work. I felt very fortunate I had managed to escape the drudgery of staff work at the division and corps levels throughout most of my career. The loud din of voices that never seemed to let up reminded me of CMATT's operations shop, only on a giant scale and without the camaraderie and humor. It was an impersonal world of outstanding people doing work of great value that was more than likely unappreciated by the fighting formations in the field. Staring at the madness, I realized how spoiled I had been to have served the bulk of my career at battalion and brigade levels or in other field assignments close to the troops.

I waved to Bob and pointed to my watch as I made my way out of the room to the deputy commander's office where General Wojdkowski greeted me with a smile and offered me his huge hand. We did not talk very long, but I appreciated the general's courtesy and advice. Things were beginning to get difficult in Iraq and, after the usual exchange of pleasantries, he told me the Multinational Division (MND) would be a huge challenge for me. He informed me the Polish-led MND would assume charge of its designated area of responsibility (AOR) early in September from the 1st Marine Expeditionary Force (IMEF) that would soon return to its home station at Camp Pendleton, California. The AOR was quite large and included most of Babil Province immediately south of Baghdad, southwest to the holy cities of Al-Najaf and Kerbelâ', south to ad-Dīwānīyah all the way to the Saudi Arabian border, and east to al-Kūt and the Iranian border. It encompassed five provinces and included 142 kilometers of border with Iran. The Marines were in firm control and had by all accounts performed their stability role in an exceptional manner. There was some understandable concern about the readiness of the MND that included contingents from 22 nations augmented with American combat support forces. The headquarters of both the IMEF and MND were co-located at Camp Babylon, a little over one hundred kilometers south of Baghdad on the bank of the Euphrates River. Listening intently, I thought 100 kilometers was not far enough from the "madness" I had seen in the CJTF-7 Operations Center, but it would certainly do for now. The general did not mince his words and told me very clearly, "Roland, we're counting on you to keep us informed of what's going on down there. Do everything you can to help the command group and keep the division moving."

He shook my hand, smiled, offered his best wishes, and returned to his paperwork. As I made my way to the door, he looked up and with a broad smile said, "Oh, and Roland, don't get your ass shot off."

I looked at him and smiled. "Yes, sir, I'll do my best."

I decided to check out the Coalition Planning Section where I met Lieutenant Colonel Sean MacFarland, USA. Sean was the lead American planner in a room heavily populated with allied officers. The atmosphere away from the loud and seemingly disjointed Operations Center appeared far more controlled and organized, but the plans shop was a busy place as well. The arrival of our Coalition partners had generated many logistical requirements and operational concerns. The rules of engagement of every contributing nation would generate considerable controversy over the next several months. These varying rules of engagement would negatively impact the fighting efficiency and overall capability of the division and prove to be a significant burden for the MND commander. Other concerns with official visits to Iraq by foreign dignitaries and generals, and associated matters of protocol, kept everyone fully engaged. Sean mentioned his brother Chris, an Apache helicopter pilot, who had served on the Multinational Force and Observers and Task Force Sinai staff as the air operations officer during my command tour in 2000–01. Chris had been an outstanding member of the Task Force Sinai staff who I remembered very well. Sean and I quickly established a friendly relationship. He provided a lot of information about the still evolving Multinational Division (Central-South). The best news of all, however, was that Brigadier General János Isaszegi, my close friend from Hungary who I had met in the Sinai when he served as the director of the Operations Control Center of the Hungarian Defense Staff, would soon arrive at Camp Victory to serve as the deputy chief of Coalition operations. János and I had stayed in contact via email since our last meeting in Rome in May 2001. I was encouraged to know I would have an influential Coalition friend on the CJTF-7 staff for the duration of my tour. Things were looking up and I was feeling better about my assignment as I settled down for another long and restful sleep in my king-size bed. It had been less than a week since I had left my chaotic life at the Republican Palace headquarters in Baghdad and I was anxious to get back into the war.

The following morning, I attended a series of briefings regarding Coalition operations to gain more insight into the magnitude of my impending task. My office call with General Miller was very informative. The Multinational Division (Central-South) staff included positions in operations, intelligence, and logistics designated for Americans. These embedded American staff officers and NCOs would be provided by the Illinois National Guard. He told me I was expected to monitor and coordinate their efforts and assist them as required. I have always had a high regard for the National Guard. During my assignments with the 101st Airborne Division in the mid to late 1970s, my battalion had trained with units from Arkansas, New York, and Wisconsin. I admired their fundamental tactical skills, but I always thought their planning and general staff work left a lot to be desired. The general's comments made sense to me. I told him I understood the mission and would do my best to deliver the results he expected. Other Americans worked in direct support of the division but were not embedded into the division structure.

These people were primarily transporters and communicators and came from the Regular Army. Several Americans specifically designated as liaison officers would work directly for me, but in August only a captain and a staff sergeant were available, and no liaison personnel were assigned to the division's brigades. My responsibilities, therefore, were not limited to the division staff and command group. The lack of liaison personnel dictated we move throughout the division's vast AOR and position ourselves at brigade or battalion level to observe operations, advise commanders, influence the action, and render reports. General Miller encouraged me to get out and do whatever was necessary to ensure CJTF-7 had good situational awareness of the division's activities. My reports would be made directly to him. Our discussions were productive and ended with a firm handshake. I was proud and happy for Tom Miller who I considered another one of the "good guys" who had broken into the general ranks. He had a tough year ahead of him, but I assured him the least of his concerns would be the liaison effort in the MND and that my team would do everything it could to mitigate his operational concerns.

As I left General Miller's office, his aide informed me I would leave that evening and fly to Camp Babylon via a Marine CH-46 helicopter. I quickly left the headquarters to inspect and pack my gear. Colonel MacFarland informed me in passing that it would be a good idea to attend Polish Army Day ceremonies on 16 August as one of my first official duties. I thanked him for the heads up and ran back to my quarters. By nightfall I would be back in the field with a division again. It was a nice thought.

The Iraq–Iran Border Region. (U.S. Central Intelligence Agency)

CHAPTER 17

Serving with the Multinational Division (Central-South)

Our words have power. They impact others, but they also impact us.
—MICHAEL S. HYATT, CEO AND FOUNDER OF HYATT & COMPANY

The helo pad at Camp Victory was a short walk from the distinguished visitor quarters. Several CH-46 helicopters sat on the pad as I dragged my bags to the edge of the road and began to poke around looking for any pilots or crewmembers. The Marine CH-46 Sea Knight was the butt of many jokes by aviators and infantrymen alike. It first entered service in 1964 to provide assault transport of combat troops and supplies and equipment. It had undergone many modifications over the years but was nonetheless regarded as a "dinosaur." A crew chief emerged from the cargo compartment of the lead aircraft and informed me our departure time had been moved several hours to 10 pm. Our departure was delayed because Major General Stalder, deputy commander of the 1st Marine Expeditionary Force (IMEF), had several unexpected briefings and office calls to attend before he could return to Camp Babylon. I was surprised to hear the general's name. General Keith Stalder, USMC, had served as the deputy director of the Plans and Policy Directorate at Central Command prior to his current assignment. He was a highly respected leader and a true gentleman. We had become good friends during my tour in the Joint Security Directorate and I looked forward to seeing him again. Certainly, his thoughts regarding the situation in our area of operations would be valuable. I spoke with several other pilots and crewmembers until we were suddenly informed the general was en route to the pad. Good crews always have the rotary blades turning by the time the boss arrives, and these guys were not going to be caught short. Any discussions with General Stalder would have to wait another day.

We lifted off into the darkness and headed due south for Camp Babylon. The combination of the heat, my body armor, weapons, combat equipment, and the stifling air of the helicopter's closed cargo compartment, bathed me in sweat. It was dark, but the compartment's dim red lighting allowed me to survey my immediate surroundings. The briefings and office calls of the last two days aside, I really knew very little about what awaited me at Camp Babylon, but I was thrilled with the opportunity to serve in a combat division. As an infantry officer, the prospects of a combat infantry assignment were professionally very satisfying to me. It had not come easy. My orders were simple and succinct and, like the others I had been given, purely "VOCO" or verbal orders from the commander. There was no accompanying paper. The orders were from Lieutenant General Ricardo Sanchez, USA, the Combined Joint Task Force-7 (CJTF-7) commander:

"Proceed to Camp Babylon, report to the Polish Division Commander, and assume the duties of the Coalition Joint Task Force-7 Senior Liaison Officer to the Multinational Division Central-South."

I sank as comfortably as I could into the canvas cargo seat, attempting to dodge the hydraulic fluid that steadily dripped onto the bill of my patrol cap. I closed my eyes, thinking of the exciting events of the past year and the challenges that lay ahead. It had been all of 30 minutes before a loud voice caught my attention:

"Stand by, sir, we're only a few minutes out from Camp Babylon."

That was all I needed to get fired up. We landed in our self-made sandstorm from the rotor wash. The cargo ramp was slowly lowered, and the crew chief and gunner began to move boxes of supplies off the aircraft. The Camp Babylon airstrip was several ball fields long, but it was impossible to see much beyond my nose as I struggled to get off the ramp and move away from the aircraft with my bags and equipment. I could barely make out several sedans, trucks, and Humvees lined up parallel to the airstrip as I stood by my gear awaiting instructions as to where I should go. The noise of the still-churning helos, the sandstorm, and the absolute darkness of the strip disoriented me. There was a brief moment of helplessness until I heard a gruff voice piercing the darkness and calling my name:

"Colonel Tiso, right this way, sir. I've got a pickup truck to haul you and your gear to your quarters."

The voice belonged to Staff Sergeant Chris Stewart, a big man who had volunteered to join the Division Liaison Team, having already served on the V Corps and CJTF-7 staffs in Iraq for over six months. He had had about all he could stand of the noise and stress of the command's Operations Center, something I totally understood. He was all business as he took my duffel bag and heaved it into the truck. We were quickly loaded and on our way down a road that turned away from the airstrip and into a built-up area with several large buildings. I could not see much. There were no lights and any traffic I saw moved on "black out drive." As we continued down the road, we passed what I later found out were the walls of the ancient city of Babylon, many storage containers, and a vehicle park. Sergeant Stewart then turned into a road with a long row of tents. Pulling up next to a large, white, general-purpose tent, he announced in that same gruff voice:

"Alright, sir, end of the line. This will be your home until the Marines pull up stakes and they sort out the hardstands. I imagine you'll get some better digs next month."

Sergeant Stewart pulled the tent flap back and I entered a small well-lit area that was marked "OFFICERS." The bulk of the tent behind the next flap was marked "ENLISTED." There were 10 Marine junior and field-grade officers in the tent, but there were enough bunk beds to house at least twice that many. I took the first bunk I saw without any bedding or personal equipment on it, dropped my gear, and sat on the thin mattress. I looked up to find everyone staring at me. I guessed it was my rank that got their attention, but I mustered up a smile and announced:

"Men, my name is Tiso and I'll be bunking here for a while. I'll do my best not to mess up your routine. Have a good night."

Several of the young Marines welcomed me with a characteristic naval "Welcome aboard, sir" as I kicked off my boots, wiped and oiled my rifle, and laid my head back to catch my breath. As usual, I quickly fell asleep.

The large tent cities had been erected by the now famed contractor Kellogg Brown & Root. They were air conditioned and comfortable and situated a short distance away from a series of shower trailers and porto-johns. People moved about in various modes of dress as the day's activities began to take shape. The troops I saw were mostly U.S. Marines. Some of them wore body armor and combat equipment, but most were wearing their physical training uniform and appeared to have just completed a unit run. Just like the Marines of the 15th Marine Expeditionary Unit prior to the withdrawal of UNIKOM (United Nations Iraq–Kuwait Observation Mission) from the demilitarized zone in March, these Marines conducted physical training whenever they could. Physical excellence and personal readiness was their callsign, a part of their daily regimen. They reminded me of the paratroops I had been privileged to command and the Army Rangers whose physical fitness in the U.S. Army is renowned. The landscape was dotted with chin-up bars that are inevitably constructed by Marines wherever they camp for more than 24 hours in one place. This place did not have too much to offer and it briefly occurred to me I was probably looking at the longest six months of my life. It did not matter though; I was happy to be in the field again. I got cleaned up, made my bunk, secured my equipment, and made my way up the final mile to the headquarters of the IMEF and the Multinational Division (Central-South).

I had not mentally linked the word Babylon to anything historical at that point but, staring at the rebuilt walls of the ancient city, it finally occurred to me I was camped next to one of the most magnificent structures of the ancient world. Babylon had been the city-state capital of the famous King Hammurabi who had dictated his famous Code of Laws inscribed on huge stone plaques that were recovered by French archaeologists and are currently on display in the Louvre in Paris. The Iraqis identified more with King Nebuchadnezzar II who, between 604–562 BC would build most of Babylon's existing buildings, walls, and the famous Hanging Gardens.[1] I remembered that Alexander the Great had made Babylon the capital of his empire at one point and had reputedly died there. People spend thousands of dollars to see and experience sites like these and I made a mental note to explore the ancient ruins at the earliest opportunity.

The end of the paved road was the center of a built-up area. Two large buildings housed the headquarters of both the IMEF and the 1st Marine Division. IMEF was roughly equivalent to an Army corps. In addition to the 1st Marine Division, the IMEF consisted of the 3rd Marine Aircraft Wing (its close air support and transport arm), and the 1st Forward Support Group, its logistical arm. IMEF had provided command and control to several Army and Navy units during the maneuver phase of the war and its strength at one point had exceeded 86,000 personnel. The Marines had occupied their area of responsibility (AOR) for nearly five months and had executed immensely successful nation-building operations. They had provided security, refurbished hospitals, rebuilt schools, and had seen to the needs of the Iraqi people. It was a new role for the Marines, and they had performed it superbly. Elements of the IMEF had been in the thick of the fighting from the beginning. The unit had been credited with the destruction of nine Iraqi divisions and would later receive the Presidential Unit Citation, the highest unit combat award, for its heroic achievements during the maneuver phase of the campaign and follow-on operations.

The Seabees, naval combat engineers who manned the famous construction battalions (CB) of the U.S. Navy, had constructed a number of temporary wooden structures for the Marines, and had provided power throughout the camp. These structures and many mobile containers were adjacent to the headquarters and served as overflow working spaces for the staff as well as quarters for officers and senior noncommissioned officers. Large tentage provided temporary working space for the Multinational Division (MND) staff. Looking upward, I saw a huge palace-like building that served as a communications center and a barracks for troops of a variety of nations. It was a literal antenna farm, the "roots" of which could be traced by miles of cable that ringed the palace from every direction. Swirling about me as I stood at the end of the road was an endless sea of men in a smorgasbord of uniforms. The MND consisted of troops from more than twenty nations, including the United States. The proximity of the mess hall to the headquarters eventually brought everyone to the central point of the road on which I stood. The multitude of uniforms, the different languages, the heat and dust, the vehicle traffic, and the incessant noise of it all contributed to a seemingly chaotic scene in which I felt temporarily lost and terribly small. It was a literal whirlwind of activity.

I had had enough of the crowd and entered the larger of the two headquarters buildings, hoping to pay a call on General Stalder. I was in luck and the general's aide ushered me in for a quick visit. Always a gentleman, General Stalder was happy to see me. He had been a big supporter of my efforts to get an overseas assignment after September 11, when we were assigned to Central Command Headquarters, and he expressed a great deal of interest in my experiences in southern Iraq and Baghdad. IMEF was pulling out of Iraq and going home. Its principal mission now was to orient the MND and prepare to redeploy. He told me assisting the "stand up" of the MND and ensuring its smooth transition of authority were the key goals toward which I should strive in the near term.

"Throw yourself in that direction, Roland, and you'll be a real hero."

I assured him I would do everything I could and then, recognizing how busy he was, thanked him and asked if he could spare someone to show me around. He laughed and offered the services of a young Marine corporal.

"Recommend your next stop be the IMEF G-3 shop. Dave Brown will provide you the details about the upcoming transition of authority, proposed timelines, and things like that." I thanked him again and asked the corporal to show me the way.

The heart of any military headquarters is its operations shop. The IMEF G-3 shop was affectionately known as the "House of Angst." The stress level in the G-3 is always high in peace or war. It is the place where the commander's desires and instructions are articulated in the form of operations orders, policies, directives, briefings, and never-ending efforts to coordinate activities up and down the chain of command. It is literally a "beehive" of activity. The cramped quarters of the G-3's trailer featured several desks, an array of computers, stacked boxes of everything from administrative supplies to rations, and several coffee makers. The G-3 and his closest assistants rarely took the time to go to the mess hall; evidence of hot chow and ration packs, as well as foodstuffs and "pogie bait," Marine slang for candy and other nice-to-have snacks from care packages, was everywhere. Like any deployed operations shop, it was a 24/7 operation. I introduced myself to Colonel Brown, the IMEF G-3, and I was immediately taken by my reception. He and the other Marines were glad to see me; I assumed my presence was clear evidence they were close to going home. I smiled and told Colonel Brown, "I never expected the Marines to be so happy to see the Army."

These battle-hardened Marines would have welcomed anything or anyone that could expedite their redeployment. Dave briefed me on IMEF's current operations and unit dispositions. He then invited me to attend two meetings regarding the planned relief in place of the Marines by multinational units. They were interested in my views regarding the transition of authority from the start. After listening to a variety of issues concerning rules of engagement, unit boundaries, communications shortfalls, and the availability of multinational units to serve as quick reaction forces, among a host of others, Colonel Brown asked me what I thought. I had been on the ground less than a day and I had not even met the MND command group or members of its staff yet. Normally, an officer with any smarts at all would simply look around, listen to what people had to say, and develop a sense for what was really going on before offering any solutions. They wanted answers now and all I knew was what Dave Brown and a few briefing heads had told me and the information I had picked up at CJTF-7 Headquarters. I concluded with a smile that it must be my intelligent, good looks that force me into these situations while I thought about how to respond. I said, "You know, Dave, a meeting of the respective commanders of both IMEF and the MND regarding command-and-control issues and timelines for the relief in place may be the best way to work through the outstanding issues.

They may feel some pressure to provide the decisions you need to pull this off and promote the parallel planning required to ensure both commands are in sync." If nothing else, I thought, it sounded intelligent enough.

After a moment of silence, he smiled and enthusiastically agreed with my comment. General Stalder had been right. I had gotten an earful about the situation from the G-3 and Marine solutions for a quick and efficient relief in place of their units. There was much to do and, according to the schedule, there was barely three weeks to make it happen. It was up to Dave Brown to get the two commanders and their staffs together; about the only other thing I could think of at that point was how to get to the mess hall. It was well past the noon mealtime, but thankfully Dave offered me an opportunity to rummage through his collection of care packages and stacks of pre-packaged "happy meals" that often substituted for "meals, ready to eat." It was the American logistics system at its best. These "happy meals" consisted of a cardboard tray with cans of tuna or BBQ, and spaghetti or some other pasta, chips, cookies, a soft drink, crackers and cheese or peanut butter, and several other delights, all packaged in plastic wrap. It was not something I wanted to do every day, but having not eaten in over eighteen hours, I was happy to have it.

I was anxious to meet and speak with Staff Sergeant Stewart and Captain Tom Lowman, the CJTF-7 operations officer who had volunteered to serve on the Division Liaison Team. I found them in a huge canvas operations tent, one of many similar tents housing the MND staff. The tent floor was organized in a similar manner to the dreaded CJTF-7 operations floor that had given me the creeps at Camp Victory. The briefing area to the rear of the tent, as one entered through the primary entry point, had a large screen to depict the same array of PowerPoint slides used by everyone, I assumed, for every occasion and operation. There were 10 rows of tables and chairs along which were arrayed the computer stations from which the division's operations officers monitored current operations. Areas to the left and right of this area housed the intelligence and plans shops. I vowed not to spend any more time in this environment than was necessary, but I knew there was no escaping it.

I recognized Sergeant Stewart; he immediately introduced me to Captain Lowman. Tom was the kind of junior officer anyone would like. A fit-looking infantry officer, he had risen to the rank of sergeant and had served in special forces before he was selected for Officer Candidate School. Tom was older and more seasoned than most captains. Mature and knowledgeable, he had served at corps headquarters and was as thoroughly oriented on the commonly used computer programs as he was with small-unit tactics and weapons. I could not have asked for a better officer. Tom gave me an orientation and tour of the tent and the staff areas, as well as a "who's who" of the various characters that worked there. We would be closely familiar with all of them before too long. Our liaison team was allocated a portion of one of the tables to the rear of the briefing area. We had three chairs and access to three computers that allowed us to operate on three nets: the U.S. classified SIPRNET, the multinational classified net known as

CENTRIX, and our unclassified NIPRNET. All of them were critical to successfully executing our mission. There were several field phones on the table that provided landline connectivity to CJTF-7 Headquarters. Except for the U.S.-only SIPRNET, everyone had access to the computers and phones. Our area was particularly busy as computer-smart officers and enlisted personnel used them for both professional and personal business. The NIPRNET was particularly popular for officers to send and receive messages home and access the internet. It was a good way to get to know people, but conducting classified conversations was a non-starter. The operations, plans, and intelligence staff members were a diverse lot. Officers from Spain, the United Kingdom, Kazakhstan, Ukraine, and Bulgaria, mingled with those from Denmark, Norway, and, of course, Poland. I was anxious to meet the man tasked to organize this multinational group into a cohesive, functional team. He had to be a leader, a commander who truly commanded the respect of every contingent and soldier. His name was Major General Andrzej Tyszkiewicz.

The commanding general of the Multinational Division (Central-South) occupied a modest office at the end of a long series of buildings that ran parallel to the canvas tents that housed his staff. General Tyszkiewicz had led an advance element of his division to Kuwait on 2 July and had entered Iraq several weeks later. His group had been preceded by a secret Polish formation known as the GROM, the Polish acronym for Operational and Mobile Reconnaissance Group. The unit is the equivalent of the American Delta Force and the British Special Air Service.

The elite, combat-tested GROM traces its lineage to 1939 and the defeat of the Polish Army by the Germans at the start of World War II. Polish exiled paratroopers were selected to form a special military unit and were trained by British special forces to enter Poland, train the Polish resistance, and fight the occupying German forces. These Poles were trained like the British special forces with emphasis on intelligence and reconnaissance, sabotage, partisan warfare and covert operations, communications, and English training. They re-entered Poland early in 1941 and remained engaged against the Germans until the end of the war and continued the struggle against the Soviet Army. Poland, however, was subjected to the Soviet influence zone established at the Yalta Conference in 1945.

Special Unit GROM was established in July 1990. Lieutenant Colonel Petelicki, a colorful, highly accomplished special operator, was tasked to create the special operations unit from existing special units within the Polish Armed Forces. He became its first commander. The unit remained completely secret for the first several years of its existence. It was first reported to the press in 1992 and became known to the public in 1994, after its first major military operation in Haiti. Petelicki was reassigned in December 1995 but returned to GROM two years later as the commanding officer. In August 1998, he was promoted to brigadier general by President Kwaśniewski. He gave up command of GROM and retired in 1999.[2]

Today, GROM is considered to be among the top special forces in the world. It is organized with three squadrons, two of which, along with the force's logistics unit, are based in Warsaw, the other being a maritime element based in Gdańsk. GROM's missions are not unlike U.S. special forces and include counterterrorism, special reconnaissance, direct action, unconventional warfare, and combat search and rescue.

GROM had been in the Central Region for months before the invasion of Iraq and had conducted operations to secure Iraqi oil platforms and the port of Umm Qasr. In March 2003, its operators had assaulted the Khor al-Amaya Oil Terminal about thirty miles southeast of the al-Faw Peninsula in the Arabian Gulf, while U.S. Marines and Navy SEALs seized the Al Başrah Oil Terminal. Both of the terminals were seized with no casualties. Following the initial phase of their operation, GROM were assigned to Task Force Thunder, under Combined Joint Special Operations Task Force–Arabian Gulf, as a counterterrorism unit.

By the end of August, General Tyszkiewicz would command over nine thousand troops; 2,300 were Polish. This was a major deployment for Poland, its first since the end of World War II. Its details had been coordinated by NATO and agreed upon late in June. The United States had agreed to fund the deployment and the sustainment of the Polish-led division including all deployment costs, strategic lift, and operations support for eight base camps. Base support included rations, laundry, and fuel. The U.S. had also agreed to provide theater-level general support that included civil affairs, intelligence, theater communications, and meteorological support. The division was also backed by American medical and military police units. The deployment had attracted a great deal of media coverage in Poland. His frequent television appearances and interviews had made General Tyszkiewicz a Polish "rock star."

Shortly after I was announced by his aide, he stopped what he was doing, got up, welcomed me, and ushered me into his office as if I was a long-lost friend. General Tsyzkiewicz was a big man, well over six feet tall and fit-looking at 187 pounds. He wore his grey hair closely cropped. He impressed me as a survivor after I quickly reviewed his bio. He had graduated from the Polish Wrocław Army Academy in 1973 and had by all accounts had an amazingly successful military career. He had been schooled at the Frunze Army Command and Staff College in Moscow and later attended the Voroshilov Armed Forces College. He had commanded two mechanized regiments and in the late 1980s commanded the 6th Air Assault Brigade, Poland's elite paratroops. What struck me was how he had reinvented himself after the breakup of the Soviet Union. He had learned to speak English at the age of 44 and, in addition to serving as the Polish defense attaché in Ankara, Turkey, had served as the Polish military representative at Supreme Headquarters Allied Powers Europe from 1999 to 2002. He had attended the NATO Defense College General/Flag Officers Course in Rome as well as the NATO Senior Officers Policy Course. The general's broad smile and charming accent largely contributed to what I thought was a most friendly personality. I liked the man almost immediately and left his office after our initial "get to know each other" conversation feeling I was a part of his team. It was clear I would be more than just a liaison officer. The general was impressed by my operational background and suggested I would be of great service to him and the division as his senior adviser. He encouraged me to interact with his staff and assist in whatever way I could. Most importantly, he recognized his brigades would operate independently and he encouraged me to visit and assist their commanders as well. During the conduct of operations, he said he would attach me to a brigade staff as both an adviser and, when necessary, as the operations officer. It occurred to me that some commanders would undoubtedly have a problem with that arrangement, but it was not my place to argue with him. I had every confidence I could work well with General Tyszkiewicz as well as with his diverse brigade commanders. The meeting was a great start to my mission.

As encouraging as the commanding general's welcome had been, I knew that acceptance as an adviser and as a respected and equal member of the division staff required a lot of work. It was essential my team insert its views and expertise at the proper times and in the proper settings. The idea is not to detract from the officers assigned to positions, but to influence with reason and offer to assist, while ensuring any credit for a particular job well done is attributed to the advised counterpart. It is a tall order, but success in multinational operations often means leaving your ego at the door.

In the multinational setting, an American officer automatically brings a great deal of credibility to the table. In November 1994, I was briefly seconded to the United Nations and deployed to Somalia as a planner with a military advisory and fact-finding team. I was the only American soldier in Somalia. The United States had not committed to supporting the withdrawal of the United Nations Operation Somalia II (UNOSOM II) force at that time, but my presence seemed to reassure our allies of our nation's eventual support. It is generally a good idea to be a good listener in these situations, take good notes, and defer from making comments that commit your command or country to anything operational, but on one occasion I was asked by a Pakistani brigadier general on the UNOSOM II staff to brief a reasonably possible concept of operations the Americans might employ to support their withdrawal. The Pakistanis, the Indians, and the Egyptians were very apprehensive about their future in Somalia; they hung on every word I said. I briefed how an unnamed supporting force would doctrinally execute an amphibious withdrawal given the port and beaches available and the international airport currently secured by the Egyptians. An overhead projector allowed me to show slides I carried of several amphibious ships our Marines and Navy could use to support the operation. It may not have been the best briefing I ever gave, and I emphasized there had been no decision regarding American assistance, but it was extremely well received. A week later in Nairobi, Kenya, I was directed to brief Ambassador Daniel Simpson on my actions in Somalia and particularly the briefing I had given to the military commanders and staff members at UNOSOM II Headquarters. He and his staff had been withdrawn from Somalia in September and had established a consulate in Nairobi. He was deeply interested in the UN team's mission, and he greeted me with enthusiasm. Ambassador Simpson had been the State Department's representative to the U.S. Army War College before he left in the summer of 1994 to assume his ambassadorship in Somalia. We had had several discussions about the future of Somalia during my tenure as a student at the War College and had developed a friendly relationship. In his dispatch to the State Department shortly after my departure, he stressed the importance of a quick decision to support the UNOSOM II withdrawal and referred to how the recent presence of a single American officer in a UNOSOM II conference concerning the withdrawal had "Filled the room." Reflecting on the experience, I concluded that, handled correctly, the impact an experienced, reasonably well-prepared American military officer can have in a multinational setting is huge.

In the Multinational Division (Central-South), I recognized the world's appreciation for American military "know how" could only take us so far. Ultimately, solid personal relationships with commanders and staff members are critical elements that allow an adviser to get into the details of operations and the decision-making process. I fully appreciated the value of Captain Tom Lowman's and Staff Sergeant Chris Stewart's presence on the division staff. Both were "wizards" on the computer and quick to assist the officers on the operations floor with technical challenges, PowerPoint-slide production, and military reports. Armed with his special forces training and warm personality, Tom was particularly adept at developing friendships and professional relationships with junior and senior officers alike. While they focused their attention at the "worker bee" level, I focused on the staff directors. The relationships and procedures we developed, during this period before the transition of authority from the Marines to our division, were critical to whatever success we achieved afterwards.

The next several days were a whirlwind of briefings and preparations for the relief in place. There was much to do. We were fortunate the military situation in our AOR was relatively calm. The growing insurgency and security challenges I had seen in Baghdad were not as evident in our Shia-dominated region. Many of the division's units had not yet arrived and the division staff was heavily engaged in coordinating their movement from Kuwait to Iraq, a military mission referred to as Reception, Staging, Onward Movement and Integration. Particularly important was the arrival of the Polish aviation contingent which was critical to the division's ability to operate independently. The anxiousness of the Marines to leave meant the MND's staff could never move fast enough. The dynamics were interesting and, in retrospect, totally understandable. General Tyszkiewicz was no fool. The deployment of the Polish Army to Iraq was its first in 60 years and was clearly its largest military mission. He needed to establish a firm foundation for the division's success and it was clear no amount of pressure for an early transition of authority would make it happen before everything was ready. As we moved closer to the end of August, this caused significant friction between the two commands and particularly about the transition of authority in the Spanish brigade sector. The situation there would eventually require the intervention of the U.S. Central Command commander.

The Poles were particularly proud of their contribution to the Coalition's effort in Iraq. They are a fiercely proud people. The beginnings of a Polish state is traced to over a thousand years ago, when the Kingdom of Poland was founded. Poland became closely aligned with Lithuania upon the signing of the Union of Lublin that formed the Polish–Lithuanian Commonwealth. It was one of the largest and most populous nations of 16th- and 17th-century Europe. Its unique liberal political system adopted the Constitution of 3 May 1791, Europe's first modern constitution. Poland's fate in the 18th and 19th centuries was decided by Prussia, Russia, and Austria who feared its existence and power. Poland would be partitioned three times, the second of which occurred following the 1792 Polish–Russian War that left Poland deprived of territory and incapable of independent existence. In 1795, the Commonwealth was partitioned for a third time and Poland ceased to exist. The last Polish king abdicated the throne. The Polish people rose against the partitioners and occupying armies several times. An unsuccessful attempt to defend Poland's sovereignty took place in 1794. The popular and distinguished General Tadeusz Kosciuszko, who had served under George Washington in the American Revolutionary War, was ultimately defeated, ending Poland's independent existence for 123 years. Remnants of the country fought on through a series of insurrections during the Napoleonic campaigns of the early 18th century and vestiges were created, such as the Duchy of Warsaw, by Napoleon, only to be abolished when he was exiled. Its territory was divided into Russian Congress Poland, the Prussian Grand Duchy of Posen, and Austrian Galicia with the Free City of Kraków. The Poles in Warsaw in 1830 and in 1848 rebelled against its occupiers only to see the last vestiges of old Poland integrated into the German Empire in 1871. In Russia, the January Uprising in 1863–64, prompted severe political, social and cultural reprisals, followed by deportations and pogroms of the Polish–Jewish population.[3]

Poland's service and sacrifice in World War II has always fascinated me as both a soldier and a historian. Poland made the fourth-largest troop contribution in Europe, and its troops served both the Polish Government-in-Exile in the west and Soviet leadership in the east.

The wartime resistance movement, and the Polish Home Army, fought heroically against German occupation. It was one of the three largest resistance movements of the war. The resistance was loyal to the exiled government and generally resented the idea of a communist Poland. During the Yalta Conference, Joseph Stalin insisted on the formation of a new provisional pro-communist coalition government in Moscow which ignored the Polish Government-in-Exile based in London. This angered many Poles who considered it a betrayal by the Allies. In 1944, Stalin made guarantees to Churchill and Roosevelt that he would maintain Poland's sovereignty and allow democratic elections but, with victory in 1945, the elections organized by the Soviet authorities were falsified and used to provide a veneer of legitimacy for Soviet dominance of Polish affairs. The Soviet Union instituted a new communist government in Poland. The Poles resisted from the outset and continued into the 1950s.

The new Polish Government accepted the Soviet annexation of the pre-war eastern regions of Poland and agreed to the permanent garrisoning of Russian Army units on Poland's territory. Its military alignment within the Warsaw Pact throughout the Cold War was a direct result. Poland, however, never ceased to identify with the West. The Russian failure to enter Warsaw during the Polish uprising against the Germans in the summer and fall of 1944, years of Russian occupation of Polish territory, and Stalin's betrayal of the Poles right to self-determination in 1945, was clear to every Pole. The Polish people never saw themselves or their country as a part of a communist brotherhood. Ultimately, their religious faith, love of Polish culture and independence, and identification with democratic values would never allow them to bow to "Godless Communism" and Soviet Russia.

Labor turmoil in 1980 led to the formation of Solidarity, the independent trade union that became a political force. Despite persecution and imposition of martial law eight years earlier, in 1989, Solidarity decisively won Poland's first partially free and democratic parliamentary elections since the end of the World War II. Lech Wałęsa, a Solidarity candidate, won the presidency in 1990. The Solidarity movement contributed to the collapse of communist regimes and parties across Europe. Poland joined NATO in 1999 and became a full member of the European Union in 2004.

The Multinational Division (Central-South) attracted a great deal of interest in the early days of its deployment in Iraq. The multitude of its national flags and contingents gave a different face to a war that had been dominated by the United States and, to a lesser extent, Great Britain. There was overwhelming participation by the CJTF-7 staff and commanders on 16 August when the Poles held their Army Day ceremonies. The ceremonies commemorated the Polish Army's magnificent victory over the Russians in the decisive battle of Warsaw in 1920 that the Poles refer to as "The miracle on the Vistula." The victory preserved Poland's statehood and the Second Polish Republic, something it had acquired only a year before the battle in the aftermath of World War I and confirmed by the Treaty of Versailles in 1919. The Poles are proud of their Army and value their personal freedom and independence as much as Americans. They take great pride in their national identity. Deeply religious and proud of their Roman Catholic faith, the Poles have always identified with Western culture.

The ceremonies provided me an opportunity to take in the magnificent ruins of Babylon. General Tyszkiewicz had wisely chosen a field inside its reconstructed walls to conduct the simple, but dignified observance. Arriving dignitaries and senior commanders included Generals Sanchez and Miller. They had the pleasure of walking through the famous Istar Gate, a replica of the original door to Babylon complete with its decorations of bulls and dragons and blue enameled panels, and walk a series of passageways and steps to the parade field. Following his short speech, General Tyszkiewicz invited everyone to join him and his soldiers to a series of small open tents filled with various Polish foods. The festive mood made it hard to believe we were in Iraq as we enjoyed an array of red peppers and sausages, mushrooms, bread, sweets, and variety of soft drinks. It was an excellent chance for our senior leaders to relax, but the challenges of Baghdad cut their visit short. In a brief conversation with General Miller, I learned he had received my initial report that focused on the challenges we faced and the actions we were taking with the transition of command. He encouraged me to do everything I could to speed up efforts to accomplish the transition of authority. Getting the MND fully on board was significant both militarily and politically, and, for now, it was the CJTF-7 Liaison Team's number one priority.

The IMEF G-3 did not waste any time following up on my recommendation to have the IMEF and MND commanders discuss the details of the relief in place. Their discussions were preceded by a briefing that captured IMEF's recommended schedule of events. General Tyszkiewicz was clearly uneasy with the timelines. His argument, with which I fully agreed, was that timelines should be conditions based as opposed to time driven. In his view, the readiness of his still-arriving units did not support a transition of authority in August. General Stalder agreed in principle. The meeting of these gentlemen eased the pressure on the IMEF staff, but every effort was needed to facilitate the readiness of the MND. Everyone committed to doing whatever could be done to "step up" operations in a coordinated manner. General Tyszkiewicz stated very clearly that he was not interested in artificial delays to the transition of authority and would welcome the responsibility by the end of August assuming all preparations were in place.

The MND was a commanding general's nightmare. The melding of 23 national contingents' worth of standard operating procedures and rules of engagement was enough to drive a professional soldier crazy. Language was an issue. English was the base language, but Russian was a legacy of the Cold War that bonded the Poles, Ukrainians, Bulgarians, Romanians, Hungarians, Kazakhs, and Mongolians. The division's structure was built around three national infantry brigades. The Polish brigade included a Bulgarian infantry battalion. The Ukrainian brigade included a small support unit from Kazakhstan and an attached Polish aviation section. The Spanish brigade included battalions from Honduras, the Dominican Republic, and El Salvador, and a detachment from Nicaragua. Interestingly, the Nicaraguan detachment commander had studied in Moscow in the 1980s during the heyday of the Sandinista regime and spoke fluent Russian. The commanders of these units were under orders in almost every case to consult with their Ministry of Defense before they executed any orders given by division headquarters. A dictatorial style of leadership in this division could never be successful. General Tyszkiewicz had to master the persuasive form of leadership and deal with the eccentricities of each of his subordinate commanders. It was easy to understand the commanding general's discomfort with going too fast. Operationally, he could not so much as take a Ukrainian battalion and task organize it under the Polish brigade commander for an operation requiring additional troops in the Polish sector. The agreements made by each nation to commit troops to Iraq were rigid. Offensive operations were not in the division's playbook. Iraq was supposed to be a peacekeeping mission and the national aversion to casualties by every contingent was a huge operational burden. The MND was a far different kind of "animal" than its U.S. Marine or Army division counterpart, and far less efficient. It required, as Americans would say, "Special care and feeding." It would be much later, however, before CJTF-7 Headquarters fully appreciated the division's limitations and the political fragility of its national contingents.

General Tyszkiewicz met frequently with his staff prior to the transition of authority and relief of the Marines. In a command and staff meeting following his IMEF G-3-arranged discussions with General Stalder, General Tyszkiewicz surprised everyone by introducing me as his American adviser and a senior member of his personal staff. I was pleasantly surprised, thrilled at the prospects it offered, and truly honored. I spoke briefly, thanking the general for his confidence and promising my best efforts to secure the division's success. He put me to work immediately. The MND was chock full of generals and one of the commanding general's initial burdens was to determine what their responsibilities would be. Each brigade was commanded by a brigadier general. Additionally, the Poles and the Ukrainians provided a second brigadier general equivalent for the division staff. The Spanish provided a major general. There was also a brigadier from the Philippines who was not assigned to the division and functioned solely as his nation's contingent commander and as an observer. General Tyszkiewicz wanted options to determine how best to organize his generals and get the most of their experience. It was a small but necessary task that allowed me to engage with my liaison officers, the staff directors, and the chief of staff to develop several options that we captured on PowerPoint slides and presented to the commanding general the following morning. He complimented our efforts but made a few changes. He agreed that the Polish and Spanish generals should be his deputies for operations and logistics respectively, but he created a deputy position for force protection for the Ukrainian general—to account for "His exceptional tactical experience." Significantly, he said he would not designate the Spaniard as the ranking deputy and insisted all the staff generals be shown equally on the chain-of-command diagram. The Spanish general exercised authority as a major general only with regard to his national duties. This relatively minor project had the positive effect of opening the division G-3 and other members of the staff to seek advice and assistance from the American

Liaison Team on other projects. The Director of Operations, Spanish Colonel Javier Cabeza, and his G-3/Chief of Current Operations, Polish Colonel Mieczyslaw Gocul, were not inclined to talk with me initially. After being complimented by the commanding general on the general officer project, however, they requested assistance with everything from the preparation of command briefings to the development of orders and directives, to discussions of issues pertaining to the relief in place. Almost overnight, we were totally involved with nearly every task and challenge that confronted the staff.

One of the best and obvious weapons an American on a multinational staff brings to the table is his fluency in English. Our Polish and Eastern European counterparts understandably struggled with the language. We used to joke with them that their slides were prepared beautifully in Polish or Ukrainian English with a unique style of word usage and grammar. Once we knew each other, the G-3 and I would often enjoy a good laugh as we performed massive "surgery" on nearly every briefing he presented. Our allies were almost always baffled by the American use of acronyms, but they enjoyed learning and using them during division briefings. Our willingness to work with, mentor, and learn from our various counterparts significantly improved the staff's efficiency, the quality of its work, and our personal and professional knowledge. Everyone looked good and General Tyszkiewicz was quick to notice and compliment his staff directors. It reinforced the single greatest rule for an adviser to understand—that is simply that credit for a unit's success always goes to the advised commander or staff leader with whom he works. But General Tyszkiewicz knew his American officers were an asset and never failed to acknowledge us with a nod and a smile.

The commanding general expected me to visit him every morning. Our discussions were often opportunities for him to review issues and seek input to pending decisions. Closing the door one day, the general sat next to me on his office couch and explained in detail his reasoning regarding the duties he had assigned to his generals.

"Roland, you must understand that I can absolutely rely on General Kwiatkowski. He is a Pole, my friend, and my classmate. We grew up together in the Army. He must be my operations deputy. General Sobora is a great soldier, but he speaks no English. As deputy for force protection, he will work closely with General Kwiatkowski and me and we will take advantage of his strong tactical expertise. We all speak Russian. The Spaniard will be heavily involved in national matters. I will have to rely extensively on Colonel Hejna, the Polish G-4, and the American logistics officers for their advice and staff work."

The general wanted me to totally understand the basis of his decision. His reasoning was as brilliant as it was practical. I appreciated the commanding general's exceptional grasp of the political/military challenges of his multinational command. In fact, General Tyszkiewicz had taken a very active role in the division's development long before he had deployed to Kuwait. The heavily weighted Polish presence on the division staff was no accident. He had carefully crafted its design, ensuring the chief of staff, the G-2 (Intelligence), G-3/5 (Operations/Plans), G-4 (Logistics), and G-6 (Communications) were Poles. The G-3 section was led by a senior Spanish director, but a Pole of equal rank did the lion's share of the work. The more I got to know the commanding general, the more I liked him. At his invitation, I began to spend more time in his office. Like the staff directors, he was particularly appreciative of my ability to provide a quick translation of military correspondence and explain any military jargon and acronyms. Significantly, as my credibility with the commanding general grew, so did my credibility and influence with the staff. It was professionally very satisfying and I was determined to ensure our developing multinational staff was viewed by CJTF-7 as a professional entity that "had its stuff in one bag."

The period that preceded the transition of authority was filled with countless briefings to our respective commanders and their counterparts in IMEF. The division "PowerPoint gurus" were busy and Sergeant Stewart and Captain Lowman were fully employed assisting them both technically and professionally. There is no substitute, however, for the operational experience that allows an officer to explain simply and rationally what his command is doing and what its requirements are. There is a tendency to build slides and briefings that clutter our commanders' thoughts with irrelevant form including cartoons, photos, unnecessary maps, and whatever else the computer can generate. A focused and concise Word document augmented with a simple chart can be far more effective. As we drew closer to briefing General Sanchez on post-transition operations throughout the division's AOR, Tom Lowman and I found ourselves totally involved with the staff. We had to be careful not to do the work, but to guide the staff to ensure it captured the division's missions and its subordinate units' activities with doctrinally accepted words that everyone could understand. We recommended that, regardless of the American military's fascination with computers, a map of our AOR appropriately marked with correct military symbology and augmented with simple, bulletized PowerPoint slides was the best way to conduct operational briefings. "Ultimately," I said, "generals of all armies understand maps regardless of the language we speak or how well we speak it." Our heavily accented counterparts speaking English as a second or third language fully appreciated the concept.

Our activities with the staff were operational, professional, and downright fun. The focus of our team's efforts, at least for now, had to be at division level (consistent with General Miller's guidance). The critical three weeks to formal transition were about soldiering with maps, missions, unit capabilities, rules of engagement, reporting, and a host of other issues that taxed our professional knowledge at every level from platoon to brigade to division. It would not be long before our duties would reach beyond the division staff and into military/diplomatic affairs. I looked forward to getting the staff to where I could get back in the field and fulfill my duties at the tactical level. It was why I had hoped to get to a division but, for now, my team and I were welcome in the MND Headquarters where we were genuinely needed. Professional knowledge was important; we had shown we were qualified military professionals. We also understood we had a diplomatic mission as well.

National recognition days like America's Independence Day on the Fourth of July are major events in the multinational environment. The celebrations or observances conducted by the respective contingents are a matter of pride and honor. Attendance by senior officers is expected; with that in mind, I boarded a Polish Mi-8 (NATO name *Hip*) helicopter on 23 August for an hour-and-a-half-long flight to Al-Kut, some one hundred miles southeast of Baghdad, on the far eastern flank of the division's AOR, to attend the National Day observance of Ukraine. Also on board was the assistant G-4, Colonel Dula Hautzinger of Hungary, the senior Ukrainian contingent commander and deputy commanding general for force protection, Major General (one-star equivalent) Antoliy Sobora, and several Polish officers. Looking at everyone during the flight, it struck me that for nearly twenty years my contemporaries and I had diligently studied and trained our minds and bodies to battle the Warsaw Pact and defeat its forces in detail on the plains of Europe or anywhere else they might challenge us. Flying in a Russian-built helicopter in the company of Poles, Hungarians, and Ukrainians, all of whom conversed in Russian, made my head spin. I could not help shaking my head and smiling to myself once again. It was a scene as surreal as those mini-skirted girls and the party I returned to one evening in Baghdad after a reconnaissance mission last June. My tours of duty with the United Nations in Iraq and Somalia, and the Multinational Force and Observers experience in the Sinai, had provided some exposure to Russians and Eastern Europeans, but nothing like this. The world had changed and the force of it all was now totally in my face. Over the next several months, these guys would become my best friends. General Sobora would become a brother.

The air base at Al-Kut had been a significant facility for Saddam's air force with its immense tarmac and landing strip. The U.S. Air Force had not certified the nearly 10,000-foot strip for large transport aircraft, but the Ukrainians were comfortable with routinely landing their Russian-built transport aircraft to deliver national supplies. Nearby Polish helicopters were in direct support of the Ukrainian brigade and the aviation detachment commander greeted General Tyszkiewicz and our party along with the Ukrainian brigade commander, Major General Sergei Bezluschenko. A long line of vehicles accommodated our move to the brigade cantonment area where several lines of white canvas tents, porto-johns, and shower trailers set the area apart from the looted and otherwise run down, decrepit buildings we had passed during the drive. These temporary facilities serviced 1,600 men of the 6th Ukrainian Mechanized Brigade and its attached reinforced company of paratroopers. Regardless of how far we got from Baghdad, it was clear the Iraqi people had not spared any facility that once served the vaunted Iraqi military. Plans were being made to refurbish the barracks and selected other structures but, in August 2003, tentage provided the headquarters, barracks, and messing facilities for the officers and men of this fine combat brigade. We were quickly given a billeting assignment for the night but, as I moved to my designated tent, General Tyszkiewicz motioned to me to come with him.

"Roland, you will stay with me and General Sobora in the general's quarters."

I thanked the general. I was honored to be invited, but my Cold War mentality could not help me from thinking that it was also a good way to keep a close eye on their "Amerikanskyi Colonel." The brigade commander's quarters also served as both his office and conference space. A large desk and living room-like furniture provided a comfortable setting. I placed my gear and weapons by a large, soft couch. There was plenty of daylight left and I thought about getting out and looking around as the generals conversed in Russian; I could only sit, smile, drink tea, and contemplate my escape. General Tyszkiewicz smiled at me as I worked the action of my assault rifle to pass the time. He said it was time to go, but I didn't have a clue where we were going. Always with a smile, he asked me, "Roland, is your rifle ready for combat?"

I smiled back and replied simply, "Yes, my General, it longs for action."

General Tyszkiewicz laughed, "Ah, but first we must prepare. Come, we go to hear the Ukrainian brigade's plan to command their area of operations."

We moved to the operations tent where a briefing area had been prepared, including a series of large operations maps that covered the Al-Kut area north to the vicinity of the town of Al-Suwaira and east to the Iranian border. The Ukrainians patrolled 142 kilometers of a porous avenue the Iranians used to enter Iraq and move to the Polish and Spanish-patrolled holy cities of Kerbelâ' and Al-Najaf. General Bezluschenko presented the command briefing in Ukrainian with his entire staff and principal subordinate commanders present. General Tyszkiewicz assumed the role of translator and spoke to me throughout the briefing to ensure I was included. I was very appreciative of this and listened intently as I studied the military graphics that divided the Ukrainian area of operations into manageable unit sectors. I wanted to pick up at least one point that could make a positive difference in their operations while simultaneously impressing them with my tactical acumen. I thought it was important to strike early and impress the Ukrainians with what I could bring to the table. I found it!

The Ukrainians had outlined a superb plan for patrolling and stabilizing their area of responsibility. They had not thought, however, to link their Quick Reaction Force (QRF), a company-sized element of about 100 men ready to move on short notice to address any contingency, to their attached Polish aviation element. Following the general's briefing, General Tyszkiewicz asked me to comment on the brigade's plan. It was a sincere request and I stood up in front of the hardest-looking group of men I had ever seen. There was not a smile in the place. I thought it best to extol the virtues of the plan and finish with a recommendation that would warrant further consideration. Words are important. The last thing an adviser needs to do is turn off his target audience with unbalanced criticism. In this situation, it was not hard to do. It was a proud, tough crowd. The Ukrainian plan made excellent use of the brigade's available manpower and ground transport. It addressed security concerns and task organized the command in what appeared to be a well thought out and responsible manner. I limited myself to the aviation matter, pointing out the efficiencies gained by creating an aviation-infantry task force to facilitate command, control, and communications should the QRF need to deploy by air. I further added that the development of such relationships between air and ground units had been very common in my experience in the American 101st Airborne Division, a unit with which they were very familiar from their Cold War days. My comments generated a series of exchanges in Ukrainian as I stood silently not understanding a word. Finally, in a great moment of relief, General Bezluschenko smiled at me and nodded. General Tyszkiewicz laughed as he stood up, put his arm around me, and, in a booming voice, said, "It is an excellent idea, Roland! You see, they like you already."

Suddenly, everyone was smiling. The Polish aviation commander, Colonel Darius Kostrzewa, thanked me for my comments. General Sobora managed a rare smile, muttered something to me in Ukrainian, and shook my hand. I was happily surprised by the difference a few well-placed comments and recommendations could make with this tough crowd.

I did not venture far from the general's or the operations tents. Lunch and dinner were served by Ukrainian soldiers who arrived with paper plates covered in silver foil. A warrant officer always stood by us at the rigid position of parade rest and was quick to fill an empty glass with a cold drink. The conversation was in Russian in deference to General Tyszkiewicz who spoke fluent Russian as opposed to the similar, but different Ukrainian. He would translate from time to time when he sensed my discomfort at being left out of the conversation. At nightfall, I once again checked and oiled my weapon as General Tyszkiewicz looked at me and shook his head. I never really sensed that he understood my interest in weapons or desire to operate with his battalions, but I knew that good soldierly habits are respected in every army. I always slept easier knowing my equipment and weapons were combat ready. In Al-Kut at that time, I was only one of a handful of Americans in the immediate vicinity and I was yet to bond with the Ukrainian troopers who guarded our base camp. I carefully tucked my 9-mm pistol under my pillow and fell asleep.

Daylight in Al-Kut brought the usual morning sounds and activities a soldier would expect to hear in a troop area: officers and sergeants barking orders; troops scrambling from one detail to the next; formations marching and running; and guys returning from the showers and porto-johns. The arrival of more dignitaries had every leader in the brigade checking for trash and unkempt areas. It all swirled around me as I headed toward latrine row. Standing at parade rest by one shower trailer was our stoic warrant officer. When he saw me, he pointed toward the trailer, pulled out a set of keys and unlocked the door. Only the best for the brigade's senior officers and guests, I assumed. It is not unusual for armies to maintain separate facilities for its officers. In my traditional military mind, I thought it was the right thing to do. Officers are best not placed in informal settings and in various modes of dress where they may not be recognized. Liberties taken by the troops in these situations could be viewed as breaches of discipline. Since I had arrived in Iraq, however, separate accommodations had not been practical. At Camp Babylon, there were crowds of soldiers and officers of all ranks who vied for a position to shave and shower every morning. In the Ukrainian Army, an officer is highly regarded, and extra efforts are made to separate the ranks.

I looked forward to the National Day ceremonies. A military review was scheduled, including the brigade's home-grown brass band. It was not uncommon in the Ukrainian Army to issue instruments to talented, trainable soldiers or experienced musicians in the ranks. In a short period of time, they are expected to learn a few appropriate martial tunes and serve as the unit band. What a concept, I thought. Ukrainian National Day was a major event with visiting Lieutenant General Petrok and the Iraqi Governor of Wasit Province in attendance. Ukrainian presence on the world stage in Iraq made the event even more important. The band would have to out-do itself.

General Tyszkiewicz led his group of officers and a host of local Iraqi dignitaries to a reviewing stand; I quietly took a place far to their rear. There were only a couple of rows of seats and I was happy to stand. The sound of the brigade's band initiated the ceremony and the troops looked as regimental as any I had seen as they marched to their place in front of the reviewing stand. Unfazed by the hot August sun, the troops stood at parade rest while they listened to speeches by Generals Petrok and Tyszkiewicz and the governor. Following his remarks, General Tyszkiewicz turned and motioned to me to come forward. I could not believe it!

"Roland, it would be very nice if you spoke to our Ukrainian soldiers as the American representative to their National Day celebration. You should not speak very long, just a few appropriate remarks."

It was an order and once again I was reminded that a senior American officer in any venue can "fill a room" and be called upon to speak on any subject at a moment's notice. I grabbed an English-speaking Ukrainian officer named Andriy Lischynskyi, the brigade commander's interpreter who I had met the previous evening. Andriy was a sharp soldier whose angular good looks and huge muscular frame reminded me of Dolph Lundgren as "Drago," the Russian boxing champion in Sylvester Stallone's blockbuster movie *Rocky IV*. I told Andriy in no uncertain terms he was to translate my remarks exactly as I said them. The gentle giant nodded with a smile and calmly replied he would do the very best he could. General Tyszkiewicz introduced me as his American adviser and the principal American representative to the National Day ceremonies. My feelings at that point were an odd mix of pride, nervousness, and confidence in my abilities to handle any situation. Failure is not an option when you suddenly find yourself representing the entire United States of America. After recognizing the leading figures on the reviewing stand, I turned to the troops on parade and said, "It is an honor to stand with you in support of this important mission in Iraq. The world is proud of you, and I know you will acquit yourself well in combat in the finest traditions of your predecessors in the Great Patriotic War. On behalf of the American people, I wish you good luck on your mission, and offer my sincere congratulations and best wishes on your National Day."

There is nothing that stirs the blood of the peoples of the former Soviet Union quite like a reference to their nation's sacrifice and heroism in World War II. Turning from the podium, I was greeted with loud applause and the smiling face of the stoic General Petrok who vigorously shook my hand. I had hit a "home run" and as the troops passed in review the claps on my back by my Polish and Ukrainian "comrades" made me feel like a "million bucks." The long helo ride back to Babylon did not seem half as long as our trip out the day before. Things were beginning to look good even as the challenges of the impending transition of authority from the Marines stared the division, and all of us with anything to do with it, in our collective faces.

Now less than a week away from accepting responsibility for its mission, the commanding general sent representatives from the staff to all the division's assigned units to assess readiness and make final preparations. The commander's concerns focused squarely on force protection, placing General Sobora in the forefront of the action. He summoned me to his office and asked me to accompany him on an inspection tour of the division's units and key installations. In al-Hillah and Camp Babylon, Polish and Romanian engineers were improving barracks, clearing refuse, and installing wire and concrete barriers. The division was rich in engineers, but in stability operations you can never have enough of them. In addition to Poland and Romania, Slovakia, Thailand, and Mongolia contributed engineer platoons to our diverse force. The demands on their talents and skills were nearly overwhelming, particularly given the priority on force-protection projects. Their hard work and dedication to the mission impressed the entire command. The Slovaks were true combat engineers who cleared mines and were experts with explosives. The Mongolians built walls with sandbags and eventually bunkered the entire headquarters. Sandbagging is tough work, a lost science in many Western armies that, when done correctly, provides excellent barriers. The Thais and the Romanians were vertical construction experts. When I compared my poor, but adequate plywood hut to the sturdy construction of the quarters the Romanians had built to house themselves at Camp Babylon, I could not help being impressed, and very envious.

In the city of Kerbelâ', the Bulgarian battalion under the command of Lieutenant Colonel Petko Marinov was gaining valuable experience and confidence. They had already come under mortar fire and there had been a roadside bombing of one of their vehicles. Fortunately, there had been no casualties. Their Marine mentors worked closely with their leadership and earlier Bulgarian complaints that the Polish brigade did not care about them and provided inadequate support were clearly behind them. Bulgarian force-protection concerns had been largely addressed, but the standoff distance from the secured entrance to their cantonment area to the public road that ran parallel to it was nowhere near adequate. Efforts to mitigate the lack of standoff could only go so far. Much like my experience in Baṣrah with the New Iraqi Army recruiting facility, they would have to do.

Visitors to the high-profile MND were common. Helicopters in Iraq were a high-priced and rare commodity, but the arrival of Romanian Minister of Defense Ioan Mircea Paşcu on 26 August merited a large U.S. CH-47 Chinook. General Tyszkiewicz and I were on hand for the minister's arrival as the helicopter landed in the Romanian cantonment area and caused a major "brownout" from the blowing sands. The minister's entourage created quite a stir in other ways. In addition to his wife and defense officials and staffers were several good-looking young ladies who received a considerable amount of attention from their Romanian countrymen. One female journalist was particularly "interested" in the American colonel; General Tyszkiewicz, always the gentleman, insisted I serve as her escort. I cannot say I wasn't flattered; the photographers had a ball taking pictures of us. These well-intended distractions from our work were politically and diplomatically essential to the continued support of many countries that contributed troops to the Coalition and the MND. The minister was genuinely interested in the welfare of his soldiers and the division's work. He had a particular interest in communications, and we briefly discussed the characteristics and strengths of HF and VHF radios. His technical questions to the division staff about the reliability of our tactical communications were answered with "deafening silence." I waited a few seconds and, absent any comment, simply said that in my nearly ten years of service in the Central Region, redundant communications had proven essential in view of the extreme heat and its effects on our systems. Both HF and VHF are good systems, but the impact of the operational environment on one or both at any given time dictated we operate with both capabilities. The minister acknowledged my comments and thanked me. General Tyszkiewicz appeared very pleased.

Escorting dignitaries came with the job; it included conducting briefings, sipping cool drinks, and responding to questions that ran the gamut from troop morale and welfare to combat operations. The CJTF-7 staff was understandably frustrated by the need to provide aircraft and we received many irate phone calls from the C-3 (Operations) section at Camp Victory to do what we could to turn the visits off. I do not think they understood how much we dreaded these visits but, regardless of how demanding and stressful they were, each one was executed with maximum effort and professionalism. With so much work to do and the transition of authority only days away, all of us wished there was a way to turn the visits off. We always responded that we would try, but everyone knew these events were inevitable, important, and inescapable. Ultimately, it was worth the cost of maintaining international interest and support to our mission. The senior officers on the staff understood that. The visits were not all bad and could even be fun, particularly when you got to escort beautiful women.

Regardless of the difficulties and distractions, the Polish and Ukrainian brigade areas of operation were ready for transition of authority by the end of August. Trouble in the Spanish and Latin American sectors, however, threatened to torpedo the division's reputation, operational readiness, and ability to complete the transition. The next several weeks were painful.

Captain Owens, Captain Loman, Colonel Tiso, and Captain Reed.

With an El Salvador platoon following a patrol in Al-Najaf, December 2003, shortly after the announcement of Saddam's capture.

CHAPTER 18

The Challenges of Multinational Command

Advisers have to be empathetic to their counterparts and understand their culture while being honest about the units and their leaders.

—Lieutenant Colonel James Willbanks, USA

The Polish and Ukrainian brigades had deployed to Iraq for the purpose of conducting peacekeeping and stability operations. They could conduct limited combat operations, but they were not nearly as robust or capable as American formations. They could shoot, move, communicate, and sustain themselves to a limited degree. The Ukrainians had their armored personnel carriers but neither brigade had artillery or any substantive indirect-fire assets. The Soviet-built Polish helicopters were sorely lacking anti-missile defenses. Armament on the large Mi-8s was limited to door guns. The United States had committed several units and assets to back up the Multinational Division (MND) including a battalion of military police, air medical-evacuation support, a communications company, and considerable transportation assets. It could all be summed up as the cost of diplomatic and political credibility that comes with waging Coalition warfare as well as an effort to facilitate operations and reinforce vulnerabilities. By the end of August, however, it was evident the American military had not done enough to facilitate the division's operational effectiveness.

On 27 August, the MND staff received a report from Brigadier General Cardona, the commander of the Spanish brigade, that the Latin American battalions (El Salvador, Honduras, and the Dominican Republic) and the Nicaraguan detachment were non-mission capable and transition of authority (TOA) in Al-Najaf by 3 September was unlikely. The ramifications of this report prompted as much consternation and gnashing of teeth as a major enemy breakthrough of a critical defensive position. Efforts to address General Cardona's concerns were made immediately and several members of the division staff, under the leadership of Spanish Director of Operations Colonel Cabeza, flew to Al-Najaf on the 28th. I had planned to go as well, but was informed, when I arrived at the airstrip at the specified time, that the aircraft had already departed. The Polish G-3, Colonel Gozul, later told me Colonel Cabeza was not comfortable with having another member of the staff present for this mission. I had already sensed the proud Spaniard had grown uncomfortable with my relationship with the commanding general. I respected his decision to leave me behind, though I quietly resented being deceived. Putting myself in his position, however, I thought having a little "space" to act independently of the command group or its senior adviser was a good thing. Someone had to get to the bottom of this problem and sort it out. Solving the TOA challenge would be a major coup for the director of operations and a tremendous boost to his credibility. Javier Cabeza wanted the credit; no one wanted him to have it more than I did. A good adviser seeks to promote confidence in the people with whom he serves. I decided to let it go and talk to Javier when he returned to gain his perspective on the problem and, if he was amenable, discuss solutions and offer my assistance. There were other issues to work. The challenges facing the division were growing substantially.

By the late summer of 2003, the developing insurgency facing the Americans in Baghdad and northern Iraq was beginning to make itself felt in the MND's area of responsibility. Shortly after returning to the operations tent, Captain Lowman informed me the Ukrainian brigade had been ordered to search and clear three weapons caches reported in and around the city of Al-Kut. The mission did not strike us as particularly difficult, but whether it constituted a combat mission commensurate with Ukrainian rules of engagement was an issue. With both Colonels Cabeza and Gozul at Spanish Brigade Headquarters in ad-Dīwānīyah, several junior members of the division operations staff were pleading with the Ukrainian brigade operations officer (S-3) to accept and execute the mission before nightfall. The absence of helicopters that would enable us to fly to Al-Kut quickly put a damper on any thoughts I had about going there. Captain Lowman suggested we rewrite the order and put the mission in the context of a stability operation consistent with Ukrainian national guidance. It was not as simple as it might seem, but it reinforced our understanding that words are important, and that missions and tasks had to be properly written to deal with national sensitivities. Instead of obvious offensive language like "attack to seize or destroy …," a more palatable mission could be "Patrol the following sectors or sites, report suspicious activities, and seize contraband." Working with his multinational counterparts, Lowman edited the mission statement, and a reworked and finessed order was passed to the Ukrainians. The mission was quickly accepted, and we were thrilled to learn several hours later that the three sites had been cleared and several rifles and grenades captured. The power of the pen in this case had made possible the power of the Ukrainian sword. The operations officers and we advisers had learned a good lesson, but in the grand scheme of things it was a pyrrhic victory, a mere sideshow compared to the developing challenge of a timely transition of authority of the division's Spanish brigade area of responsibility.

The Spanish commanders and the division staff had tasked the Latin American commanders to assess their requirements and shortages, but there had been no definitive report submitted and verified at the end of August. General Miller was at the end of his patience. He informed me in no uncertain terms and angry tones on the evening of 30 August that he was sending an assessment team to my location with the expressed purpose of obtaining "ground truth" on what we needed to move forward. I could not blame him; I sensed his displeasure with me. I was there to provide more than liaison and advice and I had come up short on this issue. General Miller expected me to influence decisions even if the actions required to do that were well above what could be reasonably expected. Lieutenant Colonel Sean MacFarland flew into Camp Babylon the next day with two highly coveted UH-60 Black Hawk helicopters and wasted no time in informing me the C-3 did not intend to waste any more time on "rumor." He was there to gather the facts and make recommendations to the C-3 that would ensure a total transition from the Marines to the MND in a timely manner. His meeting with Colonel Gozul produced nothing of any substance. The Latin Americans had not produced a report of any real value and he could add very little to what had already been said about their readiness. MacFarland was livid, but in a calm, measured voice he asked me to accompany him to Al-Najaf where he had coordinated a meeting with Lieutenant Colonel Woodbridge, commander of the 1st Battalion, 7th Marines, and the commanders of the Honduran and El Salvadoran battalions. I agreed to go, but I did not think the meeting would be productive and I told him so. The key to the transition was convincing the Spanish commander to proceed with it and I reiterated he was determined not to move before the Latin Americans were fully equipped. Sean knew I was right. I thought his mission was intended to send a message that the Combined Joint Task Force-7 (CJTF-7) commander was growing impatient with his MND's failure to act more than anything else.

The 30-minute flight to Al-Najaf, followed by the usual sandstorm and "brownout" upon landing in the 120-degree temperature, was enough to make anyone want to lay down and call it a day. Lieutenant Colonel Woodbridge and a handful of Marines were standing by to greet us. Lieutenant Colonels Carlos Andino of Honduras and Santiago Monterrozza of El Salvador greeted us when we entered the Marine Battalion Headquarters. The cordial greetings and professional courtesies aside, it was clear the meeting would go nowhere. Neither commander was prepared to discuss a definitive list of requirements, but shortfalls of several types of communications equipment were identified in our discussions. These and other items of equipment had supposedly been promised to Honduras and El Salvador in a predeployment agreement but had not been provided. At one point, both commanders indicated they could assume responsibility for their battalion sectors. The mixed signals seemed to point to Spanish Brigade Headquarters at ad-Dīwānīyah; it was clearly all over Monterrozza's face. The Latin American commanders were very professional and proud of their units. They did not care for the attention they were getting about the transition issue or anything else that would cast aspersions on the efficiency or pride of their units or their countries. Colonel Monterrozza was a particularly tough soldier. His command of English and physical fitness spoke well of his special forces background. He had seen action as a young officer in his nation's civil war. The facts were not totally clear, but the deplorable conditions under which the Latin American soldiers lived in their recently occupied barracks and base camps spoke volumes about what they had been promised and what CJTF-7 was yet to deliver. In my view, the absence of General Cardona or the Spanish brigade commander's representative made our discussions a waste of time, effort, and assets. MacFarland had a few notes to take back to Camp Victory, and we ended our meeting cordially, but not a word was said during our flight back to Camp Babylon. Everyone knew the problem was far from solved.

Equipment requirements for the MND were slowly making their way to the Marines who were hard-pressed to respond. They fully expected to return to their home bases with all their assigned equipment. The snag in achieving transition of authority in Al-Najaf did nothing to enhance the reputation of the MND and the resentment was beginning to show both at CJTF-7 Headquarters and, particularly, at 1st Marine Expeditionary Force (IMEF) Headquarters. Everyone was polite and courteous, but it was difficult for the Marines to hold their sentiments back from me. Colonel J. C. Coleman, a proud and distinguished infantryman serving as the IMEF chief of staff, held several lists of equipment requirements and told me each was different and increasingly demanding. Some effort had been made to provide some communications equipment from excess stock, but the proud Marines were not willing to provide items at the expense of their own combat readiness. J. C. was a gentleman and particularly respectful of me. A Virginia Military Institute graduate of the class of 1976, he had been a fourth classman during my first-class, or senior, year. Our discussions were always courteous, but I knew that his and the Marine command group's frustration level was high. What was not clear, however, was what IMEF was doing to address the MND's requirements through the chain of command. I was not convinced the Marines took a sympathetic and helpful view of the division's situation, nor did I think they voiced any serious concern to CJTF-7 about the operational deficiencies these shortfalls of equipment potentially represented to the division's ability to achieve mission success. Perhaps unfairly, I sensed in their zest to redeploy the same selfishness and lack of teamplay that characterized the Army's reluctant support of the New Iraqi Army project. General Conway, the IMEF commander, was particularly displeased a CJTF-7 representative had met with one of his battalion commanders. The "House of Angst" could not have been unhappier as it began to draw up plans for continued operations in Al-Najaf and adjust redeployment schedules for the 1st Battalion, 7th Marines, and its supporting elements. The frustration at CJTF-7 was evident in the phone calls I received from General Miller and members of the CJTF-7 operations staff pressing me and the liaison team to find a solution.

It was clear the CJTF-7 command group would have to accept a delay in transitioning responsibility in the Latin American sectors and that a battalion of

Marines and its support elements would have to remain in place until a solution could be found. Four days after the ceremony activating the MND and its acceptance of command of its area of responsibility minus Al-Najaf, Marine Brigadier General John F. Kelly, General Kwiatkowski, Ambassador Krystosik (the division political adviser), and I flew to Al-Najaf to meet with representatives from the Spanish brigade and the Latin American commanders. The generals inspected the battalions' garrison facilities and, much like I had noted a week before, saw first-hand the deplorable conditions in which these soldiers lived. The absence of air conditioning, the overcrowding of the barracks' open bays (upwards of forty men with nothing more than an Army cot), and filthy, unserviced porto-johns was as disappointing as it was dangerously unhealthy. Kellogg Brown & Root contract engineers and builders were working to improve the camps, but there was no doubt in anyone's mind that living conditions were poor by any standard. Neither Colonel Andino nor Monterrozza expressed a need for equipment, but Andino told us his battalion required another week of reconnaissance and familiarity with his area of operations. The generals and I returned to Babylon empty handed. The equipment issue remained unresolved and, later that evening, General Cardona told General Tyszkiewicz that transition of authority in Al-Najaf was not possible under the current circumstances.

The Al-Najaf problem added to the feverish pace of activity in the MND Headquarters as final arrangements for the transition of authority were made. The change-of-command ceremony was scheduled for 3 September. Our liaison team monitored every development and issue in the division headquarters and, not surprisingly, we were also pinged to provide other data as well. The office of the CJTF-7 chief of staff (Brigadier General Hahn) requested talking points concerning positive points and challenges about the MND. Division Chief of Staff Colonel Zdzisław Antczak requested talking points to provide Polish Deputy Division Commander General Kwiatkowski for a meeting scheduled with local Iraqi leaders on the same day as the change-of-authority ceremony. The division commander asked me to review and edit his remarks for the ceremony. These tasks and a growing number of reports to CJTF-7 Headquarters required considerable work, but our efforts were appreciated by CJTF-7, the division command group, and most of the staff. Each report required meticulous care about style and wording. I was genuinely concerned about the division's credibility in view of the Al-Najaf issue. The commanding general's credibility was dependent in large measure on flawlessly prepared and delivered remarks and briefings. Reports and PowerPoint slides required substantial review and editing for content and proper English. Our frequent reference to "Polish English" always drew laughter from our Coalition counterparts, but everyone acknowledged the need to check and recheck word usage and ensure professional presentations. The hours of work per day grew longer.

Our small American liaison team had a major boost on 1 September when a contingent of officers and noncommissioned officers from the Illinois National

Guard arrived at Camp Babylon. The Illinois Guard had a training relationship with the Polish Army. The great state of Illinois, and particularly the Chicago area, has a large population of Americans of Polish descent. Several of the guardsmen were conversant in Polish. Unlike my liaison team, the guardsmen were officially assigned as embedded members of the MND staff. They were assigned to every staff section including operations, logistics, and intelligence. Colonel Terry Downem, a veteran Guard officer with over 35 years of service, was assigned as the deputy chief of staff with focus on the Division Logistics (G-4) Section. Terry was older than me, soft spoken, and steady. I welcomed him to my plywood hut. Our duty hours were significantly different, but I was happy to have a roommate with whom I could talk from time to time. He seemed like a good guy and I admired him and the other Illinois guardsmen for their patriotism and readiness to serve. I thought their presence might allow my liaison team to leave the division headquarters every now and then and spend time with the infantry in the field. It was a nice, but overly optimistic, thought.

The impressive ceremony that officially transferred authority of the Central-South area of responsibility from the IMEF to the Multinational Division (Central-South) was conducted in the massive amphitheater at Camp Babylon on 3 September. Our small airstrip was the busiest airport in Iraq that morning as a host of military and civilian dignitaries, including nearly every general who had access to a helicopter, flew in for the show. The stage was adorned with the colors of 23 nations whose forces comprised the division at that time, and the V Corps band was on hand to provide appropriate honors and entertainment. General Sanchez, Commander CJTF-7, presided over the ceremony and Generals Conway and Tyszkiewicz signed documents officially acknowledging the transition of authority. His remarks highlighted the ceremony as a key step in the continuing development of security and stability throughout Iraq. The MND would be a major factor in helping the Iraqi people rebuild their country and create an environment conducive to the establishment of a free and democratic Iraq. General Tyszkiewicz reiterated that the purpose of his division was to create conditions conducive to the reestablishment of civil order and democratic rule, to coordinate and provide military assistance and support for humanitarian organizations, and to assist local civilian authorities to maintain law and order. His remarks were delivered in an exceptionally crisp and proud manner. He had practiced his delivery the previous evening, reading his remarks aloud and having me critique his pronunciation. He had learned to speak English only 10 years before this moment, but his slow and deliberate delivery was brilliant. He was complimentary of the Marines who he cited as his "Division's mentors." Following the benediction by Major General Glodz, the Polish field bishop, and the playing of the Polish Army Song and the Marine Hymn, the flag bearers and generals marched off the stage. General Tyszkiewicz reached for my hand as he walked off and thanked me for my assistance. He was a man anyone could easily admire, but I knew he would be sorely tested in the coming months. The insurgency was growing to our north and it appeared likely to engulf the entire country. I took note of the ceremony's program that provided the following quote from George Washington:

> The moment is critical, the opportunity precious, the prospect most favorable.

The quote could not have been more appropriate. Iraq was a long way from being stabilized and the work to be done was enormous. I walked away from the ceremony consumed by thoughts of the failures and frustrations of the summer in Baghdad and wondered just how favorable Iraq's prospects really were.

The day had barely passed when one of the MND's major weaknesses became blatantly obvious. A few days before the change-of-command ceremony, Ayatollah Mohammed Baqir al-Hakim, a highly respected Shia cleric, had been gunned down in Al-Najaf by gunmen allegedly operating under the orders of Muqtadā aṣ-Ṣadr, a young, fiercely anti-American Shia cleric. Muqtadā aṣ-Ṣadr was the son of the famous Grand Ayatollah Mohammed-Sadiq al-Sadr who had been assassinated by Saddam Hussein's gunmen in 1999. An Iraqi warrant for aṣ-Ṣadr's arrest had previously been issued for the murder of a moderate Shia leader named Abdul-Majid al-Khoei in April 2003. American and Iraqi authorities concluded aṣ-Ṣadr, barely thirty years old and lacking years of religious training required of senior ranking Shia leaders, was simply eliminating his competitors. He would become a subject of immense controversy and his disregard for the Coalition and the Iraqi Interim Government would lead to a major battle in Al-Najaf between his Madhi Army militia and American and Iraqi forces in April 2004. At the present, however, there was little the MND's units in Al-Najaf could do, or were willing to do, about aṣ-Ṣadr or his militia.

The MND's immediate challenge was to escort a bus convoy of Ayatollah al-Hakim mourners from the Iranian border to Al-Najaf. The mission itself was not particularly difficult, but the Ukrainian brigade had national orders not to cross its brigade boundaries. The division staff had to coordinate a link up at a designated contact point at the boundary dividing the Ukrainian-garrisoned Wasit Province and the Spanish-controlled Al-Qadisiyah Province where the convoy would be handed over to the Spanish for final transport to Al-Najaf. It was well after nightfall when the Ukrainians finally arrived at the coordinated contact point. Confusion reigned as the two units attempted to link up without communications, a standard operating procedure, and the difficulties their vastly different languages must have presented. The operation took several hours longer to complete than we would have normally expected. Planning the movement had been poor from the beginning and reporting from the convoys to their respective brigade headquarters, and subsequently to the Division Tactical Operations Center (TOC), was nonexistent or poor at best. It was obvious the division was far from combat ready. I was particularly concerned about its ability to command and control its brigades. Clearly, the lead time to coordinate any operation in a multinational organization would be significantly greater than a homogenous American or British one.

In my report to General Hahn's office on 1 September regarding five weaknesses and strengths of the MND, I noted the following:

a. Cross boundary movement by the maneuver brigades is prohibited.
b. Rules of engagement are not standardized in the division.
c. Tactical communications are poor.
d. English comprehension is limited.
e. Night operations are limited by inadequate numbers of night-vision devices.

These weaknesses and others had serious readiness implications for a division involved in peacekeeping or combat operations. I reported these weaknesses to General Miller as well, emphasizing that unreliable communications at both brigade and division headquarters, coupled with national restrictions on maneuver beyond brigade boundaries, deprived the division commander of the ability to task organize his division for contingency operations and to effectively command and control complex operations of any kind. In fact, the only troops at his disposal to maneuver were the Poles. Recognizing his limitations, General Tyszkiewicz wisely maintained a Polish company in reserve at Camp Babylon that he could employ anywhere in his area of responsibility. The dearth of sophisticated weapons and fire-control items such as night-vision devices, heavy direct-fire weapons, armored vehicles, indirect-fire assets, and poor or noncompatible communications equipment was challenging enough in the division, but the austerity of modern combat equipment in the Latin American battalions was particularly bad. Tactical communications and transport stood out as the predominant shortfalls that immediately impacted their ability to perform the most fundamental tasks.

General Tyszkiewicz was well aware of these readiness challenges. During our daily meetings, he would share his thoughts on the difficulty of "multinationality" in military operations. He was painfully aware the deployment of every national contingent was subject to what he referred to as a "Delicate balance of military necessity, political maneuver, and international diplomacy." There was not a day that he did not take a call from a high-ranking government official or general from one or several countries with troops in the MND who wanted to demonstrate their interest and caring for their nation's soldiers. General Tyszkiewicz was understandably stressed by each call and he was quick to tell me any misunderstanding could have a negative effect on the future of that national contingent's deployment in Iraq. He could ill afford to take a hard stance on most issues or appear as bellicose as the American commanders. The failure to transition authority in Al-Najaf bothered him immensely, but he could not risk alienating the Spanish by pushing them to do anything before their units were ready or conditions allowed. He opined on several occasions that the Spanish commander had received national guidance from Madrid to delay the transition and he had to manage the situation, "Very delicately." General Tyszkiewicz was a very loyal and dedicated commander. He wanted to satisfy General Sanchez and the CJTF-7 staff, as well as any American division commander, but he was steadfast in his belief the Americans did not fully understand the challenges of his fragile division. He was clear that, if American intent was to keep an international face on Operation *Iraqi Freedom*, far more attention needed to be paid to each nation's requirements and concerns. He said it was particularly important we respect the conditions under which each contingent agreed to deploy. Combat operations were not in their equation and, as the situation in Iraq continued to worsen, General Tyszkiewicz knew his decisions and actions regarding direct combat with insurgents or former regime elements would be questioned by the Americans and 22 other nations, including his own.

Brigadier General Kelly had been given command of the Marine units that remained in place pending Spanish acceptance of authority in Al-Najaf. He appreciated the difficulty of commanding an MND. His friendly relationship with General Tyszkiewicz and their previous assignment together in NATO had made him the perfect choice to command the small Marine brigade in Al-Najaf while the bulk of IMEF redeployed to their bases in the United States. By 8 September, however, American patience was running low. The issue had risen to the four-star level. General Sanchez had discussed the matter with the Central Command's commander, General Abizaid, who was scheduled to visit Camp Babylon and the MND on 14 September. On 9 September, a report from Spanish Brigade Headquarters, signed by Brigadier General Cardona, provided yet another required list of items including vehicles, communications, and navigational aids that his Latin American battalions required to operate with an acceptable level of efficiency and readiness. The changes in both numbers and types of requested items infuriated the Marines. A solution had to be found that would provide command and control of the three Latin American battalions and allow them to take charge of their areas of operation in the event the Spanish refused command even after some or all the equipment demands were met. An option the MND staff offered was to form a command-and-control element with vehicular-mounted tactical communications, several additional operations officers, and a senior officer as the ad hoc brigade commander. It was further suggested a TOC and small battle staff be established at either the Honduran or El Salvadoran base camps. No one thought the solution would fly diplomatically but, in the absence of a decision, the division staff was obligated to develop courses of action should the division commander ask for them. The situation only got worse with time and the absence of any positive movement.

On 12 September, the Honduran and El Salvadoran commanders reported a dire shortage of medical supplies. These reports, coupled with angry reports from CJTF-7 Headquarters that General Sanchez intended to order a transition of authority in Al-Najaf on 21 September and false reports (allegedly from CNN) that elements of the MND were under enemy fire and engaged in combat operations, caused an unusual level of stress in the Division Operations Center. There had been no reports of combat activity of any kind at this point in time. Late that afternoon, General Tyszkiewicz invited me and General Kwiatkowski to his office to discuss the division's challenges and possible solutions. Our discussions immediately turned to the problem in Al-Najaf. I was not aware he had already ordered General Kwiatkowski to go to Spanish Headquarters in ad-Dīwānīyah to sort out the Al-Najaf problem when I proposed we confront the Spanish and Latin American commanders about their requirements at General Cardona's headquarters. The general smiled:

"It is an excellent idea, Roland. You will accompany General Kwiatkowski tomorrow to ad-Dīwānīyah and solve this problem once and for all, okay."

It occurred to me the good general had this planned all along. I smiled and suggested he tell General Sanchez of his intent to send a team to ad-Dīwānīyah and that a report of its findings would follow. We had to quash the rumors that CJTF-7 thought we were ignoring the problem and doing nothing. He agreed and made a note to include it in his TACSAT report to General Sanchez.

The tactical satellite (TACSAT) report was the commanding general's daily operations report to the CJTF-7 commander. It was normally conducted on or about 6 pm and was preceded by the brigade commanders' reports to the division commander. Communications were always "touch and go" and General Tyszkiewicz would normally have his American and Polish signal officers by his side to address any technical failure. If one radio or phone would not function, we would quickly move to another system. One of the more effective systems we had was the Polish Storcik telephone. It was superior to the American phone system in clarity of voice and overall reliability, a small point about which the commanding general took great pleasure.

"Roland, you see we Poles have a few items of equipment that are even superior to the American equipment."

His comments never failed to include a smile or a good laugh. Good communications in Iraq were a blessing for which every commander prayed. The extreme heat and other environmental factors often wreaked havoc on everything from simple tactical radios to sophisticated satellite systems. I described communications to the commanding general as a "Crap shoot. Sometimes we win, general, and sometimes we lose. The idea was not to lose when it was absolutely critical, when you needed fire support, and when you were talking to your boss."

Communications challenges in the MND, however, went above and beyond its equipment. Both the Polish and the Ukrainian commanders reported in their native languages; I admired the way General Tyszkiewicz would maneuver from English, to Polish, to Russian, and back again. It was a phenomenal effort as he carefully clarified or added to the report we prepared in the Operations Center, utilizing the daily log of events reported from the three brigades. He would then read his final report, asking me to correct his English pronunciation. All the division commanders would then render their report in a specified order of briefing to General Sanchez. On the evening of 12 September, General Tyszkiewicz briefed his intent to send a general-led team to ad-Dīwānīyah the next day to attempt to eliminate any confusion about the requirements of the Latin American battalions and the intent of his Spanish brigade commander. As we had hoped, this seemed to put General Sanchez at ease, and I sensed he had bought a little time to at least properly frame the problem and render an accurate report. After dinner, I met with General Kwiatkowski to discuss the best way to approach the Spaniards. We agreed I would lead the discussions to determine the operational requirements and that he would frame the issue with introductory remarks. I thought we made a very good team as I left his quarters to coordinate a helicopter for our flight to ad-Dīwānīyah.

The Camp Babylon airstrip was a deceptively quiet place when it was not receiving or launching aircraft. The seemingly slow pace suited the typical weather of the late Iraqi summer. At mid-morning it was typically "Clear, blue and a hundred and two (degrees)," as our soldiers would say. American and Polish aviation crews were working on the medevac Black Hawks, the Polish Mi-8s, and reconnaissance helicopters known as Falcons. The operations tents for the American medevac unit sat off to the side of the strip and staff officers and pilots on alert could often be found in or around there studying maps, drafting flight plans, playing cards, or catching a few rays. The scene was not unlike the ones you often see in World War II movies of Royal Air Force pilots waiting for an order to scramble, relaxing one minute and running to their aircraft the next to do battle against the Germans. War has not really changed all that much. There is always a lot of time spent waiting around, broken up by periods of extreme stress, excitement, and fear.

The crew of our Mi-8 was standing by to receive us when General Kwiatkowski and I scrambled aboard. The Polish pilots were great guys, and I was getting to know many of them pretty well by now. They were all business this morning as they sharply saluted the general and strapped us into our seats. We knew how we wanted to approach the Spanish and Latin American commanders, but we did not know how General Cardona would take it and what, if anything, he would have to say, but, for the first time since this drama had begun, I thought we were going about the problem correctly. Arrangements had been made to have all the major players present at Spanish Brigade Headquarters, including General Cardona, his chief of staff, and the commanders from Honduras, El Salvador, the Dominican Republic, and Nicaragua. All of them waited for us as we touched down at the headquarters helipad and moved to vehicles for a short ride to the Brigade Operations Center.

By July 2003, the Spanish Multinational Brigade Plus Ultra had nearly 2,500 troops; some 1,300 were Spanish and the remainder were from the four Central American units. The brigade operated from five operational bases, two of which were located in ad-Dīwānīyah Province while the other three were in Al-Najaf Province. In ad-Dīwānīyah, Base España was the brigade's command post and housed a majority of the Spanish and Nicaraguan contingents. The other, Base Santo Domingo, was manned by forces from the Dominican Republic. In Al-Najaf, Base El Salvador was home to the Salvadoran troops, while Base Tegucigalpa accommodated the Honduran soldiers.

The Al Andalus Base was the site of the brigade's alternate command post and the Al-Najaf Coalition Provisional Authority. The brigade's area of responsibility was the provinces of Al-Qādisiyyah and Al-Najaf, two largely Shi'ite regions. The Spanish, like the bulk of the Multinational Division (Central-South), thought they were deployed as peacekeepers with primarily humanitarian missions. The brigade's five camps were hit by mortar and other small-arms attacks throughout its deployment, forcing the Spanish to deploy additional combat units to better secure their medical, engineer, and logistical units. There was no group of men more proud of their respective countries and their military reputation than the Spanish and Latin American officers of the Multinational Brigade Plus Ultra.

There was no time wasted on the usual pleasantries, but everyone was cordial and professional. Brigade Chief of Staff Colonel Viega made introductions and turned the floor over to the brigade commander. General Cardona was a tough, no-nonsense soldier who was the commander of Spanish special forces in Spain before he was selected to command in Iraq. He was not a man to be pushed around. We were very conscious of the fact his decision to delay transition of command in Al-Najaf was consistent with his government's position. He was on solid ground and this was his "house." We would have to tread lightly. Not surprisingly, he thanked General Kwiatkowski and me for visiting his headquarters and quickly reviewed the disposition of his forces and their readiness status. He told us the serious shortfalls in equipment promised to his Latin American units precluded their ability to effectively assume responsibility for their respective areas of operation. In his professional opinion, American forces had to remain in position until the shortages were rectified. His briefing was emotionless, sharp, and concise. You could hear a pin drop when he was not speaking. After his short remarks, he sat down and asked General Kwiatkowski whether he had any questions of his staff and commanders.

General Bronisław Kwiatkowski was the epitome of a Polish gentleman. Physically tough and athletic, he was a classmate of General Tyszkiewicz and, like him, had commanded the famed Polish Airborne Brigade. He was conversant in English and Russian, and his German was fluent. He was a pleasure to be around and we were already good friends. After making a few brief remarks about the importance of determining the exact requirements of the Latin American units, he introduced me and asked me to proceed as we had discussed the night before.

You could have cut the tension in the air with a knife. I introduced myself in Spanish and provided a little information about my background and experience.

Both General Cardona and Lieutenant Colonel Monterozza were paratroopers and I was quick to highlight my tour in Panama as an airborne infantry battalion commander and the training exchanges my battalion had conducted in Honduras, Argentina, and Uruguay. My Spanish held up rather well, but in deference to General Kwiatkowski and recognizing my own limits, I reverted to English to address the real purpose of our visit. Colonel Viega had a chart on the overhead screen that listed key items of equipment required by each national contingent. I adapted it to my needs. I asked each commander to fill in the chart using a grease pencil with the definitive numbers that would satisfy their operational requirements. I made it clear the numbers had to be final, consistent with their professional assessment and personal honor. This was no small point. Honor is everything to Spanish and Latin American officers. Expressed in this manner, I knew I would get the truth. The commanders were prepared to talk. There were no weapons requirements. Their needs fell into three fundamental categories: vehicles, communications, and navigational equipment or global-positional systems (GPS). The numbers were staggering, but I hid my uneasiness as each commander moved line by line through the chart. Some battalions were better off than others, but the final tally of requirements at the end of the exercise stood as follows:[1]

ITEM	REQUIREMENT
Humvee	27
5-ton truck	38
Water truck	4
Fuel truck	3
Ambulance	6
Maintenance truck w/crane	3
VHF radio	68
HF radio	9
Thuraya phone	7
Iridium phone	1
Motorola radio	24
VHF amplifier	10
OE-254 antenna	5
GPS	23

The Latin American commanders insisted they simply wanted the same capability the Marines had. As far as they were concerned, that capability was what they had been promised by the United States prior to their deployment to Iraq. General Cardona sat quietly and without emotion as we discussed possible substitutions, the operational criticality of each item, and the numbers desired. I noted the presence of an American maintenance team with a vehicle recovery capability at a battalion headquarters would negate the requirement for another maintenance recovery vehicle and that Motorola radios were acceptable substitutes for VHF radios in most cases. The commanders emphasized that their national representatives had been promised the items they had specified. They expected nothing less. In addition to these requirements, they confirmed the report that their units were critically short of medical supplies. I noted everything in detail and assumed my report to CJTF-7 Headquarters and General Miller would go over like a lead balloon.

I concluded the exercise by reverting to Spanish and thanking General Cardona for giving me the opportunity to address his commanders and develop the "Definitive requirements that if provided would allow the transition of authority to the Spanish brigade in Al-Najaf." I chose my words carefully and the good general knew it and smiled. I expressed my sincere hope that, armed with these definitive numbers, the United States would make good its promise to outfit the Latin American battalions accordingly. I had the last word and the meeting concluded with smiles and handshakes.

General Cardona invited General Kwiatkowski and me to lunch. The multinational mess halls attempted to accommodate the cultural tastes of the troops and the Spanish mess hall was big on fish. Dining with the tough Spaniard was a good sign our cordial and professional command relationships were intact; I felt relieved as I wiped away the sweat from two of the most intense hours of pure staff work I could remember. General Cardona was a smart man. He knew he was pushing his limits with the Americans and, to a lesser extent, his Polish division commander. I sensed he knew how many "buttons he could push" and how often. Following our seafood lunch, he invited General Kwiatkowski and me to his tent where he presented each of us a beautiful drinking mug decorated with the Spanish colors and crown. He then reached for a bottle of Spanish wine, turned to me, and with a broad smile said, "Colonel Tiso, please present this bottle to General Sanchez on my behalf. Let him know that the Spanish are honored to serve under his command and seek the best possible relations with our American comrades in the future."

He knew what I was attempting to do would not go over easily and he smiled as he handed me the bottle. I assured him I would get it to General Sanchez, but I doubted anything good would result from the list of requirements we would present to General Tyszkiewicz upon our return to Camp Babylon. I could only imagine what General Miller would say. I had no idea where we were going to get this amount of equipment. The Marines were dead set against leaving anything behind. The answer was well above our collective pay grades. It was an answer only the theater commander could provide.

General Tyszkiewicz took our report in his usual calm manner and asked me to draft a letter to General Sanchez stating the transition in Al-Najaf from the

Marines to the Multinational Division (Central-South) remained in doubt for the near term. General Sanchez had ordered the transition of authority to occur no later than 21 September. General Tyszkiewicz told me to emphasize the transition was wholly dependent upon the operational readiness of the Latin American units. He liked our chart and directed it be attached as an enclosure to the letter and sent to General Sanchez that evening. General Tyszkiewicz wanted his boss to have a complete appreciation for the range of requirements that had to be met before General Abizaid visited the division the next day. It was as much a professional courtesy as it was a report.

By mid-September, I was nearly as exhausted by the stress and difficulties associated with my duties in the MND as I had been when I left the Coalition Military Assistance Training Team in early August. It appeared to me that everything we were doing in Iraq was a desperate struggle to get a massive project under control with too little time and human and material assets to do it. I took my work seriously, but there were times I felt like I was running on empty. By this time, our country had been at war for two years. The events of September 11 were as clear to me as if they had happened the day before. Those events had occurred only three weeks after I had returned from my command tour in the Sinai. The long hours at Central Command, the deployment to Egypt in support of Exercise *Bright Star* in November 2002, multiple trips to Saudi Arabia, the mission in Afghanistan, and the nearly non-stop stress of the past six months in Iraq were taking a toll I had little time to think about. I was tired, my weight was down, and I had trouble sleeping at night. My mind was in overdrive thinking through the issues. Failure was not an option, and I cursed the "shoe-string" economy of force-like situations in which I continually found myself.

The poor regard held for the MND by the Marines and the CJTF-7 staff bothered me. The division's operational readiness seemed to be a low priority on CJTF-7's long list of tasks, yet international participation and operational success in Operation *Iraqi Freedom* was a major strategic concern. There seemed to be a serious disconnect. The Al-Najaf issue was consuming me. The logistics fix to the problem was out of my hands and I did not have a lot of confidence it would be addressed. During a phone conversation with General Miller, I proposed the command-and-control arrangement for the Latin American battalions in Al-Najaf that did not include the Spanish brigade. I suggested an effort be made between CJTF-7 and the Multinational staff to form an ad hoc staff and command group. A senior officer could assume command of the El Salvadoran, Dominican Republic, and Honduran battalions and coordinate the activities of the Nicaraguan detachment. It would not be pretty, but if he augmented my liaison team with several operations and signal officers and the minimum equipment to run a TOC, I was reasonably certain the Latin American commanders would accept the interim fix until the equipment issue could be satisfied. He listened intently. He was as desperate as anyone to find a solution and relieve the

Marines of their responsibility in Al-Najaf. He never said, "No," but the idea was far more operationally, than politically, expedient. It did not bother me. I did not get paid to offer political solutions to operational requirements. I was totally confident we could put a command team together and make it work. It was a tactically viable solution I suspected no one wanted to propose to the CJTF-7 commander. Regardless, the phone calls from the CJTF-7 staff requesting information about Al-Najaf and the status of the Latin American battalions continued unabated, and the MND staff continued to respond with the same, unacceptable answers.

CHAPTER 19

The Power of the Theater Commander

Never forget that no military leader has ever become great without audacity.
—CARL VON CLAUSEWITZ

The activity on the Camp Babylon airstrip was at its highest level ever on 14 September as many vehicles, high-ranking staff officers and the commanding general assembled to greet the new theater commander, General John P. Abizaid, USA, and the powerful congressman from Missouri, Ike Skelton. General Abizaid had assumed command of U.S. Central Command (USCENTCOM) early in July, having previously served as its deputy commander under General Franks. He was intimately familiar with his new command. Congressman Skelton had served in the Congress for over 25 years and was one its major leaders on defense issues as the ranking Democrat on the House Armed Forces Committee. I had briefly met him and Congressman Murtha of Pennsylvania in Washington, D.C., during one of General Zinni's many visits to Capitol Hill. During this visit, he would be content to observe, listen, and learn. He had voiced considerable concern in letters to the president about the absence of an occupation plan prior to the invasion of Iraq, and now had a very strong interest in the activities of the multinational forces participating in the occupation effort. There was no denying the importance of this visit and I had briefed General Tyszkiewicz accordingly. What I did not know was how the new theater commander would address the Al-Najaf issue. Several officers on the Combined Joint Task Force-7 (CJTF-7) staff had told me General Tyszkiewicz would be "counseled," the Army's way of telling an officer he is not getting the job done. I discounted that possibility. The fact that over twenty nations had come together under one command, regardless of how different or less lethal than the American or British formations, was a major achievement. General Tyszkiewicz had a major role in making that happen as General Abizaid was certainly aware.

General Abizaid's reputation as a soldier was solid. His career had been nothing short of phenomenal. A West Point graduate, he had served in airborne and ranger units as a junior officer and had commanded a company in the 1st Ranger Battalion during its parachute assault on Grenada in 1983. He had risen rapidly through the officer ranks and commanded at every level including the famed 1st Infantry Division in Germany during the Kosovo crisis. An Arabic speaker with significant multinational and coalition experience in both the Middle East and Europe, I was confident he would handle any discussions with our Polish friends in a professional and friendly manner. When I briefed him on the organization and mission of USCENTCOM's Joint Security Directorate early in 2002, he had impressed me as a gentleman. I had suggested to General Tyszkiewicz that this visit was an opportunity for him to tell the division's story and outline its operational requirements. The visit could not have been timelier.

The general's and congressman's arrival at Camp Babylon airstrip was announced by the high-pitched noise and sand-blasting effect of three UH-60 Black Hawk helicopters that carried them and members of various staffs. The problem with any VIP's visit is not the VIP as much as the entourage that accompanies him. In addition to the commander and Mr. Skelton were a couple of two-star USCENTCOM staff directors, the commander's political adviser, and a variety of administrators and aides. General Abizaid was conscious of the burden an entourage could be and did better than most to hold "strap hangers" to a minimum. As usual, I kept to the background, content to lean against a tent pole and watch the customary handshakes and "how do you dos." After the buses and vehicles were loaded and the procession began to move, I hitched a ride to Division Headquarters. I thought I would stand by in the unlikely event I was called to comment on anything. I did not wait very long. As everyone began to file into the entrance and lobby of the headquarters, General Tyszkiewicz saw me and shouted, "Roland, come and join us!"

He immediately introduced me to General Abizaid who offered his hand and addressed me by my first name. Rear Admiral "Rookie" Robb, then serving as the director of the Strategy, Plans and Policy Directorate (CCJ5), the general's political adviser, and several others acknowledged my presence with a smile. It had been over six months since I had left USCENTCOM for duty in Kuwait, but most of these gentlemen remembered me and I felt comfortable in their company. Not surprisingly, transition of authority in Al-Najaf quickly became the focus of the discussions. I was impressed by General Abizaid's friendly manner and intent to get to know the division commander. There were no bully like tactics or anything of the sort. We had assumed he had been briefed on the memorandum that General Tyszkiewicz had sent to General Sanchez the previous evening. When he asked for specifics concerning the readiness and general status of the Latin American battalions, General Tyszkiewicz looked at me and smiled. It was a clear signal for me to speak. I handed General Abizaid a copy of the equipment-status chart that had been forwarded to the CJTF-7 commander, briefly discussed each line item of equipment, and told him previous reports had inaccurately stated the type and amount of equipment requested by the Latin American commanders.

"These items and numbers," I said, "Were agreed upon in a meeting with all of the unit commanders present who have all but sworn to their accuracy. Provide these items of equipment in the numbers indicated, General, and the Spanish brigade will be operationally ready to assume its responsibilities in Al-Najaf and will do so without further delay."

General Abizaid quickly looked over the document and broke the silence with a calm, emotionless reply.

"We should be able to provide this equipment from prepositioned stocks in theater."

He was referring to assets in Kuwait, Qatar, or prepositioned afloat assets in the Arabian Gulf. This equipment had been carefully placed in theater since the end of the First Gulf War to enable Army and Marine units to quickly fly into the theater during a crisis or an exercise and draw the combat vehicles and other rolling stock, and special equipment they needed consistent with their normal "go to war" configuration. A lot of it had been issued and used by the Army's 3rd Division during its initial deployment to Kuwait and campaign in Iraq. Turning to Major General Sattler, USMC, USCENTCOM Director of Operations (CCJ3), General Abizaid handed him the document and simply said, "Fix it." He thanked me for my contributions to the discussion and said my comments had been a big help to him. Other discussions addressed a variety of subjects pertinent to the theater and the outlook for Iraq. It was all quite secondary to what had just happened. The tension was broken and the meeting adjourned shortly after with a lot of friendly banter and handshakes.

The meeting had been as cordial and business-like as any I have seen. Only the theater commander could tap prepositioned assets in this magnitude for multinational troops. He did it with a mere wave of a document and two simple words to his J-3. The process of getting to this meeting was as frustrating as it was necessary, but I was convinced the critical step had been taken to properly equip the Spanish brigade's Latin American battalions, relieve the Marines in Al-Najaf, and lift the veil of doubt that hung over the Multinational Division's (MND) senior leadership.

I was alone with General Abizaid for a few brief moments as the aircrews made their final checks of his aircraft. We exchanged a few friendly words, he wished me good luck, and walked to his aircraft amid the high-pitched sound of the engines and the blowing sand. Our trouble in Iraq had not yet exploded into the insurgency and sectarian violence that would characterize the next several months. The situation for now was manageable despite any poor strategic decisions that may have been made before and after the fall of Baghdad. As I watched the general strap himself into the aircraft, I didn't know whether to envy him or feel sorry for him. He undoubtedly carried a huge weight of responsibility on his shoulders. General Zinni had once told me, after I had presented him with an ambitious schedule of briefings and talks for a typical travel day in the Central Region, that "I did not feel his pain," a reference to the stress associated with his position and rank. The inference was that if I did, I would not coordinate such difficult schedules. The commander is "on parade" 24 hours a day and the schedule he maintains, even on a relatively easy day, can wear down the best of men. I knew what he meant and appreciated it better than most. Looking at General Abizaid, I did not doubt he was feeling some "pain" himself. But there is no denying the awesome power a four-star general wields as a theater commander. Orders would soon be issued to address the MND's requirements and the frustration, angst, and embarrassment of the Al-Najaf affair would end within a week.

I walked away from the airstrip satisfied I had helped to solve a potential crisis. I was proud of the actions General Abizaid had taken, but I questioned whether the drama, the operational delays, and the accompanying anger and disrespect had been necessary. The Latin American units were ill-equipped, and it was obvious to the Marines and the MND command group. The units relieving the Marines were expected to perform the same stability mission. The military leaders in their respective countries were apparently told the contingents they contributed to the Coalition would be properly equipped for the mission. There was an apparent disconnect regarding the availability of the required assets that should have been addressed through proper channels to CJTF-7 and beyond as required. Poor reporting by the Spanish brigade and the Latin American battalions confused the issue, but little was done by either the American units on the ground or CJTF-7 to truly come to grips with the units' requirements. No one expected the Marines to give their equipment away. The commanders of both the 1st Marine Expeditionary Force and the MND did not aggressively pursue the issue with CJTF-7. I believe that had they reached consensus on the requirements and addressed them together to the CJTF-7 commander, the solution to solve the problem would have occurred much sooner and without the stress and anger that had caused a lack of confidence in the efficiency and professionalism of the MND. The Marines wanted to go home, the Army expected the MND to accept the mission timeline regardless of its readiness, and the division did little to aggressively pursue its requirements with either the Marines or CJTF-7 Headquarters. I saw a dangerous pattern in all of this. This event was not unlike what had characterized my experience with the New Iraqi Army project. The civilian and military senior headquarters were desperately short of resources. Rather than establish priorities, allocate precious resources accordingly, and report additional requirements to their higher authorities, they selfishly turned within themselves and unfairly criticized those who sought the means to accomplish their respective tasks. Careerism and selfishness always seemed to prevail, and the absence of teamwork, selflessness, and leadership at the senior-executive level in an extraordinary wartime environment spoke of a peacetime mindset that threatened any chance for mission success at the operational and tactical levels of the war.

On 19 September, large amounts of equipment began to flow to the Spanish brigade in ad-Dīwānīyah for distribution to the Latin American units. Generals Kelly and Tyszkiewicz agreed to pass authority in Al-Najaf to the Spanish brigade on 23 September. The exceptionally good relations between these old friends had effectively defused any serious problems that may have developed between the Marines and the Spanish-led forces in Al-Najaf. The Marines worked with their Latin American counterparts throughout their extended deployment. The officers and men of the Latin battalions were ready to assume the mission in large measure because of the exceptional patience and professionalism of the Marines in Al-Najaf.

In a simple, dignified change-of-authority ceremony, General Kelly passed the responsibility of command to General Cardona with General Tyszkiewicz presiding as the senior ranking officer. Local Iraqi dignitaries and senior members of the CJTF-7 staff attended. Everyone appeared upbeat. What could have been a disaster with the potential to dissolve a portion of our vital Coalition had been resolved with some timely staff work and the decisive intervention of the theater commander. Following the last joint Marine brigade–MND tactical-satellite report to General Sanchez that evening at Camp Babylon, General Kelly quietly presented me with a 1st Marine Division coin in recognition of my work to support the Latin American units and facilitate the relief of the Marines in Al-Najaf. The Marines do not routinely hand out awards; I was proud to receive it. Earlier that day, as we prepared to leave Al-Najaf, General Cardona's aide passed me the general's compliments regarding the successful conclusion of the "Al-Najaf affair." I was happy the "affair" was finally behind us and that I could now get on with the pressing concerns in other parts of the division's vast area of operations.

CHAPTER 20

Patrolling with the Ukrainians on the Iranian Border

Soldiers admire leaders who are tactically competent, physically fit, and willing to "mix it up" with soldiers in the field.

—Lieutenant General J. W. Crysel, USA

The Multinational Division's (MND) immediate needs in August and September had kept me close to its commanding general and headquarters at Camp Babylon. American and international interest in the MND kept the staff occupied with numerous official visits even as it planned and executed operations. My liaison team assisted in every possible way. It was very gratifying to see that the commanding general and many other senior officers considered us an extension of the staff as well as their connectivity with Combined Joint Task Force-7 (CJTF-7). General Tyszkiewicz and I had dinner, either in his office or in the mess hall, on a regular basis. He was genuinely interested in my thoughts and opinions. He particularly valued my ability to write and frequently asked me to review his memos to CJTF-7, official remarks, and general correspondence. The liaison team had accomplished a lot with the division staff, but I was anxious to get out to the infantry to see firsthand how we were conducting business in the field. Frequent visits to the brigade areas of operation were essential for our situational awareness given the absence of liaison officers and noncommissioned officers (NCO) at the brigade and battalion level. General Tyszkiewicz respected my desire to work with the brigades and totally understood doing so was an important part of my team's overall mission. Once the Al-Najaf problem was solved, he somewhat reluctantly allowed me to leave Camp Babylon, though I remained on a "tight string" to respond to his call at all times.

Wasit Province and the Iranian border was the most overtly active area in the division area of responsibility in the early fall of 2003. By the third week of September, the Ukrainian brigade had reinforced its paratroop company on the border to nearly two hundred men. The company covered 142 kilometers of the mountainous Iraq–Iran border with extended mounted patrols and reconnaissance operations. Their mission was to control illegal smuggling and immigration from Iran. Iraq had heavily fortified the border during the Saddam era and had ceased

Iranian visitation of the Iraqi holy cities of Al-Najaf and Kerbelâ'. Now, with the Iraqi Army gone and the border wide-open, Iranian Shi'ite Muslims long denied access to holy shrines for worship, such as the Imām 'Alī Mosque in Al-Najaf, were coming across the border in large numbers. They were undoubtedly accompanied by men of questionable and nefarious intent. It was not surprising intelligence reports indicated many foreign fighters had entered Iraq from Iran to infiltrate, influence, and eventually dominate the Shi'ite community in southern Iraq. Iranian infiltrators later sought influence with Sunni Muslims in central Iraq as well.

The Ukrainians had increased their presence in the city of Al-Kut by patrolling throughout its numerous streets and market areas. Al-Kut, like so many Middle Eastern towns and villages, was a fascinating place with its port on the banks of the Tigris River and its numerous street markets where everything—from grain, fruit, and vegetables to clothing and furniture—is bought and sold in open-air store fronts. The town had experienced war for many years by this time as it was well inside the southern "no-fly" zone and, since 1996, had been subjected to air strikes by American and British fighter-bombers as well as surface-to-surface Scud missile strikes by the Iranians in pursuit of the Mojahedin-e-Khalq (MEK) in the spring of 2001.

During World War I, Al-Kut had figured prominently during the British Mesopotamia campaign against the Turks in Iraq, which included several pitched battles in 1916 and 1917 that saw the British lose and recapture it.[1] Now a city of over three hundred thousand people, it had been liberated by the 3rd Battalion, 23rd Marines, in early April 2003 and turned over to the Ukrainians in August. The Ukrainians initially steered clear of the city, but gradually assumed a more aggressive presence. The Supreme Council for Islamic Revolution (SCIRI), an historically Iraqi insurgent group backed by Iran and financed directly by the Iranian Revolutionary Guards, maintained a strong presence in Al-Kut. At one point during the Iran–Iraq War, the Iranians considered SCIRI the government of the Islamic Republic of Iraq. Iranian Ayatollah Khomeini had named Ayatollah Baqir al-Hakim as its titular head. SCIRI rose to prominence among Shi'ite Iraqis with the fall of Saddam. The party maintained an armed wing known as the Badr Corps, and later the Badr Organization, with a strength of upwards of ten thousand men. Many of its members were Iraqi exiles who had settled in Iran and had fought against Iraq in the 1980–88 Iran–Iraq War. They were known to conduct maneuvers with units of the Iranian Revolutionary Guards. The Badr Corps' principal operating area by the fall of 2003 was Kerbelâ', but it had set up its elaborate intelligence apparatus initially in Al-Kut in April 2003. With its intentions unclear in the fall of that year, SCIRI was a major concern to the Coalition. Additionally, the MEK had maintained a training camp near Kut for many years. The MEK was anti-Iran and had drawn its support from Saddam. It had fought against the Badr Corps throughout the 1980s and had assisted the Saddam regime quell the Shia and Kurdish uprisings in

1991. It had since focused its efforts totally against Iran. The MEK had essentially stood down with the Coalition triumph over Saddam in May, and the bulk of its members were confined to Camp Ashraf, 96 kilometers north of Baghdad in the Diyala Governorate. In the fall of 2003, however, their small presence in Al-Kut did not mix well with SCIRI. Finally, Al-Kut's location so close to the Iranian border made it a logical way station for Iranian Ministry of Intelligence and Security agents who routinely crossed the border into Iraq. Many of them moved to Al-Najaf and Kerbela' which were nerve centers for Iranian operations in Iraq. There was no doubt Al-Kut was a potential powder keg and had to be watched closely.

Late on the afternoon of 20 September with all but the change-of-authority ceremony in Al-Najaf behind me, I enthusiastically boarded a Polish Mi-8 helicopter for the long flight to the Ukrainian camp at Al Hayy Air Base and the Iranian border. It had been nearly a month since my first visit with the Ukrainians to celebrate their National Day. General Sobora had approved my request to go to the border and regretted that his duties at Camp Babylon would not allow him to go as well. I had previously relied on the general's translator, Lieutenant Alex Kanus, to translate for me, but for this trip I was accompanied by Sergeant First Class George Gogolewski, an intelligence NCO from the Illinois National Guard, now serving in the division's G-2 (Intelligence Section). Sergeant Gogolewski had found his way into the Army at the age of 36 after gaining a waiver for his age to enlist from President Reagan. Born in Poland, he enlisted in the National Guard out of pure patriotism and love of his new country. He spoke fluent Polish and Russian. I was lucky to have him for this trip. We were about the same age, and he was one of those guys with whom you could talk about anything. The Poles and Ukrainians respected him immensely as much for his jovial personality as his professional knowledge.

It was not customary for a passenger aboard these aircraft to sit in the gunner's position by one of the two machine guns mounted on each side, but I always insisted on it. It was a great place to sit and observe the countryside. Far more diverse than just desert, central Iraq is green with an abundance of trees and plants. Groves of palm trees, irrigated fields, and swamplands speak to the potential of the land. The Iraqis work well with the land. Even in southernmost Iraq, the Iraqis near the port city of Umm Qasr did amazing things with their desert land. With water pumped from the Shatt al-Arab, they managed to grow an abundance of vegetables that UNIKOM (the United Nations Iraq–Kuwait Observation Mission) purchased for its mess halls prior to the Coalition's invasion. The Iraqis would often wave to us as we flew by. It was not uncommon to see herds of cattle, goats, and camels. Not until you begin to close on the Iranian border does the landscape turn a sandy light brown and a once fiercely contested land becomes evident. From one end of the 800-mile expanse of border to the other, the land is scarred with a series of forts that figured prominently in the Iran–Iraq War. The front-line posts, that accommodated at most a platoon of perhaps forty men, were as close as a couple of kilometers from the

Iranian border, while larger supporting posts and logistics centers were built further to the rear. The border structures were spartan outposts that closely resembled the French Foreign Legion forts in the movie *Beau Geste* with turrets at each corner. The border itself is not clearly marked but, during the war, the Iranians almost matched the Iraqis in construction, fort for fort. They had fought each other from these fixed positions and massive artillery duels had been common.

During my tour with UNIKOM, I had frequently flown reconnaissance missions with our Bangladeshi pilots in their Huey 212 helicopters over the al-Faw Peninsula. Some of the largest and most devastating battles of the Iran–Iraq War had occurred there. The Iranians often assaulted the heavily prepared Iraqi positions with human-wave attacks that left thousands of casualties in a dead-locked World War I-like environment. I was impressed by the long lines of trenches and bunker systems as well as abandoned barrier materials and pieces of equipment. The waste of the war was everywhere. The scars in the earth outlined where everything from the front lines to the command centers, to the logistics centers, and everything in between had been located. This once beehive of activity with more than 100,000 Iraqi troops in 1987, was nothing more than a ghostly field of trash and death 10 years after the battles had been fought. I suspected a close-up inspection of the border areas would reveal something similar.

I continued to study the military architecture and the terrain when our pilots flew over several armored vehicles on the desert floor that I recognized as Ukrainian BTR-80s, formidable, armored personnel carriers that would transport us to our destination for the day. The Ukrainian company that patrolled the border was commanded by a paratroop major named Valeryi Semenets. A ruggedly handsome and fit-looking man, Val spoke some English and he welcomed me and Sergeant Gogolewski after the helicopters departed. Visitors to his unit were rare, and he seemed to be genuinely happy to have us. We spoke briefly and I assured him the sole purpose of my visit was to gain an appreciation for, and participate in, his unit's operations. I told him I was not an inspector from higher headquarters looking to find fault with him. Sergeant Gogolewski translated for me, and Val was surprised and relieved the big sergeant could speak native Russian. I told Val I wanted to learn from him and his men and that hopefully he would invite me back in the future to participate in his operations along the border.

Val nodded his approval and suggested we mount up and move. It was getting near nightfall and he wanted to be back at his base before dark. Val issued a few quick orders and the vehicles moved from their hasty defensive perimeter into a column formation. Included in his armored column was a four-seat civilian truck he pointed out to me. I would have preferred the armor of the BTR-80 but did not say anything. We had about a half hour of daylight and that was about how long it would take to move along the border road to Camp Fort, the barracks and headquarters of Val's company. Our uneventful drive was my first on-the-ground look at the mountainous terrain that separated the two countries and the vast Iraqi desert that straddled the border road. It was not unlike the desert in southern Iraq except for the immense sand dunes that were not characteristic of the landscape along the southern Iraqi border. The immensity of the desert reminded me of my conversations with General Peay who, reflecting on his experiences in the Gulf War, once told me the desert would literally "Swallow up an entire mechanized brigade." To the east was Iran and the mountains, but everywhere else we looked was a seemingly endless, uninhabited, and unforgiving desert. It struck me how small it could make a man feel.

We turned east on to a worn vehicle path after a 30-minute drive; atop a dominating piece of high ground was a large fort. Below was a row of porto-johns and makeshift latrines. A parking lot filled with civilian vehicles was cordoned off and I wondered what it was all about. There were pickup trucks, vans, a couple of school buses, and sedans of all makes and sizes. After we dismounted and secured our gear, I asked Sergeant Gogolewski to ask about the parking lot. It was a secret I assumed Val wanted to keep quiet, but he smiled at me and told Gogolewski the vehicles had been confiscated from both Iraqi and Iranian smugglers. The Iranians would move Shi'ite pilgrims across the border where they would be met by Iraqis who transported them to one of several places, but most likely the holy cities of Kerbelâ' and Al-Najaf. Val looked at my reaction, laughed, and told us he was never short of transportation when he had to get supplies or move personnel to the rear. It sounded to me like a great plan to put smugglers out of business; I was not there to criticize, engage in politically correct American solutions, or otherwise tell him what to do with confiscated property. I have always thought there was something to say for the "spoils of war." This Ukrainian major and his company of paratroops were doing a great deal to control their piece of the war as far as I was concerned. I thought it was great and told him so.

"Val, I think I'm going to like it here."

He laughed, turned toward the fort and, as we started walking, he said in English, "First we eat, then we plan patrol for tomorrow."

The entrance to Camp Fort was a tunnel integral to a labyrinth of dank passageways that led to barracks rooms, bays, a communications room, and ladders to the turrets that were manned 24 hours a day. I asked Val for a tour and he gladly started to show me around. Infantrymen of every nation had it rough in Iraq, but anyone would have been impressed with the rugged way the Ukrainian paratroopers lived in this isolated, spartan environment. There was no entertainment to speak of although Val had a television rigged in his quarters. Everyone slept on a cot. Chow was trucked out to the company twice a day from the brigade mess hall in Al-Kut. The dank and dark passageways provided the air conditioning. The engineers must have had an extremely difficult time getting electricity in the place. It occurred to me that if everyone lived in expeditionary conditions like this, including the commanding generals, and the CJTF-7 and Coalition Provisional Authority staffs in Baghdad, we would wrap up operations in Iraq very quickly and save the American people billions. I have always believed our extreme concern for our soldiers' welfare, as defined by creature comforts and the niceties that burden warfighting logistics, gives us a less-than-efficient expeditionary mindset, makes us too comfortable with the status quo, and more apt to stay in places long after we should be gone. Stories of special beds and various other creature comforts ordered on Ebay and delivered to American soldiers in the combat zone was a bit much for me, a form of decadence that spoils soldiers and ruins armies. On the Iranian border, however, I was among the true Spartans. Val introduced me to his officers who struck me as competent, rugged, and professional. The soldiers appeared tough, fit, and disciplined. Soldiers on watch in the turrets used a telescope, but I noted night-vision devices were in short supply. The Ukrainians were a competent and honorable people, and they were proud of their mission, but their lack of communications equipment and night-vision capability concerned me. I made several notes to accurately report these shortfalls to the division. The mountainous terrain directly to our east included an Iranian fort that was occupied by Iranian border police. Parts of it appeared to have been hit by artillery fire. As tough as things may have been for the Ukrainians, I suspected they had it a lot better than the Iranians living in the bombed-out hell hole of a fort immediately across the border that I viewed through my binoculars.

A small open area in the center of the fort with a table and several chairs served as the officers' mess. Sergeant Gogolewski and I joined Val and his platoon leaders to an American meal served on paper plates and covered in foil that had been transported from the brigade mess hall at Al-Kut. Soldiers everywhere see chow time as an opportunity to socialize. Even in the field during tactical maneuvers, soldiers gather to enjoy the company of their buddies, much to the chagrin of their officers who fear they present a lucrative target to hostile indirect fire. Val's officers and soldiers were no different. The officers were very interested in me and what I was doing there. My impression was that senior officers in their Army did not often participate in tactical operations or spend much time in the field. In fact, Val told me it was unusual for a senior colonel or general to want a tough field assignment. He suggested that senior officers desirous of field duty were an exception. He added with a laugh, "They are very fat, and they do not talk to soldiers in the field."

I reminded him of General Sobora who I thought of as a real warrior and a soldier's general. Val agreed and acknowledged my comment in English: "We are very lucky that he is our commander."

I was impressed by the high regard these Ukrainian soldiers and officers had for those leaders who are tactically competent, physically fit, and willing to "mix it up" with soldiers in the field.

Following dinner, Val broke out a map of his area of operations and gave his order for tomorrow's patrol. Sergeant Gogolewski quietly translated for me. His intent was to cover the entire length of the border road within the Ukrainian sector. We would take up fixed reconnaissance positions along the route at designated locations and observe. Suspected illegal activity would be checked with two BTR-80s and dismounted infantry from an overwatch position. Two other vehicles would move to the activity, dismount, and engage as required. Val explained to me later that most activity was addressed without combat action. Our actions might involve as little as an identity check. The time schedule was an eye opener. Wake up was scheduled for 3 am and we were scheduled to depart an hour later for what he anticipated would be a 6–8-hour patrol. Val arranged cots for me and Sergeant Gogolewski. I checked my gear, wiped my rifle with an oily rag, and laid out my bed roll. I was unconscious as soon as the light went out.

My Ukrainian comrades were up long before I was. I quickly dressed and made my way to the latrines. There was a lot of movement as soldiers conducted what in American parlance are preventive maintenance, checks, and services on their vehicles, weapons, and communications equipment. Breakfast would be eaten on "the go" as the chow wagon from Al-Kut was scheduled to arrive long after our departure. I carried MRE (meal, ready to eat) packets and some granola bars with me to account for moments like these. I have always thrived on the excitement generated by mission activity and today was no different. A soldier doesn't think about being tired and the morning wooziness is quickly overcome by the excitement and the adrenalin it generates. Sergeant Gogolewski and I took our gear outside so as not to disturb those guys not participating in this operation, checked the action on our weapons, and ate some of our chow. It was not long before Val showed up with his usual wide grin. He was all business, however, and directed us to our respective carriers. It was a little before 4 am and still quite dark. Val's orders were to remain inside the BTR-80 until it was light. It made sense—a soldier could fall off and not be seen or heard between the darkness and the roar of our engines.

The BTR-80 is a formidable, armored personnel carrier. It is a four-axle, eight-wheeled vehicle with seats to accommodate 10 infantrymen. Soldiers have limited vision via the vision blocks on the sides of the vehicle and they can fire their individual weapons through firing ports. The turret mounted a 14.5-mm or 12.7-mm caliber machine gun and a smaller co-axial 7.62-mm machine gun. It was outfitted with grenade-launcher tubes designed to fire smoke grenades to conceal the vehicle's movement under fire. The vehicle has a powerful diesel engine and eight-wheel drive. The driver told me through Sergeant Gogolewski that it could sustain an anti-tank mine hit and its frontal protection could absorb hits from 7.62mm and 12.7mm machine-gun fire. It was all very comforting, but I was just as happy to see these things tested in the lab. Sergeant Gogolewski shared my thought with the driver who laughed in agreement.

The early hour and the darkness accounted for the lack of activity during the first two hours of the patrol. There were no vehicles or evidence of people as we made our way down the border road. I was relieved when light conditions allowed us to come up for air and ride on top of the vehicle. After the adrenalin rush of the initial movement had worn off, I had found myself dozing in the cramped space I occupied inside the vehicle. We stopped at a point Val wanted to use as a fixed reconnaissance site. A worn path leading to the Iranian border provided numerous indications of its use by illegal Iranian immigrants and other unauthorized personnel. Torn clothing and other abandoned personal items lay strewn on boulders on both sides of the path. We dropped off two men with a radio and orders to avoid contact and report any observed activities in the area.

After nearly three hours into the patrol, we came upon what appeared to be men and vehicles biding their time to pick up illegal Iranians and smuggle them somewhere in Iraq. Val halted the column about two hundred meters from three sedans some one hundred meters south of the road. The Ukrainians were well briefed and rehearsed in their procedures; the two lead BTR-80s moved into an overwatch position from where they could provide supporting fire if necessary while the other two vehicle commanders ordered their maneuver teams to dismount and check things out. The likelihood of combat was slim, but the Ukrainians moved as if they were preparing to attack. Like all soldiers in a potential combat situation, my senses were in overdrive. We moved to a dune less than fifty meters short of the sedans where three men sat around a small cooking fire. The section leader directed his men to take up a good firing position and then indicated he and one other would go forward, talk to the men, and signal us to come forward at the appropriate time. The section leader approached the encampment from an angle to avoid masking our fires if the Iraqis opened fire on them. Between our overwatching machine guns and the small-arms fire our dismounted infantrymen could bring to bear, we could quickly "dust" these guys if we had to fire. The lieutenant was smart. We could engage the target area almost immediately if something went wrong. His men were veterans by now, and this wasn't the first time they had done this. The lieutenant casually but cautiously walked up to the campers and through his Arabic interpreter asked them who they were and what they were doing. He signaled us almost simultaneously to come forward. The Iraqis appeared docile enough. They were directed to get up and "spread eagle" on the cars. A body search revealed several knives including one with an 18-inch blade. The cars were searched thoroughly for other weapons and contraband, but none were found. The lieutenant radioed to the overwatch force to come forward. Val was all smiles as he saw the results of our work. He instructed three men to drive the cars back to the Ukrainian "parking lot." The Iraqis were told to start walking back to their village. If they had been picked up with illegal Iranian immigrants, we would have taken them into custody as well. They were told they could pick up their cars at the Ukrainian fort in a month. Val explained to me that some did, but most did not bother. It seemed odd considering what a car was worth, but fear can be a great weapon. The Arabs respect those who they fear, and this and later experiences on the border showed me the Iraqis feared and respected the strange-speaking soldiers who were neither American nor British and played by a different set of rules.

As luck would have it, this was the only incident of note on this patrol. We checked out one of the former Iraqi forts that had been damaged by artillery fire during the Iran–Iraq War. The grounds in and around the posts were littered with unexploded ordnance. Lying among the ruins were tattered Iraqi uniforms, helmets, shoes of all types, and protective masks for chemical warfare. As I had thought during my air reconnaissance, the post would have accommodated between forty and fifty men. The forts would prove useful again someday as border-control sites, border police headquarters, and logistical centers. Our return along the border road was completed a little faster and we rolled back into the Ukrainian fort just shy of seven hours since our start. Several miles before our turn off the border road, our lead vehicle stopped to pick up a pistol belt with an attached American bayonet. None of our fixed reconnaissance sites had seen any unusual activity and the belt remained an unexplained mystery. One thing was for sure—there were plenty of folks out there and, regardless of the fear they held for the Ukrainians, they were determined to enter Iraq or help those who desired to do so. Iraqi border police would not establish legal entry sites to manage immigration and patrol the border for at least another six months, and the illegal entry problem would continue long after we were gone. The Iraqi problem with illegal Iranians is not unlike the American problem with Mexicans along the U.S. southern border. My sense was it would take an army, much like the one Saddam used, to man these "ghost" forts before the illegal immigration problem could be brought under control; such an army would not be available for years.

I was impressed with how thorough the Ukrainians were with debriefings and after-action reports. Sergeant Gogolewski translated my comments; I complimented them on the excellent battle drill used to take and secure the Iraqi encampment. Another patrol would leave in a couple of hours. It was a never-ending cycle of patrol, maneuver, search, seize, and drive on. I did not think our senior leadership had a good feel for the difficulty of these border operations, the superb efforts of the Ukrainian troops, and the tough conditions under which they lived day to day. I made a mental note to ensure I reported everything I had seen to General Miller. It was hot as hell, and I had practically sweated through my armor. Patrolling the Iranian border was as good a weight-reduction program as any I had ever experienced. I must have been down 10 pounds or more after the exhausting physical activity, combat-related stress, and the extreme desert temperature of this long patrol. Showers were at a premium at this isolated post. These guys were hard. I knew my time at the fort was nearly up, so I did not give showering a second thought. I was happy to break out an MRE and have lunch. Sergeant Gogolewski and I were expected back at Al-Kut Air Base late that afternoon to link up with our scheduled helicopter ride to Camp Babylon. Before we left, Val shook my hand and invited me back. I told him I intended to come back as often as I could. The accommodations weren't all that great, but a man could soldier here, and I was very comfortable soldiering with these rock-hard paratroopers from Ukraine.

We arrived at the air base shortly after General Sobora landed. The Mi-8 that had taken him to Al-Kut was scheduled to fly me and Sergeant Gogolewski back to Camp Babylon, but my good friend wanted a complete debriefing about the patrol and insisted we join him at Brigade Headquarters. We were accompanied by General Bezleschenko and his interpreter, Andriy Lischynskyi, the gentle giant who had translated my remarks at the Ukrainian National Day parade. Our discussions lasted several hours and included a hot lunch. I had not realized how much of a hit I had been with them the previous month, but I knew they appreciated that someone had an interest in their mission and the work they were doing so far from the division "flagpole." I complimented the Ukrainian soldiers on the border and their leadership. I explained the patrol in detail using my map and I could see the general was jealous. Big Andriy translated the general's comment with a smile and told me, "The general is very sad that he could not take part in the action this morning on the border, but he promises that he will be with you in the future."

In fact, General Sobora was a frequent visitor to the border and participated in patrol activities in and around Al-Kut as well. He carried an AK-47 rifle variant known as the AKM, a sweet, shorter version of the famed Russian assault rifle often carried by paratroops and special forces. He always looked angry and most soldiers that did not know him avoided him at all costs. I had never met a general who cared more for his soldiers. He sincerely appreciated that I had participated in an operation with his soldiers. By 4 pm, however, I had to get on the helicopter if we were going to get back to Camp Babylon in time to help prepare the general's tactical-satellite (TACSAT) evening report. The pilots kept their eyes on the clock for two reasons: crew rest and nightfall. Airmen can only be operational for a designated crew day that normally does not exceed eight hours. It makes sense since mistakes at altitude by an exhausted aviator can often be fatal. Additionally, the Poles were concerned about their limited night-vision capability. The Polish aircraft were limited in other ways, most notably the absence of an anti-missile capability. This troubled General Tsyzkiewicz, whose concern for force protection eventually led him to ban all helicopter flights to Baghdad.

Sergeant Gogolewski and I piled into General Sobora's vehicle and drove back to the airfield where our patient pilots were waiting for us. I took my position behind one of the door guns and enjoyed an uneventful trip back to Camp Babylon where I joined my friends in the Operations Center to write the general's evening TACSAT report. Finessing this report was something in which I took great pride. I emphasized to my officers the importance of word selection to accurately convey the specifics of relevant, operational aspects of the division's activities. Analyzing our data and writing the reports was both an art and a science that required the utmost care. We agonized at times to ensure the division's reports were as complete and as accurate as they could be. I think we were more appreciated by the staff for helping to complete the evening report than for anything else we did.

I was satisfied with the day's work. It is not everywhere a soldier with the rank of colonel can operate with a reinforced platoon in combat, fly over the Iraqi countryside as a door gunner, and prepare a division commander's operational report all in one day. I resolved to get back to the border as soon as I could, but there was work to be done everywhere we looked in our vast area of responsibility. The Multinational Division had a lot to learn and a growing list of responsibilities on its plate. All things being equal, however, I felt pretty good about how we were contributing to the division and the role we would undoubtedly play in the future.

CHAPTER 21

Preparing the Occupation of Iraq

The best form of welfare for the troops is first-rate training.
—Erwin Rommel

The early days of fall provided a tranquil interlude for the Multinational Division (MND) between the trials of assuming command of its area of operations and the insurgency that was slowly making its way into central-south Iraq. The end of the controversy in Al-Najaf had raised the morale of the division staff. People at all levels felt better about the division and the stabilization role it was playing in central Iraq. The division received many visitors including my old boss and friend General Eaton. He was genuinely interested in the MND. The first battalion of the New Iraqi Army would soon complete its training at Kirkush Barracks and be placed under the operational control of the U.S. 4th Infantry Division. I assumed General Eaton wanted to familiarize himself with the MND's organization and operations, and perhaps find a good fit for future available Iraqi formations.

General Eaton asked me about the Polish ground transport vehicle the Poles referred to as the "Honker." The Honker was a small, light truck with a cargo bed that could seat up to ten men on two troop benches. The vehicle was underpowered, but it was an acceptable administrative troop transport that served the Poles well enough. General Eaton loved it. The original blueprint for the New Iraqi Army called for a light force of 40,000 men that would not have armored vehicles or artillery. It was not intended to be a powerful military force. Its original organization and number of troops were still in effect at the time of General Eaton's visit. He had successfully argued for a significant increase to his budget but was still looking for equipment that could support the force and not break the bank. The American Humvee was far too expensive. I promised to get him the specifications he needed on the Honker and coordinate as required to arrange a possible purchase from the Polish Government. This was music to General Tyszkiewicz's ears. A defense contract would financially aid Poland immensely. It was a good project and I worked closely with Polish Logistics Officer (G-4) Colonel Pauvel Hejna to make it happen. Though it did not occur during my tour with the MND, the Honker was eventually purchased for the Iraqis. The growing insurgency and the eventual senior-level decision to develop a credible force of nearly a quarter of a million Iraqi troops eventually led to purchases of more modern, up-armored combat vehicles to support the Iraqi Army's expanded combat role.

Much like when I left it in early August, the Coalition Military Assistance Training Team (CMATT) staff was still grossly undermanned. The first Iraqi battalion would not be fielded before mid-October. Without so much as a single Iraqi battalion to show for its efforts, the Coalition Provisional Authority (CPA) looked for quicker, less expensive ways to produce Iraqi security forces. Given the large number of demobilized Iraqi soldiers in the streets, the CPA thought it could create units that, with minimal training, could remain in their communities and integrate into Coalition military units. The Iraqi Civil Defense Corps (ICDC) was a Combined Joint Task Force-7 (CJTF-7) initiative formally established by the CPA early in September 2003. The senior leadership in Baghdad envisioned a force of about 15,000 men organized into nearly twenty battalions by the end of January 2004. The ICDC was to be trained by elements of each division in Iraq, including the Multinational Division (Central-South).[1] General Tyszkiewicz and I flew to Kerbelâ' on 25 September to attend an ICDC graduation sponsored by the U.S. 1st Armored Division and gain a better appreciation for the program. ICDC training called for a six-day training program that focused on basic rifle marksmanship, drill and ceremonies, field craft, and other basic military classes that allowed these men to participate in joint patrols with Coalition Forces, conduct fixed-site and route security operations, and conduct general-assistance missions not involving significant combat. The training was later expanded into a three-week program. We were impressed by the spirit and morale the troops demonstrated on the parade field and the classic British way they marched to the sounds of the U.S. V Corps Band. Great Britain's long association with Iraq was indelibly marked by the training and influence it left behind as it had in all the countries in which its soldiers had served. Brigadier General Scaparetti, the assistant division commander of the 1st Armored Division, told me after the simple, but impressive, graduation ceremony that breaking the Iraqis of their British upbringing was a near impossible task that was not worth the effort. The ICDC soldiers wore the same uniform of the former Iraqi Army except the olive drab material had been dyed a dark brown. We had made a considerable effort in the CMATT to develop a combat uniform with a camouflage pattern that would be unique to the New Iraqi Army. The former Iraqi Army uniform was very bulky and uncomfortable and lacked any distinctive insignia. Most significantly, the uniform was despised by the bulk of the trainees who did not want to be identified with the former regime. The uniforms would have to do for now. I later suggested to General Miller's chief of operations that he should consider adding a shoulder brassard of some kind to the uniform that could provide a distinctive insignia for the ICDC; I was pleasantly surprised when an orange-colored brassard with an Iraqi flag and white letters spelling "ICDC" was introduced by CJTF-7 the following month for wear by units trained by the MND.

The ICDC was not the only security forces project underway in Iraq. On 27 September, I accompanied General Tyszkiewicz to Al-Kut Air Base to attend the Iraqi Police Academy graduation at the city's Police Headquarters. The academy's training program was supervised by the 101st Airborne Division's 716th Military Police Battalion under the operational control of the Multinational Division (Central-South). The battalion was commanded by Lieutenant Colonel Kim S. Orlando, USA, a former enlisted military policeman and Officer Candidate School graduate with over twenty years of service. He had commanded the battalion in Iraq since March when it was under the operational control of the 1st Marine Expeditionary Force. In addition to its responsibilities in Al-Kut, the battalion was now responsible for training, advising, and supervising Iraqi police forces throughout the MND's area of responsibility including Kerbelaʾ, Al-Ḥillah, ad-Dīwānīyah, and Al-Najaf. Kim Orlando's battalion, in coordination with the Iraqi police chief, orchestrated a simple, but very dignified ceremony conducted in a small auditorium. The new policemen were sharply dressed in an appropriate light-blue uniform with rank insignia similar to those worn by the Iraqi armed forces. The policemen held their American instructors in high regard and the smiles on their faces spoke well of the pride they felt in their appointment. Colonel Orlando was the graduation speaker and his carefully chosen words focused on concepts of service, dedication to country, community, and respect for the law. His impressive remarks made me think perhaps there was hope for this country. There was still a chance Iraq could rise above the growing chaos and the police forces we were training would play a major role. Kim Orlando had made my day.

We returned to Ukrainian Brigade Headquarters where General Bezluschenko had arranged a working lunch to discuss border security, the development and employment of the Iraqi Border Police, and construction projects on the border. The Coalition was aware of the almost unabated infiltration of Iraq by illegal Iranian immigrants, al-Qaeda agents, and foreign fighters. It was a significant security issue for the CPA; it had to get the border under control. The Iraqi Army, however, was essentially non-existent, the local police were just beginning to stand up in places like Al-Kut, and Iraq's long and rugged borders were guarded by a thin line of Coalition Forces feeling the initial stabs of a growing insurgency and sectarian violence. The Ukrainian brigade, already on tap to train ICDC units, had been directed to assist the training of the Iraqi Border Police. This project also called for the refurbishment of several Iraqi forts to facilitate housing, office space, and logistics for the border police along the 142 kilometers of border the Ukrainians patrolled. The sooner the Coalition projects on the border could be completed and border police and customs agents trained, the sooner responsibilities on the border could be handed over to the Iraqis. The operational concept of standing Coalition forces down as Iraqi forces stood up would be sorely tested over the next several years but, at this point in Iraq's reconstruction, we were very excited about the positive prospects these plans held for Iraq's security, the success of the occupation, and the MND's overall mission success.

I was happy to be eating a hot meal at the general's table instead of an MRE (meal, ready to eat) on a hot Polish helicopter to Camp Babylon. Generals Tyszkiewicz, Sobora, and Bezluschenko conversed in Russian. I was content to eat and speak if I was asked a question. The presence of my favorite Ukrainian warrant officer, who had to have been born at the rigid position of parade rest, ensured I had plenty to eat and drink. Colonel Orlando and his command sergeant major were as conversant in Russian as I was, and I smiled as I watched them trying to appear engaged in the conversation. General Tyszkiewicz saw me smiling and changed to English to explain the Ukrainians' concerns with the border project. The concept called for the reconstruction of several border forts in the Ukrainian-patrolled sector of the border and a new customs checkpoint to facilitate legal visitation and departure from Iraq. This major project was actually a small part of a program associated with the creation of a CPA-directed Iraqi Department of Border Enforcement that would eventually include the construction or refurbishment of hundreds of border forts and deploy and equip over eight thousand Iraqi border police by the spring of 2004. The intent was to ultimately double that figure. Eventually, over three hundred million dollars would be allocated to this project from a special U.S. Congressional allocation to rebuild Iraq.[2]

The CPA, CJTF-7, and every senior leader from President Bush on down had taken about as much heat as they could stand over the occupation of Iraq. The looting of Baghdad, the dissolution of the Iraqi Army, the failure to secure critical sites and national borders, and countless other issues were haunting our senior leaders as the violence and insurgency in northern Iraq continued to worsen. Even the Grand Ayatollah Ali al-Sistani, the most important Shi'ite cleric in Iraq and one of the most respected in the world, had issued a strongly worded condemnation of the failure of the U.S. to provide security in Iraq. Controlling Iraq's borders was a huge challenge. The problem was not limited to the 1,500 kilometers of border with Iran. There were more than 800 kilometers of border with Saudi Arabia, 600 with Syria, 350 with Turkey, and 180 with Kuwait. These borders were mostly along desert regions not unlike what I had experienced in the former demilitarized zone between Kuwait and Iraq during my tour in the United Nations Iraq–Kuwait Observation Mission (UNIKOM). The MND treated the border with Saudi Arabia in the southeast corner of the Spanish brigade's area of responsibility as an "economy of force" area; it was patrolled by air as a secondary mission when helicopters were operating in the vicinity. Iraq's borders were not patrolled on a routine basis and movement across them was essentially uncontrolled.

General Tyszkiewicz said the Ukrainian border sector could expect to receive enough money to support the construction of up to twelve forts. Money for the first three was currently allocated. The three generals studied the map outlining the 142-kilometer border in their area of responsibility and eventually agreed to establish three battalion-equivalent commands under which the border police would be organized. Administratively, I thought it was a good idea, but I suggested we view the border in terms of a defensive line and draw the proposed units' areas of responsibility and other coordination symbology accordingly. We needed to study the terrain in terms of natural lines of drift and routes into Iraq, determine where forts should be from a tactical perspective, as opposed to where they were currently located, and link them to our interior lines of communication and our main logistics hub at Al-Kut Air Base. This was a simple "preparation of the battlefield" exercise which would provide a better appreciation for our challenge on the ground, determine which posts were best suited for our purposes in the near term, more efficiently allocate available forces, and delegate responsibility for command and control. I suggested it may be desirable to require a unit commander in an area with numerous natural routes from Iran to patrol less terrain. More stationary posts or fixed reconnaissance sites may be required in this case as opposed to another commander with a more wide-open area who would have more terrain to actively patrol. Given my recent experience with the Ukrainians on the border, I knew the far eastern portion of their sector was open terrain requiring far more mounted patrolling than the central part of the sector. General Tyszkiewicz translated my comments and General Sobora agreed with me. He suggested I work with him directly as his operations officer for this project; General Tyszkiewicz tacitly agreed. It meant I would spend more time on the border developing a vitally important project. I was thrilled with the prospect, but sensed General Tyszkiewicz was not pleased with his senior adviser having more extended absences from his headquarters at Camp Babylon.

My ability to assist and advise the brigades and battalions in the field was inhibited by my responsibilities at the division's headquarters. We needed more officers and noncommissioned officers (NCO) to assist the division staff and simultaneously maintain situational awareness in the field, respond to requests for information, and render our own reports to CJTF-7. I was happy to learn that my team would be reinforced by a Marine officer. Captain Ken Owens arrived at Camp Babylon on 29 September, and I was immediately impressed by his physical bearing and professional deportment. Like Tom Lowman, Ken was a former NCO, older than most captains, and vastly more experienced. Ken had managed to break away from his posting as a logistics officer to the U.S. Marine Central Headquarters, at MacDill Air Force Base, for a temporary assignment in Iraq. He was not the only marine that would add a splash of naval color to the MND. The division was scheduled to be augmented by a detachment of the 4th ANGLICO (Air and Naval Gunfire Liaison Company), a Marine fire-support team from the Marine Forces Reserve out of West Palm Beach, Florida. Lieutenant Colonel Doug Beals, USMCR, arrived with Ken and several of his men to coordinate his unit's mission, deployment, and quartering. A short, feisty, and unusually mustachioed marine, Doug was full of energy. His team was not scheduled to arrive until 15 October, but the division was happy to see him. Our sense that the general situation in Iraq was turning sour grew more intense each day. Regardless of the division's weak rules of engagement, any of its brigades could be tested by the growing insurgency and we were always uneasy with the absence of indirect-fire assets. The ANGLICO was outfitted with the communications and "know-how" to bring any form of supporting fires on the enemy; without artillery in the division, its ability to deliver aerial fires would be particularly important for us. There was not a day that went by that I did not think about the division being tested in a big way. The "Battle of Baghdad" had already begun and the 82nd Airborne Division was frequently in action just above our northern boundary in Babil Province. I walked the perimeter of Camp Babylon nearly every evening ensuring we were secure and hoping a significant insurgent effort would not occur in our region. I did not think the division was ready for it mentally or physically at this point in its deployment. I told Doug we looked forward to his unit's arrival and I quietly asked him to do anything he could to speed up operations.

"Things are quiet at the moment, Doug," I said, "But it's only a matter of time before the situation in our AOR [area of responsibility] turns 'brown.' We're going to need you."

I did not realize at the time just how correct I was.

Another welcome arrival to Camp Babylon was a British liaison team. The British-led Multinational Division (South-East) was south of us with its headquarters in Baṣrah near the border of Kuwait and the port of Umm Qasr. British presence in CJTF-7 Headquarters was growing with the addition of Major General Figgures, a distinguished Royal Engineer, who was assigned to duties dealing with posthostilities and Coalition operations. It made sense therefore, to have a British team with the Multinational Division (Central-South) and I anxiously sought them out to work with us and ensure our efforts were coordinated. The Brits were quartered with a small NATO communications unit located adjacent to the division staff's work area. After finding my way around a series of wire obstacles and bunkers, I found Major Charlton, a well-conditioned, good-looking officer of the Parachute Regiment, and a British logistics officer sitting by a small field table. I introduced myself and they quickly invited me to sit down to a cup of fine British tea. As a general rule, I avoided tea, coffee, and alcohol. My physical fitness regimen did not support the drinking habit, but good relations with Coalition partners inevitably dictated some sacrifice. Charlton was a pleasant fellow; he told me he had been selected for promotion to lieutenant colonel and command of the 4th Battalion of the Parachute Regiment. Our relationship was excellent from the start. Having had the good fortune of commanding an airborne battalion, we shared a lot in common. Charlton and I agreed to share information and assist each other whenever possible.

I informed him I would soon be spending more time at brigade and battalion level. I emphasized our need to assist the division staff and command group to the maximum extent possible, while ensuring we had the situational awareness at all levels critical to our responsibilities as liaison officers. It was a pleasant meeting. We even agreed to join each other for physical training one morning, an agreement both of us would later regret.

The division had no major recreational facilities in September and October. Weightlifting equipment, treadmills, and other physical training gear now common in the American divisions and higher headquarters' areas, had not arrived in central Iraq. Our existence was relatively spartan. Shower tents were few and crowded, and the mess hall served only one hot meal per day. MREs and "happy meals" were still the norm. I was always concerned about my team's physical conditioning. Late hours in Division Headquarters, the heat of the day, and the absence of facilities, made it difficult to keep our physical edge. We looked forward to morning runs and we were grateful for the pull-up bars our marine friends had left in place. I encouraged my officers to participate in a particularly rugged form of calisthenics I developed from drills routinely performed by Navy SEALs, Marines, Army paratroops, and Rangers. I led the drills every morning when I was not away from Camp Babylon. These drills could be performed for periods of up to an hour or more and were particularly stressful on the mid-section and upper body. A few days after meeting Major Charlton, I asked him to join me for a physical-training session, thinking it would add to our sense of camaraderie. Charlton agreed and brought his logistics officer with him the next day. Perhaps for reasons of national pride, neither officer suggested we slow down or ease up the requisite drills and, thinking both were very hardy fellows, I mistakenly poured it on. Charlton held up rather well, but the logistics officer became ill and vomited. I could not have felt worse about what had happened and, though we parted on a high note, we never got together for another physical-training session. In fact, the logistics officer departed a week later and returned to England for personal reasons. So much for my team-building efforts. I had to be more careful in the future with ensuring newly arrived personnel were fully acclimated before they engaged in excessive physical training and operations in the field.

The highlight of this quiet period was the announcement of the graduation of the first battalion of the New Iraqi Army at Kirkush Barracks on 4 October. All the Coalition division commanders including American Major Generals Swannack, Petreaus, Odierno, and Dempsey, and CJTF-7 commander Lieutenant General Sanchez, were invited to the ceremonies. I encouraged General Tyszkiewicz to accept the invitation. He was more than willing to attend, having established a warm relationship with General Eaton during their meeting at Camp Babylon only a few weeks before. He had received a briefing on the development of the New Iraqi Army from Brigadier General Riley at Camp Babylon on 29 September. He also recognized the Iraqi Army project as one of the more important security programs currently in progress.

The remote, but ever-developing training base at Kirkush Barracks was alive with activity as the Mi-8 helicopter carrying General Tyszkiewicz and I circled the landing strip already filled with American Black Hawks. Our Russian-built chopper attracted a lot of attention from the growing crowd assembling near the parade field. The growing difficulties with the former Ba'ath Party and Al Qaeda-led insurgency made this visibly positive event for the CPA and the Iraqi Interim Government the place to be for everyone who was someone in Iraq. We were greeted by an excited and happy General Eaton as we made our way to the parade field. His life since his arrival in Baghdad had been a series of frustrating setbacks, disappointments, and misunderstandings as he went about the business of developing his command, building a foundation for an army, and coordinating the efforts of his contracted civilian trainers in large measure with only limited and often reluctant support. Paul Eaton had performed a minor miracle and the day belonged to him as much as it did Iraq's new Army.

The 1st Battalion of the New Iraqi Army, 700-men-strong, including 65 officers, stood on the parade field in the unique battle-dress camouflage uniform we had designed several months before. The troops wore a tan beret, a marked contrast to the black beret of Saddam's Army. About three-quarters of these graduates had been soldiers of that 400,000-man force that had fallen apart during the Coalition's offensive only six months before. This was not an army poised to deal with the growing internal strife and insurgency that would tear at Iraq's soul over the next several years. Its mission was to defend Iraq's borders from external threats; none of its training, organization, or general orientation addressed an internal role. The Iraqi Army was expected to reach its intended end strength of 40,000 men by October 2004. By that time, a sovereign Iraqi government could decide on the eventual size and organization of its military. The 1st Battalion was destined in the short term to be assigned to the U.S. 4th Mechanized Infantry Division to conduct border-security missions commensurate with its training as light infantry.

I took a seat in the bleachers, watched the ceremonies, and listened to speeches by Iraq's American Administrator, L. Paul Bremer, and the President of the Interim, U.S.-appointed Iraqi Governing Council, Iyad Allawi. Ambassador Bremer's remarks noted that this battalion would be the core of "An Army that will defend its country and not oppress it." Allawi echoed the same theme stating that "Our Army will be devoted to the defense of our nation and all of our citizens, regardless of ethnic background," and he denounced the old Army as a force that had terrorized the people and ensured Saddam's grip on power.[3] Like any spectator, I particularly enjoyed watching the troops as they marched past the reviewing stand swinging their arms in the finest traditions of their original British upbringing and carrying their AK-47 assault rifles to marches played by the U.S. 4th Infantry Division band. They appeared to be a proud and competent; remembering the actions of my "desperate" band of officers at the CMATT that did everything to make this moment possible, I proudly stood at attention and saluted as the color guard with the national colors of Iraq passed by the reviewing stand. At the front of the battalion was Colonel Ali Naim Jaber carrying an Iraqi ceremonial sword. Following the parade, he commented to several reporters that, "Iraq needs an army of at least 120,000 men within three years."[4] It would be no small task, as I looked at the second battalion to be trained being marched off the parade field by their contracted Vinnell trainers. Iraq had plenty of manpower, but the facilities and assets available to train, equip, and house them were very limited. Still, what occurred on the parade field that day was promising. Junior officers in the 1st Battalion lauded their training and the cooperation between Arabs and Kurds in the ranks. One officer commented that he and his men had found the human-rights training particularly worthwhile. I was pleased my team's efforts during the grueling summer months appeared to have paid off. If nothing else, the historical event we had just witnessed was a source of hope for a badly beaten and demoralized nation.

General Tyszkiewicz was pleased with what he had seen. General Eaton asked us to attend a reception in a nearby mess hall and I was happy to meet and speak with some of my old teammates. General Crocker greeted me with a smile; he seemed to be a much happier person than the man I remembered in July and August. Thoughts of that period still made me shake. General Crocker's sincere handshake and kind remarks made my day. We spoke briefly about the training experience with the 1st Iraqi Battalion and I asked him specifically about the way the Iraqis marched. He told me his trainers had done everything they could to teach the American manner of marching, but to no avail. Like General Scaparetti had explained to me at the 1st Armored Division's ICDC graduation ceremony in late September, it was evident their former ways were too firmly ingrained to be worth the additional effort to change them.

Food service, transportation, sanitation, and housing issues had been corrected over time and the hard-pressed Mr. Underwood, the CMATT food-service and general-services contractor, appeared to be the happiest man in the room. The progress the CMATT had made over the past two months was truly remarkable. The sun-burned and weathered faces of Generals Eaton and Crocker, and trainers like Australian Army Major Doug Cumming and the Vinnell contractors, were testament to the first-class leadership the CMATT team was providing the Iraqi Army training effort. The Iraqi Defense Support Agency, the beginning of a Department of the Army, was also beginning to develop. Its existence was significant considering the Iraqi Council excluded the Defense Ministry when it reconstituted an interim cabinet. The Iraqi Defense Support Agency would be responsible for the daily bureaucratic demands of an emerging army, including recruiting and contracting, and eventually lift some or all this burden from the manpower-strapped CMATT.

The United States Army was blessed to have Paul Eaton in command of the vital, but still badly undermanned CMATT. Its personnel shortfalls were not corrected until well after his departure from Iraq the following summer and after Iraqi units had performed badly during street battles in Al-Najaf against Muqtadā aṣ-Ṣadr's Mahdi Army militia in April 2004, and later in Falluja in operations they were never trained or equipped to fight. It was not until after these watershed reality events that the powers in Washington and Baghdad began to get serious about training, equipping, and fielding a credible Iraqi Army. Colonel Jaber's prediction of Iraq's need for an army of 120,000 men in three years was not too far off the mark. The CMATT and New Iraqi Army had a long way to go and, as the internal challenges in the country continued to task the occupation forces, it was becoming clearer the Coalition's eventual withdrawal from Iraq would be linked to fielding strong, fully equipped, and combat-ready Iraqi security forces.

The Coalition's mission to secure and stabilize Iraq had made General Eaton's mission as the CMATT commander one of the most important of the occupation in my view. Whether CJTF-7 or the CPA saw it that way is debatable. Reflecting on the situation from my desk at Camp Babylon, I saw the growing challenges in Iraq stemming from a significant shortfall in American and Coalition troops on the ground, the loss of the Iraqi Army following the capture of Baghdad, and what appeared to be a lack of senior-level enthusiasm and, above all, resources to get Iraqi manpower trained and deployed. Perhaps somewhat naively, I thought it was not too late to commit additional forces to the occupation and training effort currently ongoing. It appeared Washington had not yet come to grips with the sheer volume of tasks to rebuild Iraq and the manpower needed to execute them. The loss of a partially intact Iraqi Army and police force, compounded with exclusion of former Baathists from the Iraqi Government, made the challenges of occupation and governance increasingly difficult.

Denied personnel and other training assets by the CPA and U.S. Army, General Eaton increasingly turned to our Coalition partners for military trainers and assistance, many of whom responded positively. Later, in an appearance before a Congressional committee, General Eaton would recall the Al-Najaf, Kerbelā', and Falluja debacles in 2004, and criticize himself for not instilling in the Iraqi units he had trained a greater appreciation for Iraq's enemies. He said his personal failure was that he had not instilled in the Iraqi soldiers an "internal sense of legitimacy" that would have allowed them to fight alongside Coalition forces.[5] I doubt it would have mattered. What mattered in 2003–04 was a gross lack of assets required to organize, man, and equip an Iraqi Army that could fight and win in modern combat. American senior leadership had not, for all intents and purposes, taken seriously the possibility of an insurgency, sectarian violence, or any significant instability in

Iraq. It had hoped for the best after the fall of Baghdad and had received something far less. In the ensuing chaos that followed, the development and training of Iraqi security forces took a back seat to the combat and stability operations required of the Coalition forces that were immediately available. Though understandable, it was inevitable Iraqi units would be undermanned, underequipped, poorly supported, and ultimately embarrassed in their first battles.

Indications of a Growing Insurgency in Central-South Iraq

Gooks in the Wire

—AMERICAN SLANG FROM THE VIETNAM WAR

The calm in our division area of responsibility (AOR) except for the Iranian border contributed to a false sense of peace and tranquility. My team's efforts were focused on situational awareness and staff assistance. The Multinational Division (MND) was still a new and developing organization and staff activities included the design and approval of such things as the division's colors, a decoration for service in Iraq, and an organizational patch to wear on the combat uniform. Similar items for the United States Army would have been the work of the Department of Heraldry at the direction of the Defense Department. I participated in these endeavors at the invitation of General Kwiatkowski who moderated the staff working groups. His challenge was to find apolitical and simple designs that did not speak to a specific national preference. The Spanish officers submitted a patch design dominated by the Spanish lion. As sharp as it was, it was quickly placed in the dead file. Eventually, the good general selected a design for both the patch and the colors that featured a palm tree and a crescent with the words, "Multinational Division CS-Iraq" in English and Arabic. The service decoration included a ribbon with the red, white, and black national colors of Iraq, and a medal featuring a dove carrying an olive branch on a map of Iraq and the Iraqi flag with the words, "Stabilization Forces; For Service in Iraq." The obverse included a map of the world and palms with the words, "Multinational Division Central South." The patch and flag were quickly approved and introduced to the troops, but the decoration was not approved by the Poles until two years later.

As interesting as these and the operationally focused staff work may have been, I wanted a greater sense of situational awareness that only comes from being in the field. Captains Lowman and Owens had a great handle on things; I was confident in their abilities to handle any staff contingency. In fact, the only work I was ever uncomfortable not doing myself was the dreaded evening tactical-satellite report that required a senior-level review of intelligence and operations reports and experience in technical military writing. I turned to General Tyszkiewicz to seek his permission to visit units in the Spanish brigade and he reluctantly allowed me to go to Al-Najaf to participate in patrolling operations with the El Salvadoran battalion. The general appreciated my need to see beyond the division's headquarters, but he asked me to keep my departures short. As his American adviser, I was growing more aware of the difficulties of his command. Some of them were mindboggling. No other division commander had to deal with a work stoppage when a national engineer commander decided the conditions under which his men were working were not to his liking, or a chief of his civil affairs section who arbitrarily decided not to employ the division's civil affairs teams in the manner specified in his orders because he did not like them. I often commented to General Miller that General Tyszkiewicz had one of the toughest jobs in Iraq, something I do not think he fully appreciated or agreed with me. I appreciated the division commander's sense of fair play and promised to return to Camp Babylon within a couple of days.

Colonel Monterrozza wore a broad smile when he greeted me in Spanish at the entrance to the headquarters of the Cuscatlán Battalion in Al-Najaf. He spoke superb English and quickly used it when I asked him to repeat something he said in Spanish or to speak more slowly. The transition of authority in Al-Najaf and the welcome arrival of promised American equipment had, unbeknown to me, made me very popular with the officers of this fine battalion. Most of them were selected from special forces units and had combat experience. They greeted me as if I was an old friend.

The Cuscatlán Battalion had been sent to Iraq in August 2003. El Salvador's President Antonio Saca considered his nation's contribution to the stability of Iraq as an honorable act, particularly in view of the war it had fought in the 1980s against terrorist forces supported by the Soviet Union and communist Cuba. He appreciated the support of the international community in his nation's struggle, particularly that of the United States. No nation more proudly served in Operation *Iraqi Freedom* than the soldiers of El Salvador. Most of the battalion's duties focused on humanitarian missions and the rebuilding of the Iraqi infrastructure. Its operations in 2003 included the distribution of food and clothing and the reconstruction of schools, roads, medical facilities, and water-treatment plants, while also leading security patrols and escorting convoys. Several of its soldiers would receive an American decoration for heroism defending a convoy late in 2004. They were, by any standard, superb combat soldiers.

On the floor of the operations section were several AK-47 rifles the men had confiscated during their sweeping patrols of the city and its surrounding road complex over the past week. The weapons ranged in readiness from very good to something I would not want to shoot. It was clear, however, that Al-Najaf was a potentially dangerous place with plenty of armed men. This was not particularly surprising. Al-Najaf is the center of Shia power in Iraq. Located 190 kilometers south of Baghdad, it is considered a holy city among Shia Muslims. Central to Al-Najaf is the Imām 'Alī Mosque, burial place of 'Alī, the cousin and son-in-law of the Prophet Mohammad and the man whom Shia Muslims believe should have succeeded Mohammad in leadership after his death. Significantly, Al-Najaf is home to many Shia scholars and a "wannabe" named Muqtadā aṣ-Ṣadr. His presence and the Mahdi Army militia he commanded caused significant concern to the Combined Joint Task Force-7 (CJTF-7) command group. In the fall of 2003, the Coalition was obsessed with his capture and it brought significant pressure to bear on the MND to get him. CJTF-7 had designated Operation *Stuart* to manage and direct as necessary those actions to be taken by troops on the ground to eliminate Sadr's influence. The Spanish brigade and the El Salvadoran battalion were its lead actors by virtue of location. This did not sit well with the Spanish who considered the mission rash, unnecessary, and detrimental to the stability of their AOR. I was confident the "El Sals" could perform any mission they were given, but I was mindful they were under the command of the Spanish brigade commander.

Colonel Monterrozza told me I would participate in a night patrol that would be conducted initially in Humvees, and then dismounted. At a designated location, the patrol would establish a checkpoint to search vehicles. The operations briefing that outlined the entire battalion's patrol plan for the evening was given by the Battalion S-3 (Operations). The young lieutenant designated to lead the patrol then briefed his plan. I was impressed by the detail with which he described his routes, formations for dismounted movement, actions in various situations, actions at the objective, command and control, and the logistics plan. His patrol order was textbook perfect and I complimented him on its thoroughness. The patrol was scheduled to go out after nightfall at 7:30 pm, establish a checkpoint on a major road leading into the city, and inspect vehicles for contraband, essentially weapons and drugs. Prior to returning to base, the patrol would check for any unusual activity at designated checkpoints in the city. Colonel Monterrozza recommended I take my gear into a section of his headquarters where a cot and an end table were situated for my use. I told the lieutenant I would attend his last rehearsal after supper chow and settled in for a short power nap. The heat of the day and the long drive from Camp Babylon to Al-Najaf had tired me enough to want to kick back and recoup before our 5–6-hour patrol. Opportunities to sleep were becoming more important to me. I was only just beginning to realize I was not a 20-year-old Ranger student or scout platoon leader, but, at nearly fifty-three, I took great pride in my overall fitness and conditioning. It is a young man's "game," but I still felt I had more than a few good "plays" left. There was no better way to see what the division was doing in the field and report accordingly.

Our patrol moved out in three Humvees, passing through the city and quickly moving beyond its ambient light to the darkness of the unpaved, gravel access roads utilized by heavy vehicles and large trucks. At a designated point, the lieutenant ordered his men to dismount, and we moved off the road to an assembly area while the vehicles turned and drove off. We would link up with them at a predetermined time later that evening. It was pitch black as we moved in a disciplined tactical formation about one hundred meters to the side of the road toward our checkpoint 1,000 meters away. The lieutenant wisely elected to walk to the designated checkpoint rather than drive to it and alert anyone in the vicinity of our presence. The soldiers moved without a sound. Their equipment was secured to their bodies and there was no talking. The platoon occupied an objective rallying point (ORP) some two hundred meters short of the intersection where the checkpoint was to be established. We then moved to a position concealed from the road by a row of trees and bushes. Its elevation above the road afforded us excellent observation of the intersection. Several men moved closer to the intersection and positioned themselves to quickly flag down a moving vehicle. All we could do at that point was wait. It is always like that—a flurry of excitement from planning to briefings, to inspections and rehearsals, to movement, and then the wait. Leaders and soldiers alike can relax, lose their edge, and even fall asleep if discipline or leadership is lacking. In this platoon, however, a senior sergeant slowly made his way to every man to encourage him and ensure he was awake. Thank God for sergeants, I thought, as I stared into the darkness, tensing my legs from time to time to fight off my own fluttering eyelids.

The tell-tale lights of an 18-wheeler loomed ahead and the flashlights from the checkpoint team signaled it to stop. Only then did the lieutenant direct a team to move toward the truck. A supporting element remained in place to provide supporting fire in the event anything went wrong. I moved forward and peered into the window of the cab. The fear on the driver's face made me think he had just seen the devil himself. I directed him to get out of the vehicle and a soldier frisked him for any hidden weapons. He was dressed in traditional Arab garb and sandals; he was visibly shaking with fear. After he opened the trailer, two young paratroopers climbed aboard and inspected it. I stayed with the driver and attempted to put him at ease by offering him a cigarette. I always carried a pack or two with me. American cigarettes are a big hit with Arab men, and they tend to be more friendly and talkative after they light up. In the meantime, our young troopers turned up two AK-47 rifles that they quickly confiscated. There was not anything else suspicious about him, his papers, or his cargo, so we let him go. Before he drove off, I gave him another cigarette. Not much of an exchange for the rifles, but he looked relieved to be alive and unhurt. It was a lot of effort for two rifles, but this country had to be pacified one weapon at a time. We packed up the checkpoint and moved to the ORP, then back to our dismount point. Throughout the entire process, the only sound I heard was the lieutenant on the radio ordering the patrol vehicles to begin their movement to our dismount point where we linked up with them precisely at midnight. It had been like clockwork. We devoted another hour to patrolling designated streets in Al-Najaf proper, but the city, including the vicinity of the Imām 'Alī Mosque, was asleep at 1 am. I was happy to head back to the El Salvador garrison for debriefing and some much-needed rest. The morning patrol was scheduled for 7 am and wake up was scheduled for 5 am. I kicked off my boots after the debriefing, lay back on my cot, and fell almost immediately to sleep.

I was still running on adrenalin when a young sergeant shook me awake. I washed my face, grabbed a quick bite of chow, and stood by the briefing room at 5:30. The morning patrol promised to be much different from my experience on the night patrol. This patrol would reinforce civilian security personnel and escort a convoy of vehicles carrying new Iraqi money. After linking up with the convoy at a designated link-up point on a city access road, we would move into the city to make deposits at several local banks. I listened intently, fascinated with what I was hearing. It was all about rehabilitating this beaten nation into something that could survive the global economy. I remembered entering southern Iraq with my long-range reconnaissance unit in April and being greeted by long lines of Iraqi kids looking to trade their practically worthless Saddam-era dinar for anything we were willing to pass to them in exchange. This security mission was a small, but important piece of Iraq's economic rehabilitation.

The Iraqi dinar was worth $3.20 U.S. dollars prior to Saddam's ill-fated invasion of Kuwait in 1990 and the United Nations embargo that followed. The dinar was a total disaster and practically worthless by April 2003, having slipped to anywhere between 3,500 and 4,000 against the dollar. It recovered to 1,500 by July 2003, but the dinar was printed poorly, and many forgeries had been made.[1] U.S. officials had already agreed a new currency was needed to introduce some stability and get money with real value into the hands of the people. The fact the Iraqi dinar had Saddam Hussein's image on it hastened that decision. In July, Ambassador Bremer announced the Coalition would print and distribute new banknotes for Iraq and that the "Saddam" dinar and other variations were no longer suitable for the new Iraq. In August, the Central Bank of Iraq advised Iraqis to deposit all their dinars in local banks to facilitate their change into the new currency, and in early October the new currency was unveiled during a press conference in Baghdad. An exchange rate had been established to account for the variety of dinar in the economy and the new currency was to be made available to the Iraqi people on 15 October. Our mission was to simply ensure a portion of the nearly two billion notes that comprised the original order of new dinar was safely delivered to designated banks in Al-Najaf. Over six trillion new Iraqi dinars were scheduled to be in the economy by mid-January 2004.

Unlike the night patrol, there was a lot of talking and members of the platoon were curious about the "gringo" colonel with them. I spoke with several soldiers as we prepared the vehicles and made final premission inspections. My Spanish held up well and they appreciated that I could speak and laugh with them. We moved out and linked up with our convoy on the outskirts of the city. The civilian security guys were dark, large, young men in gray, unmarked uniforms; several of them were manning M240 machine-guns mounted in the beds of their trucks. One of them cried out to me and I could not believe what I saw. These guys were former Fijian soldiers who had been caught up in the United Nations' decision to stand-down the Fijian battalion that had served in Lebanon for over twenty years. They had quickly volunteered when their services were avidly sought to conduct contract security missions in Iraq.

"Colonel Tiso, hey, Chief of Staff!" I was suddenly surrounded by several Fijians with whom I had served during my tour of duty in the Sinai with the Multinational Force and Observers in 2000–01. I had always been impressed with the "Fiji boys." I enjoyed their humor, military discipline, island culture, and love of athletics. I had always had a soft spot in my heart for the Fijians, but particularly since the wonderful dinner they had thrown in my honor prior to my departure from the Sinai. I had spent a lot of time with them at various outposts in the desert, but most notably after we had established observation posts to oversee the Gaza Strip in the spring of 2001. They were tough guys who handled discomfort well. After my first trip to one of these outposts, where I spent the night observing and reporting fire fights and pyrotechnic displays until dawn the next day, I directed and helped coordinate additional supplies to improve their living conditions. The Fijians were very appreciative and their friendship was genuine. Their pats on my back and nice words brought tears to my eyes, but our reunion was short-lived as the civilian contractor in charge signaled us to prepare to move. He, the lieutenant, and I quickly looked at the map and reviewed procedures regarding how to secure the bank locations. I was able to roughly translate his instructions into Spanish for the young lieutenant. The mission did not appear to be particularly difficult, but I suggested to the senior Fijian and my young lieutenant that we take the time to rehearse our actions at the banks. Our civilian contractor could wait, particularly if he wanted to ensure a smooth and secure delivery. "No time is ever wasted in reconnaissance"; I would add, "And rehearsals" to that old British dictum. The potential for trouble at the banks dictated a thorough rehearsal of actions at our respective objectives. The lieutenant took charge and I watched him and the senior Fijian brief their troops. They designated an area along the road as the location of one of our banks and the officers led their drivers and the gunners through their paces. Little things like rehearsals are often the difference between failure and success. Through hand signals and head nods, they worked things out and even the contractor agreed it was a good idea to rehearse their security and battle-drill actions at the objective sites. It took all of 30 minutes.

Our convoy of civilian security vehicles, the money trucks, and our Humvees made a very impressive sight to the Iraqi crowds as we made our way through the streets and marketplaces of the city. The streets of Al-Najaf were filled with shoppers and the small sidewalk businesses that characterize all Middle Eastern cities and towns.

There were plenty of onlookers as we drove to a designated local bank to deposit the new Iraqi money. Our vehicles quickly moved into place and our gunners remained alert behind their machine guns. Our presence slowly attracted a crowd nearer to the bank. I took up a casual position next to the lieutenant's vehicle, quietly hoping the deposit would go quickly. The soldiers and Fijians were tense. Our position was not the best and the crowd continued to grow as more curiosity seekers came by to have a look. There was an older gentleman standing only a few feet from us and I decided to divert the crowd's attention from our gunners and the bank by approaching him and offering a cigarette. I moved toward the old guy, greeted him with a customary Arab greeting, and held out a pack of Marlboros with one cigarette exposed at the top. He smiled an old broken, gap-toothed grin and accepted my offer. I reached for a match and lit it up. We did not speak, but I extended my hand and smiled. The crowd fixed its attention on us and not a minute later our contractor came out of the bank and gave me a "thumbs up." I waved him over to me and introduced him to my old Iraqi friend. "Care for a smoke," I asked the contractor. He figured out from the tone of my voice what I was doing and lit up one of my cigarettes. I handed the old guy another cigarette which he quickly accepted. We shook hands and, in a sign of friendship and respect, I placed my hand over my heart. The contractor and I moved to our vehicles and waved goodbye. We were off in a cloud of dust and the crowd gave way without incident. It was not until after we were well away from the bank and the ominous crowd that I realized how fast my heart was beating. The other bank deposits were made smoothly and without the drama the crowd at our first location had provided. Our mission was completed by 10:30 am and I felt a sense of relief as our contractor bankers and my Fijian friends said their goodbyes. I had been hard at it for nearly 36 hours with only a few hours of sleep. It was already a long day and after-action reports for this mission and the usual staff work at Division Headquarters still awaited me. I was grateful for the long ride from Al-Najaf to Babylon. I slept all the way.

The need to rely less on aggressive or kinetic behavior and more on a passive approach in potentially tense situations involving civilians was a lesson reinforced by my experience at the bank. It is amazing what a smile and a kind offer of a cigarette to an Arab can do to alleviate a stressful situation. The behavior of soldiers toward civilians during the conduct of counter-insurgency operations is often the difference between success and failure. It was exactly the point British Major General Lamb, commander of the Multinational Division (South-East) shared with our division staff when he visited Camp Babylon and General Tyszkiewicz on 7 October. General Lamb had a tough reputation. A veteran of the First Gulf War and a noted sportsman, he had commanded the 1st Battalion, Queen's Own Highlanders, and the 5th Airborne Brigade before assuming command of the 3rd (United Kingdom) Division in Iraq in June 2003. The division formed the headquarters of the Multinational Division (South-East) that included Italian, Dutch, Danish, and Romanian formations.

General Lamb was a dynamic speaker. After making his way to the front of the assembled staff in the briefing tent, he removed his body armor and surveyed his audience. He noticed me in the back of the audience and, with his eyes firmly fixed on me, began to speak.

"Good afternoon, gentlemen," he said. "Let me assure you that George Patton is alive and well in the U.S. Army."

I knew very well to what he was referring as it was generally well known the British way of dealing with an insurgency was far less kinetic than the American approach. Our methods at the time emphasized killing and capturing the enemy rather than securing and engaging the populace. General Lamb was resentful of the American approach and considered it counterproductive. His views were not unlike most British officers who consider one of the greatest strengths of the British military is its ability to conduct unconventional warfare against asymmetric adversaries. Not surprisingly, they view that same ability as the single greatest weakness of the American military.[2] A noted Australian military writer, David Kilcullen, wrote that Americans are very good at big, short conventional wars, but not very good at small, long wars and even worse at big, long wars. The implication was that Americans do not allow themselves the time or effort to effectively incorporate the necessary political, economic and informational factors into an effective military campaign to wage insurgent warfare. The insurgency to our north had found its way to the predominantly Shia south and the British were already engaged. It was clear our division would be engaged soon as well. It was all very disappointing to me. The hopes for stability that we had in the aftermath of the invasion had begun to fade during my tour in Baghdad. General Lamb's comments convinced me we were headed for another protracted undertaking and an open-ended commitment in Iraq. He pointed out to us that these types of wars require patience, something Americans are not particularly well noted for having in any great quantity. The people had to be convinced to reject the terrorist insurgents and support their government. Our efforts had to convince the people of our good intentions. He stressed cultural awareness and the need to establish harmonious relations with the people in our area of responsibility. The "George Patton" comment referred in large measure to an "elitist attitude" Americans often portrayed at the time. I smiled as I thought of the type "A" personalities that dominate the fighting arms of the U.S. Army. I certainly was not innocent of type "A" tendencies, but I knew interpersonal relationships, so important to getting things done in the Middle East, were hard to develop in our "get to the point, bottom-line approach" to business. In the general's opinion, Americans were too quick to use excessive force, act without sufficient intelligence, and fail to provide adequate security to the general population in the process. The Brits, on the other hand, were inclined to apply the minimum force required to attain operational objectives, believing excessive force is ultimately counterproductive. The key point with which I left the tent was the British concept of graduated response that essentially starts with no action, moves to some action, then to major action. It was an approach I thought would sit well with my Polish counterparts. I took careful notes. General Lamb's visit was not the usual "General Officer drive by." He comments had a significant impact on the division staff and we began to think about how we could apply his thoughts to the division's operating procedures.

The central-south region of Iraq showed some signs of stabilization and reconstruction. I attended several meetings at the Coalition Provisional Authority (CPA) office in Al-Ḥillah with General Tyszkiewicz during which provincial governors from our area of responsibility addressed their challenges to CPA representatives and senior military officials. Major General Charles Swannack Jr., commander of the 82nd Airborne Division then operating in Babil Province to the north of the MND, attended these meetings and he and General Tyszkiewicz enjoyed each other's company and shared similar views with CPA officials regarding reconstruction and security issues. During a meeting on 9 October, the governors of both Kerbelâ' and Al-Najaf Provinces expressed satisfaction with the security Coalition forces and developing Iraqi police forces were providing. These men and the members of their respective staffs impressed me with their intelligence and sophisticated manners. Their sophisticated appearance and deportment provided another ray of hope for a country that had once boasted a large middle class and a relatively mature education system. The governors and several members of their staffs spoke English and appeared enthusiastic about getting on with the business of governance in the post-Saddam era.

A buffet-style lunch following the meeting allowed me to meet and speak with these gentlemen. They expressed hope for the future. They were complimentary of the Polish and Spanish troops that secured their cities and countryside. One subject they did not raise was the growing concern with Muqtadā aṣ-Ṣadr, whose growing influence in Al-Najaf was leading to a parallel system of law and governance. The outlaw cleric had reportedly established Sharia, or Islamic, Courts in Al-Najaf and Kerbelâ' and his negative, anti-Coalition position was beginning to become a major challenge to the CPA and local Iraqi governments. Ṣadr was a thorn in General Miller's side that irked him to no end. The fact that Ṣadr was still "at large" and the MND was not acting aggressively to "take him down" was a particularly bad subject. I got an earful from Miller that night over the phone that the division was not executing its responsibilities in accordance with Operation *Stuart*. General Tyszkiewicz was not keen to pursue Ṣadr. He believed it would incite violence in Al-Najaf and eliminate any gains the division had made in stabilizing the province. The lack of action did not enhance the division's or his image at CJTF-7 Headquarters.

Adding insult to injury, Brigadier General Isaszegi, my Hungarian friend in CJTF-7 Coalition Operations, submitted a damaging report earlier that day condemning the MND for not fulfilling its mission to patrol the Iraqi–Saudi border along the southern boundary of its AOR. He was essentially correct. An occasional flight by one of our Spanish helicopters that just happened to be in the area was the only asset the Spanish brigade was willing to spare in what was probably the most remote, inhospitable region of our AOR. We clearly needed something down there, but General Tyszkiewicz viewed the region, and any reconnaissance in that region, as an economy-of-force mission and did not press the Spaniards for additional efforts. General Cardona was fiercely against sending any troops to the border given the logistical and communications difficulties it presented. I understood General Miller's frustration as I held the telephone away from ear to avoid going deaf. He was upset and I was as good a target to vent his frustration and anger as anyone. It also reminded me that, in the CJTF-7 staff's collective mind, my team was more than just a liaison element rendering reports. We were expected to make things happen. General Lamb was right about American patience. I knew things would not happen too quickly in this outfit and all the anger and frustration in the world was not going to change that. I told General Miller I would address his concerns with General Tyszkiewicz and he thankfully hung up. My assessment of the challenges we faced in Iraq was disheartening. A raging insurgency in the north, growing sectarian violence in the south, porous borders, growing Iranian influence, warring clerics, a broken economy, and poor infrastructure—the list was seemingly endless; it was apparent to everyone we were critically short of personnel and resources to fix them anytime soon. I sat quietly for a moment shaking my head. Tom Lowman looked at me and asked, "Gooks in the wire, sir?" It was a Vietnam-era way of asking whether the enemy was about to over run our position.

"Tom," I replied, "It's bigger than they know."

CHAPTER 23

Dealing with Generals

No time is wasted in reconnaissance (or rehearsals).

—Old British Dictum

I was deep in thought behind one of the door-mounted machine guns when the Mi-8 helicopter transporting us to Al-Najaf settled into the Honduran base camp where General Tyszkiewicz and I were scheduled to greet British Major General Andrew C. Figgures, the newly arrived Combined Joint Task Force-7 (CJTF-7) deputy commander and senior British military representative in Iraq. The situation in Al-Najaf concerned a lot of people these days and I guessed General Figgures was no exception. He was, by all accounts, a brilliant engineer. I had read his bio prior to leaving Camp Babylon that morning and could not help but be impressed by his broad military engineering background and record of achievements. The Brits probably figured they needed one very bright fellow to assist CJTF-7's stability and reconstruction efforts; they had him in General Figgures.

The sound of two UH-60 Black Hawk helicopters announced his arrival and he landed in the usual sandstorm the Black Hawk's powerful engines generated. After a brief exchange of pleasantries with General Tyszkiewicz on the landing zone, we jumped into a couple of Humvees and took an extensive tour of the city. It was clear from the beginning General Figgures was no "stuffed shirt." No sooner did we turn into the marketplace did he turn toward his driver and order him to pull over. The streets were crowded with local sidewalk merchants doing business in their seemingly wild and disorganized manner. There is nothing calm about street business in the Middle East. It reminded me of the seemingly angry, but friendly bantering at the local vegetable stores in the predominantly Italian section of Mount Vernon, New York, when I was a kid. The streets were filled with all sorts of goods the Iraqis had long learned to live without, and they now gazed in amazement upon everything from new bicycles to Sony radios. The port of Umm Qasr must have been booming with ships and cargo. I could not have guessed what was coming next as the general looked back at me and, in his best British accent, said, "Let's get out among the people, shall we?"

There was not time to suggest otherwise as he bounded out into the crowd wearing his helmet, body armor, and side arm, seemingly unaware he was giving his security detail an absolute fit. That's all I needed, I thought, a mad Englishman hell bent on getting me killed. I moved next to him and General Tyszkiewicz, all the while cognizant of the security detail by our side and rear, and kept my eyes moving as we moved through the sidewalk crowds. The general walked as though he was out for a countryside stroll and conversed with several Iraqi merchants and customers who wanted desperately to speak to him. They spoke passionately about how grateful they were that we had saved them from Saddam Hussein. They spoke of the need to build and to recover their wealth and asked for our help. In every group, someone could speak English, reminding all of us that an educated middle class had once existed in this country. I would have liked to have listened to all the conversations, but my concern for the growing crowds distracted me. I briefly thought of the old man at the bank during my patrol with the "El Sals" several days before and comically thought there were not enough cigarettes among us to placate everybody. General Figgures seemed to enjoy himself and, while I was concerned with the crowds, I was genuinely impressed by the fearless way he engaged with the Iraqi men who approached him.

I was relieved when the vehicles pulled alongside. We mounted up and drove to the El Salvadoran garrison for lunch in their new mess hall. General Tyszkiewicz asked me to join him and General Figgures at their table and I listened to their small talk until General Tyszkiewicz was called away to answer a phone call. General Figgures then spoke to me, focusing his questions on the division, the Spanish brigade, and Operation *Stuart*. I explained the difficulties we had experienced with the Spanish brigade in August but, on balance, I told him the equipment shortfalls that existed at the time would have severely hampered the brigade's ability to effectively operate and accomplish its mission. I suggested the actions the Spanish commander and General Tyszkiewicz took could just as easily be viewed as highly responsible and even praiseworthy. I was concerned about CJTF-7's perception that the division was unreliable and suggested the unique differences between the Polish-led MND and American and British formations dictated that CJTF-7 Headquarters make every effort to communicate on a more personal basis, commander to commander and staff to staff. I further suggested he carry that message to General Sanchez. Regarding Operation *Stuart*, I reminded him the problem with the mission was that the MND's contingents had deployed under peacekeeping rules of engagement. The commanders in large measure did not think they had the national authority to engage in offensive operations and there was not any enthusiasm in the division's national contingents, therefore, to engage Muqtadā aṣ-Ṣadr. The Spanish had agreed to maintain surveillance of his likely locations, but I seriously doubted they would move on a reported sighting. If the Americans were casualty adverse, the multinational contingents were so to a much higher degree. It was very evident to me that whether a national unit stayed in Iraq was dependent on how high a cost they paid in casualties. I strongly suggested Operation *Stuart* be reconsidered and that any effort to seize Ṣadr be American led with multinational troops in support. Finally, I told him very emphatically that the division and its commander were valuable assets that merited the utmost respect.

General Figgures was a good listener. He acknowledged my comments and thanked me for my, "Frank assessment," but our conversation made it increasingly clear to me the MND was perceived by our higher headquarters as ineffective, more a distracter from a tactical and operational perspective than an asset. We went our separate ways after lunch, the Black Hawks and the Polish Mi-8 creating a sandstorm that engulfed our El Salvadoran friends who proudly stood at attention and rendered a hand salute. The military is high on protocol and respect, but there was something about these arrivals and departures that struck me as one of the silliest things we did. I smiled as I watched Colonel Monterozza and his staff turn away just before the blast of sand hit them full in the face. Fine soldiers, I thought.

Back at Camp Babylon, I moved to my plywood sea hut to relax and get some rest. My complete trust and confidence in Captains Lowman and Owens at this point allowed me to stay away from the operations floor for longer periods of time, something for which I was immensely grateful. A phone call from General Miller, however, could be handled only by me and the young messenger at my door informed me that I was, "Urgently needed at the operations center." My concern I had said something that had insulted General Figgures quickly faded as General Miller wasted no time informing me of a rumor that a meeting had apparently been scheduled between the Ukrainian brigade commander and an Iranian Army commander somewhere on the Iranian border. As usual, General Miller did not mince any words,

"Roland, we don't need any loose-cannon brigade commanders conducting uncleared meetings with the damn Iranians. What the hell is going on down there? Find out what's really going on. If they have arranged a meeting, I want it quashed."

No such meeting had been reported to the Division Operations Center and the Ukrainian brigade commander had not reported a meeting with the Iranians in his report to the division commander earlier in the evening. Major General Bezluschenko did not strike me as a man who would do anything out of line or take any unusual risks, but Wasit Province and the Iranian border were a long way from the division flagpole and the illegal-immigrant crossings along the 142-kilometer Iranian border his reinforced company patrolled were increasing significantly. It would not surprise me if a local commander would take action to mitigate the problem by meeting with Iranian border-guard officials. I told General Miller I would investigate it and take the necessary action to prevent any meeting of that sort. Clearly, his patience with the division was growing increasingly thin. Small talk about old times in our conversations was a thing of the past. I hung up wondering what else could go wrong.

Major General Bezluschenko answered to Major General Sobora, the Ukrainian contingent commander and senior Ukrainian representative in Iraq. General Sobora was one of the toughest, hard-bitten men I had ever met in any Army. Slow to smile, he was once described by one of the American National Guard officers on the division staff as a man with a "Perennial case of the ass." My dealings with him had been civil since the Ukrainian National Day ceremony in late August, so I did not think much of it as I made my way through the series of small buildings in the center of our camp and found the Ukrainian Headquarters. Several Ukrainian staff officers were manning the phones and poring over various papers and forms when I walked in and requested to see the general. Not many officers or soldiers other than Ukrainians normally came into General Sobora's headquarters. Some of these guys, undoubtedly still entrenched in the Cold War, had to wonder what this "Amerikanskyi colonel" could possibly want with their general. Fortunately, First Lieutenant Alex Kanus, the general's interpreter, was present and quickly addressed me in English. I enjoyed speaking with Alex and did everything I could to make him smile and occasionally laugh. Alex was the most stilted character I have ever known. His taciturn mannerisms and military correctness were as funny to me as they were professional. I told him I needed to see the general on a matter of important business and asked if he would make the necessary arrangements. After a few minutes, Alex ushered me into the office where the general was sat behind a computer writing a report to his national headquarters. He spoke little English so Alex sat down and joined us around his conference table to translate.

Major General Anatoliy Ivanovych Sobora was a man who had avidly lived the soldier's life. In my mind, he was the quintessential Warsaw Pact soldier we had trained to fight throughout the Cold War. He had entered the Army in the early seventies and graduated from the Higher Military Armor College in 1972. He had moved steadily through the ranks to command a division in the Odessa Military District from 1994–98. He had come from Ukraine's Northern Operational Command, after nearly five years as its deputy commander, to serve as his nation's contingent commander in Iraq. There was nothing that seemed to amuse him. Stoic and as serious as a heart attack, he was a no-nonsense, straight-talking soldier. My experiences with him in August and September had been positive. Captain Owens and I had attended several of his force-protection sessions and he had impressed us with the attention to detail he placed on securing Camp Babylon. He was known to frequently walk the camp's perimeter at all hours and make corrections. He was hard on his officers and men. In many ways, I likened him to General Robert C. Kingston, USA, commanding general of the 2nd infantry Division in Korea in 1979 when I was a young captain serving as his aide-de-camp. There was general agreement in that division that attacking enemy machine-gun emplacements was far preferable to getting an "ass-chewing" from General Kingston. Professionalism and a disciplined, respectful manner are the keys to successfully approaching such men.

"General, I am very grateful that you would see me at such a late hour, but I have been advised of a meeting that is scheduled to occur soon between the Ukrainian brigade commander and an Iranian Army commander on the border. I respectfully request that you confirm this information."

The general did not confirm or deny the report. He did not respond after Lieutenant Kanus translated my question, but rather stared straight ahead with his hands around a cup of coffee. I thought I had touched a nerve, but I stared at him about as hard as he focused on the wall to his front. His face softened enough for him to speak.

"Such a meeting will be conducted only with CJTF-7 and Multinational Division Command approval."

It was as if the general knew what I wanted to hear. I acknowledged his comment and asked if he would approve my passing his words to General Miller. He shook his head in a positive manner and then surprised me.

"Tiso, I would like you to have Ukrainian water. We received a stock of it aboard a Ukrainian Il-76 that landed in Al-Kut. I think you will like it."

The water was in attractive blue and green bottles, and I enjoyed its carbonated and naturally sweet taste, having drank several bottles in Al-Kut in August. I thanked him for the water and told him I looked forward to future discussions and professional exchanges. I left the office with a snappy salute and headed back to the Operations Center. It was clear to me a meeting had been arranged with the Iranians, but I trusted General Sobora would cancel it. I was confident the issue was closed and I put CJTF-7 at ease with a phone call before heading back to my hooch for the night. I did not get very far before Colonel Gocul, the Division G-3, called me just as I reached the building's massive doors.

"Roland, I almost forgot to tell you. General Sanchez will soon visit the Ukrainian brigade and the commanding general wants you to go to Al-Kut and help the Ukrainian commander coordinate the visit. You will fly out tomorrow with General Sobora."

Mike Gocul's smile said it all. The Poles knew I liked the Ukrainians and particularly their tough mission on the border, but they also knew General Sobora was a tough guy to live with.

"Commanding general's orders, Roland. You will leave after breakfast."

Tom Lowman looked at me and smiled. "It's okay, sir, we have things covered here." I was feeling guilty about Tom. His relationship with the junior officers and young field-grade officers on the division staff was exceptional. He was an invaluable source of professional knowledge and know-how, but I had promised him an opportunity to serve at battalion level and I had not made good on it, nor did it look like I could. Always the professional, Tom never said a word. I could not have asked for a better deputy.

General Bezluschenko greeted us as our Mi-8 came to a rest on the Al-Kut tarmac. We quickly made our way to his headquarters where General Sobora and I reviewed the proposed briefings and itinerary for CJTF-7's visit. Andriy Lischinskyi, the gentle giant who had served as my translator in August at the Ukrainian National Day ceremonies, now served as the principal briefing officer. Andriy cared about his work and wanted more than anything to speak fluent English, a second language relatively easy to learn for many non-English-speaking people, but extremely difficult to master. My face gave away my displeasure as Andriy went through slide after slide of poorly worded, misspelled, and poorly presented information that would never pass muster with an American three-star general. Once he was done, General Sobora looked at me as if to ask what I thought.

"General, I recommend that you allow me to work with Andriy for an hour. With a few adjustments, I'm confident that we will have a superb briefing for the Amerikanskyi General Sanchez."

Regardless of the setting, the requirement for a unit to demonstrate to its chain of command that it has a good handle on things is a never-ending fact of life. We had to develop a first-rate American style "dog and pony show" that would be both impressive and informative of the brigade's operational mission, readiness, and requirements. As my words were translated, I noticed a slight smile on the general's face. He knew what I meant, and he enjoyed my reference to the "Amerikanskyi general." He nodded and walked out with the others, content to leave me with Andriy. Good generals know when to get out of the way and let people work.

Dynamite PowerPoint presentations are a must in any business. Since the late nineties I had somewhat cynically concluded that high-ranking people expect to be entertained as well as informed. A beautifully formed briefing without substance cannot cut it in a true professional setting, but good staff work inevitably involves enough form to sell the substance. General Sobora wanted the briefing to accurately present the unit's activities and accomplishments, the challenges it faced in light of the increasing threat in Al-Kut and on the border, and provide an accounting of its shortfalls in equipment and manpower. He wanted to make a case for additional support that would enable the brigade to better control its area of operations. Wasit Province was a long way from Coalition Headquarters in Baghdad. Its actions on the Iranian border, Al-Kut, and northeast Wasit Province were not as well known as the growing challenges in Baghdad and northern Iraq, but it was a tough place to operate. With Andriy by my side and a Ukrainian junior officer working on the computer, we went through the slides, crafting a coherent briefing that was simple, understandable, and informative. Andriy took careful notes and asked me the meaning of certain words and questions regarding word usage and grammar. Much like at Division Headquarters where my liaison team mates and I translated Polish English into American English, we were translating Ukrainian English into American English. Several other Ukrainian staff officers, anxious to see what we were doing, joined us. The Ukrainians, perhaps more than any other contingent's officers, were very anxious to learn Western staff procedures and, like the Poles, wanted to improve their English-speaking skills. Our session to build the Ukrainian briefing was more than simply improving slides. It was also a class on military presentation and English conversation.

We exceeded the hour and the final presentation still required rehearsals with the brigade commander. When Generals Sobora and Bezluschenko returned to the tent, a confident Major Andriy Lischenskyi explained what had been done and recommended a rehearsal at the brigade commander's convenience. The smile on his face after the commander's approval said a lot about how a little training and "know-how" instills confidence in a soldier. General Sobora was pleased with the slides, but he was clearly anxious to get back to the airfield and fly to the border. A big part of the day with General Sanchez would be spent on the border and a series of briefings and site visits were planned. After directing General Bezluschenko and Andriy to remain behind to refine and rehearse the briefing, General Sobora signaled me to come with him and we quickly departed for the airfield where our Mi-8 crew was standing by to take us to the border.

The vast emptiness of the eastern Iraqi desert suddenly revealed several vehicles and a platoon of infantry securing our designated landing zone. We were long overdue, and I could not tell if the general was angry at me for our extended stay in Al-Kut or if he was just being himself. Our operational concern was always the availability of daylight and the lack of night-flying capability. We had to work fast if we were to get to see everything we needed to see, make adjustments, provide additional guidance, and make the long flight back to Camp Babylon. This was not the first time I wished for additional liaison teams for duty at brigade level. Our reporting and advisory assistance would improve a thousand-fold if we could provide a two-man cell with each of the division's brigades. The constant liaison requirement at division and the high level at which staff work was accomplished meant I had to bridge the gap by getting to the brigade headquarters as often as possible and assisting as required or requested. I would later address the shortfall of manning in my after-action report to General Miller but, for now, there was no alternative to my "on the go" advisory and liaison service. It was as frustrating as it was exciting and fulfilling.

The Ukrainian platoon commander greeted us as we moved away from the aircraft. General Sobora wasted no time. The itinerary for the border visit scheduled us to move to Camp Fort, then to a reconstructed border post and finally to a new Iraqi-run customs checkpoint. Briefings would occur at each site. The long drive to Camp Fort along the difficult border road was a huge time consumer and I noted the need to relocate the landing zone for the General Sanchez visit. Mine clearing would be an issue, but the importance of this visit would give us priority on the required engineers and equipment to get it done in a timely manner. The company commander greeted us at Camp Fort. Major Val Semenets appeared to be in good spirits as he provided an orientation briefing using a map that highlighted key structures and locations as a young lieutenant translated Val's presentation into English. The briefings and tours at the follow-on locations indicated the paratroopers had done their homework. I shared my time concerns with the general. He quickly adjusted the program by scratching the drive to the border post and organizing a tour of a similar construction at the customs point. This cut over a half an hour of driving time and made the entire program flow in an efficient manner. We agreed the initial landing zone had to be adjusted. The general was never one to mince words. After I explained my concern, he simply replied, "Da," Ukrainian for "Yes."

The briefings and proper reconnaissance had taken a lot of time and we were approaching the "witching hour" to get back to the aircraft and take off when we turned into the access road to Val's headquarters at Camp Fort. Several soldiers were gathered around the entranceway as we got out of our vehicles for what I assumed were final instructions for the upcoming visit. Val emerged from behind the crowd carrying a 16-inch, slightly curved blade. With his characteristic smile, he presented the blade to me as a souvenir of our last patrol. These blades and other assorted crude weapons were routinely confiscated from illegal Iranian immigrants and Iraqi smugglers that his patrols picked up. I was proud to have it and thanked Val and his men for honoring me in such a special way. General Sobora placed his hand on my shoulder and thanked me for my efforts on what had already been a busy day. I walked back to our vehicles thinking that these folks truly appreciated whatever assistance we provided. Their tough, isolated, and seemingly unappreciated mission merited more attention and I thought General Sanchez's visit would be a positive event for them. I had no doubt his visit would be successful operationally and increase the Ukrainian brigade's credibility. Efforts like these validated that no time is ever wasted in reconnaissance or rehearsals.

CHAPTER 24

The War Comes to the Multinational Division (Central-South)

The most precious resource we all have is time.

—Steve Jobs

Any good infantry soldier will tell you it is always preferable to be in the field with the troops and as far away from the flagpole or headquarters as he can get. In the field, life comes down to the basics of soldiering, and a focus on mission, the enemy, operations, and training. It is a simple, often dangerous, life that real soldiers prefer and appreciate. Life for a soldier at a headquarters above battalion or brigade level is complicated with all the other factors of a military campaign for which no one studies and wishes did not exist. It is the politics and constant bickering over complex issues other than combat that may or may not be important the next day that drives a good man batty and makes him want to escape it all. The bad news is that a senior officer can never totally escape it. It did not surprise me, therefore, when I entered the Multinational Division (MND) Operations Center at Camp Babylon and was immediately informed by the G-3 (Operations) that General Tyszkiewicz wanted to see me right away. Tom Lowman, carefully reviewing operations reports from the brigades and plotting unit locations on the operations map, looked up at me and smiled that wide grin of his that always suggested he was glad he was not me. I headed to the commanding general's office and found him preparing to deliver his tactical-satellite (TACSAT) report to General Sanchez. I suspected he simply wanted his team with him. It was more than that. Operation *Stuart* and Muqtadā aṣ-Ṣadr were again on the major-issue plate. General Miller's frustration level with the Multinational Division (Central-South) over not executing this mission was about as high as it could get. General Tyszkiewicz informed me we would fly to Camp Victory in the morning for what amounted to a "showdown" with General Sanchez. This was a "no-win" situation for me. On the one hand, the restrictive rules of engagement under which the division operated, coupled with the reluctance of the Spanish brigade to do anything of an aggressive nature, put General Tyszkiewicz in a box. On the other hand, Al-Najaf and Kerbelā' were in his area of responsibility and Ṣadr was a wanted man. General Tyszkiewicz wanted no part of Operation *Stuart*, but the pressure from the American headquarters was undoubtedly weighing hard on him. The TACSAT report was uneventful and the meeting regarding Ṣadr was not mentioned. The commanding general told me to be ready to fly to Camp Victory. He was not happy.

General Miller advised me the next morning that General Tyszkiewicz was expected to meet with General Sanchez that night at 7:30 pm. We were not surprised by the renewed concern with Ṣadr. The reports from Al-Najaf and Kerbelâ', where the young cleric spent the bulk of his time, were filled with the activities of his militia known as the Madhi Army. The militia issue in Iraq would grow larger in the months ahead, but the presence of the thugs who rallied to Ṣadr's militia was already very prolific. What was particularly troubling was they had begun to wear a semblance of a uniform, complete with insignia of rank, arm bands, and other assorted military regalia. Their presence in and around the mosques threatened the authority of the police. It was strongly believed Ṣadr had established a Sharia, or Islamic, Court in Al-Najaf, an action that, if true, flew in the face of the legitimate justice system the Coalition Provisional Authority (CPA) and the Iraqi Interim Government were trying to establish. The long-range militia threat was undoubtedly felt by the Iraqi Interim Government. In October 2003, the New Iraqi Army consisted of one battalion with another in training. The thought of competing military arms vying for power in Iraq at this point was unthinkable and, for the interim government, very unrealistic.

These thoughts were tormenting General Tyszkiewicz as we approached the Camp Victory landing zone. His limitations as a commander of a division with over twenty national contingents burdened him like no other commander in Iraq. The rules of engagement of these contingents in this environment lacked the flexibility he required to do the things Combined Joint Task Force-7 (CJTF-7) was asking him to do. Clearly, the Spanish would not move against Ṣadr. I did not envy him for what he had to do with General Sanchez, but I knew this exceptional man would handle himself well.

Vehicles were standing by to take us to the Joint Visitors Bureau where we received rooms in my old haunt, the distinguished visitors quarters (DVQ) that I referred to as "the Cat House." Things had not changed. My spacious room was not unlike my visit in August with all the ardor of a 19th-century New Orleans bordello. Dinner was available in the adjoining building, and we enjoyed a quiet meal together before we walked to CJTF-7 Headquarters. I had orders to see Major General Wojdkowski, who surprised me with a smile and an enthusiastic handshake when I walked into his office. We spoke very little about the situation with Ṣadr. The deputy CJTF-7 commander was interested in my impressions of the MND and general observations about the troops. I reviewed my operational concerns while extolling the virtues of the soldiers in the field. My stock with General Wojdkowski must have still been high because our brief discussions ended with his sincere compliments of my work, particularly my efforts to bring the transition of authority in Al-Najaf to a successful end. General Wojodkowski had an excellent understanding of the complexities of command that we faced in the MND. I suggested the rules of engagement that "handcuffed" the division commander might ultimately force CJTF-7 to carve out an area of operations within the division's zone to conduct specific operations with U.S. troops. He acknowledged the point and made note of it. Nobody wanted to see that happen, but it was a viable option and the possibility of exercising it was very real if CJTF-7 was serious about pursuing Ṣadr, dealing with his militia, and closing the Sharia courts.

General Tyszkiewicz's meeting with General Sanchez did not appear to have stressed him and he seemed at ease with himself as we walked back to the DVQ. He described his meeting as simply, "Good," and informed me the CJTF-7 commander had given him 24 hours to respond to him about whether or not the MND would execute Operation *Stuart*. I'm not sure the response was ever made, but I never doubted Ṣadr would test us. I was certain the challenges of Baghdad and northern Iraq would eventually threaten the relative peace in central Iraq. It was simply a matter of time before foreign infiltrators, former regime loyalists, and the Shia militias clashed with our forces in the more populated, significant cities. There was not much time to reflect on it. We had to plan for it! The generals also discussed General Sanchez's scheduled visit to the Ukrainian brigade on 14 October. General Tyszkiewicz directed me to return to Al-Kut and ensure all preparations were made to receive the CJTF-7 commander. He was more concerned with the visit to the Ukrainian brigade than anything else; Operation *Stuart* and Muqtadā aṣ-Ṣadr could wait. I told him I would fly to Al-Kut in the morning.

The Polish pilots had laughingly suggested I be awarded Polish crew wings to recognize the flying hours I had accumulated since my assignment to the MND in August. They were great guys, and I enjoyed their company and camaraderie. Captain Britt Reed, the American aviation liaison officer, often flew on my missions. Britt's relationship with the Poles was exceptional. He had trained in Poland and had deployed to Iraq with the Polish pilots and crewmembers. A superb pilot, he would amass a significant number of flying hours in both the Mi-8 and the smaller Polish Falcon and more than qualify for his Polish wings.

Generals Sobora and Bezluschenko greeted me on the tarmac at Al-Kut. I was happy to see Andriy the interpreter was present as well. There had been a lot of work on the proposed itinerary and briefings for General Sanchez since our first review. The process was not unlike preparing for a brigade quarterly training briefing to an American division commander. This presentation had the same feel to it because it would undoubtedly set the tone for the CJTF-7 commander's perception of the brigade's operational efficiency and overall competence. The Ukrainians deserved to be recognized for their work. Their efforts to stem the tide of illegal immigration on the border with Iran, to patrol Al-Kut and other population areas in Wasit Province, to train Iraqi civil defense and local police forces, and to secure and destroy stores of old Iraqi ammunition were all worthy of praise. We finetuned the briefings and manner of presentation, discussed and agreed the border briefing and visitation program were solid, and, following a late lunch, I climbed in behind one of the machine guns of the Mi-8 and flew back to Camp Babylon. It had been a good day and I was confident the CJTF-7 commander's visit with the Ukrainians would go well. Unfortunately, Muqtadā aṣ-Ṣadr and his followers had other plans that would change our schedule considerably.

I had learned, after two months with the MND, that any calm evening was susceptible to a crisis that inevitably interrupts a good night's sleep. The night of 13 October was no exception. The reports from Polish Brigadier General Marek Ojrzanowski's 1st Brigade Combat Team Headquarters in Kerbelâ' did not provide enough information to give the division's operations staff a clear picture of what was going on. The skimpy information it was given indicated a mosque had been seized by Ṣadr's supporters. If it was true, then Ṣadr's expanded influence in Kerbelâ', in addition to his base in Al-Najaf, was more than enough to make the CPA and CJTF-7 nervous and more desirous of aggressive action against him. General Sanchez cancelled his trip to Al-Kut to monitor the situation more closely in Kerbelâ'. General Tyszkiewicz directed several members of his intelligence and operations staff to accompany him to Kerbelâ' in the morning to have a look and determine ground truth for himself. Colonel Gocul, the Division G-3, informed the Ukrainians of the change in plans and that the commanding general's tour of the Ukrainian brigade's area of operations would be rescheduled. I could imagine their disappointment, but Kerbelâ' had the makings for the division's first combat operation. General Sobora would understand.

The headquarters of the 1st Brigade Combat Team was in the Hotel Karbela, a large and well-maintained structure with a lobby furnished with sofas, easy chairs, coffee tables, and a pool table. It was our first stop after touching down at the brigade helo pad. Several vehicles were standing by to lift the commanding general's staff to the hotel. I climbed aboard the back of a Polish "Honker" along with the G-2 (Intelligence) and G-3, Colonels Przekwas and Gocul. The truck was sandbagged, and two Polish riflemen were aboard to provide security. It was a clear indication the situation in Kerbelâ' was serious.

General Ojrzanowski personally conducted the initial brief, pointing out an estimated thirty supporters of Muqtadā aṣ-Ṣadr had sought refuge in the Al-Mukhayyam Mosque after a gun battle with followers of a rival cleric. Tension in the city had been growing. Iraq's mostly moderate Shi'ite leadership had maintained good relations with American and Coalition troops and had tempered the actions of radical elements such as Ṣadr's gunmen. In recent weeks, however, armed militias associated with Ṣadr, and a lesser-known senior Shi'ite cleric sheikh named Mahmoud al-Hasani, had grown increasingly belligerent. Criminal groups in Kerbelâ' were vying for power; control of the mosques ensured the availability of cash for weapons and anything else they required. A gun battle on the 13th as well as lesser incidents that had preceded it had caused the CPA to place Kerbelâ' under a 9 pm curfew. The situation, though tense, was under control and local police and city leaders were attempting to resolve the occupation of the mosque peacefully. American, Polish, and Bulgarian troops continued to patrol the city's streets and neighborhoods.

The Polish brigade staff briefed a variety of other topics related to the situation in Kerbelâ'. General Tyszkiewicz quietly suggested with a smile that I spend some time with the brigade staff to, in his words, "Make them more like the American presentations." The situation in Kerbelâ' was calm for now, but the general knew things could change quickly and he wanted to be prepared to brief General Sanchez when it did. After the generals departed for additional consultations, the staff worked another hour improving their situation maps and slides. It was a good drill, and, like General Tyszkiewicz, I thought there was a very good possibility we would have to brief General Sanchez sooner than later. It appeared we had some time for now. General Tyszkiewicz elected to return to Camp Babylon and render a report to General Sanchez via the evening TACSAT gathering of the division commanders. Colonels Gocul, Przekwas, and I quickly huddled to prepare the general's report when we got back to Camp Babylon. It looked like we had "dodged a bullet" for the short term. It made sense to allow the local authorities and sheikhs to solve the problem; General Sanchez agreed.

By the next day, our senior leadership at CJTF-7 Headquarters had changed its mind. The situation in Kerbelâ' was still calm, but the locals had not convinced the gunmen to leave the mosque. The Iraqis did not want to provoke anyone and the police chief, an old, rather overweight survivor of the previous regime, did not want to make any arrests. The problem we were experiencing would plague Coalition forces for as long as we were in Iraq. Iraqi officials could not separate their civic duties from the respect they held for the clerics. Al-Hasani was a well-known religious figure and the police chief steered clear of a confrontation with him. The phone calls from CJTF-7 to the MND staff demanding information were non-stop, but late that evening I decided to get some rest, leaving word with our watch officer to wake me if anything significant developed. I had managed a few hours of sleep before I felt a hand on my arm shaking me awake in the darkness of my plywood hut. I was half asleep, but the news brought me around quickly.

"Colonel Tiso, there has been shooting in Kerbelâ'. American soldiers have been killed. You're wanted in the Division Operations Center, sir."

The Operations Center was alive with excitement. The reports were not as detailed as I had hoped, but the watch officers were working the phones and the picture was becoming clearer. There had been a firefight in the vicinity of al-Hasani's headquarters in Kerbelâ'. Several American soldiers had been killed and several more wounded. At least two Iraqi National Policemen had been killed. Several Shi'ite gunmen were killed as well. The American soldiers were members of the 101st Airborne Division's 716th Military Police (MP) Battalion. One of those killed was the battalion commander, Lieutenant Colonel Kim Orlando, who had spoken so brilliantly at the police academy graduation in Al-Kut in late September. There was little we could do at that point except continue to monitor reports. The G-3 told me to be ready to fly to Kerbelâ' at first light. It was still early on the 16th and it occurred to me I better grab a few more hours of sleep. Ken and Tom were both on duty. I told them not to hesitate to get me and suggested one of them turn in as well. They knew the drill; the next several days would be brutal.

The Camp Babylon airstrip was as busy as I had ever seen it. The word was out about an ambush in Kerbelâ' that had left several Americans dead, including the MP battalion commander. Kim Orlando's death had shocked the 716th MP Battalion and the looks on the faces of the battalion executive officer and other members of the 716th's staff were a mix of horror, anger, and frustration. The battalion operations officer (S-3) was particularly angry as he addressed General Tyszkiewicz during the operations update earlier that morning. I understood how he felt, but I called him aside after the briefing and, in a soft, but steady voice, encouraged him to keep his head clear and his eyes focused on the mission ahead of him.

"If we're going to deal with the guys who killed him, we need your battalion mission-ready and oriented on the enemy. We'll mourn his loss after we get the job done. You need to get that message to the troops."

The S-3 withheld tears of anger and acknowledged my comment with a tight-lipped "Okay, sir, I got it."

I was deep in thought about what our operations in Kerbelâ' would involve when General Tyszkiewicz arrived at the airstrip with several members of his staff and Sergeant Calley, his American communicator. The young sergeant was the general's link to CJTF-7, and he was thrilled with the possibility of having his skills tested in a combat environment. He was loaded down with his TACSAT radio and several other devices that would have stressed a pack mule, but he would not pass off a single item. He told me in no uncertain terms, "This is my gear, sir. This is what I do."

I just smiled and shook my head. The all-volunteer United States Army has been challenged with personnel and recruiting issues since its inception, but its principal strength has always been its young sergeants and combat soldiers whose motivation to serve with dignity and courage are a source of pride to everyone privileged to wear the uniform and lead such outstanding young men.

The helo pad at Camp Juliet, one of three garrisons that supported Polish and Bulgarian troops in Kerbelâ' Province, served as the entry point for most visitors to the Polish brigade. Getting to the Hotel Kerbelâ' and the headquarters of the Polish 1st Brigade Combat Team required ground transport. In the interest of time, General Tyszkiewicz chose not to move to the hotel. Instead, we moved into a small expeditionary like headquarters within walking distance of our landing zone. It was there that General Ojrzanowski privately briefed him on the continuing situation in Kerbelâ' and the circumstances that had led to the gunfight.

American MPs and Iraqi authorities had been investigating a gathering of men near a local mosque well after the 9 pm curfew was in effect. Later, in the early hours of the 16th, that same team passed the offices of Shi'ite cleric, Sheikh Mahmoud al-Hasani. These offices were guarded by an estimated twenty gunmen. The gunmen refused an order to go inside the building. At some point after their refusal, a shootout began, including small-arms fire and rocket-propelled grenades. It was unclear who started the firing although one of the Shi'ite militia men involved in the battle would later say the Americans began to shoot without provocation and that eight Shi'ite guards were killed. We thought this was highly unlikely given the guards' overt belligerence, their refusal to comply with the curfew and refusal to disperse, and the MPs and Iraqi National Police being outnumbered and outgunned.

Anxious to see for himself, General Tyszkiewicz directed us to get into our vehicles and move to where he could conduct a personal reconnaissance of the area near the headquarters of Sheikh al-Hasani. Our reconnaissance element was not particularly large, but the addition of Polish security personnel made me a bit concerned about the size of our presence as we surveilled the house and vicinity where Colonel Orlando and members of his battalion had been gunned down earlier that morning. We stood at the end of the street approximately 250 meters from the multi-storied house. It was a large structure with several other smaller houses to its flanks. It was not unlike a city street in a mid-size American town. Capturing the headquarters would require clearing and securing the homes from where we stood along both sides of the street to Hasani's headquarters before an assault could be made. The general was standing in the middle of the intersection when a gunman emerged on the roof of the headquarters and sighted his rifle in our direction. The general's personal security men quickly grabbed him and moved out of the line of fire as the rest of our crowd moved almost as quickly away from the intersection. The reconnaissance was over. The general had seen enough; he quickly ordered us to mount up and move to police headquarters.

There were many local officials, Civil Affairs personnel, and CPA officials gathered in the police chief's office when we arrived. We did not meet very long. General Abbas, the police chief, spoke softly and somewhat timidly about the situation. Everyone listened intently, but no one contributed anything substantial. My sense was the local militia owned this town and the police were more like "window dressing" than anything substantive. There was no capable local force to turn to and it was clear there was no alternative but to confront the gunmen with overwhelming force. General Tyszkiewicz moved to his vehicle where Sergeant Calley had set up his TACSAT and called General Sanchez to apprise him of the situation. I stood by closely and listened as General Sanchez directed his MND commander to report to him in an hour with a detailed, "Mission analysis and back brief." General Tyszkiewicz handed Calley the headset and, with a broad smile, looked at me and said, "Roland, I have rendered my first combat report!"

The general had outlined his activities and observations since his arrival in Kerbelâ', but the CJTF-7 commander now wanted to know how he intended to take the gunmen down. There was work to do, and I strongly suggested we get back to our headquarters and start our mission analysis. It took us 20 minutes to get back there; I was painfully conscious of the time. Sitting at a table with the Division G-2, G-3, and Generals Ojrzanowski and Tyszkiewicz, I politely listened to their discussion before suggesting that if they would provide a general concept of operations or explain in plain simple language what they had in mind, we could convert it into the operational language I was sure General Sanchez expected. I reminded everyone that General Tyszkiewicz had less than forty minutes to call the CJTF-7 commander.

A moment of silence followed my comment before General Tyszkiewicz began to clearly articulate his intent to place a cordon around Hasani's headquarters and its adjoining street and cut off all access to the designated operational area. The assault would be conducted by heavy (mechanized) infantry and that we should request such a unit from CJTF-7. The security mission would be accomplished by General Ojrzanowski's 1st Brigade Combat Team. Collateral damage should be kept to a minimum. He saw the need to have aerial fires on standby, but he did not want to strike the headquarters from the air if it could be avoided. Steady and confident, the general outlined other key points of guidance. He thought the deployment of a heavy combat team to Kerbelâ' would probably delay any kinetic action for two or three days.

I listened intently while simultaneously reviewing the particulars of an outline of "Commander's Planning Guidance" in the battle book I had always carried since I was a battalion commander. I had developed these points under the tutelage of then Colonel Lawson Magruder in the 2nd Warrior Brigade of the 25th Infantry Division when I served in that great unit in 1988–90 as the executive officer of the 1st Battalion, 21st Infantry. The outline was an invaluable reminder of key points a unit commander should articulate, and that subordinate commanders and members of the staff should know in order to initiate detailed planning for combat operations. These key points included:

1. A general outline of the commander's intent.
2. Sequence or phases of the battle.
3. Where to accept risk.
4. Command-and-control arrangements.
5. Specific guidance on a portion of the battlefield.
6. Planning Assumptions.
7. Reconnaissance and security considerations.
8. Restrictions on operations.
9. Emerging intelligence requirements.

10. Safety considerations.
11. Type of reserve force.
12. Logistics requirements.
13. Use of fire support.

I used the points to outline and shape the division commander's words into a doctrinally correct statement of intent and used the applicable battlefield operations systems of command and control, maneuver, fire support, intelligence, mobility, and combat service support, highlighting the key specifics of each system. It was clear he wanted to isolate Hasani's headquarters and utilize the firepower and protection of a heavy force of infantry to attack and seize it with minimum collateral damage. He wanted the operation to be conducted at night. Fire support from aerial platforms should be requested and remain on standby, but in his strong interest to limit collateral damage, he stated very strongly that direct fire from ground systems was preferred. He directed that continuous reconnaissance of the site, and the employment of sniper teams, commence immediately. General Ojrzanowski offered that the bulk of the security force would be provided by the Bulgarian battalion backed up by snipers and troops as required from a Polish battalion he would hold in reserve. He strongly suggested his brigade headquarters be used as the central location for command and control of the operation. The hotel had the space and parking area necessary to stage our forces, including a large American task force. It was a great suggestion as I looked around the hovel of a temporary headquarters we currently occupied. "Geez, what a dump," I silently thought, recalling that famous quote from the vintage Bette Davis movie *Beyond the Forest*. General Tyszkiewicz acknowledged his brigade commander's suggestion and nodded approval.

This was a no-frills exercise—no computers or fancy charts, limited communications, and minimal staffing—really nothing except my hip-pocket reference, that officers often refer to as a "brain book," and a note pad. General Tyszkiewicz asked me if I had enough to work with and I assured him I did, saying in no uncertain terms that, "What I needed now was 20 minutes without interruption." Like most good commanders, the general understood what I meant and quickly cleared the room of everyone except the communicator. He and General Ojrzanowski stepped outside to talk.

Three unit deployments to the Joint Readiness Training Center as a battalion executive officer and battalion commander had ingrained the back-brief format in my memory and I crafted the general's guidance accordingly, providing the results of our brief mission analysis in the form of specified and implied tasks, a proposed task organization and proposed mission statement, commander's operational intent, a concept of operations that assumed the presence of a mechanized task force, and other planning considerations including logistics and command and control. I cursed my handwriting as I struggled to keep everything readable. It was as good as our limited time would allow and I asked General Ojrzanowski to quickly review my work before asking him to hand it to General Tyszkiewicz. He took all of two minutes to read it over and, with a broad smile, told me he thought it was excellent. He then gave it to General Tyszkiewicz who checked it to ensure his guidance had been noted appropriately. He did not change a word, quickly turned to his communications sergeant, and directed him to call General Sanchez.

The call to General Sanchez was placed exactly one hour from the time General Tyszkiewicz had rendered his initial report. He immediately came to the phone and, after ensuring he was audible on the other end, General Tyszkiewicz flawlessly delivered his back brief. There was one point of discussion that surprised all of us. General Sanchez was intent on destroying Hasani's headquarters and he wanted to do it by dropping a Joint Direct Attack Munition or JDAM, a highly accurate smart bomb. A JDAM is a general-purpose bomb with a tail kit that provides it with both a global-positioning system and an inertial navigation system. The variety available to the U.S. Air Force in 2003 was a 2,000-pound bomb with limited penetrating capability. Assuming an accurate grid of Hasani's headquarters was programmed into the bomb, it would have undoubtedly landed on target. General Tyszkiewicz's assessment of the situation did not merit such action, however, and he clearly preferred the presence of an AC-130 gunship for on-call fires as required during the operation. Emotions were running high at that point. Several Americans, including a highly valued battalion commander, had been killed by the thugs in that building. I thought about what I had said to the 716th's operations officer earlier that day. Flexibility and perspective were important in an operation that could potentially make more enemies than friends if it was not conducted intelligently. I thought of the highly effective, though limited, *Desert Fox* campaign conducted by U.S. Central Command against Iraq in December 1998. The target selection and concern for collateral damage had impressed me with the need to exercise restraint while nonetheless applying the right weapon to a given target to accomplish the desired result. Clearly, the decision to use fires of any type in our case had to rest with the commander on the ground. The conversation ended inconclusively on that point, but a mechanized task force of the American 1st Armored Division was ordered to Kerbelâ' in accordance with the general's desires and proposed concept of operations.

The mission analysis and the decisions made in such a brief period was clearly a victory for our makeshift battle staff and I noted the look of satisfaction on the general's face as he extended his hand in my direction and said, "Well done, Roland."

Turning to General Ojrzanowski, he reminded him to get reconnaissance and sniper teams in the vicinity of the target immediately. These teams were to maintain a low profile, render reports, and fire only in self defense. His intent was to isolate and fix the target area while we waited for the arrival of the American mechanized brigade. In the meantime, we would return to Camp Babylon, pack for a long stay, and return later that day. The war had finally come to the Multinational Division (Central-South).

CHAPTER 25

Defeating the Enemy with Overwhelming Force

My strategy is to attack with overwhelming force.

—General Colin Powell

The division's operations and intelligence staffs were already preparing for the move to Kerbelâ' by the time we landed at Camp Babylon. The general decided to limit the size of the division staff in Kerbelâ', considering the bulk of the division's efforts would be executed by the Polish 1st Brigade Combat Team and the limited space available for billeting and work. The chief of staff chose a small element to help focus and assist the Polish brigade staff. Tom Lowman was ready to go forward, but there was only room for our vital communications section. Tom, Ken, and Sergeant Stewart would manage requirements and reports from the Division Headquarters at Camp Babylon. I quickly loaded my rucksack with additional clothing, ammunition, several meals and snacks, and personal items, and slipped a bed roll through the outer straps. The increased activity around the general's headquarters added to the controlled confusion that normally characterized the area as I made my way down the road back to the airstrip.

It had already been a long day, but I was very upbeat as I reflected on the day's earlier activities with a tired smile. It is a rare event that brings a requirement for an officer to take nearly everything he has learned in over thirty years of military education and tactical experience and capture it all in a single report without the assistance or input of a trained staff. My work that morning had required a review of nearly everything I had studied and practiced regarding operations and planning—from the principles of war to the combat imperatives, to the battlefield operation systems, to concepts of operations analysis, to specific weapons capabilities and logistics concerns, and finally to the development of the commander's intent and planning guidance. I was proud of what I had done in Kerbelâ' and wondered what other challenges awaited me.

Things were happening fast. Before I had left the division headquarters, I verified the 2nd Brigade Combat Team of the U.S. 1st Armored Division was moving to Kerbelâ'. The increased activity at the airstrip spoke to the renewed sense of purpose the events in Kerbelâ' had brought to the Multinational Division (MND). As usual, I found a shady spot under the palm trees by the air operations office and waited for the general to arrive. These brief minutes would be the last for calm and quiet reflection for quite some time. We were in the air and on the way to Kerbelâ' within the next 20 minutes.

General Ojrzanowski's 1st Brigade Combat Team Headquarters was not a bad place to stay under normal conditions. The entranceway to the hotel was alive with plants and flowers. The lobby was a comfortable place to conduct small meetings. The general maintained his office in a room that adjoined the reception area where hotel receptionists had registered guests a seemingly long time ago. The office was modest at best with a large desk, several chairs, and an area rug. General Ojrzanowski offered the office to the division commander and our secure communications were set up in an adjoining hallway that led outdoors to an area where tentage accommodated the Multinational and American staffs. The Polish brigade staff had not wasted any time to coordinate additional facilities. Even the all-important porto-johns had been moved into place. The large parking and maintenance area beyond our planning area could accommodate many vehicles; other marshalling areas were nearby. The Polish staff members were preparing charts and monitoring reports from sniper and reconnaissance teams in the operational area. Patrolling in the city had been increased and security elements had already occupied positions from which they would prevent the escape or entry of any armed or otherwise suspicious men in the target area. The lead elements of the 1st Armored Division's 2nd Brigade Combat Team arrived after nightfall and by morning the wide-open parking and maintenance space would be teeming with armored and wheeled vehicles of all types. It occurred to me that this might be our last quiet night for a while and that I better take advantage of it to get some sleep. At the division commander's invitation, I spread my bedroll on the rug in his office, informed the communications sergeant where I was, and called it a night.

I awoke just after first light. General Tyszkiewicz was wisely still asleep when I silently left the room and headed for the latrines. The parking area was alive with combat vehicles and there was already some activity in the operations tent. The 2nd Brigade Combat Team had moved into Kerbelâ' under the command of Colonel Rob Baker, a West Point graduate and a veteran of the First Gulf War where he had seen action with the 82nd Airborne Division. Rob had deployed to Kuwait in late 2002, and later commanded the V Corps Forward Command Post in Baghdad. He had assumed command of his brigade in early July 2003, after a short stint in the States to attend several precommand courses. The 1st Armored Division had its hands full with its mission to stabilize Baghdad. Its soldiers were already hardened combat veterans. I briefly thought the unit's movement to Kerbelâ' might be viewed by many at CJTF-7 Headquarters as a sideshow and perhaps a distraction, but the death of several American soldiers gave a significant amount of impetus to the mission and I sensed the excitement among the soldiers. They knew why they were there and it would not be long before their specific mission would be known as well. General Sanchez and General Dempsey, the 1st Armored Division commander, were expected in Kerbelā' that day, and we expected that operations would commence within the next 36–48 hours.

After eating a quick breakfast, I walked into the large general-purpose tent that served as the operations and plans area. It had been filled with tables and chairs and a briefing area had been established on one end of the tent. Areas had been sectioned off to accommodate both the Polish and American staffs. At the entrance to the tent sat the stoic MND chief of staff, Colonel Zdzislaw Antczak, peering over a stack of papers. I cannot recall "Chief" having ever smiled since I had met him two months before. He was a professional officer who went about his task of coordinating the staff without emotion or fanfare. The movement of the division staff into the former 1st Marine Expeditionary Force Headquarters at Camp Babylon when the Marines rotated home in September was quietly and competently carried out under his watchful eye and direction. In the same manner, this forward division tactical operations center had been established and made ready for action. Colonel Antczak never really knew how to take me, but I sensed he thought I was valuable enough to treat well if for no other reason than because I helped to manage the commanding general's requirements. It was no secret that General Tyszkiewicz was a taskmaster of the highest order and, to some anyway, a tough guy to get along with. Colonel Antczak acknowledged my presence and told me high-ranking visitors were expected that afternoon. The Polish staff was currently working a situation briefing and refining a general security plan for the operational area as well as developing expanded patrol plans throughout the city. General Ojrzanowski was already in the briefing area, and I took a seat in a corner and reviewed several reports from the previous evening. We had time and I wanted to be available should questions arise or help be requested. I believed General Ojrzanowski would not hesitate to use me after the experience on the previous day at the expeditionary operations center. I used the time to introduce myself to the American staff officers and ensure we had good communications to Camp Babylon. Sergeant Calley's communications area was ready for action. The tough young sergeant had been up most of the night ensuring his "Gear was squared away" and I suggested he get a few hours of sleep after I spoke to Tom Lowman at Camp Babylon and the CJTF-7 Operations Center at Camp Victory. Our communications were enhanced by another American force multiplier. The Marines of the 4th Air and Naval Gunfire Liaison Company (ANGLICO) were on board and had set up an area in the foyer of the rear entrance to the hotel. If the situation dictated the use of that F-16-delivered JDAM that General Sanchez had suggested, or any other aerial fires, the Marines would ensure they were delivered on target. During the operation, elements of the ANGLICO would be with both the American and Polish forward tactical headquarters to call and direct fires as required.

The impending arrival of the American commanders had planning efforts moving at a frenzied pace when I returned to the operations tent later that morning. The Polish brigade staff was reviewing a proposed series of slides that outlined the current situation, command-and-control arrangements, force availability for the operation, and a general concept for security. General Ojrzanowski announced he would personally brief the CJTF-7 commander. The briefing was not ready for an American three-star general. The concepts were sound, but timelines had not been coordinated with the American staff and, once again, the "Polish English" would not cut it. I suggested to the Brigade S-3 (Operations) that I be allowed to make a few adjustments to the briefing. Unlike the Polish division staff officers who knew me, the brigade staff officers were hesitant. General Ojrzanowski entered the room and broke the silence. In very authoritative Polish, he ordered the staff to, "Do what Colonel Tiso directs." I stood by the charts and briefing area and started barking orders. There was no time for niceties. The computer operator looked stunned as I directed the changes to his hard-worked briefing. "Faster," I said, "Do what I tell you." Never a talented "PowerPoint Ranger," as staff officers refer to the more computer-literate, I knew the program well enough to know what it could do and I "beat up" the young Polish major manning the computer about as badly as I had any American officer during similar situations in my battalion and brigade experiences. As we fixed and refined the last slide, someone called the place to attention and in walked Generals Sanchez, Dempsey, and Tyszkiewicz. I was sweating profusely when General Ojrzanowski took his place at the podium; I made my way to the rear of the briefing area.

The articulate Brigadier General Ojrzanowski spoke as if he was thoroughly rehearsed. It was important for this session of briefings and discussions to go well to ensure a more positive perception of the Poles and the MND. A briefing by the American 2nd Brigade Combat Team staff followed the Polish brigade commander's presentation outlining its general plan of maneuver and fire support and the use of the JDAM. The Americans and the Poles had reached consensus on keeping the JDAM strike "on call" and we were relieved when General Sanchez acknowledged, essentially backing off from a pre-ground attack strike that may have caused a large amount of collateral damage to the other structures in the neighborhood. Perhaps the most important result of the reconnaissance that General Tyszkiewicz had conducted on the morning of the 16th was his appreciation for the proximity of the other structures to Hasani's headquarters. Given the limited penetrating ability of the JDAM at the time, we believed the debris and blast effect would have potentially caused significant damage to the neighboring homes as well as civilian casualties. The reports we had from our sniper and reconnaissance teams assured us Hasani's gunmen were still in his headquarters building and that activity around the neighboring homes and the business area appeared normal. The intent, therefore, was to secure the neighboring structures and take the headquarters down with infantry. This was not Stalingrad. Victory would ultimately be measured in terms of how effectively we dealt with

Hasani's thugs while demonstrating to the local populace that we respected their property and meant them no harm. Recognizing the possibility of some damage to the structures and environment beyond the target building, General Tyszkiewicz mentioned that postoperations planning included a damage-assessment survey of the maneuver area by his division's civil affairs teams, and that his engineers would make immediate repairs of any damaged property or facilities.

The time required for detailed planning, coordination, and rehearsals at all tactical levels of command pointed to the evening of 18 October as the most likely for mission execution. By attacking at night, we would maximize the exceptional advantages of the American task force to fight under low-visibility conditions while simultaneously achieving the element of surprise. General Sanchez thanked everyone for their work, signaled the "go ahead" to continue planning and the meeting broke up. Both staffs had performed admirably, and the respective commanders had the orders and guidance they required to execute the mission. I sat in the back quietly satisfied we had a handle on the security and reconnaissance role the Polish brigade would have in this fight. The operation was setting up in almost precisely the same way General Tyszkiewicz had envisioned in his initial back brief to the CJTF-7 commander. General Ojrzanowski thanked me for my assistance. His broad smile told me I had made a friend and that I had his complete confidence.

The planning effort continued throughout the rest of the day. The American task force staff was assisted by the presence of the 1st Armored Division's Assistant Division Commander for Maneuver, Brigadier General Curtis M. Scaparrotti, USA. General Scaparrotti impressed everyone with his quiet, friendly, but business-like demeanor, and willingness to work. He was a near-permanent fixture in the Operations Center but was careful not to get in the staff's way. He was there to help and coordinate assistance as required. General "Scap" had been with the 1st Armored since July. The seemingly mild-mannered general was another tough infantryman who had extensive service with airborne forces since his graduation from West Point in 1978. He had commanded the 3rd Battalion, 325th Airborne Combat Team, in Vicenza, Italy, had seen action in the Balkans, and had gone on to command the 2nd Brigade of the 82nd Airborne Division. The Brigade Task Force officers, including Colonel Baker, appeared to be very comfortable in his presence and they all worked very well together. Equally important was the comfortable relationship he enjoyed with General Tyszkiewicz. They were often seen together, inspiring a sense of confidence throughout both national staffs during the planning process.

Planning and briefings continued into the night, but by 10 pm the staffs were confident their plans were sound and fully coordinated. The next day would test everyone's endurance. I retreated to the general's office where Generals Tyszkiewicz and Ojrzanowski were about to complete their discussions and turn in for the night. General "Scap" came in a few minutes later. "Great minds think alike," I thought, as we laid out our bedrolls and put out the lights.

Morning brought the no-nonsense, business-like pace one would expect of a headquarters at war. Final briefings were conducted and time schedules finalized. The sound of engines and troops engaged in everything from maintenance activities to physical training filled the air. Reports from our security and reconnaissance teams continued to indicate Hasani's men were still in his headquarters building. Our guess was they were waiting us out. They had to know by now the Americans had come to Kerbelâ' in force; no one was interested in talking at this point. Our mission was a go.

I had done everything I could do from a planning perspective. As I watched units moving to alternate assembly points for the road march to the objective area, I considered where I could do the most good during the operation. Generals Tyszkiewicz and Scaparrotti would be airborne, but there was little room available for anyone else on their helicopter. I frankly did not like the idea of participating in the operation at 500 feet and I was dead set against monitoring radios at the hotel. It was time to call in a few "chips." Joining General Tyszkiewicz and Ojrzanowski just before nightfall for a quick dinner in the office, I asked the division commander if he would attach me to the Polish brigade to assist the brigade commander during the operation. I had spent more time with the Polish brigade staff throughout the planning effort than any other group; General Ojrzanowski appeared comfortable with my presence. I was relieved when he told General Tyszkiewicz that he thought it was a very good idea. He further suggested I would be an immense help to him at his forward command post which he intended to position near the objective area. Though hesitant at first, General Tyszkiewicz agreed and with a smile told General Ojrzanowski to, "Keep an eye on our Amerikanskyi friend. I am afraid he will be killed attempting to capture the enemy by himself."

It was pitch black when General Ojrzanowski and I climbed into his command vehicle to commence our move to his forward headquarters. Captain Lowman's presence at the hotel at that point would have been invaluable and I cursed myself for not insisting he accompany the staff to Kerbelâ'. Knowing Tom, he would have found room on the wheels or skids of a helicopter, or in the trunk of a vehicle, to be closer to the fight. Sergeant Calley would handle all the reports and maintain the logbooks. We moved to the main route of march and pulled off to the side of the road. Not a few minutes later, the combat power of a reinforced mechanized infantry and armored task force was moving past us en route to the objective. It was an awe-inspiring sight. The tank commanders stood upright in their turrets and infantry fighting vehicles that seemed to stretch for several hundred meters down the road. The streetlights provided enough illumination to detect the grim looks of determination on our soldiers' faces. During a short stop in the movement, I asked a young sergeant if he was clear on what his mission was and what in general was going on. I should have anticipated his response.

"Fucking A, sir, we're gonna kick some ass!" You have got to love these outstanding, young men who epitomize the spirit of America's fighting Army.

The Polish Brigade Forward Headquarters was in a fenced-in parking area. It was small compared to what an American headquarters might look like, but it was secure, and the Polish communications van was operational and capable of monitoring all the tactical nets. As the de facto Brigade S-3, I was relieved to know we could talk to everyone including the Americans and the Bulgarian 1st Infantry Battalion that was providing the bulk of the security that isolated the objective area. I also checked to ensure the radios with the general's vehicle were operational. I was grateful the Polish communications officer spoke English. The common language of the Poles and the Bulgarians was Russian. My Russian was limited to saying, "Yes" and "Thank you," but he assured me we were "Good to go," in perfect English. I suggested to General Ojrzanowski we make a personal check of our major checkpoints in the objective area and the general nodded his agreement. By this time, the entire city of Kerbelā' was aware of what was going on and I dreaded the thought of the Polish brigade failing to stop any attempt by Hasani's men to escape from our security net or allowing other fighters of his militia to reinforce the men in the headquarters. The amount of firepower the U.S. task force could bring to bear ensured the objective would be quickly subdued one way or another. The Poles and the Bulgarians had to ensure its inhabitants were still there when the attack occurred.

The Bulgarians, like their Polish counterparts, were good soldiers. I never asked, but I guessed the men of the 1st Battalion were volunteers from an Army that relied heavily on compulsory service. Bulgaria had always been on the wrong side during the great struggles of the 20th century, having been allied with the Kaiser in World War I and with the Axis powers during World War II. In the aftermath of the Cold War and its long association with the Soviet Union, it anxiously sought membership in NATO, a goal it would attain in April 2004. Bulgaria's Army was currently undergoing the difficulties of modernization and reform. Its goal was to produce a smaller, more efficient force of some 50,000 personnel. The fact that Bulgaria had sent a battalion to Iraq as a part of the Coalition spoke highly of its desire to participate in NATO as a serious and capable partner.

Along the various narrow streets of Kerbelā' that provided routes to and from the objective area, the Bulgarians stood at their posts in full battle gear and weapons ready, checking vehicles and pedestrians for weapons and other forms of contraband and directing them away from the area. General Ojrzanowski spoke to the squad and platoon leaders at each checkpoint in Russian. The Bulgarians and the special Polish teams had more than adequately secured their respective areas and we were confident the objective site was entirely isolated. The American task force's efforts would be totally focused on the occupied building and its immediate surroundings.

Several hours passed, though it had not seemed that long, as we continued to monitor reports from our sniper and security teams and the ongoing operation at Hasani's headquarters. The reports were encouraging. The attack was accomplished with minimal resistance and no need for major caliber weapons or air support. The American assault had bagged 27 gunmen and a large number of weapons. There had been little damage to the building or the surrounding area and there were no friendly or civilian casualties. The decision to go at night had ensured few, if any, civilians either interfered or innocently got in the way. It was, by nearly every measure, a perfectly executed operation, but there was more work in store for us.

Two days prior to the gun battle that had resulted in Colonel Orlando's death, several of Muqtadā aṣ-Ṣadr's followers had taken refuge in the Al-Mukhayyam Mosque after they had engaged in a gun battle with followers of a rival cleric. It was possible Sheikh al-Hasani himself was there as well. Ṣadr and al-Hasani were the most visible of what was becoming a number of local religious figures who had assembled small armed militias over the past several months. Iraq was awash with weapons and arming these groups was not a problem. It had been a satisfying night, but on the morning of the 19th we went back to the drawing board for another round of planning to finish off the thugs at the mosque. The planning cycle was nearly identical to the previous mission. Two days of planning preceded the hit on the mosque. The gunmen were taken completely by surprise on the morning of the 21st and, by 4:30 am, it was over. There were no casualties, 21 gunmen were captured, but the elusive cleric was not found.

There was no time for back slapping or high fives when we returned to the hotel later that morning. The situation in Kerbelâ' was calm for now and the 1st Armored Division's task force began to pack up and redeploy to Baghdad. General Tyszkiewicz was anxious to recover his division staff and get back to Camp Babylon. The Polish brigade remained on a higher-than-normal alert status and maintained an increased number of patrols throughout the city. Vigilance of this nature after a significant action is particularly valuable in an insurgency. We knew a large number of Ṣadr's and al-Hasani's men were still in the city. They had been hurt, but they would undoubtedly lick their wounds and strike again.

It is not uncommon to have injured gunmen turn up at nearby hospitals after the violence subsides. Later that evening, from my post at the division's Operations Center, I suggested by phone to General Ojrzanowski that he consider checking hospitals that serviced people in the vicinity of our recent operations for any gunmen that may have been wounded in the gun battles in Kerbelâ' throughout the previous several days. He advised the division staff several hours later that one of his patrols had policed up two additional wounded gunmen who were seeking medical treatment. It was yet another small victory in the "cat and mouse" game of counterinsurgency the Poles were now into up to their necks.

On the afternoon of the 21st, with our mission in Kerbelâ' completed, at least for the present, it was time to reflect on the loss of Kim Orlando and the other American soldiers who had been killed in action. The 716th Military Police (MP) Battalion arranged a memorial ceremony in his honor, and it was not long after the helicopter bearing General Tyszkiewicz and Colonels Gocul, Przekwas, and I landed at the Camp Babylon airstrip that a number of others began to arrive. High-ranking commanders who flew in included General Sanchez and Major General Petraeus, the commander of the 101st Airborne Division (Air Assault), to which the 716th MP Battalion was assigned. We gathered at the large amphitheater where the division's major events were conducted, including the division assumption-of-authority ceremony in September. I have attended and participated in a number of these services over the years, but I remember this one as being particularly difficult. I had not felt so badly about the death of a fellow officer since we had lost Marvin Jeffcoat and the bulk of his command in the Gander disaster in 1985. Kim Orlando's battalion had done a good job. On the stage were the helmet, rifle, and boots of a fallen comrade. The ceremony included appropriate Bible readings and special music including "Freedom isn't Free" and "Amazing Grace." A final roll call, a firing of volleys, and the playing of *Taps* brought the solemn ceremony to a close. As the commanders began to depart, each of them laid their unit coin at the base of the weapon, a final tribute to a fallen hero and a great commander. Kim Orlando left a wife and two sons behind. I said a prayer for them and walked away shaking my head, feeling a little numb, but proud I had played a significant role in avenging his death.

CHAPTER 26

Fighting the Battle for Central-South Iraq

Strategy without tactics is the slowest route to victory. Tactics without strategy is the noise before defeat.

—Sun Tzu

The action in Kerbelâ' was a wake-up call for every soldier in the Multinational Division (MND) regarding the seriousness of the situation in Iraq. Even before Kerbelâ', occasional mortar fire and an RPG-7 (rocket-propelled grenade) fired at the division's logistics base in Al-Ḥillah on 10 October signaled the end of the relative summer calm. The insurgency and the sectarian violence that challenged the Coalition's occupation of Baghdad and northern Iraq were now clearly present in Al-Najaf and Kerbelâ'. Muqtadā aṣ-Ṣadr and his Mahdi Army wanted to dominate the political scene in defiance of the Coalition Provisional Authority (CPA) and the Iraqi Interim Government. The Iranian influence in the holy cities was growing. The Iran–Iraq border was a sieve through which many illegal immigrants and foreign fighters entered Iraq. Clashes between competing groups were increasing and the frustration level of the Iraqi people over the lack of security and the shortage of everything, from cooking and heating oil for their homes to gasoline for their vehicles, provoked a sense of anger and frustration evident to everyone. Certainly, I thought, the Spanish and Latin American contingents, the Poles, and the other national contingents were rethinking their role in what had become a far more dangerous area of responsibility (AOR). Every national contingent needed to reconsider its rules of engagement (ROE) and accept a more aggressive posture toward the militant and criminal elements in our midst, if for no other reason than to ensure the safety of their soldiers.

Multiple ROE burdened the division and its leadership. These rules were directed by national authorities and were originally proposed for forces deployed for peace-keeping, stability operations, and self-defense, not what the combat environment in Iraq now required. CJTF-7's (Combined Joint Task Force-7) frustration with the MND was evident in the voices of the CJTF-7 operations staff and General Miller who we briefed on the Kerbelâ' operation on 22 October. The general's distaste for the large numbers of American troops needed to support the MND's operations, the division's failure to engage Muqtadā aṣ-Ṣadr, and a general sense the division could do a lot more to alleviate the stress on the Coalition effort in Iraq was always evident in our private discussions. I understood his frustration and thought extensively about addressing his concerns by convincing the division's command group to adopt a more offensive posture. I honestly thought the division could do better despite the bounds of its restrictions and discussed the matter with General Tyszkiewicz.

The Kerbelā' operation had brought me closer to General Tyszkiewicz and we more frequently met and talked about both professional and personal issues. It was not uncommon to be invited to his office in the evening for a cup of tea or a glass of wine. The general's personal quarters were in a room adjacent to his office. He insisted on being close to his work and communications and often spoke to the headquarters duty officer in the evenings to stay aware of events throughout the division's AOR. It was a lonely existence upon which he insisted.

"The soldier's life," he often said, "Was a spartan existence that placed duty to his country and his soldiers before all else."

We often watched the news on the television in his office and conversed on any number of topics. During one of these sessions, I suggested he write a concept of operations for the division and brief it to his brigade and battalion commanders and the CJTF-7 staff. It could eventually be expanded into a standard operating procedure that would coordinate the division's efforts and address differences in national ROE that, in some cases, were negatively impacting our operations, endangering our troops, and adversely affecting the division's reputation. The division was conducting a number of good counterinsurgency operations. Its units actively patrolled the streets of their assigned urban areas and surrounding countryside. The number of patrols the division conducted across its AOR was staggering. The Spanish and Latin Americans were particularly adept at generating large numbers of small-unit mounted and dismounted patrols, but all three of the division's brigade combat teams reported hundreds of patrols and civil affairs activities. The battlefield information available from these operations, properly reported and analyzed, was potentially very valuable for planning combat operations. All the brigade commanders interfaced on a routine basis with local leaders, sheikhs, community leaders, police officials, tribal chiefs, and clerics. These meetings, both formal and informal, coupled with our battlefield activities, potentially provided a wealth of information we could analyze, verify, and use to strike insurgent forces before they struck us. Doing this, I suggested, was the ultimate manner in which we could provide the force protection we required to limit friendly casualties while pacifying our AOR and maximizing punishment on those who meant us harm. Simply stated, it would provide us the opportunity to hit the enemy before they hit us.

From these and other discussions with his staff, General Tyszkiewicz developed a list of his division's key tasks and a four-point approach to the division's operations.

The tasks were consistent with his peacekeeping mission, but they also provided insight to the evolving realities in Iraq that burdened him daily as the insurgency began to pick up speed. In order to conduct effective stability operations, the general focused on the concept of providing a visible presence throughout the AOR. The division was more than capable of providing both mounted and dismounted patrols while simultaneously providing the force protection the soldiers and facilities required. These patrols would be both mobile and stationary. Checkpoints could be established to inspect for weapons and other forms of contraband. Additionally, the Multinational Division (Central-South) had to:

a. Conduct civil affairs activities.
b. Conduct an information operations campaign (activities focused on public affairs and psychological operations to influence enemy and general population behavior).
c. Assist the development of the Iraqi Civil Defense Corps and police.
d. Provide border security.
e. Restore essential services.
f. Construct/enhance local Iraqi infrastructure.

The general acknowledged the division had to conduct operations against anti-Coalition forces. How to do that, however, consistent with its multiple national ROE was a major challenge. The battlefield information our enhanced presence provided could also provide invaluable leads about planned insurgent attacks and other nefarious activities well within the division's purview to preemptively strike. We could strike the enemy to deny him freedom of maneuver and prevent unnecessary Coalition casualties. He thought it would make sense to even our most restricted national contingent commanders.

The division strategy that emerged from these discussions was as elementary as it was brilliant:

1. Maximize patrolling with our combat units.
2. Conduct civil affairs activities accompanied by tactical intelligence teams.
3. Place emphasis on local leader engagement.
4. Conduct calculated, low-profile, surgical operations designed to eliminate insurgent cells.

General Tyszkiewicz particularly liked the wording of the fourth point. In order to ensure our actions were focused and ultimately appreciated by the larger community, he sought to limit collateral damage by emphasizing the "surgical" nature of any proposed combat operation. His civil affairs personnel and engineers would address any damage to any public or private facilities that may be inadvertently damaged or destroyed by combat action. This contributed to the division's "End State" intent of providing a "secure and stable environment." I had been impressed by how fast the division had moved to repair a small structure in Kerbelâ' after an armored vehicle from the 1st Armored Division had struck it on the evening of 18 October during the raid on Hasani's headquarters. Civil affairs teams and engineers were on the scene before our major combat forces were withdrawn. If the division acted as quickly on actionable intelligence to attack and destroy insurgent cells, it could make huge strides toward defeating any insurgent activity in its area of responsibility.

It was apparent the action in Kerbelâ' had not been as loud a wake-up call as I had hoped. The division's Operations Center received a report from Spanish Brigade Headquarters that 40 gunmen had attacked a hospital in Al-Najaf on the evening of 23 October. The division reported the attack to CJTF-7 but said nothing about the actions taken by the Spanish to defeat it. Neither Colonels Cabeza nor Gocul were present or immediately available to ask questions or press the Spanish for more information. After trying without success to convince several operations deputies to call the Spanish Operations Center for more information, I put my advisory/ liaison role aside and called General Cardona to determine if help was on the way. He assured me troops would be dispatched to the scene and that information would be provided as the situation developed. The troops he selected were the proud paratroopers from El Salvador, augmented by members of the Iraqi Police Service. Their actions resulted in the capture of four gunmen who informed them only 12 men had entered the hospital grounds. Spanish soldiers, with six armored personnel carriers and American military policemen, assisted in the cordon and search of the hospital grounds. Despite the limited success, I was frustrated by what I thought had been a slow reaction to a potentially dangerous situation. I lashed out at the Spanish desk officer for being absent during the bulk of the action. It should have been him who called General Cardona, not an American liaison officer. He was undoubtedly insulted by my words, and I suspected he would inform his national chain of command. The Spanish had relied initially on the tough "El Sal" paratroops because their ROE allowed them to enter the building. The Spanish troops, in accordance with their ROE, could only provide a cordon of the premises. I thought I may have really overstepped my bounds when I received a phone call the next day from the Spanish brigade's chief of staff, Colonel Viega. Still appreciative of my actions in September to coordinate equipment and supplies and facilitate the transition of authority in Al-Najaf, he merely repeated his commander's invitation to have me spend some time with his brigade. Breathing a sigh of relief, I told him I looked forward to the opportunity.

The incident on the night of the 23rd was more troubling in view of several conversations I had with American commanders and human intelligence (HUMINT) team leaders operating in the MND area of responsibility. The reports of Lieutenant Colonel Dunn and Captain Culbertson of the 323rd Military Intelligence Battalion were particularly disturbing. The insurgent action in our AOR was increasing, but the MND was not acting on reliable HUMINT and other forms of intelligence. Turning to me in frustration, the captain said, "The division just seems to hunker down, sir."

Reports like these disturbed me for several reasons. I was proud to be associated with the MND. I was determined to ensure it contributed to the war effort in every possible way it could. I was concerned about the perceptions the Americans had of the division. The presence of its numerous national flags was important to the Coalition's image, and I worried about misplaced insults that might cause a national embarrassment. But, more than anything else, I was concerned with the growing insurgency in the division's AOR. This insurgency was not like anything our European counterparts had experienced since World War II. A two-volume study I had read years before, *War in the Shadows: the Guerrilla in History* by Robert B. Asprey, addressed the author's concern that conventionally trained military commanders cannot grasp the concept of limited war and meet the challenges of a guerrilla force.[1] The commanding general had a good strategy, but he had not yet briefed it to his commanders and put it to work in the field. I was concerned about whether or not his commanders had the will to carry it out or the combat acumen to do it efficiently. I shared these thoughts with General Miller in yet another phone conversation during which I was encouraged to "Get the division moving." I suggested we give the commanding general's new approach to operations a chance to develop targets and inspire more aggressive action from his brigades. In the meantime, he should consider sending an American task force to the MND's AOR to conduct offensive operations on reported insurgent targets. I doubt this received any serious consideration. American units in Baghdad and in the northern provinces were already stretched thin and I was well aware we had nothing close to the forces needed to stabilize Iraq. The absence of a credible Iraqi Army to assist the Coalition with fundamental security concerns, and the paucity of American and multinational troops, significantly stressed the occupation. The Coalition had been sold "Mission accomplished" and had essentially deployed under a Chapter VI, United Nations-like agreement that says that when the consent of the two opposing parties breaks down, you leave. You cannot impose peace. General Tyszkiewicz knew how I felt about our need to be more aggressive and at one point described my reporting as "Overly emotional." I took issue with that, but in the interest of good relations and my credibility to support future operations on the line, I simply let it go and promised to be more civil. It was the only time during our tour in Iraq that our relationship was stressed.

The situation in Baghdad was getting worse. I was surprised to learn that the Al-Rashid Hotel was attacked by a guerrilla force with small arms and mortar fire on 26 October and the gallant Lieutenant Colonel Buehring, my former Ranger School student who had served so brilliantly as the public affairs officer for the New Iraqi Army project when I was the operations chief (C-3), was killed. One of the hotel's occupants at the time of the attack was U.S. Deputy Secretary of Defense Doctor Paul Wolfowitz. He had visited the MND at Camp Babylon only two days before, and I had had lunch with him and Major General Bill Caldwell, his executive assistant and an old friend of mine. Doctor Wolfowitz had a long and distinguished career in the State and Defense Departments. A former ambassador to Indonesia and a prominent neo-conservative, he had served several presidents and was a firm believer in pre-emption. His experience at the Al-Rashid Hotel may have given him a few second thoughts about Iraq and the folly of conducting an occupation of such a large country with less than a third of the required manpower. I still believed we could accomplish our goals in Iraq, but the growing insurgency and the paucity of much-needed combat forces to thwart it were beginning to cast a large shadow on our chances for success.

Another visitor to the MND in late October was the former commandant of the U.S. Marine Corps and now Supreme Allied Commander, Europe, General James L. Jones, USMC. I had first met General Jones in December 1998 when he was the military assistant to Secretary of Defense William S. Cohen. He and General Zinni were good friends and I was introduced to him during one of many of the general's trips to the Pentagon. We had talked several times during two trips to the Persian Gulf aboard the secretary's airplane before and after Operation *Desert Fox*, the four-day bombing campaign of Iraq that addressed Saddam's failure to positively respond to United Nations weapons-inspection protocols. He was very concerned about the performance and reputation of the NATO contingents assigned to the MND and his discussions with General Tyszkiewicz focused on rules of engagement and the burden of their inflexibility. General Jones was no stranger to this problem, having served in Bosnia–Herzegovina and Macedonia as the chief of staff of Joint Task Force *Provide Promise* in 1992. I had hoped General Tyszkiewicz would press him to address the issue with NATO national representatives, particularly when General Jones offered to do so, but he thought better of it. There was no doubt, however, that the ROE problem inhibited a more effective performance by contributing NATO countries. In this regard, the Spanish stood out as the most "handcuffed" contingent of all. General Jones understood the commanding general's reluctance to "drop a dime" on specific countries. I hoped he would address the matter in Europe at an appropriate time.

The ever-increasing concern about security and the growing insurgency in Iraq focused the division's command group and staff on what could be done to satisfy the general populace's needs and prevent the widespread discontent that ultimately causes instability and violence. Unemployment, the economy in general, and the lack of available resources—particularly oil and gas for cooking, heating, and transportation—were huge sources of discontent. The numbers told the story. In a country with something that approached twenty percent of the world's known oil reserves, there were vast shortages of every kind of oil-based product that an urban-based society requires to live a normal existence. The shortages were at an all-time high in the August–September 2003 timeframe. The MND staff was aware of the problems these shortages caused. Long lines of cars stretching for several miles at filling stations were scenes of angry, frustrated, young men who had more resources available to them before the invasion and Saddam's fall from power. General Tyszkiewicz pursued this point with General Sanchez in his evening tactical-satellite reports and spoke passionately of his observations. He personally conducted frequent reconnaissance flights and often drove through urban areas, stopping to speak to people who said they had waited in line to purchase gasoline for hours. The shortages stemmed in part from the insurgency, but the Iraqi infrastructure for refining oil products was limited, old, and poorly maintained. More than that, corruption in the oil industry and among the oil bureaucrats had long been rampant. Strictly from a management perspective, the commanding general wanted to lobby the Iraqi Oil Ministry to transfer management of the oil infrastructure in Wasit Province from Baghdad to the al-Ḥillah or ad-Dīwānīyah-based management offices in Central Iraq. The consensus of the division staff was that locally managed oil would be more equitably and quickly distributed and less susceptible to corruption. More resources in the division's AOR meant a happier populace and less disgruntled youth interested in fighting Coalition forces and the occupation in general.

General Tyszkiewicz raised his oil management issue at a CJTF-7 Commanders' Conference at Camp Victory early in November, and I did my part by discussing the issue at Camp Babylon with former Coalition Military Assistance Training Team Chief of Staff Colonel Tom O'Donnell. Tom was now commanding Task Force *Shield*, an organization established specifically to provide protection of the oil pipelines and facilities. He had happily left the stressful chief of staff position for a more exciting life in the field. Tom was more at ease in his new role, and we discussed the oil issue in my plywood hooch over a soda, some pepperoni, and a variety of Italian cheeses my folks had sent to me. Tom was amenable to supporting the division's request to manage Wasit Province oil from al-Ḥillah or ad-Dīwānīyah, but the best he could offer was promise to present the matter to the oil ministry and voice support for the transfer. Tom was a good and honest man; I knew he would do what he could. It was ultimately a Baghdad political issue that was very difficult to change. Like in every country, power is everything and all of the common sense and facts and figures we could muster might not convince the power brokers to change the policy. We did not expect to see any oil and gasoline relief anytime soon. In a moment of cynicism, I thought the more oil the Baghdad ministers managed, the more money they could loot for themselves. The combination of factors that adversely impacted Iraq's oil wealth had turned it from being a potential oil exporter, with profits originally estimated by the CPA to be as high as 50–100 billion dollars in two–three years, to being a net importer of oil; an Iraq the U.S. Government in March 2003 fully expected to finance its own reconstruction was now a growing burden on the Coalition and the United States Treasury.

The insurgency and sectarian violence in the Central-South AOR continued to get worse and the Poles and Bulgarians began to report more enemy activity in Kerbela' and Babil Provinces. Convoys were taking sporadic small-arms fire and at least one convoy had been attacked by insurgents hurling grenades. Casualties were inevitable and on 6 November the division was shocked by the death of Major Hieronim Kupczyk, a Polish officer killed by small-arms fire while traveling in a convoy 30 kilometers northeast of Kerbela', just north of our division boundary in the U.S. 82nd Airborne Division's sector. The MND had been extremely lucky up to this point. Major Kupczyk's death was taken particularly hard by the predominantly Polish division staff. On the following day, the commanding general, several members of his staff, and I flew to Camp Juliet in Kerbela' Province where memorial services were planned. We were greeted by General Marek Ojrzanowski who led us to a small tent where tea and soft drinks were available while final preparations were made for the memorial service. Marek greeted me with a smile. We had become close friends during the action in Kerbela' and I expressed my sincere condolences to him for the loss of one of his officers. We moved onto the large, barren field that normally served as the brigade helipad where a large number of Polish soldiers stood in formation. In the center of the formation was Major Kupczyk's coffin decorated with Polish colors and mounted on the ramp of a Polish military vehicle. The division staff officers and I stood behind General Tyszkiewicz who made appropriate remarks. Poland had suffered over six million deaths in World War II. This combat death, however, was a relatively new experience for Polish soldiers, and I thought about what these brave Poles must have been thinking as Kupczyk's coffin was driven past their formation and off the parade field to the strains of a Polish funeral march. Major Kupczyk had probably not seen his killer. It was the nature of an insurgency fought in the shadows and designed to attrit the Coalition's will to stay its course one death at a time. I suspected we would experience a lot more memorial services before we went home.

CHAPTER 27

Combat Action in Al-Kut

It's a great advantage not to drink among hard drinking people.
—F. Scott Fitzgerald, *The Great Gatsby*

The focus on Kerbelā', Babil Province, and the Spanish sectors in Al-Qādisiyyah and ad-Dīwānīyah Provinces in October, had left the Ukrainian Brigade Combat Team in Wasit Province essentially on its own. The division needed a better appreciation for the ongoing challenges facing the Ukrainians on the Iranian border. By this time, the Ukrainians were also involved in the Iraqi Civil Defense Corps (ICDC) and police training programs and an ICDC graduation was scheduled for 1 November. General Sobora was anxious to have me back in Al-Kut to update and review the proposed briefings and plans for the General Sanchez visit. The on again/off again Combined Joint Task Force-7 (CJTF-7) commander's tour of the Ukrainian brigade was proposed for a date to be determined in November and, with the commanding general's permission, I took the three-hour drive to Al-Kut on the morning of 1 November with General Sobora and his interpreter Lieutenant Alex Kanus.

The use of improvised explosive devices in Iraq was not uncommon by November 2003, but it was less prolific than our soldiers would experience later in the war. I was more concerned about the possibility of being hit with small arms and rocket-propelled grenade fire. General Sobora rode in the front seat and the absence of conversation and the heat of the day had me fighting the "sleep monster" for the bulk of the trip. I was aware of the danger, however, and struggled to stay awake.

The Ukrainian soldiers were still billeted in tents, but their base was beginning to improve and it would not be long before the troops would move into renovated barracks. The focus of construction during the summer months had been the Iraqi training facilities. The expansion of Iraqi security forces was central to the transition of security responsibilities from the Coalition. The Ukrainians had a strong appreciation for this vital understanding and mission and, despite some initial difficulties stemming primarily from cultural differences, the tough Ukrainians were doing very well training both the ICDC and the Iraqi Police Service. American trainers assigned to the base were very complimentary of the support they received from the Ukrainian brigade. Generals Sobora and Bezluschenko were anxious to brief the training program's progress to General Sanchez. General Sobora's primary concern, however, was the Iranian border where illegal immigration and suspected foreign-fighter infiltration were increasing. The challenges there made patrolling the border his "bread and butter" mission. Following the impressive ICDC graduation and a short review of potential discussions and briefings for a future General Sanchez visit, we quickly got back into our vehicles and headed for the border.

We closed on a prearranged contact point where Major Val Semenets and a reinforced platoon of infantry with four BTR-80s were waiting for us. Val was pleased to have us. It had been more than a month since our first patrol and he greeted me with an enthusiastic handshake. Val broke out his maps and briefed General Sobora on the patrol route and the general situation along the border. This patrol would cover about 90 kilometers of the border. It would be nightfall before we would complete the mission. He wanted to spend additional time observing the areas near the Iranian border forts. Many of the Iranian "pilgrims" stopped at the forts for food and drink before crossing into Iraqi territory. His smile told me the "pilgrims" he was referring to were likely men of military age who meant to make trouble in Iraq.

"Perhaps tonight, Colonel," he said to me with a smile, "we will have some action."

It was not uncommon for the Iranians to cross the border under the cover of darkness in large numbers. Once past the border, they would move to the border towns and villages and then buy transportation to the holy cities of Al-Najaf and Kerbelâ' which had been denied to them during the Saddam years. The Ukrainians wanted additional facilities along the border that would support efforts to prevent illegal immigration and allow the Iraqi border police and customs agents to regulate legitimate crossings. These facilities would have computers and photo capability to document who entered the country, their proposed destination, and date of departure. It was another issue I would have to address to the CJTF-7 staff and the Iraqi Ministry of Interior during the commanding general's upcoming trip to Baghdad. But for now, the only thing that stood between illegal Iranian infiltration and the Iraqi interior in Wasit Province was a thin line of Ukrainian paratroopers and infantrymen. It was a sobering thought considering the magnitude of the job.

As expected, the daylight portion of our patrol was uneventful. The Iraqis had learned to avoid the tough-talking Ukrainians who policed them up and shook them down for weapons and drugs. It was assumed any Iraqi with a vehicle near the border road at night was engaged or planning to engage in illegal activity. For a small fee, an Iraqi would gladly haul Iranian pilgrims to Kerbelâ' or Al-Najaf and business was pretty good. For all the hapless Iraqis who had seen their vehicles taken and impounded by the Ukrainians, numerous others had undoubtedly made off with their Iranian customers. It was a living, I suppose, but the wily General Sobora had some other ideas up his sleeve to make the would-be Iraqi cabbies miserable.

He directed his men to disable any Iraqi vehicles in the vicinity of the border road clearly intended to transport illegal immigrants but before any had been picked up. This could be done in any number of ways and still allow the vehicle to be repaired in a reasonable period of time. I wondered what the general really had in mind and looked forward to seeing for myself.

Growing bored with Val's twilight stakeout of a suspected Iranian infiltration route, General Sobora decided to engage in some light physical training. The desert winds had created a huge dune to the rear of our position and the general decided he would sprint up and down the dune. He was fully attired in body armor and carried his AKM, the paratroop variant of the famous AK-47 rifle. At the top of his lungs, I could hear the general calling me, "Colonel Tiso." The general stood atop the dune waving his rifle and challenging me to run to the top as well.

Here we were on a tactical operation, deployed in an ambush position, and I was being challenged to run up a damn sand dune. "What the hell," I thought, "Go for it!"

I moved to the base of the dune and started running. We ran up and down the dune several times before we observed the headlights of a vehicle in the distance. We ran down the dune and advised Val who immediately alerted his checkpoint personnel on the road. A soldier signaled an old Oldsmobile sedan to slow down as it approached our position. The driver knew better than to attempt to run a checkpoint. The Ukrainians had been on the border for several months now and the locals knew they followed a different "play book" than the Americans. There was no doubt in the Iraqis' minds these boys would take all appropriate actions if they were threatened. The Ukrainian soldiers were all business as they searched the two Iraqi men and their vehicle for contraband and weapons while maintaining security up and down the road. Our Arabic speaker asked them a few questions and their shaky responses failed to convince us they were simply out for a drive. No one would buy that. The border road was not exactly a place to socialize. The search of the vehicle turned up a couple of switchblade knives the soldiers pocketed. General Sobora then directed the vehicle be driven several hundred meters off the road where one young paratrooper cut the vehicle's fuel lines while two others let the air out of its tires.

I looked at General Sobora and smiled. The old soldier knew what he was doing. These guys would have to walk all night to get back to their village and secure the necessary parts, tools, and assistance to repair their vehicle. They would also put the word out that going to the border road at night was bad business. Hanging out with General Sobora was like being back with the "fellas" in old New York. I suppose there's a little "street thug" in all good infantrymen. I could tell the good general was enjoying himself as he shook the Iraqis' hands and left them in the desert to do whatever they had to do. It was getting late and we had several hours yet to complete our mission and return to Al-Kut.

We intercepted several other vehicles before Val signaled his men to pack up and begin our movement to his headquarters at Camp Fort. He was genuinely disappointed in not having intercepted any Iranians, but he expected follow-on patrols that night would have better luck. At Camp Fort, I thanked Val for the opportunity to work with his men. I always thought the actions of these "hard rock" soldiers and the isolation they endured were not fully appreciated at CJTF-7 Headquarters. I looked forward to the proposed General Sanchez visit as much as General Sobora. Recognition of the Ukrainian brigade by CJTF-7 was long overdue.

I would have preferred to stay at Camp Fort that night. The long drive to Al-Kut earlier that day, the staff work we had done, the drive to the border, and our border patrol had left me yawning. The last thing I wanted was another long drive back to Al-Kut. There was no choice. General Sobora was needed back at Camp Babylon the following afternoon and he wanted to speak with his brigade commander before he departed. We were technically not allowed to be on the roads at night, but the general accepted the risk. The bulk of our drive would be along unpopulated routes. He mitigated the risk by directing Val to provide an armed escort of two squads of infantry aboard two BTR-80s.

I took a seat in the rear of the general's sedan and settled in for the long drive. It had been a good day and the excitement of the patrol had been worth the time and discomfort of driving to the border. There was nothing to look forward to at this point, however, and I did my best to make myself comfortable and placed my pistol in the pocket on the back of the general's seat where it was readily accessible. It was pitch black once we turned away from Camp Fort. I stayed awake for a while conversing with Lieutenant Kanus as we rolled over the potholes and rough spots of the desert roads. Once we turned onto the paved open roads, I had to catch myself from falling asleep. It was a desperate and losing struggle until a little over an hour into the drive when we jerked to a halt.

I was suddenly aware of General Sobora opening the passenger door of the sedan and I was instantly wide awake. Somehow, the white pickup truck that was part of our four-vehicle convoy and our sedan had gotten out in front of the BTR-80s carrying our supporting infantry. The pickup truck was about 100 meters in front of us and had driven into a ditch on the right side of the road. I moved to the left side of the sedan to join General Sobora who was crouched by the front bumper. I could see a steady stream of red tracer rounds being pumped into and left and right of the pickup truck. Opposite the truck, on the left side of the road, was a clump of palm trees. Several men were lying there, firing from the prone position. The rising ground near the palm trees masked them from us and provided a modicum of cover. During the few brief moments that we huddled in the front of the car, we were totally exposed, but they did not see us and continued to direct their fire in the direction of the pickup truck. The Iraqis were silhouetted by the ambient light coming from the direction of the outskirts of Al-Kut, and I could make out the rounded shape of someone's buttocks as he lay in the prone position. I raised my rifle and fired at his butt from the kneeling position just as General Sobora fired a burst of three to four rounds from his AKM. I thought I had a good shot and, while I was never a great marksman, I honestly thought my long hours on the range at Central Command with my enlisted mentor and friend, Master Sergeant "Q" Gingola, had paid off. The Iraqis were surprised and started to break away, but they were disciplined enough to move low to the ground and not overly expose themselves to our fires. I turned to Lieutenant Kanus and told him to stay by the vehicle. Almost simultaneously, General Sobora and I looked at each other. He grunted something in Ukrainian and I simply replied, "Let's go!" We quickly moved out in a crouch, down the center of the gravel road, and then to our right in the direction of the rear of the pickup truck. The truck's right front tire had careened into the ditch. The driver and passenger had escaped through the passenger door and had found cover in the rocks well away from the truck on the right side of the road. We had no sooner opened the passenger door of the truck to see if anyone was still inside when we came under fire from the same guys who had positioned themselves in tall grass about 25 meters to the rear of the palm trees. The general and I instinctively dove into the ditch and pressed ourselves into its dirt and gravel. The ditch and vehicle provided adequate cover for the moment, but neither of us was in a good position to see or engage the enemy. After what seemed like an eternity, the red tracer over our heads stopped, but we were now under the fires of our infantry that had maneuvered in the open area along the right side of the road and were engaging what they thought were enemy targets in the vicinity of the truck. I looked up this time to see a string of Ukrainian white tracer fire headed for the palm trees and the grass. The Iraqis returned fire and for a brief moment the sky lit up with white and red tracer. Caught in a crossfire and with no place to go, I simply laid there thankful for our ditch and taking some comfort in the thought that small arms fire at night, even by disciplined troops, tends to be high. The short exchange was followed by another moment of silence. General Sobora arched up, yelled something to his soldiers, and announced that he was, "General Sobora." The firing suddenly continued, more violently than before.

In one of those Hollywood-like comical moments, I turned my head toward General Sobora and, with all the calm I could muster, strongly suggested he simply "Shut up!"

His reply was an even more comical—"Da"—as he pressed himself into the ditch.

I crawled to the rear of the pickup truck and made my way out of the ditch using the left rear tire as cover and fired several more aimed rounds in the direction of the ambush site. A few moments later, the firing again ceased and our troops approached the truck. I moved across the road past the ambush site to a clearing where in the distance I saw a sedan silhouetted by the ambient light. I heard the doors slam shut as the ambush team attempted to get away from us and drive off. It was a long shot, but I quickly got into a firing position and fired one round at the rear window of the vehicle as they sped off along the access road. General Sobora was on his feet barking orders to the infantrymen to secure the area. I grabbed Lieutenant Kanus and told him to tell the squad leaders to establish a checkpoint and detail several men to check the grassy area from where we had last been engaged. There was evidence of blood by the clump of palm trees where the ambush had been initiated and a number of 7.62mm shell casings. I took some comfort that we had hit at least one of them, but I cursed myself for not having had a grenade to throw.

The paratroopers quickly moved into position to establish the checkpoint and within minutes stopped a large dump truck coming from the direction of the access road that our ambushers had used to make their escape. The driver was attired in typical Arab dress and sandals. It was obviously not his day. Ordered out of the cab, he was understandably very animated by the sight of a lot of men with guns speaking a language that must have sounded out of this world to him. In another moment of comical insight, I couldn't help laughing and thinking that the strange, but tough-sounding Ukrainian language was a combat multiplier that added an element of fear to unknowing Iraqi civilians wherever we encountered them.

The Iraqi driver was scared silly and babbled somewhat incoherently. One phrase that I made out was "Ali Babas, Ali Babas!!" The Arab speaker came over and calmed the poor guy down by handing him a cigarette. He had apparently caught the tail end of our firefight and had seen our ambushers drive off. There was some good news. He told the interpreter the rear window of the car had been shot out and one of the men was slumped in the back seat with his head against the window. He said there were three men in the car. "Well, what do you know," I thought. "All of those years on the rifle range for one lucky, improbable shot at a moving target in the darkness." I wondered if the driver or his other buddy in the right-front seat was nursing a bullet hole in his butt. The fellow in the back seat was either dead or badly wounded with a head wound. Regardless, I was satisfied our actions had saved the lives of the two Ukrainian soldiers who had been in the cab of the ambushed pickup truck and prevented the loss of the vehicle and the equipment in the back seat and rear bed.

General Sobora quickly decided the Iraqi dump-truck driver was not going to provide us any useful information. We remained in position for another 10 minutes, and then moved to the closest Ukrainian garrison where our sad and disillusioned dump-truck driver was handed over to the commanding officer for further questioning. The Arabic interpreter informed us the dump-truck driver thought our enemies were Iraqi bandits. The reference to "Ali Baba," was a common expression to describe bandits like Ali Baba and the 40 thieves. This, coupled with the fact that not a single round had entered the engine compartment of the pickup truck, was a good indicator they had intended to steal it. The front windshield was intact, but the windows had been shot out and several bullet holes had entered the rear cargo area. The vehicle was otherwise in good shape and drivable. The Iraqi bandits had not anticipated shooting up a military convoy escorted by infantry which probably explained why they did not see and engage the general's sedan or the BTRs. The distance between the general's sedan and the truck, the darkness of the country road, and the fact we were driving without our headlights on had made all the difference between our good fortune and the possibility of friendly casualties. The action had lasted about 12 minutes. It had been 9:10 pm when I had gotten out of the sedan after our abrupt stop. It was late by the time we left the Ukrainian garrison to drive the final leg to the air base and the headquarters of the Ukrainian brigade.

General Bezluschenko greeted us when our convoy pulled up in front of his headquarters. His sullen look of concern contrasted with his usual broad smile. The generals exchanged a few pleasantries while I took a closer look at the pickup truck. How the driver and his passenger had escaped injury amazed me. Neither had much to say and I suspected they both appreciated the opportunity to get a fresh pair of underwear. I thought it might be smart to check mine as well. I had not given much thought to the ambush. During the final leg of our drive to the air base, I had been especially alert for anything else that could happen. I was happy not to be hurt and, in the safety of the base and later in the general's tent, I felt an immense sense of pride and relief in what we had done to defeat the ambush. It was not long after I sat down, and the adrenalin began to subside, that I felt bone tired. I welcomed the comfort of a lounge chair after removing my body armor and combat equipment. I was sweating profusely. The generals took a seat at a desk and spoke privately as I began to doze off. General Sobora, however, would have none of that.

The proud General Sobora was feeling pretty good. He was now ready to celebrate having been "blooded" and surviving his first real combat action in Iraq. He had, after all, performed quite well in this action. To the best of my knowledge, he was the only Coalition general who had fired a rifle in combat. Generals and colonels firing rifles or engaging in close combat was not the norm in any army, but General Sobora was different. Calling my name, the general waved me over to his desk as General Bezluschenko got up and gave me his seat. General Sobora then reached into the lower drawer of the desk and hauled out a bottle of vodka. It was time to toast our victory and, if I read him correctly, we were about to get snockered.

I'm not a drinking man, but I learned early in my career that a little alcohol on special occasions is normal in the officer corps. The initiation rite in the 1st Battalion, 506th Infantry, challenged every new officer to chug a shot of flaming Drambuie after citing the great campaigns the regiment fought in Europe and Vietnam—"Normandy, Bastogne, and the A Shau." The 506th was my first unit and the initiation shot of Drambuie my first hard drink. Thankfully I got it right on the first shot. Others were less fortunate and either suffered the humiliation of being burned or taking several tries to get it right. Five years later in Korea with the 1st Battalion, 23rd Infantry, my battalion commander enthusiastically suggested we christen our new commanders' drinking cups with champagne. A decent and deeply religious man who had grown up in the finest traditions of the airborne, the good colonel insisted we drink up and engage in the Officers Club antics that characterized the highly charged social activities of our finest regiments of the era. These activities were followed with more champagne and everything else the club had to offer. Our lieutenants carried their drunken commanders to their quarters that night. It was my first and, I had hoped, my last drunken experience. It had taken 16 hours of sleep and a ten-mile run to put its effects behind me. I had a good idea of what I was in for this time.

I was staring at a man determined to drink his native vodka in the finest traditions of the victorious celebrations of the Great Patriotic War. To have walked away would have been unacceptable, even unmanly. Visions of Korea passed before me as I settled into the chair, determined to represent the United States Army and my country in the best possible way. Major General Antoliy Ivanoyvich Sobora of the Ukrainian Army might have had more experience and capacity, but I was either going to out-drink him or go down in the attempt. And so it began; the shot glasses were filled and the general proposed the first toast that was translated by the Ukrainian giant, Andriy Lischynskyi. Andriy had entered the tent along with the brigade commander's aide, the stoic paratroop warrant officer who took his smiling lessons from General Sobora. Senior Warrant Officer Anatoliy "Tolik" Kunitskyi was always serious looking and always at the rigid position of parade rest. He stood by the entrance to the tent and stared straight ahead, ready to immediately respond to his general's orders. Andriy explained the shots would be taken "under control," meaning the glass would be emptied in one throw. The toasts were initially serious with the general proposing a toast to Ukraine. I responded with one to the United States of America. We then toasted our respective presidents, commanding officers, regiments, families, and just about everything a soldier could possibly hold dear. The good general even toasted former President Bill Clinton whom he detested for his moral indiscretions. The session simply went downhill from there and I do not recall how many shots we had, but the large bottle was about empty and I was as "shit faced" as a drunken sailor on liberty after six months at sea. We had not had a lot to eat that day and I was about as ripe for a good drunk as a man could be. General Sobora seemed unaffected, but he thankfully called a halt to the celebration, perhaps out of fear he was going to kill me. I had done my best, slowly got up from my chair, shook the general's hand, and walked a staggering 15 feet to the couch where I passed out.

I woke up during the night covered with a blanket. My boots had been removed and a pillow had been placed under my head. I made my way to the latrines that were located directly across the brigade street, urinated into something I hoped was a urinal, and miraculously returned to the right tent where I again collapsed and fell into a dead sleep. It was nearly six hours later when I was shaken awake by General Sobora. He was holding a towel and toilet articles and I guessed it was time to hit the showers. Getting up was an effort in itself. My body hurt, my head hurt, and my legs were wobbly. I could not remember feeling so bad. We made our way slowly to the latrines and there, standing at parade rest by the senior officers' shower, was my favorite warrant officer with his same stoic look, holding a towel and some soap. He handed them to me as I approached the door. One look in the mirror told me the story. General Sobora had definitely won that round and I jokingly wondered if I qualified for a Purple Heart.

My headache wreaked havoc on my brain. I was hungry and attributed my headache as much to my hunger as I did my tremendous hangover. I stepped into the general's tent to find my uniform cleaned and pressed and a breakfast of eggs, sausage, toast, and juice waiting for me on a coffee table. Generals Sobora and Bezluschenko invited me to join them and to the rear of the tent stood my favorite warrant officer stoically standing at parade rest. Andriy sat nearby to translate. I was with my "Ukrainian family," but the last thing I wanted to do was talk. Headache and all, the chow looked good to me and I wanted to eat. General Sobora was wide awake and wanted to talk about the United States Army. The Ukrainians are great admirers of America's Army, but they could not understand why it had so many women. Surely, the general suggested, they must cause significant trouble with matters of discipline. Despite my headache, I thought about the various challenges the integration of women into America's volunteer Army had caused over the years. I have never been a proponent of women in uniform in large numbers for a variety of professional reasons, but as the Task Force Sinai commander I had done my utmost through training and administration to ensure everyone was treated equally. It was much to the chagrin of many female soldiers who resented being held to the same standards of every soldier in the unit and to the standards of our higher headquarters, the 1st Corps Support Command. My experience with female-integrated units, though largely limited to the Sinai experience, had reinforced a well-established fact that fighting units are best served by physically strong, athletic, and intelligent 18–27-year-old, single, well-trained men. I suggested to General Sobora that any attempt on his nation's part to enlist women should be measured. Though the rigors of combat organizations may not be conducive for females, there certainly are roles for women in the Army. Women can be an asset to the military if their talents and strengths are properly focused, high standards of personal fitness and discipline are maintained, and their numbers and units of assignment carefully managed. I thought it was a fair response and he appeared to appreciate it.

The general asked about physical conditioning and the U.S. Army physical-fitness test. I explained between bites of sausage the method by which our soldiers are assessed. The Ukrainians had seen me running and doing push-ups and sit-ups at both Al-Kut and Camp Babylon and the young officers would occasionally join me for a run or a weightlifting session. I explained the rating scales and time requirements for the two-mile run, and our standards of appearance. Soldiers could not be overweight or appear to be fat. I explained that American soldiers are weighed and assessed against an established standard of height, weight, and body fat every six months.

These efforts ensured individual readiness for combat. His interest went beyond the breakfast table. The enthusiastic and fit General Sobora got on the floor and knocked out 25 regulation pushups while I asked for a second helping of sausage and eggs, thinking more chow would help to soak up the "poison" I had consumed at our evening's victory celebration. My headache was still throbbing and the last thing I was interested in was physical training. Standing by the coffee table, the general then invited me to emulate his performance. It was another challenge that Andriy translated with a smile. I mustered a lot of energy just to get up from behind the table. The tent was still blurry to me as I moved to where I could assume the push-up position. Taking a deep breath, I got on the floor and started knocking out high energy push-ups, clapping my hands under my chest as I pushed up and off the floor. I had everyone's attention as I executed 50 of them seemingly without effort. My head was pounding and I probably could have added an Academy Award for faking good health to my hard won, alcohol-stained "Purple Heart." General Sobora looked at me and shook his head as I made my way around him and back to my chair. Looking up at the general with a forced smile, I pointed to my breakfast and the discussion ended. I think I won that round.

The drive back to Camp Babylon was uneventful and I was most thankful. In spite of the combat-readiness lessons of the previous evening, and with my head still pounding, it was not long before I stripped off my armor and helmet, lay back, and fell into a deep sleep. To his credit, General Sobora did not say a word to me the entire trip. The great soldier knew I was "smoked" and, like any infantryman, respected my sleep. At Camp Babylon, we shook hands and I slowly walked to my plywood hooch contemplating the error of drinking with Ukrainians and driving through "Indian country" without wearing body armor. I slept for several more hours, showered, and headed for the division's Operations Center and the evening's tactical-satellite report exercise. I was immediately informed I would accompany the commanding general to Baghdad in the morning for a series of meetings at CPA and CJTF-7 with commanders and selected members of the respective staffs.

CHAPTER 28

The American Bureaucracy in Baghdad

I'm in the business of doing things quickly but legally. That means nothing gets done quickly enough.

—Colonel Tony Bell, USA

The trip to Baghdad was a great opportunity for me to assist the commanding general's efforts to address the resource shortfalls in the division's area of responsibility (AOR) as well as to see my friends still assigned to the Coalition Military Assistance Training Team (CMATT). Accompanying the commanding general was his highly respected political advisor, His Excellency Ambassador Ryszard Krystosik. My superb relationship with the ambassador always ensured fun-filled conversations and I never failed to learn something from him or gain valuable insights regarding any number of issues. The general's meetings with the Combined Joint Task Force-7 (CJTF-7) commander and the other key commanders and staff members were held at the Republican Palace; rooms had been arranged for us on the palace grounds. By this time, the Kellogg Brown & Root contractors had managed to deliver a number of suitable two-room trailers to accommodate the ever-increasing Coalition Provisional Authority (CPA) staff, and the days of wild parties and high-living at the former family residences were long gone. The residences now housed embassies and government office space. The CIA occupied the house the CMATT staff had occupied during the wild and wholly early days of the occupation.

The palace grounds reflected the reality of the war. Surrounding the rows of white trailers were sandbag walls that protected against the ever-increasing rocket and mortar fire from Baghdad and its environs. It was sobering, but just as evident in contrast was the bikini-clad set of State Department employees and off-duty staff officers and soldiers in administrative positions who still enjoyed the luxurious pool. Life at the palace had to be pretty good between the comfortable quarters, renovated, air-conditioned office spaces, magnificent gymnasium and pool, and the best mess hall in Iraq. It appeared to me the United States was not planning on pulling out of Iraq anytime soon. These were not expeditionary conditions by any military standard, though many civilians and rear-echelon staff officers thought they had a hard life. The cast of characters I saw every time I went to Baghdad made me laugh. America's military relied heavily on the contractors who provided the general support our Army used to provide itself before it had been drawn down to its post–Cold War levels. I tried to ignore it, but deep down I always resented the poor judgment of our senior leaders who, after the fall of the Soviet Union, significantly reduced or eliminated the support structure the Army so desperately needed to conduct sustained combat operations. The United States military could not function for any significant period of time without contractors. I valued their expertise and resources, but many of them made me sick with their "get rich quick" schemes, excessive creature comforts, and force-protection requirements.

After locating the general's and Ambassador Krystosik's quarters and acquiring their room keys, I moved to the Iraqi ministries area on the first and second floors of the palace. I wanted to speak to representatives from the Oil and Interior Ministries about oil management in central-south Iraq and see what information and assistance I could get regarding the construction of the point-of-entry customs facility on the Ukrainian-patrolled portion of the Iranian border.

I was taken by the number of Iraqis working in the ministries. The ministries would eventually be integrated into the Iraqi Interim Government and the elected governments to follow. In 2003, however, they were under CPA control. The Iraqis were well dressed and educated and moved easily between Arabic and English. It was a good sign of hope for the future. I entered the Oil Ministry and met Brigadier General Robert Crear, USA, who commanded Task Force *Restore Iraqi Oil*. He was a big man with a big job. Like a number of other generals plucked from their regular stateside assignments to plug holes in the Iraq reconstruction effort, General Crear was the commander of the United States Army Corps of Engineers Southwestern Division in Dallas, Texas. He was deployed to Kuwait in February 2003 to establish his new command and assist the new Iraqi Oil Ministry to import fuel products, restore oil systems, and replace looted equipment. Friendly and courteous, he listened intently as I explained General Tyszkiewicz's desire to change the controlling offices for central-south oil from Baghdad to offices in ad-Dīwānīyah or al-Ḥillah. General Tyszkiewicz wanted to more adequately channel resources locally and perhaps lessen the growing discontent with the American occupation and the expanding insurgency in his area of operations. General Crear appeared supportive and asked me to arrange an office call for him with General Tyszkiewicz at Camp Babylon. As a show of good faith, he presented me his commander's coin for excellence and we parted ways with a firm handshake.

My call on the Ministry of the Interior was also encouraging. Building a major customs post requires money, contracting, and scheduling. The impression I had was that our much-needed customs post on the Iranian border was far down CPA's priority list. It was understandable and I did not expect much going in. It made sense to coordinate with the ministry whenever we were in Baghdad, however, just to let the staff know we were alive and waiting. I eventually spoke with a Lieutenant Colonel Burley, USA, after waiting a couple of hours to see him. Colonel Burley, like so many other people assigned to responsible positions in the CPA, was a "one deep shop" and up to his ears in work. His schedule had no breaks and he was away from his office more than he was there. A good man with what appeared to be a strong sense of purpose, Burley surprised me when his records indicated our customs post construction project was scheduled to go to the contracting office before the end of the week. He could not tell me much more, but suggested I see Colonel Tony Bell in the contracting office for more information.

I was in luck. Tony Bell was the chief CPA contracting officer who had arrived in June and helped us get the New Iraqi Army project off the ground. He was happy to see me and we talked briefly of the desperate summer we had spent sorting out the construction of Kirkush Barracks and the recruiting stations. He laughed when I told him I was involved in another desperate fight as the adviser to the Multinational Division (Central-South). His comment to me summed up the challenge we all faced in Iraq.

"Roland, everyone is desperate here. Everyone wants everything now, and I'm in the business of doing things quickly but legally. That means nothing gets done quickly enough."

I understood Tony's predicament and did not want to add to his woes. I asked him to keep an eye out for the customs station project and wished him well. I did not expect to see a customs station on the border anytime soon. I walked out satisfied I had done everything I could and very glad I was not Tony Bell.

I was happy to bring my official calls to an end for the day and call on my buddies in the CMATT. Geoff Fuller and Trey Johnson, two of the original desperate men of the summer, ensured I had a place to stay for the night in one of the CMATT-designated trailers and we had dinner together in the palace mess hall. Sitting on beach chairs by the trailers that night was a far cry from the parties and beer-drinking sessions that had characterized the late evenings at Uday's former house during the summer. Things had changed and, in their view, for the worse. It did not take long to see what they meant. Our conversation was interrupted by the distinctive sound of mortars being fired from somewhere in Baghdad. Several rounds passed over us as we watched the rear-echelon soldiers and civilians scrambling for cover. Geoff told me the evening mortar and rocket drill was becoming a regular event, but it was still amusing to watch the REMFs (a strictly unofficial term combat soldiers use to describe rear echelon personnel) scramble for their lives. I left Baghdad the next day thinking the occupation and reconstruction of Iraq was at best precarious and at worst in danger of failure. My activities of late had allowed me to gain an appreciation for our challenge in Iraq from urban warfare in Kerbelā', to a windswept country ambush site and ditch in Wasit Province, to indirect fire intended to discourage a growing American presence and bureaucracy in Baghdad. The war planners and commanders of the 1990s had never envisioned the occupation of Iraq to look like the under-resourced effort currently confronting the CPA and the Coalition, but I was more determined than ever to do whatever I could to make the Multinational Division's efforts in Iraq's central-south region achieve an acceptable level of stability.

CHAPTER 29

Developing a Strategy to Conduct the Long War

A general is just as good or just as bad as the troops under his command make him.
—General Douglas MacArthur

The Multinational Division's (MND) deployment to Iraq in the summer of 2003 had been heralded as a significant contribution to the Coalition and the development of an independent, democratic, and secure Iraq. Its presence and multiple national colors gave the overall Coalition effort a major boost in credibility. Its soldiers were proud of their mission and service in Iraq. By November, however, the sobering reality of the expanding insurgency dampened the division's initial enthusiasm. It was increasingly apparent to the division's senior leaders the commitment in Iraq would be long term.

The weather reflected the mood. The season's first rain had fallen on 29 October and it was falling with increasing intensity with each passing day. It reminded me of the intense rains I had experienced in Iraq during my tour with the UN in the fall–winter of 1997–98. The rains that year were so intense several people had drowned in the streets of Kuwait City. The water-drenched desert had turned a light shade of green and produced a vast crop of large mushrooms known as truffles that resembled, and were easily confused with, anti-personnel mines. A large number of Bedouin desert dwellers died as a result of innocently harvesting the protein-rich truffles that too often turned out to be deadly unexploded "gator mines" from the First Gulf War. The hot, sunny days to which we had grown accustomed were now overcast, damp, and cool at night. It was a welcome relief for some, but it also reflected the subdued mood of soldiers and officers far from their native lands and looking at the second half of their six-month tour in an increasingly dangerous Iraq. Their relief in January by a scheduled rotation of personnel and national units seemed a long way off.

The rain turned the sandy ground in and around the living areas of Camp Babylon into a sea of mud and filth, making us even more grateful for the new shower units the Kellogg Brown & Root (KB&R) contractors had recently installed. Getting from the shower units back to my plywood hooch, however, required some nifty walking around large ponds of water and mud. Rather than make the trip, I often bathed in my hooch with sundry pack moist bath towels that were normally provided to refugees and prisoners of war. Watching people stumble across the muddy sea as they walked to and from the showers in all forms of dress provided a sick form of comic relief as I shaved by my front door. KB&R also installed white accommodation trailers like those I had seen in Baghdad; the tents that had served as billets for the staff were taken away. I preferred my plywood hooch. Late in October, the Romanian engineers had winterized a portion of it and I was comfortable with its relative isolation and privacy. The simple, spartan life of the camp appealed to me and I laughed at the characteristic gripes of soldiers and officers about the primitive conditions in which they lived.

The loss of several U.S. helicopters by enemy action in October was troubling. Mindful of the lack of aircraft-survivability equipment on Polish aircraft (anti-missile systems designed to defeat an infra-red missile threat), the commanding general decided to forbid any flights to Baghdad. Future travel to Combined Joint Task Force-7 (CJTF-7) Headquarters would be by ground transportation only. This decision, coupled with Major Kupczyk's death, reinforced the reality of the war north of us on my Polish friends. Almost simultaneously, however, the G-2 (Intelligence Section) was seeing increased insurgent activity in the Al-Ḥillah, Kerbelâ', and Al-Najaf regions, and the reports from Wasit Province showed more hostile-fire incidents involving Ukrainian patrols in the vicinity of Al-Kut. Polish patrols were engaged in several small actions involving hostile fire and insurgent activity in and around Kerbelâ'. Working with American special forces units, the Poles conducted several successful early morning raids against suspected former regime element planning cells. Mortar fire periodically fell on Al-Ḥillah. But it was Muqtadā aṣ-Ṣadr and his growing Mahdi Army militia who represented the biggest threat to the cities of Kerbelâ' and Al-Najaf, and the central-south region. The reluctance of the Spanish brigade and the MND to deal aggressively with Ṣadr continued to burden CJTF-7. The Spanish generated large numbers of patrols throughout their area of responsibility and the presence they provided each day was as prolific as the best combat organizations in Iraq. An offensive fighting force was needed, however, if Coalition forces were going to act upon the battlefield information their presence generated.

American special forces activity in Al-Najaf was picking up. Up until this point, night activity at the Camp Babylon airstrip, now referred to as "Landing Zone (LZ) Ruins," had been almost non-existent. U.S. special forces officers had been by the division's Operations Center on several occasions in mid-November to coordinate flights of Black Hawks and Apache gunships into LZ Ruins. Tight-lipped and professional, the impression we had from their queries was their activities were focused on Ṣadr. American aircraft operated from LZ Ruins for the bulk of November and December, but Ṣadr went untouched. His survival and increased influence throughout Iraq would ultimately hold severe consequences for the Coalition and the future Iraqi Government.

The commanding general was increasingly concerned about the division's force-protection posture. General Sobora had coordinated the initial defense arrangements of Camp Babylon and met frequently with a force-protection committee that made recommendations for enhancements to the camp's security. Occasionally, General Tyszkiewicz asked me and Brigadier General Kwiatkowski to assess the recommendations and provide our views as well. We frequently walked the camp's huge perimeter. The LZ was particularly vulnerable to infiltration and attack. We recommended patrols along its perimeter be increased and that additional standoff be created by bulldozing the foliage and trees on the north and east sides of the airstrip. The pilots were very appreciative of this effort in view of the increased American use of the strip. General Kwiatkowski and I were also concerned with the built-up area on the far side of the Euphrates River where we thought mortar fire had been directed against Camp Babylon. The mess hall was a very lucrative target as was the division's headquarters, which was well in range of 60-mm and 82-mm mortars. On several evenings, we crossed the river with several Polish soldiers to recon the far side for insurgent activity. We agreed that the Polish company responsible for the camp's security should add a cross-river day and night patrol to its security responsibilities.

We put our soldiers to work sandbagging critical facilities to mitigate the effects of any mortar and rocket fire. The Mongolian engineer platoon constructed a series of "Chinese walls" that bunkered in the Division Headquarters and Operations Center. These amazing, hard-working engineers were part of a 173-man contingent from the Mongolian 150th Elite Peacekeeping Battalion. They worked night and day to satisfy this requirement. Camp Babylon began to look like a fortress.

The division command group was equally concerned about the force-protection posture of the outlying camps. This was particularly true of Camp India in Kerbelâ' Province that housed the 1st Bulgarian Battalion and Camp Foxtrot in ad-Dīwānīyah that housed the soldiers from the Dominican Republic. The access roads to these camps ran parallel to their entrance and exit points, thus exposing them to forced entry along a broad and vulnerable front. There was little we could do about the lack of standoff from the road to the camps, but the command group directed the bulk of its division engineer assets to strengthen the outer walls of the camps and reinforce key facilities. Regardless of how good our intelligence was, the initiative and ability to strike favored the insurgent. This was particularly true in the Spanish brigade areas of responsibility where offensive action was restricted by its strict rules of engagement. All of us suspected it was only a matter of time before they were hit. The million-dollar questions we thought about were when and how?

Another concern was the vulnerability of the ammunition supply points that housed tons of ammunition and explosives from the former Saddam regime.

Iraq was awash in munitions and ammunition dumps. Saddam had required tons of every imaginable type of munitions to conduct his eight-year war with Iran, the invasion of Kuwait, and his desperate attempts to hold onto Iraq in the aftermath of his Gulf War disaster. Countless campaigns against the Kurds in northern Iraq and the Shia Arabs in the south had required tremendous amounts of ordnance now ripe for theft by every militant group in the country. The explosive material contained in this ordnance, and particularly the high-caliber ammunitions such as artillery rounds, was the centerpiece of the highly lethal, improvised explosive devices (IEDs) employed by the insurgents. The growing use of IEDs had made these munitions even more valuable to an insurgent enemy that could ill-afford to fight small-arms engagements with disciplined Coalition formations. U.S. Central Command (USCENTCOM) had issued orders to secure any known arms and munitions after the fall of Baghdad, but it proved a near impossible task given the shortage of troops and the volume of stocks to be secured. In Wasit Province, the Ukrainians had secured the ammunition dumps on Al-Kut air base, but the situation in the Spanish-patrolled ad-Dīwānīyah Province was very different.

Major McKinney, an energetic American operations officer from the Illinois National Guard, was detailed by the director of operations to assess the ammunition supply points (ASPs) in ad-Dīwānīyah. His report clearly indicated the lack of security at these sites may well be contributing to insurgent stockpiles of IED components and explosives. There were two ASPs, each consisting of 100 bunkers constructed of earth and concrete. His report described them as being "In different types of condition; some could stand for years; others could collapse within the next year." The bunkers were filled to various levels with artillery and mortar rounds of different calibers and a variety of mines. Large quantities of munitions sat outside the bunkers, in some cases surrounded by earth berms, but more often scattered or stacked in the open. The ASPs had a perimeter fence in various states of disrepair and significant breaks filled with concertina wire. There was no working electricity at either site. Security was provided by 30–35 men from the Iraqi Facilities Protection Service (FPS). The FPS was by no means an elite unit though many of its men were former Iraqi soldiers. Armed with AK-47 assault rifles, they were a scraggly bunch with poor or absent leadership. Most of them did not so much as have a flashlight and many slept through a good portion of their shift. An FPS Headquarters in ad-Dīwānīyah provided limited supervision of the two ASPs and at least twenty men were available there to serve as a quick-reaction force to address a contingency at either of the two sites. The report stated that many FPS employees were corrupt and were likely selling ammunition to augment their wages. Large amounts of ammunition were probably being taken out of the ASP by the vehicle that rotated the security with every shift.[1] Spanish patrols checked the location at least once a day, but that was not nearly enough to ensure these men were performing their duties to any acceptable standard.

The deplorable situation at the ad-Dīwānīyah ASPs spoke in large measure to the magnitude of the Coalition's challenge to secure and stabilize Iraq. A contractor working for a company charged with the destruction of the countless tons of ammunition at a huge ASP in Al-Najaf informed me he expected it would take five to ten years to dispose of the ammunition and explosives in Iraq.

"It's amazing," he told me, "that the country doesn't sink under its weight."

The Al-Najaf ASP was secured with a squad of nine former U.S. military men. Their number was expected to grow to 20. They were augmented by a platoon from the Honduran battalion, but at least another platoon was needed. The Spanish Brigade Headquarters thought additional security could be made available in January as more Iraqi Civil Defense Corps (ICDC) personnel were trained. Additionally, General Cardona agreed to provide some helicopter reconnaissance support as well as more ground patrols.

A major part of the proposed security solution was to consolidate the ASPs in ad-Dīwānīyah at Al-Najaf and maximize security with the additional ICDC and FPS assets we would have to patrol the site under combined American, Spanish, and Honduran supervision. We hoped this would minimize corruption and theft. The consolidation effort was underway by late December. It troubled me that these former regime ASPs were probably a principal source of ordnance for our insurgent enemy. In Kerbelâ', General Ojranowski ensured the security of the ammunition supply points in his area of responsibility by increasing the number of Polish troops patrolling the ASPs. Good staff work and division-level supervision and inspection helped to solve some of the problems the security environment and the growing insurgency presented us, but throughout the next several months it became increasingly apparent victory in the continuing struggle to stabilize Iraq would require far more troops and security assets than were currently available if we were to attain the success our senior leaders so desperately hoped to achieve.

Manpower is paramount in a stabilization campaign, but technology is a force multiplier that can significantly enhance a unit's capability to conduct surveillance, secure a valuable site, communicate, and identify bad guys. Colonel Cabeza surprised me with his interest in biometrics, a technology that measures and analyzes human physical (i.e., fingerprints and eye retinas) and behavioral characteristics for authentication purposes. As the director of operations, he thought we could put the technology to good use tracking the identification of Muslim pilgrims entering and leaving the holy cities of Kerbelâ' and Al-Najaf, as well as on the Iranian border. The USCENTCOM Joint Security Directorate team that deployed to Afghanistan in November 2001 had used this technology with great success to monitor Afghans going to and from the Hajj, the annual Islamic pilgrimage to Mecca in Saudi Arabia that every able-bodied Muslim who can afford it is obligated to make. Colonel Cabeza asked us to investigate the availability of the technology for the division's use. We spoke to several project officers working the issue at CJTF-7 Headquarters;

they informed us the biometrics hardware was not immediately available. During the process of inquiring about it, however, we discovered that immediately available was a relatively new computer tool that allowed units in the MND to send messages, plans, and orders via a system that translated the language used on one end to the language spoken on the other end. This system was known as "Chat line" and was introduced to the MND in mid-November by representatives of MITRE Corporation who were working with the U.S. London-based Office of Naval Research (ONR) Science and Technology. This organization, a part of the ONR Global, was one of several similar offices in the Pacific and South America. Their mission was to establish and maintain liaison with scientific research and development agencies throughout the world, seek out accomplishments and trends in research, and evaluate the information for possible application to U.S. research programs.

The division staff was frustrated by the lack of speed with which it could communicate plans and orders to its front-line brigade combat teams. Couriers were often required to assist in translation. Everyone was expected to speak English, but the degree of fluency from one unit to the next almost always ensured the likelihood of a misunderstanding. We were impressed when we observed several demonstrations in the division's Operations Center. It was a great tool in trained hands. To ensure the operators in each brigade were trained, the ONR employed an interesting group of men who cut a strange appearance, even in the "Star Wars-like" diverse environment of the Multinational Division (Central-South). The group was led by Captain Jim Campbell, a professional, clean-cut, U.S. Navy officer, but that's where any semblance of military professionalism ended. His team was comprised of bearded scientists and long-haired "wire heads" who were seemingly from another dimension. They enthusiastically went about their work and turned out to be a pretty good group of guys.

I accompanied them to Al-Kut where they installed the computers in the Ukrainian Operations Center and conducted the requisite training sessions. Afterwards, several of them, including a fellow named Rod Holland of MITRE Corporation, voiced an interest in going to the Iranian border. Rod was probably the least likely guy to want to do anything physical, but he genuinely wanted to see the border region. We had the time and I agreed to go despite the long drive. There had to be something up there they could fix and I welcomed the opportunity to see Val Semenets and his paratroopers.

The scientists and Captain Campbell were taken by the isolation of the Ukrainian mission and the fort's inadequate communications with Al-Kut. Val gave them a tour and afterwards asked if the scientists could give his unit a computer and a digital camera. He wanted the items to maintain a record of illegal immigrants suspected of being foreign fighters. Their patrols could photograph the more suspicious characters they detained and attempt to get positive identification by later linking the photos back to Al-Kut. A supply of CDs would allow them to store the photos and develop working files of detainees. It was a relatively crude, but interim step they could take pending the construction of the customs station and the introduction of biometric technology. Captain Campbell did not respond positively or negatively, but he took note of the request and thanked the Ukrainian commander for his hospitality and service in Iraq.

Several weeks later, a box addressed to me arrived containing a high-speed laptop computer, a digital camera, a number of blank CDs, and a request from Jim Campbell to stay in touch with the ONR and let them know how their contribution to the war effort worked out. General Sobora, a Ukrainian communications officer, Lieutenant Kanus, and I returned to the border on 1 December to install the computer. After the Ukrainians nabbed several suspicious foreigners crossing the border, I sent a message to Jim Campbell and the ONR team that they had indeed contributed to the war effort. I included several photos of the suspected guerrillas awaiting disposition. The computer and camera did not cost all that much, but they were a relatively low-tech, simple, and imaginative approach to help secure and stabilize the Iraqi border in the short term for what looked like a long-term struggle for Iraq's border security.

The conditions at Camp Babylon continued to improve as we neared the end of 2003. General Tyszkiewicz arranged to have a Polish General Officers Mess established near the headquarters that augmented the superb mess hall KB&R operated in support of the division. The Polish mess often provided hearty soups and breads that were particularly appreciated by late returning patrols or the late shift working in the Operations Center. After a significant amount of work to the facilities, the division staff moved into the buildings that had previously served as the headquarters of the 1st Marine Expeditionary Force and the 1st Marine Division. Between the rain and the cold evening temperatures of the approaching Iraqi winter, these developments were great for the camp's morale and unit efficiency. The Romanian engineers returned to my hooch and winterized the side Illinois National Guardsman Colonel Downem occupied. The work enabled the structure to retain more heat at night. If my previous adventures in Iraq were any indication, the improved conditions meant I would be moving on soon. I assumed I would go home in January when the 1st Polish contingent was relieved and rotated to Poland. It was a nice thought, but there was much to do and precious little time to think about it.

There was cause for celebration in the camp. The 4th ANGLICO (Air and Naval Gunfire Liaison Company) marines reminded everyone that 10 November was the 228th birthday of the Marine Corps and asked me to serve as the guest speaker for their annual birthday celebration. They arranged a traditional birthday ball using the ballroom in the former summer palace Saddam had built on a hill overlooking Camp Babylon. The palace was a communications hub as well as office space and barracks for several national contingents. It is a rare honor for a soldier to speak at a Marine Ball and I enthusiastically accepted their offer. The marines filled the ballroom with guests from throughout the command and asked every woman they could find to attend. The KB&R-run mess hall supported the effort with food and the ceremonies that honored the traditions of the Marine Corps were carried out in a superb manner. As a soldier who had proudly served with elite Airborne and Ranger units, I was equally proud to be a part of these observances. Looking out to the marines and my multinational audience, I spoke about how fortunate we were to be forward deployed in combat, living the life for which we had trained, and serving where we were most needed. I spoke about the major campaigns the Marine Corps had fought, and I spoke with passion about my brief association with the gallant Marines of the 15th Marine Expeditionary Unit which had led the invasion of Iraq in March. This was a great occasion and though not as fancy as the Marine Balls I had attended previously as General Zinni's executive assistant, every bit as wonderful and meaningful. The marines were appreciative of my efforts and I left the hall to a standing ovation.

Poland's Independence Day is 11 November and it merited special recognition and celebration. Poland's existence is a very heroic, but sad story that had seen it eliminated as a national entity in the late 1700s. In the aftermath of World War I, the victorious allies redrew the map of Europe and President Wilson's Fourteen Points called for the reconstitution of Poland. On 11 November 1918, with the signing of the Armistice ending the Great War, Poland was reborn.[2] Polish patriotism is second to none; their patriotic zeal and love for their flag and symbols of national honor are renowned. We gathered at the ruins of Babylon to celebrate the life of a great nation; everyone was impressed with the ceremonies and the following party. The Poles treated everyone to a magnificent display of Polish cooking before we began to make our way to the headquarters and the reality of the war and our staff work. General Kwiatkowski took me by the arm, however, and invited me to his hooch where he broke out a few Polish beers and toasted our two countries.

It had been nearly a month since Kim Orlando's death and the subsequent combat action in Kerbelâ'. The evolving, increasingly dangerous situation throughout central-south Iraq convinced the commanding general to articulate to his commanders the strategy he had developed in writing several weeks previously. He called for a Commander's Conference at Camp Babylon on 17 November and personally briefed them. On the previous evening, he asked me to review his proposed remarks concerning the division's concept of operations, the mission statement, his commander's intent, and the desired end state. I merely clarified a few points by cleaning up the English. His words captured in a clear and concise manner his previous thoughts about the evolving threat to the division and his strategy to protect our soldiers, facilities, and equipment.

Standing at a podium in one of the camp's few remaining tents, the general told his commanders Iraq had grown significantly more hostile since they had arrived at Camp Babylon. The threat from former regime elements, foreign fighters, terrorists, and common criminals had significantly complicated their mission. He specifically cited the recent attacks in Kerbelaʾ and the ever-growing threat of IEDs along our supply lines as evidence of the increased threat level. He followed with his concept of operations, or "strategy" as he called it, to deal with the new situation:

> The Division has a balanced approach to meet the challenge of the insurgency we are currently fighting. This strategy calls for a very visible presence of Coalition soldiers in urban areas, on our Major Supply Routes, roadways, and the countryside. The strategy calls for constant engagement with local governmental leaders, sheikhs, and religious leaders, as well as a high energy Civil Affairs program. Significantly, our strategy calls for surgical strikes against targets where arms caches and bomb making materials may be stored or where bomb makers, terrorist cells, and Former Regime Elements may reside. These strikes are a critical part of our strategy to prevent the insurgent from attacking us and killing our soldiers. These strikes, conducted normally as raids or "cordon and search" or "cordon and knock" operations are based on actionable intelligence developed by our Tactical HUMINT [human-intelligence] Teams, other intelligence sources, and our patrols.

The general wanted his combat units to employ tactics to ensure the protection of his division and his soldiers more adequately. The tactics included raids and cordons of suspected enemy caches and planning cells. The "cordon and knock" was a relatively new technique and the least invasive. After a cordon was in place that blocked any attempt by someone to escape, soldiers would simply knock on doors and ask questions of people whose answers could lead to a search, an arrest, or more information. The situation and the available intelligence drove which tactic was employed. His commander's statement of intent took his concept to a greater level of detail:

> I expect the Brigade Commanders to conduct a very aggressive patrolling campaign in their respective provinces. Our presence is vital to suppress the insurgents that threaten our forces and the local population. Our patrols must operate at night to prevent the insurgent from feeling secure in the darkness. Our patrols must dismount, move among the people, and talk to them. Brigade and Battle Group (Battalion) Intelligence Officers (S-2) or their representatives, must brief our patrol leaders before the patrols depart and after the patrols return. I expect every patrol to be focused on specific routes and specific targeted areas. The patrols must stop, surveil designated areas, and report their observations. I expect every patrol to file a report and the patrol leader must be debriefed by intelligence personnel at Battle Group level. I expect Brigade and Battle Group S-2s to aggressively coordinate with Tactical HUMINT Teams operating in the Brigade areas of operation. When these teams provide intelligence information, we must act on it. We cannot wait for perfect intelligence. I expect the Brigade Commanders to have Quick Reaction Forces available that can quickly move to conduct appropriate operations to investigate the information that we are provided. These operations may be "cordon and knock" operations where the utmost courtesy with locals and the targeted house or facility is exercised, "cordon and search" operations where permission to enter an area or specific premises is not requested, or, if necessary, a violently executed raid. If questions arise regarding rules of engagement, I will find the forces at Division level that can execute the mission. We will not make excuses not to strike the enemy before he strikes us. By executing our patrolling and intelligence campaign in this manner, we will keep the insurgents on the run and defeat him before he can attack our base camps and kill our soldiers and innocent civilians.[3]

General Tyszkiewicz knew his words would get back to the senior military and political authorities of each contingent's country. He made everyone understand that his more aggressive posture was designed to protect the lives of his men. He was very conscious some contingents would be more aggressive than others, but they could not afford to sit back and think their presence was enough to ensure their unit's welfare and pacify their area of responsibility. His remarks could not have been timelier. This meeting was the single best appreciation for the situation in Iraq his commanders had heard. It was time to soldier. If they did not respond to the battlefield information produced in the field, he intended to use his division reserve to get the job done. His comments did not change things with regard to his desire to move against Muqtadā aṣ-Ṣadr; I was convinced that if Ṣadr was going to be brought to justice it would have to done by an American task force. But General Tyszkiewicz had taken a critical step to address the evolving threat to his division and he clearly wanted his brigades to act in a proactive, more aggressive manner.

The general's comments were timely for another reason. His successor and selected members of the second Polish rotation division staff arrived in Iraq for a predeployment site survey on 21 November. This gave the current staff the opportunity to familiarize them with the evolving threat in Iraq as well as the division's concept of operations that was now in effect. The original decree, signed by Polish President Aleksander Kwaśniewski, authorized 2,500 troops for six months. Remarks by President George Bush in early September, indicating that reconstruction of the Iraqi state would take longer than had been expected, triggered new discussions in Poland about the participation of Polish troops. Despite polls indicating that upwards of sixty percent of the Polish people opposed its military's participation in the Iraqi mission, national-level decisions were made to remain in Iraq.[4] The visit by the second rotation's commander and members of his staff generated excitement throughout the camp. The Poles expected to rotate in mid-January and, like any soldiers away from home, they were anxious to leave. It was understandable since being the first to do anything is always difficult. The troops that would follow them would have far more comforts than they had experienced. The presence of their future relief picked up morale considerably.

The colorful Major General Mieczysław "Mike" Bieniek was designated to command the Multinational Division (Central-South). Short, physical, and full of energy, General Bieniek was Poland's most noted paratrooper with over two thousand jumps to his credit. He had served in several UN and NATO peacekeeping assignments, including command of the Polish contingent on the Golan Heights and the North Polish Brigade in Bosnia–Herzegovina. He had also commanded the elite Polish 6th Air Assault Brigade and the 25th Air Cavalry Division. Perhaps most significantly, he and Generals Tyszkiewicz and Kwiatkowski were cadet classmates. He was quite different from General Tyszkiewicz, outwardly more fun-loving and seemingly less serious. He was very likeable, but General Tyszkiewicz was highly respected and admired by everyone in the division and a tough act to follow for any new commander. I enjoyed talking with the prospective commander about the current situation in Iraq and the challenges of multinational command. He was a good listener as we prepped him for his meetings with the CJTF-7 staff for several hours. My sense was that our senior leaders at Camp Victory looked forward to the opportunity to meet and work with the new Polish commander. In spite of the division's tougher, more offensive posture, it was considered by many officers at CJTF-7 to be too little, too late, and that a new commander would more aggressively pursue the threat in the MND's area of operations. It was a grossly unfair perception of General Tyszkiewicz by senior Americans who were fundamentally ignorant of the rules of engagement and other national parameters under which the various national contingents had agreed to deploy. General Bieniek could not change things very much if he wanted to. Quite the opposite, he would later tell General Sanchez that he considered force protection his primary responsibility as the MND commander.

Time was running short for our liaison team as well. Ken Owens was scheduled to return to his assignment at Headquarters, Marine Central (USMARCENT) at MacDill Air Force Base in December, and Tom Lowman was scheduled to return to Germany and the V Corps Staff in January. I attempted to have Tom reassigned to a combat assignment with the 173rd Airborne Brigade in northern Iraq at his request, but his boss at CJTF-7 Headquarters insisted he redeploy to Germany. I never did get Tom the combat experience he wanted at brigade and battalion level and I felt terribly about letting him down. The expected turmoil the division staff and liaison team changes would create concerned me, and I was not surprised when the commanding general asked me to stay longer to assist the transition of the command group and division staff. It was the logical and honorable thing to do; I told him I would do whatever I could to help.

The division approached the end of November with guarded optimism. A number of people visited the division. Hungarian Vice Chief of Defense Staff Lieutenant General András Havril toured the division with my old friend from the Sinai, Hungarian General János Isaszegi, Deputy for Coalition Affairs (C-9) at CJTF-7. After learning of my association with the Hungarian contingents in both the Sinai and Iraq, he honored me with a small memento of his visit. I was pleased to receive it, but disappointed by the harsh restrictions on the Hungarian transportation unit that essentially limited it to internal division support. It was one of the more casualty averse units in the division, a fact that significantly impacted its overall worth and reputation.

General Peter Pace, USMC, United States Vice Chairman of the Joint Chiefs of Staff, paid a call on the commanding general to discuss equipment shortages and operational challenges confronting the division. The cordial and polite conversation between the two generals revealed an issue that had rubbed the Poles the wrong way for quite some time. In the myriad of discussions and agreements that led to

Polish leadership of the MND, General Tyszkiewicz stated that 200 Humvees were supposed to have been shipped to Poland or Iraq for the division's use. After he arrived in Camp Babylon, he thought he would receive the vehicles from 1st Marine Expeditionary Force. General Pace made note of the comment and said he would investigate it further. The vice chairman's executive officer made several phone calls to me over the next several weeks seeking more information about the alleged agreement. He later told us the U.S. had never committed to filling the vehicle requirement with in-theater assets. The Poles were scheduled to receive 200 Humvees as part of a Foreign Military Sales contract and that a percentage of the 200 vehicles would be shipped to Iraq at a date still undetermined. Apparently, someone had signed a lot of checks to get an international force to Iraq and there were still a lot of loose ends to cover. The increasingly hostile environment merited up-armored vehicles for fundamental force protection, but these were in short supply throughout Iraq. The division's poor material combat readiness and inadequately protected air and ground mobility assets remained a major concern for the commanding general and every unit commander in the division who were continually pushed to engage in more aggressive, offensive operations.

On another occasion, General Tyszkiewicz met with several men who identified themselves as former Iraqi generals and now represented an organization called "The Free Iraqi Officers and Civilians Movement." The commanding general listened politely to their desires to meet with senior authorities who could restore their former stature and assist their efforts to provide jobs to locals, then stood up and cut them off with a raised voice demanding they turn in the "Murderers of Major Kupczyk," the Polish officer who had been killed by a sniper's bullet early in November. He could not have been more blunt.

"Give to me his murderers and then we will talk about how I can assist you."

The former generals were initially amused, then very concerned by the commanding general's outburst. They offered nothing, claiming they had no knowledge of who was involved in Kupczyk's death. General Tyszkiewicz had them ushered out of his office and escorted to the perimeter gate. Many of these former military leaders knew more than they were apt to admit. Many of them provided leadership and technical assistance to various former regime elements operating throughout Iraq. They could have undoubtedly provided a lot of valuable intelligence information about various insurgent cells operating in Babil and Kerbelâ' Provinces, but this particular group elected not to cooperate and never returned to Camp Babylon.

The division's increased operational tempo did not change the fact we were experiencing a lull in enemy activity throughout most of central-south Iraq. We attributed this partially to the weather. Temperatures at the end of November were unusually cold and wet. Engineers tried to make our swampy area of the camp more livable by spreading huge amounts of crushed rock over the standing water and mud. My plywood hooch stood above it all, a veritable island in a sea of mud and water. Looking out from the entrance of my hooch on Thanksgiving Day, I thought it would take at least a week for the evening's rainfall to drain. It was cold, gloomy, and just plain miserable. But it was Thanksgiving and the mess hall went to great lengths to bring the great American tradition to the troops with holiday dishes and all the trimmings. It was a good day with death seemingly taking a holiday. Reports were relatively benign, but this was Iraq and the respite did not last.

CHAPTER 30

False Hope for Peace in Iraq

Hope is not a plan.

—GENERAL TOMMY FRANKS, USA

On 29 November, several Spanish military officers assigned duties in Baghdad were ambushed in Babil Province while traveling south toward Al-Ḥillah in two civilian sedans. The vehicles and the Spaniards' bodies were badly burned. Though technically not a Multinational Division (MND) affair, the loss deeply disturbed our Spanish comrades and I expressed my condolences to General Isadoro, the Spanish assistant division commander for logistics. The long and difficult insurgent war we faced as an occupation force would undoubtedly result in many more such tragic incidents. We had no idea how long the Coalition intended to stay in Iraq, but many members of the Combined Joint Task Force-7 (CJTF-7) and Coalition Provisional Authority (CPA) staffs thought that if the Coalition could capture Saddam Hussein the pattern of violence would level off and meaningful progress could be made that would lead to our withdrawal. It was a reasonable assumption and Saddam's capture was a top priority for all Coalition forces.

General Tommy Franks once told the U.S. Central Command staff that "Hope is not a plan." He was merely pointing out that when we think through requirements and make the necessary arrangements and decisions to facilitate them, events are more likely to happen in the manner we intend. I was concerned the Coalition had lost sight of this kind of fundamental thinking. We did not appear to have a blueprint for success. We were "digging in" for a long fight that made no sense to me. I reflected on the development of the original war plan in the mid/late nineties. Disbanding the Iraqi Army and de-Baathification policies essentially ignored Iraqi and Arab culture, the ethnic makeup of Iraq, and the geography of the country. Securing Iraq was a nightmare scenario that required large numbers of troops. Long porous borders, unemployment, criminal activity, a bitter Sunni minority, and bitter former regime loyalists were the ingredients of an insurgency and a long-term commitment for the United States and its allies. The original war plan envisioned a period of occupation followed by a transition to an international body with multinational troops and a credible and large Iraqi Army. A legitimate Iraqi Government would then accept responsibility for its country and people. The more creature comforts and permanent-like facilities I saw in Baghdad and elsewhere, the more the environment spoke of a forward-deployed U.S. Army preparing for a long occupation and not an expeditionary one with near-term plans to withdraw.

A good soldier stays in his lane and does not concern himself with matters above his level, but I knew too much not to think about the trouble I saw. I sought escape from my troubling thoughts and the petty staff work generated by the CJTF-7 and division staffs by participating in operations as often as I could. Our liaison team had been reinforced by a lieutenant colonel whose presence enabled me to have even more flexibility with regard to my staff responsibilities in the headquarters. Colonel Wise was close to retirement and was serving in V Corps Headquarters in Germany when his seniors in Iraq decided he should share the burden of their deployment. An intelligence officer who spoke fluent Spanish, we welcomed him to the team, hoping he would maintain good relations with the Spanish and Latin American officers on the division staff. It was not the easiest thing to do for Captains Lowman and Owens, who were often frustrated by the seeming lack of energy they saw in some of their counterparts, but they never lost sight of their personal professionalism, military bearing, and courtesy. Armed with minimal guidance, these trained veterans performed their duties superbly. Colonel Wise would significantly contribute to the staff-assistance mission and his friendly manner and fluent Spanish helped to ease the friction that inevitably occurs on any staff. He was content to work with the staff and I spent more time with the brigades and battalions in the field.

General Tyszkiewicz and I flew to Al-Kut to attend a series of briefings for Ukrainian Colonel-General Petro Shulyak, commander in chief of the Ukrainian ground forces, on 12 December. General Shulyak's visit was no small event for the Ukrainians, the division, or CJTF-7. There were several governments already beginning to reconsider their commitment to the Coalition in Iraq. Ukraine's commitment of a combat brigade was too significant to take lightly. The briefings he was given were the standard briefings we had developed over the past several months. They were presented totally in Ukrainian and I sat in the rear of the room and smiled a lot. To my rear was my favorite warrant officer standing, as usual, at a rigid position of parade rest. When General Shulyak asked a question, General Tyszkiewicz would courteously translate it into English and seek my input. General Shulyak was scheduled to be in Al-Kut for several days. He planned to see the paratroops on the Iranian border, and then visit Division Headquarters at Camp Babylon and CJTF-7 Headquarters at Camp Victory for official office calls with General Tyszkiewicz and General Sanchez.

General Shulyak's primary goal was to seek support to improve and expand the landing strip at the Al-Kut air base and to secure approval for Coalition airlift of Ukrainian helicopters to Iraq to support operations along the Iranian border and throughout Wasit Province. American aircraft larger than a C-130 were not cleared to land on the Al-Kut airstrip, but the Ukrainian Il-76, a rough equivalent of the U.S. Air Force C-141 Starlifter with a payload of approximately forty tons, routinely landed there with the brigade's national supplies. Expansion and improvement of the strip would allow follow-on Ukrainian rotations to fly directly into and out of Al-Kut, eliminating ground transportation from Baghdad and the force-protection requirements associated with long ground movements. The helicopter issue was not new. Before the Ukrainian brigade had deployed to Iraq, the Ministry of Defense was prepared to send six all-weather helicopters, including four assault Mi-24s, (the counterpart to the U.S. Apache attack helicopter, but with the additional capability of transporting eight combat soldiers) and two Mi-8s, to facilitate the brigade's operations. General Tyszkiewicz had supported the deployment of these aircraft in a memorandum to General Sanchez in mid-September, but it was not favorably considered. General Shulyak was also interested in getting more items of special equipment for the Ukrainian brigade including night-vision devices, perhaps the most sought-after piece of equipment by all multinational units. General Tyszkiewicz suggested he focus on the first two issues which were three-star, operational level concerns. I concurred with the commanding general's assessment and suggested to General Shulyak he couch his request for airlift of additional helicopters in terms of the increasing threat to Coalition soldiers in Wasit Province and along the Iranian border. I further suggested he give General Sanchez a document that described the Ukrainian brigade's operations and provided the number of illegal immigrants Ukrainian patrols had detained and the number of Iraqi and Iranian vehicles they had confiscated. Ukrainian patrols were under fire in Al-Kut, Al-Suwaira, and other towns and villages throughout the eastern portion of the province. I suggested he document these actions, particularly since most of them took place at night, but that he address his desire for additional night-vision devices in an informal or social setting and only if the opportunity presented itself. The painful Al-Najaf transition in September with the Spanish brigade was still a sore point with CJTF-7 and the last thing he needed to do was make what American commanders might consider an outrageous demand for equipment. The general's translator carefully recorded and translated my words. The general's smile suggested he appreciated my remarks. I made a mental note to advise General Miller of what was on General Shulyak's agenda and then moved into an adjoining dining room where Warrant Officer Kunitskyi had prepared our lunch.

Kunitskyi was a great cook and the spread he prepared was impressive. There was a variety of meats, vegetables, breads, and fixings of all kinds on display, but I was less concerned with the food than what was sitting on the table directly in front of me. Several bottles of vodka were prominently placed for what I knew would be a series of appropriate toasts. Everyone at the table would be expected to make one. I was looking at no less than eight shots of vodka before this lunch was over. At least this time, I thought, I would have some food in me to soak it up. Everyone seemed to be in great spirits when General Sobora stood up and proposed the first toast. Our shot glasses were filled and someone announced the shots would be "under control," no sipping allowed. After the four generals had given their toasts, all eyes turned toward me. General Tyszkiewicz nodded his head and asked me to speak. General Shulyak's military assistant translated my remarks. Standing up and looking directly at Generals Shulyak and Sobora, I began to speak slowly and deliberately.

"Gentlemen, no one trained harder than I did as a young officer to fight and kill men like General Sobora and destroy the Warsaw Pact in battle."

I definitely had their attention as I listened to the translation and watched them straighten their backs. But their stoic looks softened as I spoke about the friendship I had forged with General Sobora on the battlefield and the friendship of our two great nations since the end of the Cold War. I spoke of brave Ukrainian soldiers serving with distinction in our nations' common cause in Iraq just as they had in Europe during the Great Patriotic War. Then, after a short pause, I raised my glass and said, "I propose a toast to the continued comradeship of two great nations: the United States of America and Ukraine."

When the final words were translated, General Shulyak stood up and held his glass to mine, downed his shot, and applauded. He reached for a small jewelry box containing The Armed Forces of Ukraine Badge and presented it to me. General Bezluschenko took the badge from the box and pinned it to my uniform. It was a great moment. I felt like I had hit another "home run." General Sobora was all smiles and General Tyszkiewicz enjoyed a good laugh.

Three shots later and it was time to head back to the airfield. I was clearly under the influence as I struggled up the steps of the Mi-8. I was not "wasted," but I was feeling pretty tipsy. There had not been time to do anything after lunch except leave and about twenty minutes into our flight to Camp Babylon my bladder was filled to the brim. Another ten minutes and it was clear to even my cloudy judgment I was not going to make Camp Babylon without relieving myself. My desperate thoughts on how to urinate while maintaining a semblance of dignity in the presence of the commanding general helped to clear my head. While the general's attention was focused on the terrain below us, I turned toward the bulkhead of the aircraft and managed to direct my aim into a small water bottle I had removed from a trash bag in the rear of the aircraft. I gladly deplaned at Camp Babylon with my combat equipment and a small bottle of "lemonade" that I quickly tossed into a dumpster. This was not exactly what I had in mind about getting away from the staff work at Division Headquarters and clearing my head, but my duties as the division's senior adviser and liaison officer never allowed a total escape. Several hours later, as I walked toward the Operations Center, Sergeant George Gogoleski, the Russian-speaking intelligence noncommissioned officer (NCO) from the Illinois National Guard, told me he had overheard several Ukrainian officers say I was to be decorated by their minister of defense in January.

"Well, what do you know George," I said jokingly, "I guess getting drunk with high-ranking general officers has its merits." I quickly dismissed his comment and went to work.

My well-oiled liaison team could do just about anything the division demanded of it, but when it came to general officer correspondence and official remarks, the commanding general looked to me. I took great pride as his "ghost writer" but, on 14 December, seemingly free of reports, general paperwork, and requests for translations and speech writing, I took off for Al-Najaf and a scheduled day patrol with the El Salvador paratroopers. I appreciated these guys as much as I did the Ukrainians on the Iranian border. Tough, professional, and genuinely happy to see me, I enjoyed their camaraderie and friendship. Colonel Monterozza introduced me to Lieutenant Carlos Emilio Erazo Aleman who would lead a patrol of 17 men and three vehicles into Al-Najaf that day. The patrol order had already been issued, but there was still time to participate in his platoon's mandatory rehearsals before beginning the patrol. Carlos briefly familiarized me in Spanish with the proposed route of the patrol that would take us past the famous Kufah or Great Mosque of the City of Al-Najaf with its beautiful golden dome. The city had been quiet lately despite the presence of Ṣadr's Mahdi Army militia. The patrol was expected to be routine, but the paratroopers planned for the worst possible situations. Carlos personally checked the combat readiness of each trooper and his equipment before ordering them to mount up. He directed me to ride "shotgun" in his vehicle and an NCO sat in the back seat. We charged our weapons as Carlos called the Battalion Operations Center on the radio to report our departure. Quiet or not, Al-Najaf was a dangerous place and every man was alert and ready for action.

The Coalition had hoped Saddam Hussein would be killed or captured soon after the fall of Baghdad. We did not know that on 13 December the infamous Iraqi dictator had been captured. He was found hiding in a hole some six feet underground in the vicinity of his hometown of Tikrit in northern Iraq by soldiers of the U.S. 4th Infantry Division and a Special Operations Task Force. The announcement of his capture was made about three hours after we had departed to conduct our patrol. As we passed the Kufah Mosque and drove through the normally crowded streets that surrounded it, we heard the report of a rifle to our left front. Straining our eyes to find who may have fired a weapon, a second round passed inches above our vehicle and we all reacted to its sound. Carlos and I spotted the gunman as he took off running toward a residential area. He immediately gunned his vehicle and the others followed. Flicking the selector switch on my rifle off safe, I yelled to Carlos in Spanish, "Vamos a combate" or, loosely translated, "Let's go get him!"

Carlos responded with a simple, "Si, mi Colonel," as he deftly handled the vehicle, negotiated the road, and avoided hitting any pedestrians.

The indirect route we were forced to take to where the gunman had fled cost us several precious minutes. Kicking down doors was not an option, but Carlos instructed his men to dismount and we began a systematic search of the neighborhood. There was no doubt we had been engaged by aimed fire, but the celebratory fire that now filled the air convinced me that finding our gunman was not going to happen. There was shooting everywhere. Carlos was clearly disappointed as he ordered his men to return to the vehicles. Our patrol was nearly over and the crowds and gunfire made the city an even more dangerous place. We decided to return to headquarters where Colonel Monterozza greeted us with the good news of Saddam's capture. Our decision to return had been a good one. The Iraqis are as famous for firing weapons when they celebrate as Americans are for shooting firecrackers on the Fourth of July. The predominantly Shia population of Al-Najaf was thrilled with Saddam's capture and celebratory gunfire was heard throughout the rest of the day and night. We had had a close call and the soldiers were motivated by the experience. I gladly accepted an offer from Carlos to stand with his platoon for an after-action photo that reminded me of something out of *Soldier of Fortune* magazine; I was relieved our exciting experience had not resulted in any friendly casualties.

It was a great way to end our patrol, but I left the camp even more pessimistic that we were closer to achieving stability in Iraq. I believed Saddam's capture offered a false hope of peace. The CPA decisions regarding demobilizing the Iraqi Army and de-Baathification had essentially alienated the predominantly Sunni former regime loyalists and disallowed them from military and government service. I believed they would fight even harder to recover their lost dignity and sense of honor. The rise of the competing Shia militias to fill the power void was ominous. The next two weeks would prove my gloomy thoughts correct.

CHAPTER 31

Christmas on the Iranian Border

To get the best out of your men, they must feel that you are their real leader and must know that they can depend upon you.
—General John J. Pershing, U.S. Army

The Spanish contingent was in all its glory when it turned out for General Cardona's change-of-command ceremony on 15 December. I personally liked this tough, but nationally constrained brigade commander. I was disappointed Spanish rules of engagement had kept him from accomplishing more. His brigade's orders to not pursue Muqtadā aṣ-Ṣadr had soured his and the Multinational Division's (MND) reputation at Combined Joint Task Force-7 (CJTF-7) and Coalition Provisional Authority (CPA) Headquarters. The Spanish soldiers had performed as well in the field as they were allowed. The brigade had seized over 400 rifles and pistols since its arrival in Iraq, and a significant number of schools, medical centers, and municipal buildings had been built or reconstructed in the areas in which it provided security. The issue of what to do with Muqtadā aṣ-Ṣadr and the Mahdi militia remained an unanswered challenge, but I also knew the issue was greater than one brigade or the MND could handle.

My days as a war planner at U.S. Central Command were long behind me, but it was clearer to me than most, I thought, that the postmaneuver war decisions the CPA had made in Iraq, however arguable, were now threatening any chance we had to facilitate a stable and peaceful country. The lessons a generation of planners had built into OPLAN 1003-98 for the invasion of Iraq and its occupation had been cast aside in the hope of achieving our national goals on the cheap. The absence of the requisite forces required to secure key facilities, and simultaneously pursue former regime elements, rebuild, reorganize, and quickly field the Iraqi Army, and secure Iraq's borders was a recipe for disaster. Our lack of combat strength emboldened Iran. Its influence in southern Iraq from Al-Najaf and Kerbelâ' to Baṣrah and Umm Qasr was as prolific as it was frightening and appeared to threaten another war. The fact thugs like Muqtadā aṣ-Ṣadr were allowed to thwart our efforts to stabilize Iraq with rag-tag, armed militias that killed Coalition soldiers and administered religious courts, occupied mosques, and threatened city and provincial officials, reflected a poor American and Coalition policy that did not allow what few forces we had to clamp down Iraq in the martial manner Iraqis understood. Democratic ideals and practices do not facilitate law and order when everything around you is broken and lawless. Iraq was broken in the fall of 2003; I was disgusted with what I saw. The American military and CPA leaders often blamed its multinational forces in southern Iraq for its failures there, but clearly U.S. failure to establish martial law in Iraq in April and May 2003 and eliminate militant groups, rogue clerics, former regime leaders, and foreign influence, had all but eliminated the opportunity for true peacekeeping and stability operations, instead opening the door for a violent insurgency. Peacekeeping now meant aggressive combat action the bulk of the multinational forces in southern Iraq were ill-equipped to take on. I was frequently reminded of that old Army saying, "When you don't know where you're going, any road will get you there." My sense was our senior leaders did not know, or would not admit, that our shortfalls in soldiers and equipment, coupled with the absence of strong, realistic, and aggressive policies, had our mission in Iraq on a road to failure. If they did know, I suspected they did not voice their view in an effective and collective manner to their national-level seniors.

Rules of engagement (ROE) that governed what each multinational contingent could and could not do were not changed by their respective national governments to allow more flexibility. Our senior American military leaders did not know or simply chose to ignore that many contingents had highly restrictive ROEs that prevented them from taking decisive offensive action. As a result, a considerable amount of unfair criticism was directed at the MND which impacted its morale and, in some cases, threatened the long-term deployment of several contingents. The U.S. Army would eventually fight Ṣadr's militia in the spring of 2004, but the same indecisive policy that failed to deploy adequate combat forces to destroy his militia in the fall of 2003 would prevail again and the Coalition would fail to destroy his forces or bring him to justice. Muqtadā aṣ-Ṣadr would survive to burden the Coalition and the Iraqi Government. No one had a good feeling about the future of Al-Najaf and Kerbelā' with Ṣadr on the loose.

General Tyszkiewicz invited me to fly to Al-Najaf where I was honored to meet the Spanish minister of defense and the chief of staff of the Spanish Army prior to the ceremonies. On the parade ground, the Spanish soldiers proudly welcomed their new commander, General Fulgencio Coll Bucher. Perhaps this general, I thought, would interpret his rules of engagement with more imagination and flexibility and find a way to have a greater impact on achieving peace and stability in his area of operations.

We returned from Al-Najaf to find the division's Operations Center alive with activity as the staff monitored and reported demonstrations in progress on the streets of Al-Ḥillah, less than ten miles from Camp Babylon. It was a relatively rare event when there was action in our immediate vicinity instead of in Al-Najaf, Kerbelâ', Al-Kut, or the Iranian border. Over four hundred people stood outside the perimeter walls of the City Hall that served as the seat of CPA South-Central, Mr. Bremer's subordinate command headquarters in the MND's area of responsibility. Mr. Mike Gfoeller was the CPA's regional coordinator. A veteran diplomat and Arabic speaker, he was highly respected for the relationships he had developed with Iraqi officials and his wide-ranging projects to stabilize the region. He was supported by a small staff including U.S. military personnel. Army Colonel Mike Whitehead, a civil affairs officer, worked closely with the CPA staff and I had spoken with him on a number of occasions concerning the division's operations and support of the CPA's regional projects. I contacted Mike by phone later that night to get a personal report on the demonstration at City Hall. He considered the situation manageable; I left the Operations Center somewhat cynically convinced the Iraqis were simply exercising their rights as citizens of a future democratic society. These demonstrations were always subject to infiltration by former regime loyalists, Mahdi Army thugs, criminals, or anyone with nefarious intent, and it was prudent to monitor them. The MND did not over-react to these events, perhaps because of the numerous demonstrations the Poles had staged in the 1980s to break the communist hold on their own country. By 17 December, however, the division staff was advised the CJTF-7 commander would soon issue an order to clear the streets of demonstrators in the vicinity of the City Hall. We were convinced he was receiving bad information about the seriousness of the situation. Late that afternoon, Ambassador Krystosik, the commanding general's political adviser, asked me to accompany him to City Hall where he intended to a make a personal reconnaissance and discuss the matter with members of the CPA staff.

Our driver wisely avoided driving down the main street of Al-Ḥillah and turned down a side street that allowed us to arrive unimpeded at the City Hall and enter the grounds through a side entrance. American soldiers guarded the facilities and everyone wore body armor and carried weapons. Ambassador Krystosik was quickly ushered into the building for a meeting. I intentionally fell behind the group and ventured up to the roof of the headquarters where I could get a clear view of the crowd. Military Police were in place staring at a crowd of people that seemed to be enjoying themselves. The original estimate of 400 people appeared reasonable. There was chanting and one guy held a loudspeaker proclaiming various demands for jobs, fuel, and electricity, among other things. The CPA's concern was prompted by several small tents erected to have people rest during the day and allow some presence during the night. Several women were preparing food in one of the tents and another tent blocked a portion of the street that ran in front of the building. Traffic had to be diverted by the local police but, other than that, it did not seem to present a major problem. Looking at the spectacle below me, I saw what appeared to be a peaceful crowd, but my presence seemed to pick things up a little. The guy with the loudspeaker and I made eye contact and he smiled at me. I started to laugh as he began to yell another chant that the crowd echoed in return. Turning to an older platoon sergeant who had noticed my presence had caused the crowd to come to life, I could not resist saying "Well, Sergeant, I guess they like me."

Humor is important in tense situations. It inspires confidence in the men and their leadership. He laughed and told me they must have thought I was some kind of a celebrity. All joking aside, I suggested his men not display their weapons to the crowd and maintain as low a profile as possible. He nodded in agreement and I left the roof to join Ambassador Krystosik and report on what I had seen. I found him drinking tea with members of the CPA staff. His calm manner had the desired effect of cooling bad tempers and restoring their perspective. The old warrior-diplomat appreciated my report, but I could tell he had already assessed the situation the same way. He was confident the demonstration would end by nightfall and strongly suggested any reinforcement of the City Hall or attempt to clear the streets by force was ill-advised. As we prepared to leave the building, I saw Mike Whitehead and suggested he call CJTF-7 and discourage any orders to end the demonstration by force in the near term. He nodded his head in agreement and we drove back to Camp Babylon. By 6 pm, the demonstration was over and the tents were removed. Cooler minds had prevailed and I was reminded that stability operations often dictate a different approach to various challenges and crises than just decisive military action. Patience is a virtue; knowing when and not to act is invaluable.

As the excitement of the demonstration in Al-Ḥillah died down, someone in Division Headquarters reminded me it was nearly Christmas. It had hardly occurred to me. I tried to sleep whenever I was not on the road, on patrol, or in the Operations Center, and I had not noticed the camp's U.S. Army-run post office was busier than usual with holiday packages coming in and out. The postal unit was out of California and several of the younger enlisted men were fitness buffs. They had a bench press and enough weights for some serious training and I slipped in the back door from time to time to work out with them. One night, I noticed a large supply of goods stockpiled against the wall and gathering dust. There was everything from boxes of Kool Aid to personal hygiene items, to Christmas candies and cakes. The postal commander noticed my interest and told me the background story that I found hard to believe.

"Sir, we receive this stuff from a number of different sources and put it out for anyone who wants it. Problem is, no one takes it and it's beginning to get in the way."

I immediately thought of the Ukrainian paratroopers on the Iran–Iraq border. Camp Fort had to be the loneliest, most desolate outpost in Iraq. The men there were among the least thought of in Iraq. They lived much like warrior monks in an isolated, hostile, and spartan environment. No single group of men would appreciate these goods more than they would. I could not resist asking, "How about holding on to this stuff for several more days? I know some guys who would really appreciate it and you'll make their Christmas." He agreed and over the next several days the stockpile grew considerably.

The division was besieged with well-wishing Christmas guests from all over the world including the presidents of Spain and Poland. General Tyszkiewicz introduced me to Poland's President Aleksander Kwaśniewski when he visited Camp Babylon on 22 December. This charismatic leader had been elected in 1995 and played a major role in securing Poland's membership in NATO. A strong ally of the United States, he supported the American request for Polish troops in Iraq despite the controversy it had sparked in Poland. He was a brave man with a strong vision of Poland's future. The war and Iraq seemed distant for several hours as soldiers of all ranks gathered for photos with their popular president, shook his hand, and enjoyed Polish hors d'oeuvres. The president's departure signaled an unfortunate return to reality. A report from Kerbelâ' verified a Polish soldier had been killed by another soldier's negligent weapon discharge. The sad event had a significant negative impact on everyone's morale. It was one thing to accept a battle casualty, but a preventable and unnecessary death seemed even more difficult to process and accept. It was particularly hard at Christmas.

The winter rain, coupled with the unusual cold and incessant mud, made Camp Babylon a miserable place. More to pick up my spirits than anything else, I wrapped up several buck knives and delivered them to Ambassador Krytosik, and Generals Tyszkiewicz, Kwiatkowski, and Sobora as Christmas gifts. Between the events in Al-Ḥillah, the stress-filled, high-level visits, and the death of another Polish soldier, I knew their spirits were low. I admired and respected all these men. They had become like family to me. General Tyszkiewicz had an aide deliver some Polish sausage to my hooch later that night. Between the sausage and a package I had received from home that day, I had a feeling of Christmas that had not existed up to that point. It was a feeling I wanted to share. General Tyszkiewicz had reluctantly granted me permission to spend Christmas with the Ukrainians on the Iranian border. He thought I should spend Christmas in a comfortable setting with good food and my "Polish friends," but he could not resist not giving me the one Christmas gift I had requested: to be with the Ukrainian paratroopers for the holidays. There was another reason. General Sanchez's tour of Al-Kut and the Iranian border was again scheduled for 27 December and it made sense for me to go there to assist with final preparations for his visit. General Sobora and I left on Christmas Eve with a truck full of gifts courtesy of the U.S. Mail and Army post office.

I never looked forward to the three-hour drive to Al-Kut. Sleeping was no longer an option and every passenger looked for signs of ambush and dreaded improvised explosive devices. We arrived in time for a late lunch with General Bezluschenko who briefed us on the border situation. Illegal crossings by Iranian nationals had significantly increased and he had reinforced the paratroops with another rifle platoon. It was a prudent fix, but the mission required at least a full battalion and dedicated helicopter support. The impression he gave us was that the Iranians were pouring across the border. The Ukrainian garrison near Al-Suwaira, about one hundred kilometers northeast of Al-Kut, was frequently mortared, and Farsi (the language of Iran) was openly spoken in town. It was another gloomy report of too few assets, too many missions, and too much territory. Iraq, once the Arab bulwark against Iranian aggression, was now wide open to Iranian and foreign-fighter infiltration and widespread, illegal immigration.

It was another two-hour drive to Camp Fort. I was surprised by the evidence of the incessant rain. The desert appeared ocean-like in places with six inches of standing water seemingly stretching for miles. Val Semenets greeted us with his characteristic smile. General Sobora had called ahead and directed him to assemble his company inside the main entrance to the fort. A detail stood by to carry the numerous boxes of Christmas gifts into the long corridor in the center of the structure. We walked into the fort's entrance to a loud regimental cheer as the company was called to attention. General Sobora could not be happier for his men. He spoke to them and then asked me to speak as well. Lieutenant Kanus stood by to translate. It was not anything I wanted to do. It was an honor just to stand with these men. I kept my remarks short.

"Men, I'm proud to be with you. I wanted to spend Christmas with you and show my appreciation for your hard work. Your service in Iraq follows in the traditions of your grandfathers who fought and won the Great Patriotic War. These gifts come from the rear-echelon soldiers at Camp Babylon who live very well. They admire and respect you. They send best wishes to you in this holiday season. I hope you will enjoy these small tokens of their appreciation. I look forward to going on patrol with you tonight."

General Sobora directed the leaders to come to the front of the formation where I handed a box to each of them. Their faces clearly showed their appreciation. They were accustomed to a life with little or no comforts. When all of the packages were presented, the men began to applaud and shout. General Sobora was smiling ear to ear. Val then gave me a traditional Ukrainian pipe, a wooden dish carved with the Ukrainian Army insignia, and a beer mug. It was a soldier's Christmas. I missed my family, but I was happy to be with such exceptional fighting men. These happy "Kodak moments" were woefully short. It was time to return to the reality of the border.

Val told us he expected a lot of activity that night. Orders for the patrol had already been issued, but he reviewed the patrol plan in detail for us and then had an officer show us to our cots where we could rest for an hour. He also gave us a few Ukrainian field rations. It was cold, wet, and about as miserable a night as any I could remember. The patrol was scheduled for 7:15 pm. I rested for about 45 minutes and spent the next 20 minutes checking my equipment and weapons before meeting General Sobora and Val at the entrance to the fort. The vehicles were lined up and ready to move. After a final map and time check, we moved to our start point and then to the border road. Val's prediction was correct and within fifteen minutes headlights appeared to our front. We were in for a long night.

Our lead BTR-80 stopped and the others moved to the left and right of the road in a maneuver known as a "fish tail." The men immediately dismounted and took up firing positions behind large rocks and dunes on the desert floor. The platoon leader and a sergeant waved their flashlight and the driver of the sedan slowed down and stopped. A search team looked over the vehicle while another team frisked the driver and his passenger for weapons and identification. Finding no contraband or anything suspicious, the vehicle was moved off the road where the search team flattened its tires. It was all business. Very little was said and Val directed everyone to mount up and move.

Two rifle teams dismounted at known foot trails along natural lines of drift the Iranians routinely used to walk into Iraq. They then took up ambush positions with orders to detain any people that entered their "kill zone." The mounted element of the platoon turned up an unimproved road, pulled off to its side and simply waited for Iranian vehicles. We were not disappointed. The Iranians drove into us by the bus and van full. It was clear no effort had been made to stop these people on the Iranian side of the border. There were middle-aged and elderly men and women and young children. The paratroopers searched the men for weapons, then loaded everyone up and escorted the vehicles to the entry control point the Iraqi customs service had established in a recently renovated border fort. The Iranians would be deported the following day. The vehicles were confiscated, driven to Camp Fort, and parked in the confiscation lot. It was as smooth a standing operating procedure as I had seen anywhere. Not much was said, soldiers just did their jobs as they were rehearsed and trained. We bagged over 100 illegal immigrants that night. At midnight, several of us searched a school bus looking for weapons and checking identification and other papers; we seized several knives of various lengths and types. When we got back to the fort an hour later, General Sobora handed me a 6-inch switchblade knife that any New York thug would have treasured. It was a Christmas gift he had taken from an Iranian and with a smile I thanked him for thinking of me and wished him a Merry Christmas!

We awoke to a cold, wet, and foggy Christmas morning. I had thrown myself into my cot a little before 2 am after wiping down my rifle and kicking off my boots. I was cold and bone tired. The morning patrol was scheduled for 9 am and the breakfast truck arrived from Al-Kut a little after first light—paper plates wrapped with foil contained a U.S. Army breakfast of eggs, bacon, potatoes, and biscuits. Our late departure for the day patrol meant Christmas lunch would come out of a can, so I filled my assault pack and cargo pockets with fruit, chocolate bars, and meats and cheeses from a Christmas care package my parents had sent to me. It had been an exciting night and the morning patrol promised more of the same.

We were two hours into an uneventful patrol when our reinforced platoon mounted on three BTR-80s and the general's 4 × 4 truck came to a sudden stop on the border road. To our right front about two hundred meters into the desert were over twelve hundred people who had illegally crossed the border and now sat on the desert floor awaiting transportation to their destination in Iraq. The platoon leader ordered the squad leaders to reposition their BTR-80s to cover the full expanse of the crowd. We were going to need the bulk of the company and its vehicles to handle this situation. General Sobora was already reaching for his phone when I strongly suggested he have the entire company brought forward. He directed the company commander to launch his quick-reaction force. We then walked toward the crowd with Lieutenant Kanus and an Arabic interpreter. We needed a Farsi speaker, but I suspected the organizers of this mass migration could speak Arabic or English and probably both. As we approached the crowd, four men neatly dressed in leather jackets and sweaters rose to greet us. One of them spoke excellent English.

"Welcome, my friends. It is a beautiful day, don't you think?"

I could not believe this guy. His words and mannerisms reminded me of a kid caught with his hand in the cookie jar. We had obviously put a significant dent in their transportation plan during the night. In addition to the Iranian vehicles we had confiscated, the border road was lined with numerous Iraqi-owned vehicles with flattened tires and cut hoses and fuel lines. Several of these vehicles were large flat beds that would have accommodated forty or more people. He brought these people across the border and had unknowingly lost his means of moving them to Kerbelâ' and Al-Najaf. I was surprised by the man's audacity.

"Don't worry, sir," he said, "We think we'll be away from here very soon."

Almost in disbelief, but with my best attempt at a friendly face, I simply replied, "Sir, you are quite correct, and to ensure you return to Iran, we intend to escort you back across the border."

The alarm on the man's face told the real story. Caught dead to rights bringing people across the border that had undoubtedly paid him according to the going rate, he was desperate for an alternative and started talking fast.

"Sir, we are poor Iranians who want to go to the holy cities. It is totally up to you."

He continued to talk while we waited for Major Semenets and our badly needed reinforcements. The major arrived with a reinforced platoon and four additional BTR-80s. General Sobora instructed him to position the vehicles behind the crowd and to dismount the infantry. We would drive this human mass into Iran as if they were cattle. I watched the maneuver and, seeing the men and vehicles in position, I turned to the Iranians. It was time to get serious.

"Gentlemen, have these people pick up their bags and order them to start walking back toward Iran. I must warn you that any attempt to run away from us and turn toward Iraq will result in very harsh consequences."

The game was over and the Iranian leader knew it as he looked around and saw our gunners standing behind their 12.7-mm heavy machine guns in the turrets of the BTR-80s. He told his lieutenants to get the word out to the people and after another 10 minutes, the "herd" started moving east. Our dismounted infantrymen moved with their weapons at the ready and the BTRs moved slowly, but steadily, along the flanks and the rear of the crowd. We never doubted the vast majority of these people were innocents seeking to visit the holy sites, but their numbers also offered an excellent opportunity for other people to infiltrate Iraq for other reasons. As some of the older men and women tired, we put them aboard the BTRs. When the crowd halted and sat down about 500 meters short of the border, General Sobora directed Val to have the gunners fire a burst over the crowd. A few short bursts of fire from our machine guns were all it took to get them up and moving again. I walked with General Sobora and the interpreters. The Arabic interpreter was laughing and, after speaking with him, the stoic Lieutenant Kanus began to laugh as well. A young Iranian woman, who was totally covered from head to toe in a black dress known as an abaya, had attempted to bribe the Arabic interpreter with sex if he would allow her to go to Al-Najaf. Our conversation just went downhill from there as soldier humor so often serves as a defense mechanism against the seriousness of a situation. The young woman sadly continued to march back to Iran with her virtue intact.

The Iranians moved over the ridge line that delineated the border and we waited another 30 minutes to ensure they remained in Iran. Several Iranian border police appeared on the ridge carrying AK-47 rifles and an RPG. They had not done anything to deny the crowd's movement into Iraq and they did not do anything to facilitate or deny their return. They studied us as I looked at them through a set of binoculars from my position by the side of a BTR. They were not there long before they disappeared beyond the ridgeline and returned to their border fort.

Our patrol was over and I shared my Christmas chow with General Sobora, Val, and Lieutenant Kanus, before we mounted up to return to Camp Fort and prepare for our long drive to Al-Kut. Subsequent patrols reported over a hundred illegal Iranians were deported on Christmas Night and several more vans and trucks were confiscated. It was just another typical night on the border in a seemingly endless struggle with no end in sight.

CHAPTER 32

Terrorist Attack and Tragedy in Kerbelâ'

The truth is that you always know the right thing to do. The tough part is doing it.
—General Norman Schwarzkopf

The excitement of border patrolling and the massive return of Iranian "pilgrims" on Christmas Day was now secondary to the long-awaited visit to the Ukrainian brigade and the border by the commander of Combined Joint Task Force-7 (CJTF-7). I was very pleased with the holiday performance of the gallant Ukrainians. The war never stopped for them, their simple life at that dank and isolated fort simply continued patrol after patrol. We drove back to Al-Kut and managed to arrive in time to have Christmas dinner with the troops in their new brigade mess hall. It was a great way to conclude the day and transition to the staff work required to ensure everything was in order for General Sanchez.

Rehearsals and briefings preceded the arrival of Generals Tyszkiewicz and Sanchez to Al-Kut airfield on 27 December. A proposed visit by the CJTF-7 commander on 30 November had been postponed due to weather and the Ukrainians had thought they would never have the opportunity to see him. The excitement they genuinely felt about his visit was as interesting to me as it was amusing. Most American officers regard these high-level visits as training or operational distracters and first-class pains in the rear. National pride and a strong desire to put their military proficiency on stage for the senior American commander to see was a huge incentive not only for the Ukrainians, but for all the national contingents of the Multinational Division (Central-South).

The general's tour of Al-Kut was flawless, including the superb luncheon that had been prepared in his honor. My favorite Warrant Officer Kunitskyi stood rigidly at parade rest throughout the meal and ensured everyone's glass was always filled to the brim. General Sanchez seemed to enjoy himself and even though we were behind schedule, he was more than willing to fly to the Iranian border and continue his tour. Major Semenets greeted the official party and we drove to Camp Fort for a detailed mission briefing, terrain orientation, and tour of the Iraqi customs station. The visit was nearly over when an aide informed General Sanchez that a bombing in Kerbelâ' had caused a significant number of casualties. The Ukrainian program came to an abrupt and disappointing halt as the general was whisked away without so much as a final word of thanks. Whatever occurred was serious and within ten minutes all of us were airborne and en route to Camp Babylon.

The Multinational Division (MND) had long appreciated the threat to its camps in Kerbelâ'. There had been a number of reports that indicated Coalition troops and particularly those in the multinational divisions would be hit hard after Saddam's capture earlier in December. An attack on the Italian Headquarters in An Nāṣirīyah in November had caused 17 deaths. Our enemies were well aware of European opposition to the Iraq war and they believed a successful strike against European and other multinational contingents would start a series of troop withdrawals that would unravel the Coalition.

We were greeted at the Camp Babylon airfield by several members of the staff who quickly took General Tyszkiewicz to Division Headquarters. Reports were still confused and casualty figures varied. The general waved everyone off and called his Polish brigade commander in Kerbelâ', Brigadier General Ojrzanowski. Members of the press were already awaiting the commanding general's comments and he wanted to restore a sense of calm as soon as possible. The report that General Tyszkiewicz received from his brigade commander was given over the phone in the privacy of the general's office. They spoke in Polish. The report was objective and accurate. He made a few notes, studied them for a few minutes, and walked to where the press was assembled to deliver a statement. He was a picture of calm under fire. As he walked, he turned to me and asked that I monitor incoming reports, gain a better appreciation for the situation, and update him accordingly.

The bombing in Kerbelâ' was a coordinated, complex attack, the largest since Saddam's capture. Suicide truck bombers gained entry to the Bulgarian garrison at Camp India and exploded near the 1st Infantry Battalion's Headquarters, killing several Bulgarian soldiers and wounding a number of others. Another car bomb killed two Thai engineers who were assigned to a force-protection project. Mortar fire hit several other Polish garrisons and city locations. Five American soldiers were reportedly wounded. The governor's office was attacked with a car bomb and mortar and rocket fire. A truck bomb slammed into a building at Kerbelâ' University, causing numerous civilian casualties. A total of 13 people were killed and nearly two hundred wounded including soldiers, Iraqi policemen, and civilians. A period of relative calm in Iraq with attacks showing a downward trend suddenly erupted in violence throughout Iraq. Deadly attacks on American forces in Baghdad, Mosul, and west of Baghdad near Al-Ḥabbānīyah occurred throughout the day.

The division staff and our liaison team worked long into the night and the next day sorting out the details of the attacks, answering questions, and rendering reports to the CJTF-7 staff. The commanding general was particularly concerned with his evening tactical-satellite report to General Sanchez. I worked closely with Colonels

Gocul (G-3) and Przekwas (G-2) to ensure the report was detailed, relevant, and precise. Recognizing the importance of our reporting, I was surprised the division staff had not made plans to establish a Division Command Post in Kerbelâ' as we had in October. A forward-deployed staff would have provided us firsthand situational awareness and unbiased ground truth, but the command group was content to have the Polish brigade handle it; General Tyszkiewicz concurred with their recommendation.

On the 29th, General Tyszkiewicz asked me to accompany him and Ambassador Krystosik to Kerbelâ' where he was scheduled to meet with Bulgarian Minister of Defense Nikolay Svinarov and Chief of Defense General Nikola Kolev. A small memorial service was also scheduled. The minister's decision to come to Iraq was undoubtedly motivated by his concern for his Bulgarian troops and the need to make a personal assessment of his country's nationally unpopular commitment to the Coalition. Like many of our European allies, Bulgaria's decision to commit forces to the Coalition was not well received by a large majority of the Bulgarian people. Bulgaria's armed forces had served beside NATO troops in 1997 during operations in Kosovo; it had agreed to serve in Iraq in an effort to show good faith and partnership with the Americans. The significant number of casualties its battalion had suffered was no small affair for the Bulgarians as well as for the Thais who thought the situation in Kerbelâ' was secure enough to consider scheduling a large delegation of civilians to visit their troops in February 2004.

The devastation from the bombing was all around us as we drove into the perimeter of Camp India. The suicide vehicle had breached the entrance point while traveling at a high rate of speed. The Bulgarian guards had engaged the driver with rifle fire, but he still managed to steer the vehicle into the headquarters before he died. We saw a large number of soldiers with bandages of one size or another indicating the last report we had of 27 wounded may have been low. The soldiers' faces showed evidence of shock and exhaustion and we were concerned about the battalion's readiness to carry on its mission. The Bulgarian battalion commander, Colonel Marinov, had been slightly wounded and appeared tired and depressed. Many of the guard responsibilities in and around the camp were being handled by American military policemen, at least for the near term. General Ojrzanowski changed the patrol schedule in the city and used Polish troops while the Bulgarians accounted for their casualties and equipment and made force-protection adjustments to their camp.

We arrived at Camp India and, after a brief tour of the camp and its damaged facilities, we entered the mess hall to have a cold drink and wait for the arrival of the Bulgarian delegation. There were several soldiers sitting quietly at some of the tables. Their silence was deafening. Morale had hit rock bottom, a far cry from the esprit de corps I had seen in October during the combined operation with the U.S. 1st Armored Division Task Force. The sullen and depressed looks on their faces reminded me of a study of the U.S. 28th Division in the aftermath of its devastating losses in the Hürtgen Forest during World War II. The division's casualties in that terrible battle had nearly broken it both psychologically and physically. I was taken by the similarities I saw in this significantly smaller, and yet similar, morale-breaking event. The Bulgarians needed to focus on things other than the tragedy, something that would help them reorganize and drive on with their mission. There was not much time for mourning. They had to refit quickly and get back in the game. I made a mental note to discuss the issue with Colonel Panayot Panayotov, the Bulgarian contingent commander, who lived and maintained his contingent headquarters at Camp Babylon. "Pani" was a good guy. His leadership, friendly personality, and encouragement to the younger officers and leaders of the battalion would later make a big difference in restoring it to full combat readiness.

Minister Svinarov and General Kolev arrived at the camp without fanfare. The generals were old friends from their Warsaw Pact days and I suspected they had studied together in Moscow. We greeted them at one of the perimeter gates and walked to where the devastation was most evident. Their conversation did not dwell on the bombing as much as on the need for additional force-protection measures for the camp, and the situation in Iraq. Both General Tyszkiewicz and Ambassador Krystosik expressed their deepest sympathies for the deaths of the Bulgarian soldiers. They spoke in Russian. General Tyszkiewicz told me later he had been invited to Bulgaria sometime after he relinquished command of the division. It was a good sign and I could tell he felt relieved this terrible event was not looked upon as bad judgment or poor leadership on his part. He had done much to ensure the improvement of the Kerbelâ' garrisons and I hoped he would be appropriately recognized at a later date for these as well as numerous other actions he had taken. General Tyszkiewicz introduced me to Minister Svinarov and General Kolev as the "Senior American representative to the Multinational Division and my senior American adviser." I took the opportunity to express my sympathies for their nation's loss. I went one step further by telling General Kolev that, according to all reports, the Bulgarian sentries had performed their duties in a magnificent manner and they had killed both of the suicide drivers with rifle fire.

"Had they not done so," I said, "the bombings would have undoubtedly caused additional Bulgarian casualties."

The general hesitated for a second and then thanked me for my "Kind words."

We did not remain in Kerbelâ' very long. The situation was stable and the Polish brigade had a good handle on things. What had happened in Kerbelâ' was another rude awakening to the reality of a growing and deadly insurgent war. My optimism for Iraq and any near-term possibility for the withdrawal of Coalition forces was fading fast. Our quick return to Camp Babylon was driven by the incessant requirement to report our findings and initiate or speed up actions to prevent similar attacks. The division chief of staff was already hard at work on the official after-action report for the Kerbelâ' bombing and he asked me to review it and make changes and recommendations when the draft was completed. Colonel Antczak rarely asked me to review his products, though he appreciated my efforts to improve or refine the staff's reports and briefings. We had grown closer over the last couple of months, however, and I was happy to do it. The division was also preparing briefings for General (Retired) Barry McCaffrey, USA, who was scheduled to visit on 30 December. His visit was nothing to take lightly. The MND battled for respect with every visitor and no staff worked harder to ensure the division's story was properly told by ensuring its presentations were informative, accurate, and rehearsed. Our liaison team was never too far away and helped wherever and whenever it could.

It was not until after nightfall on New Year's Eve that I left the headquarters to relax in my now totally renovated plywood hooch. Later that evening, I was invited to the commanding general's office where General Kwiatkowski, Colonel Antczak, Ambassador Krystosik, and several members of the division staff had gathered for a New Year's Eve drink and much-needed fellowship. All of them warmly welcomed me to their party. An invitation to join these exceptional Polish gentlemen for this occasion was a true honor. Ambassador Krystosik was particularly happy to see me and graciously proposed a toast to, "Our American adviser and dear friend." We had all grown very close and I appreciated the drinks and holiday food almost as much as their company. The war seemed distant as all of them expressed what I believed to be sincere compliments for my team's efforts to support the division and their personal thanks for everything I had done to help them. After the progress we had made in the division over the past five months, I had high hopes for it in the New Year. When we left the headquarters shortly after midnight, I stopped by the Operations Center to wish the late shift a "Happy New Year" and walked back to my hooch on a cloud of personal and professional satisfaction that my team's efforts in this strange, multinational organization were appreciated and having a positive effect.

CHAPTER 33

Transitioning to a New Commander and Division Staff

Integrity is telling myself the truth. And honesty is telling the truth to other people.
—Spencer Johnson, American physician and author

The New Year brought the sun and its warmth back to what had been some of the lousiest weather I had seen in the Middle East since the winter of 1997–98. The situation in the division's area of responsibility was relatively calm and quiet, a good thing after the excitement and turmoil the Kerbelā' bombing had caused. My staff duties included writing several speeches for the commanding general as he prepared for a variety of farewell affairs. The change-of-command ceremony required a great deal of staff preparation and coordination. General Tyszkiewicz was ordered to return to Poland immediately after passing the division's colors to his successor on 11 January.

Early January was also time to bid farewell to Captain Owens, the first member of our liaison team to return home. Ken Owens had proven to be an exceptional asset to the staff. In just four months, the entire staff, even the Spaniards with whom he had jousted from time to time over staff procedures and the security of the camp, greatly respected him and wished him well. His exceptional staff abilities and the impact he had had on force-protection improvements had significantly contributed to the division's efficiency and safety. He was a credit to his Marine Corps and our team. He would be sorely missed.

In December, the American National Guard officers in the division's Logistics Section had apparently convinced the American Morale, Recreation, and Welfare people in Baghdad that there were Americans serving in the Multinational Division deserving of their attention and, much to my surprise, Camp Babylon received a large amount of weightlifting equipment in early January that the guardsmen, my liaison team, and the ANGLICO (Air Naval Gunfire Liaison Company) Marines quickly put to good use. My replacement would have one of the best hooches on the camp and a great place to work out as well. Things were looking up!

Following the morning operations update on 4 January, General Tyszkiewicz spoke to his officers about the difficulties the Coalition faced in Iraq. The insurgency that plagued the Coalition by this time had not been anticipated. The division's subordinate units were increasingly drawn into combat situations. The general's new guidance regarding aggressive patrolling had resulted in a number of successful raids and cache discoveries in Kerbelâ' and Al-Kut but, in the aftermath of the Bulgarian bombing, he wanted the division to be even more aggressive and not lose any of the momentum it had generated late in 2003 to achieve greater stability in the central-south area of operations. There had been several significant engagements in Al-Kut involving Ukrainian mounted units, and Polish dismounted patrols had been ambushed several times in Babil Province. He invited me to speak to the division staff about patrolling and relevant small-unit tactics; I provided a 30-minute presentation using a few slides and an outline of subjects from my handy Ranger Handbook, a highly valued compendium of small-unit tactics, techniques, and procedures. I spoke about the need to plan, rehearse, and emphasize security throughout any patrol or tactical movement. Security was enhanced at night with the use of night-vision devices, but during many patrols on which I had participated in all three brigades, soldiers were reluctant to keep their goggles on during movement. In addition to significantly reducing their situational awareness, this bad habit caused patrol members to bunch up rather than maintain a good tactical distance from each other. This negatively impacted the patrol's security posture while simultaneously providing a more lucrative target to the enemy. The advantages night-vision devices give our soldiers are immeasurable, but physically adjusting to them for proper wear takes time and experience and wearing them for extended periods requires strong neck muscles. Many officers laughed when I said this, recognizing my interest in physical training. Clearly, however, between the weight of our helmets and the goggles, it takes a strong neck for a soldier to look forward and rotate his head to get a full field of vision over an extended period of time. As a young officer, I had devoted a lot of time and effort to the study of long-range reconnaissance and patrolling techniques. I had become particularly adept at planning small-unit operations. Patrolling and small-unit tactics were subjects to which I could speak with authority and I enjoyed teaching them. These were lessons that undoubtedly provided nice-to-know information at division level, but the lessons were more appropriately taught at battalion, company, and platoon level. General Tyszkiewicz directed me to prepare a memorandum to his unit brigade and battalion commanders that emphasized key points of my presentation and directed them to provide refresher training to their units on these vital combat subjects.

As much as I enjoyed the opportunities I was given to teach and influence the division staff and units in the field, the welfare, morale, and combat readiness of the Bulgarian battalion that was still mourning its recent losses were a major concern of mine and the division commander. It had not fully returned to its duties and something needed to be done to get it going. I had talked with Colonel Panayotev in the mess hall and in other places around the camp, but I wanted to visit him at his headquarters to emphasize the need for him to influence the battalion to "get back in the game." It took a while, but I found the Bulgarian billets after negotiating the labyrinth of communications equipment, cables, and wire that covered the paths in and around Saddam's former summer palace on the hill dominating Camp Babylon. Colonel Panayotev and his contingent staff lived and worked in several small office spaces and he was at his desk recovering from a severe cold when I finally saw him. "Pan" had spent a year at the U.S. Army Command and General Staff College at Fort Leavenworth and he spoke excellent English. He was in a deep funk. Between his illnesses, the recent deaths of his soldiers in Kerbelâ', and the continuous questions he had been asked by Bulgarian authorities regarding the battalion's training, force-protection posture, rules of engagement, and force readiness, he was understandably under a lot of stress. Pan was happy to have a visitor. He welcomed me and quickly offered a few Bulgarian delicacies including chocolate and bread. He also shared a number of photos of his family and American friends from Fort Leavenworth that undoubtedly provided him some comfort in these unhappy times. Pan had been an avid soccer player as a younger man and had played on several teams during his stint at Leavenworth. We talked about sports and family, but he was mostly concerned about how to address the circumstances of his soldiers' deaths to his minister of defense. Underlying the terrible loss the Bulgarian battalion had suffered was the question as to whether or not the Poles had adequately supported it and done everything it could have to prevent such an attack. There may have been some folks in high places who suggested the Poles were at fault for not paying enough attention to Camp India and the Bulgarian battalion's needs. It is not uncommon to play the "blame game" in the military when an unfortunate event occurs. In Pan, however, I saw a man who could rise above the nonsense and, over a cup of green tea and chocolate, I calmly suggested he just tell the truth. Speaking "soldier to soldier" I said, "Pan, the simple fact of the matter is that our soldiers are at war. Bad things happen in war. The force-protection concerns we had at Camp India were addressed several months ago and mitigated as best as possible under the circumstances. Your battalion's relationship with the Poles is very good and your men performed bravely in defending their camp. You have nothing to be ashamed of. Just tell them the truth."

Pan seemed relaxed by the time I excused myself and started down the hill. Before I left, I suggested he go to Kerbelâ' and surprise the battalion by challenging the officers to organize a few soccer games to restore morale and to get the troops' minds off the tragedy. Pan liked the idea and I was happy to learn he followed through with it. The Bulgarian battalion would soon rotate home. Its soldiers would return to Bulgaria like every soldier of all the division's contingents with a strong sense of mission accomplishment. Pan's report to the Bulgarian minister of defense made no excuses for the bombing of the barracks in Kerbelâ' nor did it blame any person or group. Honest and objective, the report stated Iraq was an increasingly dangerous place and that Bulgaria's soldiers, like all Coalition soldiers, were in harm's way. Commended by General Tyszkiewicz, Pan's exceptional service in Iraq was officially recognized by the minister of defense upon his return to Bulgaria.

The arrival of fresh Polish troops and members of the second rotation of division staff was a source of encouragement that raised the spirits of the veteran Poles. Unlike previous visits, their presence this time meant the veterans were going home. General Kwiatkowski was tapped to remain with the division for an additional month. I had already agreed to stay and assist the transition to the new command group until the last group of Polish veterans left in February. General Tyszkiewicz asked me to fly to Poland with them and stay as a guest of the minister of defense for several days. Unknown to me at the time, it was an official invitation.

During this lead up to the change of command, there were numerous social gatherings and I was frequently called to various generals' quarters to watch television and relax. Guys being guys, one of the more popular shows to watch was *Fashion TV*. The allure of beautiful women on the catwalk in various forms of undress turned the head of every self-respecting warrior. The jokes were always a great source of laughter. Inevitably, someone would break out the Polish whiskey and vodka, but there was always food to balance it out. The new guys had plenty of sausages, cheeses, and breads. General Bieniek's arrival was cause for another informal party and the three Polish Military Academy classmates enjoyed each other's company. They appeared like carefree cadets in Poland again. But appearances belied the seriousness of the growing insurgency, sectarian violence, and their genuine concerns. All of us knew the new command group would be tested. The parties and accompanying humor merely camouflaged the stress associated with change and the difficulty of war. The new officers had much to learn and there were numerous questions. I suspected my team would be very busy over the course of the next month.

The change-of-command ceremony attracted the usual crowd of commanders and dignitaries. Helicopters from every division and major command made the Camp Babylon airstrip the busiest place in Iraq on the morning of 11 January. The transition of the command group and staff had kept me close to Division Headquarters for nearly two weeks. I was anxious to see it pass so I could get back out to the brigades. General Tyszkiewicz had been adamant about keeping me nearby and I was frequently called into his office to write or review various remarks, speeches, and orders pertaining to the change of command or other related events. The commanding general was very upbeat as he approached the end of his tour of duty. At dinner on the day before the ceremony, he asked me to look over General Bieniek's proposed remarks and make recommendations or changes. I had long established that my effectiveness as an adviser and a liaison officer was dependent on doing anything I was asked to do whether it fit the job description or not.

The commanding general wanted the ceremony to be a perfect event right down to his successor's speech. I was happy to support his requests. He was a humble man who appreciated my work. Shortly after dinner, I gave him another hip-pocket buck knife as a small token of my appreciation for his leadership and the trust he had shown me as his adviser. We simply shook hands; no words were necessary.

As the generals and assorted dignitaries gathered in the amphitheater, several Polish officers started saying their goodbyes. I was checking on preparations and greeting people when the commander of the unit that had served at Camp Babylon as the division reserve pulled me aside and presented me an engraved bayonet with the words, "From the 7th Lancers Regiment's Commander." Lieutenant Colonel Marek Sokolowski was a tough, special forces officer with whom I had spoken frequently about force-protection measures for Camp Babylon and special combat missions in support of the division. It was another rare honor I proudly accepted. The ceremony was conducted without a hitch, a tribute to detailed staff planning and rehearsals. The smile on the commanding general's face was enough to satisfy anyone who helped put it together, but there wasn't time for any back slapping and compliments. The division had a new commander and the same old war was about to get even more interesting.

With American troops observing Iraqi demonstrations in Al-Ḥillah, Iraq, January 2003.

Teaching the New Command to Conduct Combat Operations

Advisors walk a tightrope. They had to be involved and proactive without stifling the initiative of the commanders.
—Unknown Security Force Adviser in Afghanistan

General Bieniek wasted no time making his presence felt. The next several days were spent touring the brigades and meeting his subordinate commanders on their turf. On 12 January, he presided over the change of command of the Polish 1st Brigade Combat Team in Kerbelâ' and passed the unit colors from General Marek Ojrzanowski to General Edward Gruszka. Shortly after the ceremony, General Bieniek was informed by a U.S. Tactical HUMINT (human-intelligence) Team operating in Kerbelâ' that a "reliable source" had provided information on a potential terrorist cell in al-Husiniyah, an area approximately twenty kilometers north-east of Kerbelâ'. Several buildings in a country-like setting supposedly held an unknown number of foreign fighters who may have conducted the 27 December attacks against the Bulgarian base at Camp India. The source said other attacks against Coalition forces in Kerbelâ' were likely being planned and staged from this location. Elements of the new Polish brigade were still arriving and settling into quarters, and little else was said about the site until the afternoon of the 14th. General Kwiatkowski called me to his quarters shortly after lunch and, in his usual nonchalant manner, informed me of a new mission.

"Roland, we must go to Kerbelâ'. There is a problem there and we must assist the new brigade commander and his staff to plan an operation. You must pack for a few days."

I did not question him. Kerbelâ' had been a thorn in our collective backsides since September and I assumed we would get a full briefing once we got to the Polish Brigade Headquarters. I simply acknowledged his words, saluted, and departed to go to my hooch. I always kept a small assault pack ready to go with a ration, toilet articles, a towel, a change of underwear and socks, and a sweater. I added several nice to have articles including my "brain book," a few handy tools, and a flashlight. I grabbed my body armor and weapons and took a few minutes to talk with Tom Lowman. Tom kept a steady hand on the Operations Center and he confidently told me he would handle things in my absence, including the evening tactical-satellite (TACSAT) report. The blades of the chopper were turning when we arrived at the airstrip and we were airborne within a few minutes.

General Gruszka greeted us when we landed at Camp Juliet. A tall, good-looking soldier with a mustache, he had commanded the 25th Cavalry Brigade in Poland. He was cheerful and confident; I sensed working with him would be both professional and easy. We drove to the headquarters escorted by a platoon of Polish infantry. Kerbelá' was a dangerous place and we appreciated the extra firepower and security the platoon offered. The appearance of the hotel was essentially unchanged since our last visit in October. The tents that had served as the tactical operations center for the operation with the U.S. 1st Armored Division were gone, replaced by several hardened trailers. The hotel's lobby looked the same and General Gruszka maintained the same office space as his predecessor. The generals conversed for a while and I was happy to wait in the lobby and play a little pool. They emerged from the office just as I was finishing a game of eight ball with an Iraqi groundskeeper and General Kwiatkowski asked me to accompany them to an operations briefing. The staff was standing by when we entered the operations trailer. We sat down and listened as a young Polish major briefed the details of the proposed objective site using a whiteboard drawing and a large map. His English was flawless and I later found out he was a graduate of the U.S. Coast Guard Academy. I also learned he had been temporarily brevetted to his current rank for the mission in Iraq and that he was actually a lieutenant. He was bright, articulate, well trained, and inexperienced. His briefing familiarized us with the nature of the target based on information the source had provided and a map reconnaissance conducted by the staff. Little planning had actually been done to address the details of a raid or any sort of combat operation. Significantly, there had been no effort to place reconnaissance and surveillance assets in the target area, a major shortfall that placed the validity of any information we had in doubt. I strongly suggested we get scouts into the target area immediately to render current reports, but the command group wanted to wait, talk to the HUMINT team's "source" and use him as a guide to the target site. I was skeptical and told General Kwiatkowski a delay would cost us the timely information we needed to move aggressively if circumstances changed. Once again, I was reminded of that old British dictum that "No time is wasted in reconnaissance." Reconnaissance teams were alerted and briefed, but the order to insert them was delayed pending the arrival of the "source." I strained to contain my frustration. The most frustrating thing for an adviser is that he does not command. Sometimes the commander accepts and actions your advice completely, in part, or not at all. In this case, I had to be satisfied with an alert order that placed several reconnaissance teams in a "ready status" but with no orders to go.

Later that evening, General Abbas, the Iraqi police chief with whom we had worked in October, arrived at the headquarters. The "reliable source" we had been assured would come did not show, so we hoped the good general would have some credible information to get this operation going. He did not. General Abbas was a decent man and he understandably lived on the edge. Kerbelâ' was a hot bed of activity. Between the criminal elements, the Mahdi Army, the influence of the clerics including Muqtadā aṣ-Ṣadr, and the foreign fighters, Abbas was hard pressed to get anything done with the limited resources he had available. General Abbas provided more details about the proposed target area, but nothing about the presence of foreign fighters or people who may have occupied the buildings. He was more concerned with the growing Iranian population in the city. Much like we assumed with the Ukrainians on the Iran–Iraq border, the vast number of the Iranians illegally crossing the border were innocent pilgrims seeking to pray at the holy shrines, but a small percentage of the men were foreign fighters poised now to stir up trouble for Coalition forces and the Iraqi police. We had wasted a lot of time. General Gruszka elected to launch an aerial reconnaissance in the morning. He directed his staff to develop several courses of action to attack the buildings and provided the initial command guidance it needed to begin planning. I enjoyed working with the staff and later that evening we briefed several courses of action to Generals Gruszka and Kwiatkowski. All of them were sound options to secure and isolate the objective area and attack to clear the buildings where the foreign fighters were allegedly staying. There was no decision made to choose and develop an option pending the results of the reconnaissance, but the staff had done a good job and was poised to act positively in the morning.

Unlike in October when there were not enough rooms available in the hotel to house everyone, General Gruszka had arranged rooms for General Kwiatkowski and me. A room with comfortable bedding and hot chow from the mess hall made our stay far more pleasant. I was content to call it a day when General Gruszka invited me into his office and gave me a book titled, *A Question of Honor, the Kosciuszko Squadron, Forgotten Heroes of World War II*. It is a fascinating account of the brave Polish aviators who left Poland after it fell to Nazi Germany in September 1939 and flew with distinction in the Battle of Britain. The book introduced me to an unusual American named Merian C. Cooper. Cooper's great-great-grandfather had been friends with the renowned Polish cavalryman, Kazimierz Pulaski, who had fought in the American Revolution. Cooper had grown up listening to stories of their adventures in the war that had been passed down to the family, as well as stories of the great Polish engineer, Tadeusz Kosciuszko. Cooper became a bomber pilot, flew with the American Expeditionary Force over the Argonne in World War I, and was cited for heroism. He was anxious for more action when the war ended and volunteered his services in the defense of Poland against the Soviets in 1919–20. He told Marshal Jozef Pilsudski, Poland's new head of state, that his desire was to act in Poland as Kosciuszko and Pulaski had acted in America. He formed a squadron of volunteer American pilots who he personally recruited and named it the Kosciuszko Squadron. He was eventually awarded Poland's highest decoration for his heroics in the defense of Warsaw during which he was shot down, captured, and eventually escaped back to Poland. This fascinating man went on to fame and fortune as a Hollywood producer and as General Claire Chennault's chief of staff with the U.S. Army Air Forces in China during World War II.[1] Poland had been abandoned by the Western powers to satisfy Stalin. From a military standpoint, Poland had had little contact with the United States during its years under Soviet influence. I read the book long into the night and, somewhat egotistically I suppose, identified with Merian Cooper. I did not believe any American officer in the modern era had been closer to the Polish Army, and certainly not in combat, than me and the members of my team. It was a nice thought. I was certain of one thing—my team was needed and appreciated, and although our advice was not always accepted, it was always respected. The Poles were good people and we were proud to be with them.

The aerial reconnaissance was flown the next day by scouts who reported to the Operations Center throughout the mission. Their reports were detailed and the debriefing they received upon landing was quite thorough. The target area was described as a quiet setting of several buildings with a large number of palm trees that would adequately provide concealment for our ground surveillance teams. A road complex that surrounded the area made it very accessible, but only one road, a major highway, could handle heavy trucks. Only a few women and children were seen during the reconnaissance. There was no evidence of any activity that would lead anyone to think anything unusual was going on there. I saw no reason not to send in ground teams and verify the aerial reconnaissance with a long-term presence of several days, and I advised the brigade commander to infiltrate the reconnaissance teams at the earliest opportunity. The information available for now, coupled with the absence of the HUMINT team's source, was enough for General Gruszka to abandon any thoughts of mounting a hard-hitting raid or a reconnaissance in force. Instead, he directed we develop a detailed reconnaissance plan that would ensure the area was routinely surveilled by air and ground elements. This particular area had not been patrolled for nearly two months. General Gruszka's intent was to develop the situation over time but, for now, the situation did not merit a strike in his view. The reconnaissance plan was developed and briefed to the commander on the evening of the 15th, but teams were not inserted until the following day. Sometimes there is only so much you can do as I smiled and fought my instincts to object and force the issue. In retrospect, the fact the staff was hampered by the absence of key personnel who were yet to arrive, as well as the time to train together and develop standard operating procedures, significantly hindered what would ordinarily have been a far more aggressive approach to the problem. The offensive spirit and an aggressive nature are characteristics of cavalrymen in every Army, and I had expected more aggressiveness from the new command group, and particularly General Gruszka.

General Kwiatkowski and I remained with the Polish brigade until the following morning. Reconnaissance teams were inserted before we returned to Camp Babylon, and initial reports were benign. I believed that if the target area in al-Husiniyah had been infiltrated by foreign fighters that weapons caches may still be found. I had no doubt the teams would vigorously execute their reconnaissance mission, but I thought we had lost a good opportunity to strike when the likelihood of the presence of foreign fighters was far greater.

General Bieniek asked me to provide a report of our activities in Kerbelâ' and I wrote a scathing report that pointed to a lack of initiative and speed by the command group and staff of the Polish brigade. General Kwiatkowski, however, quietly suggested such a report would do more damage than good to the newly arrived brigade and asked me to tone it down. He was right, and I made the necessary adjustments. He encouraged me, however, to make recommendations for future operations. I provided the following:

1. Commanders must act quickly and boldly on reliable, single-source information. Reconnaissance and surveillance of a potential target (even if it is unconfirmed) must be executed as soon as the necessary personnel and resources can be deployed.
2. The division commander should provide guidance to his subordinate commanders regarding his desire to move quickly to conduct offensive operations when a target is reasonably identified.
3. When rules of engagement (ROE) do not allow strike operations by a particular unit, the division commander should have a force ready to deploy that is not burdened by restrictive ROE and carry out the mission.
4. All brigade and battle group (battalion) planning staffs should review their military decision-making process. Emphasis should be placed on developing the mission statement, commander's intent, course of action development, and detailed planning of the commander's selected course of action.

Lastly, I suggested to General Bieniek that aiding newly arrived commanders and their staffs as he had in Kerbelâ' was a superb idea. General Kwiatkowski's and my presence had been a boost to the Polish brigade staff, but I thought a special operational cell with officers from across the division staff should be formed and made ready to deploy and assist the brigades as required in the future. At Tom Lowman's suggestion, I attached a diagram of the military decision-making process to my report that outlined the staff process from the receipt of a mission to execution, and a course of action battlefield operations systems matrix. The matrix is a planning tool that assists the staff in identifying a superior course of action by applying a numerical value (normally from 1–3) on specific aspects of each of the battlefield operating systems and other applicable tactical considerations. After all of the courses of action are considered and the applied values added up, the course of action with the highest score is likely the one the staff will recommend to the commander. While not fool proof, it is an excellent method by which a staff can make a logical recommendation with supporting rationale in a short period of time.

General Kwiatkowski enthusiastically approved the second version of the report and General Bieniek was pleased with our suggestions. Following a quick read and a short conversation with General Kwiatkowski in Polish, the commanding general looked at me with a smile and said, "Roland, you must ensure that your replacement is well oriented on the division and our staff before you leave. But I think you should stay with me."

I appreciated the commanding general's compliment, but I still did not have a good idea of when I would see a replacement. The Combined Joint Task Force-7 (CJTF-7) personnel staff assured me his arrival was imminent. I assured General Bieniek I would not leave the division until I was certain the new liaison team was "good to go." Like the commanding general, I wanted our transition to be as seamless as possible.

The challenges of the diverse Multinational Division's (MND) area of responsibility did not end with each action, but simply simmered down for a while to an acceptable level of calm before it would spike. Not one day after we returned from the reconnaissance and foreign-fighter challenge in Kerbelā', Al-Najaf raised its ugly head again. The continuing controversy over what to do with Muqtadā aṣ-Ṣadr and Al-Najaf was a never-ending battle of discontent between CJTF-7 Headquarters and the MND. On the morning of 19 January, General Bieniek was informed by CJTF-7 Headquarters that elements of Ṣadr's Mahdi Army militia had occupied the Ali Mosque. I strongly advised the commanding general to go to Al-Najaf and get firsthand, on-the-ground, reports from the Spanish brigade commander and local officials that would allow him to speak with authority when he reported to General Sanchez in the evening. He agreed and we flew to Al-Najaf an hour later.

The perception and reality of the situation in Al-Najaf always appeared to be at odds with each other. The CJTF-7 command group was frustrated the Poles did not want to confront the crisis caused by the presence of Ṣadr's illegal militia in the city. The Spanish brigade and the command group of the MND did not perceive a crisis. Everyone understood the Mahdi Army and Ṣadr were problems but, from the division's perspective, the problems were manageable without the threat of violence and military action. This was the case on 19 January when General Bieniek, accompanied by Spanish General Isodoro, me, and several members of the division staff, met with General Coll Bucher the Spanish commander of the 3rd Brigade Combat Team, and Governate Coordinator Richard Olson, in a walled and heavily guarded government compound. General Coll was cool and confident. He stated the situation in Al-Najaf was tense, but under control and no extraordinary means beyond his brigade and the local police forces were required to ensure it remained that way. General Coll said that armed members of the Mahdi Army had not entered the Ali Mosque on 18 January, however, several armed men were seen well outside the perimeter of the mosque at one point for a short period of time. Local police maintained a strong presence near the mosque and his brigade maintained a significant presence in the city. He reported that "Both the police and our soldiers are positioned in a manner that allows them to search vehicles, confiscate weapons, and detain gunmen that intend to enter the grounds of the Ali Mosque."

Mr. Olson confirmed the brigade commander's comments and complimented the Spanish brigade's actions and its relationship and coordination with local authorities.

The Coll–Olson briefing was followed by a meeting with the deputy governor of Al-Najaf Province, the police chief of Al-Najaf, and the chiefs of the Facilities Protection Service and Shrine Police. Generals Bieniek and Coll emphasized their desire to act in their support but not to do their job. Ultimately, law and order in Al-Najaf was their responsibility. The chiefs acknowledged this point, but then expressed a greater need for logistics support. They particularly needed weapons, uniforms, and vehicles. Mr. Olson offered to discuss these issues with them at a later time, stating this was a matter for the Coalition Provisional Authority (CPA) and not the MND. The chiefs' concerns were legitimate ones. In January 2004, the New Iraqi Army program had trained and barely equipped two battalions of light infantry and the National Police Forces lagged sorely behind it. It was not the MND's responsibility to staff police requirements and Mr. Olson was wise to defer further discussion about them until appropriate CPA authorities could be consulted. Al-Najaf, like Kerbelâ', was a hot bed of activity with an emboldened Iraqi Shia population in the wake of Saddam's capture. If it was to be a peaceful and stable city, those consultations and decisions had to be made quickly. There was a huge burden on the local and provincial security forces that, given their limited resources, were poorly equipped and nearly always outgunned.

During the meeting, General Bieniek was informed of an ongoing, nearby demonstration by over five hundred people who were demanding elections and a trial of Saddam Hussein in an Iraqi court. The demonstration underscored Al-Najaf's tense environment. The presence of militias, Iranian influence, and criminal activity, coupled with the weakness of the city's infrastructure and its emboldened Shia population, potentially complicated any demonstration with the possibility of violence. But as one Polish officer said to me as the meeting ended, "The right to demonstrate was inherent to every legitimate democracy." He was right of course. The Poles were always quick to remind me of democratic ideals that we Americans hold so dear. I went up to the roof with a pair of binoculars to have a look around and assess the demonstration for myself. The diverse crowd of men and women carrying multicolored flags and pictures of Muqtadā as-Ṣadr were a common sight in Al-Najaf. Most of the men were dressed in white robes and the women wore the traditional black abayas. I did not see any weapons being openly carried. The presence of middle-aged men spoke to the unemployment issue that so badly needed to be addressed. Ultimately, the restoration of a viable economy was the vital requirement in restoring a sense of stability to this land, but that seemed a long way off at the moment. It was a hot day and they must have been tiring. The situation seemed benign and we were relieved to learn the demonstrators were dispersing as we prepared to return to Camp Babylon.

General Bieniek's decision to go to Al-Najaf played well in his TACSAT report to General Sanchez that evening. He told General Sanchez his intent was to continue the division's current course of action by maintaining "A very visible presence in the city and remain in close support of local police activities." The crisis in Al-Najaf for the moment was over as the CJTF-7 commander seemed satisfied the situation was stable. But the Holy City's complexities and challenges would continue to loom large on every commander's scope and a frustrated General Miller told me that dealing with the Al-Najaf problem had only once again been delayed.

On the following day, I was informed General Bezluschenko wanted to see me at his headquarters in Al-Kut about information he had received concerning weapons of mass destruction (WMD). Ukrainian sentries at the main entrance to the Al-Kut air base had been given an envelope containing information about the location of a WMD storage site by an elderly man who had asked to see their commander. I attained the necessary permissions to meet with General Bezluschenko and accompanied General Kwiatkowski and Ambassador Krystosik on a flight to Al-Kut. General Bezluschenko personally gave me the envelope as if it was a hot potato. WMDs were a sensitive subject that would have made any contingent commander uncomfortable given the attention it would draw to his area of operations. In January 2004, the hunt for WMDs in Iraq was still in progress under the direction of a special multinational task force known as the Iraq Survey Group (ISG). I was suspicious, but curious about a series of photos of a variety of canisters and radiation warning signs the general showed me. The old Iraqi man had told him he knew where the articles were located and naturally would take him there for a price. I discussed the matter with General Miller to whom I forwarded the information and photos via an American courier. Much to the relief of both the division and the Ukrainian brigade commanders, we were informed several days later that an evaluation had been made and no further investigation was warranted. The ISG surveyed hundreds of possible WMD sites during its existence but, two days after the Ukrainians gave me the information, David Kay, an American scientist and the head of the ISG, resigned his position believing that WMD stockpiles were not in Iraq. A year later, the ISG announced the end of its search.[2] If stockpiles had existed, presumably before the U.S.-led invasion, they concluded they were smuggled out of Iraq, perhaps to neighboring Syria or Iran.

The Ukrainian reaction to the possibility of WMDs in their area of responsibility was understandable for other reasons. The last thing the Ukrainians wanted was another mission to find and secure weapons of mass destruction. Their concerns clearly focused on the Iranian border with its increasing Iranian infiltration and illegal immigration, and the challenges they faced in Al-Kut and the numerous Iraqi border towns and villages in Wasit Province. The Ukrainian border force and the Iraqi border police were being overwhelmed. In an attempt to moderate the incessant flow of illegals into Iraq, General Kwiatkowski and Ambassador Krystosik met with immigration and customs officials while I pursued the WMD information with General Bezluschenko. Their dialogue was considered constructive but, recalling the more than twelve hundred people we had policed up and forced back into Iran on Christmas Day, it was not hard to believe the illegal movement was encouraged by the Iranian Government. The absence of a large, credible Iraqi force to enforce its borders and challenge the Iranians as it had in the past, had opened a flood gate through which the Iranians could infiltrate and eventually dominate southern Iraq. The influence of Iran's masses, coupled with a steady supply of Iranian weapons to Iraq's Shia militias, was a dismal prospect for an Iraq that before the invasion had been the Arab bulwark against Persian expansion. Iraq's continued instability and weakness could only portend a dangerous Iranian dominance of the entire central and southern regions of the country.

Muqtadā aṣ-Ṣadr's growing influence in the holy cities fueled the growing instability in Iraq and it was only a matter of days after the Coll–Olson meetings in Al-Najaf that CJTF-7 Headquarters again raised the issue of the existence of a Sharia Court to the MND commander. The Poles and Spanish had denied the existence of the Sharia Court since October, but CJTF-7 was adamant about its existence. Unknown to me and the division, CJTF-7 had monitored the suspected court's activities through a variety of intelligence gathering means and wanted it shut down. I suspected something was planned by the increased evening helicopter traffic that we monitored in and out of the Camp Babylon airstrip. General Kwiatkowski told me about a possible combined Polish and American special forces operation in Al-Najaf and General Bieniek informed me of a similar operation supposedly planned to occur in Kerbelā'. They had no details to share and were clearly frustrated by the absence of more information. General Bieniek held coordination meetings with American special forces teams operating in Babil and Al-Najaf Provinces, but these meetings did not reveal any details or a definitive intent to strike at any particular location. General Bieniek strongly believed that planning was ongoing, but I was clueless about any planned operation in his area of responsibility. He was genuinely concerned about what, if any, role the MND would have if these operations were being planned, as well as the second and third effects the operations would have for Coalition forces patrolling the two holy cities.

After attending the change-of-command ceremonies of the Dominican Republic battalion on 28 January, General Bieniek and I met with General Coll to discuss possible missions the Spanish brigade could be called upon to execute if special forces strikes on the suspected Sharia Court locations occurred. We anticipated the Spanish brigade would have a security mission that would isolate the Ali and Kufah Mosques and the general vicinity of the suspected targets. The generals were uncomfortable. A Spanish soldier had been wounded in a firefight during the previous week; now they faced the possibility of a major battle in Al-Najaf. Spanish and Latin American soldiers would undoubtedly be engaged in a fight if the Mahdi militia decided to respond aggressively to an attack. Asked my opinion by General Bieniek of what the Spanish brigade's actions should be in the near term, I recommended General Coll assume his brigade would be given a security mission that would respect its rules of engagement. It should increase its reconnaissance of the two mosques and the suspected location of the Sharia Court and identify potential locations for roadblocks and other positions that would effectively isolate the likely objectives. His operations staff should develop sketches of the proposed operational areas. They should proceed with their troop to task analysis and determine command-and-control requirements to include where to establish a forward command post as the Poles had effectively done during their operations in Kerbelá' the previous October. Positive head nods from both generals ended the session.

General Bieniek informed General Sanchez of his activities in Al-Najaf during his evening TACSAT briefing; he was asked to come to Baghdad on 31 January to review and assess a proposed plan for a mission of some kind in Al-Najaf. Surprisingly, I received a phone call from General Miller seeking detailed information about the MND's plan to shut down the Sharia Court in Al-Najaf that same evening. I told him I did not know any details of such a plan, but that General Bieniek had issued a warning order to the Spanish brigade commander to begin planning for a security mission in support of a proposed CJTF-7 plan to strike targets in Al-Najaf. The division not only did not have a plan, but General Bieniek did not have any details to share with his staff about a specific CJTF-7 plan. I could sense the frustration on the other end of the phone. The Al-Najaf Sharia Court issue was the one area in which I felt my old Ranger buddy and I were at odds. He clearly expected me to convince the Poles to strike, but it was very apparent to me the Poles were not convinced of a problem or a need to hit a target they were not convinced existed in the first place. I could only push the Poles so far and strongly suggested CJTF-7 push the issue with them directly. Once again, I suggested a general-led operations team from CJTF-7 come to Camp Babylon with definitive information and a proposed plan of action. It would not be until April that CJTF-7 had had enough and directed American forces to engage the Mahdi militia in a series of indecisive, but bloody street battles in Al-Najaf. Failure to move against Muqtadā aṣ-Ṣadr in the fall of 2003 had been a major mistake. He and his Mahdi Army would survive the April 2004 battles with the Americans and become a major power in Iraq during the next several years.

CHAPTER 35

A New Liaison Team Arrives at Camp Babylon

I am a Soldier; I fight where I am told. I win where I fight.
—USA MOTTO

It was a difficult and fast-moving period for the new Polish arrivals to the Multinational Division (Central-South). The activities in Kerbelâ', Al-Najaf, and Al-Kut all but consumed them. Our liaison team, and particularly Tom Lowman, did everything it could to support and advise the new division and brigade staffs. Time is inconsequential in a war zone; one day looks like the next, the hours pass by, and you hope you can get some uninterrupted sleep before the next day begins. It is not uncommon to hear someone ask what day of the week it is or what the correct date is. Returning to Camp Babylon from Al-Kut on the afternoon of 21 January, I remembered that my original liaison team members were going home. Captain Lowman and Staff Sergeant Chris Stewart were scheduled to rotate back to Germany with the V Corps staff. They were manifested on a helicopter that would return to Camp Victory in Baghdad, the same helicopter that would bring in their replacements and several other new guys that would form Combined Joint Task Force-7 (CJTF-7) Liaison Team Two. They were standing at the edge of the airstrip with all of their equipment and baggage when my chopper landed. The exceptional work and contributions of these two American soldiers, as well as the soldiers who supported the division's logistics and transportation staffs, were immensely appreciated by our multinational comrades. Captain Britt Reed, our aviation officer, was a hero among the gallant Polish helicopter pilots. We had all been through a lot together. Soldiers grow close in tough assignments, but as the blades of their helicopter started to turn, we simply shook hands and parted ways. Tom and I exchanged salutes as the helicopter lifted off. I watched it until it was out of sight and suddenly felt very alone.

"Beg your pardon, sir, my name is Major Stephan Calhoun and I'll be your deputy until Colonel Brewer arrives."

"Damn," I thought, "There's no stopping the 'Green Machine,'" as I looked over my new deputy and the other members of Liaison and Advisory Team Two from the incoming U.S. III Corps staff.

I was deep in thought for a few brief seconds before I looked up and said, "Okay, Major Calhoun, let's get you and your people billeted. We have a lot of ground to cover."

Transitions were ongoing throughout Iraq during this period. V Corps was preparing to return to Germany and elements of the Texas-based III Corps and its commander, Lieutenant General Thomas F. Metz, USA, were already on the ground. Prior to assuming command, General Metz had served as the U.S. Central Command chief of staff. We had a good relationship and I held him in high regard. The Multinational Division staff worked hard to receive him on 25 January for a series of briefings concerning the division's area of operations, responsibilities, and current operations. He was particularly surprised by my observation that Iranian Farsi was commonly spoken in the neighborhoods of Al-Najaf, Kerbelâ', and the border towns of the eastern portion of the division's area of responsibility. Iranian support to al-Qaeda in Iraq and the Shia militias was already occurring and the growing Iraqi insurgency in the winter of 2004 was fraught with Iranian influence. We did not tell him much that he did not already know, but he appeared genuinely appreciative and complimented the staff officers who briefed him.

Lieutenant Colonel Mike Brewer, USA, arrived at Camp Babylon on the evening of 29 January. An Army aviator and European foreign-area officer, Mike was a bright, enthusiastic officer who looked forward to his duties as my replacement. I had lobbied hard with Generals Wojdkowski and Miller to be replaced by a full colonel and a ground combat officer, but to no avail. I was determined to do everything I could to ensure a smooth transition and Mike's success in what I knew he would find a most challenging position. The transition process and a series of office calls to bid farewell while simultaneously introducing Mike to unit commanders and members of the command group and division staff dominated my final week at Camp Babylon.

We flew to Al-Kut and the Iranian border on 1 February where I introduced Mike to Generals Sobora and Beslezchenko, then to Major Semenets and a large formation of Ukrainian paratroops. Val surprised us with a short ceremony and presented me with a blue beret and a blue and white-striped t-shirt worn by Ukrainian paratroopers. Back at Al-Kut, General Sobora presented me with the Bulova Mace of a Ukrainian prince. But the best was saved for last. As we prepared to leave the headquarters, the stone-faced Senior Warrant Officer Antoliy Kunitskyi approached me. He had noticed the paratroop t-shirt I had been presented, and was now wearing, was faded. A paratroop veteran of the Soviet Union's long campaign in Afghanistan, he handed me one of his own brand-new t-shirts, smiled, and said something to me in Ukrainian that I assumed was a good-luck wish. I was amazed at how my world had changed and how so many of my sworn enemies of the Cold War had become beloved comrades-in-arms.

In spite of my doubts about leaving the division at an inopportune time, I was ready to go home. Colonel Brewer conducted a reconnaissance of the mosques and other key sites of Al-Najaf while I cleared my accounts, paid a few final calls, and mailed several packages. Al-Najaf would get "hot" again, but not on my watch. It was time to move on. General Bieniek had secured CJTF-7's permission for me to fly to Poland with the last contingent of Polish troops who had served during the division's first rotation. I was officially invited to Poland as a guest of the minister of defense. The last group of Polish soldiers of the first rotation and I departed Camp Babylon in a large convoy of vehicles. We were alert throughout the long drive with weapons at the ready, but we made it to Baghdad without incident. At Camp Victory, I left the Poles and went to CJTF-7 Headquarters where I was scheduled for office calls with Generals Metz, Wojdkowski, and Miller.

Tom Miller greeted me with a warm smile and a genuine handshake. We discussed my activities with the Multinational Division and our mutual concerns. I made a number of recommendations in my after-action report, emphasizing the need to expand the liaison mission in terms of both personnel and equipment. I strongly suggested that tactical vehicles, communications equipment, and enough personnel to provide permanent liaison with the three brigade combat teams would significantly improve our situational awareness, reporting, and ability to influence the commanders with our advice and assistance. He was gracious and understanding, but shortfalls in people, vehicles, and nearly every type of tactical equipment throughout Iraq made my comments in this regard less than practical. The personnel and resource issue, that had hindered our operations in Iraq since the invasion, cast a shadow on anyone seeking more men and equipment to properly do his job. I understood the reality, but I was disappointed. He shared a number of points with me regarding Al-Najaf, Muqtadā aṣ-Ṣadr, and particularly the existence of the Sharia Court. As he spoke, I politely nodded my head all the while thinking that had I been armed with this information beforehand, I may have had better luck influencing the action CJTF-7 desired. I did not ask any questions. Intelligence sources are always classified and I suspected it was the manner in which intelligence collection was conducted that ultimately kept me from the very information I needed to convince the division's commanders to act. I was convinced more than ever that a clash between Coalition Forces and the Mahdi Army was inevitable. I briefly regretted I was leaving Iraq, suspecting I would miss the engagement in Al-Najaf. It took place in April. Tom and I parted amicably; I was happy our long friendship was well intact.

My meetings with the other generals were polite and I appreciated their kind words. General Wojdkowski was particularly complimentary of my efforts to, "Get the Multinational Division off the ground." I spent the evening with General Eaton and several officers of the old CMATT (Coalition Military Assistance Training

Team) gang still hard at work training and developing the New Iraqi Army. Their work environment at the Coalition Provisional Authority's Republican Palace headquarters had significantly improved and it appeared the program was on track. The success of the New Iraqi Army was critically important to our overall success in Iraq and the eventual withdrawal of our forces. Our belief at the time was that, as Iraqi units became operational, U.S. and Coalition forces would draw down and go home. It would be almost another year before the CMATT program was adequately resourced. Our Army's failure to resource the CMATT's requirements would cost our nation dearly as sectarian violence and the expanding insurgency significantly burdened Coalition troops whose numbers never came close to adequately addressing the needs of an occupation force in a country as large as Iraq. The Iraqi training program would eventually become a three-star command and be given considerably more resources, but all of us were disappointed by the inability of our senior leaders to initially recognize the importance of this project and source it accordingly. I later learned the CMATT was decorated with the Joint Meritorious Unit Award for its actions from June 2003–June 2004. Its exceptional accomplishments—despite poor manning, inadequate support, poor facilities, and the ridiculous and unrealistic scheduling that nearly broke the back of the program at its inception—were a tribute to the outstanding officers and men who literally performed a miracle in getting the program up and operational.

PART IV

GOING HOME: REFLECTIONS ON THE LONG WAR

CHAPTER 36

Going Home via Poland

Only the dead have seen the end of war.

—PLATO

The Baghdad air terminal was a beehive of activity on the following morning when I walked in and requested a seat on the next aircraft out of Iraq. I was in luck. A C-130 had landed a few hours earlier and I was manifested for its first run to Kuwait. I was not seated in the VIP trailer for 30 minutes before I was standing on the tarmac with the heat of the aircraft's engines burning my face and the ever-present smell of jet fuel filling my nostrils. I got a lot of stares from the Air Force cargo handlers and Army support troops who worked there. It was a far different kind of war for them. My battered patrol cap, sun-bleached desert uniform, and foreign-looking assault rifle set me apart from most of the passengers they serviced at that time. An infantryman in rear areas with his weapons and combat equipment must have appeared odd. After boarding and taking a troop seat in the cargo area, a crew chief noticed my rank and invited me to sit in one of the more comfortable chairs behind the pilots in the cockpit. I took him up on his offer, but not a minute after take-off, I was out cold.

Nothing felt right as I struggled into a clean uniform and stepped outside of the Camp Doha officer's billets warehouse. I had been pleased to again find my quarters intact and my gear secure when I arrived late the previous afternoon. I had slept for nearly 18 hours after taking a bus to Camp Doha from the Kuwait City airport's military terminal area. I should have felt refreshed and ready to go. Instead, I was sick and suddenly disoriented. I was bent over at the waist when a passing lieutenant colonel placed his hand on my arm and offered to take me to the aid station. Throughout the past 12 months I had enjoyed near-perfect health. I had held up well physically despite long, stressful days, a routine absence of sleep, long hours of exposure, and combat. A female doctor stood next to me reviewing the medical sheet with my vital signs and determined I was severely dehydrated. I was given several bags of fluid over several hours. I had generated a lot of interest. My doctor could not resist asking me a number of questions once I was lucid enough to talk intelligently and I told her my story. She took a minute to think about what I told her and shook her head. "You've been living on adrenalin for quite some time. You look like you've lost a lot of weight, but we'll have you hydrated soon. You'll need a lot of rest, but your vital signs are good and I'll release you to your quarters as long as you promise to stay there." I began to feel better and talk more as I became more situationally aware of the people around me. I must have been quite an attraction. She signed my release and reminded me to get a lot of rest. It was late in the afternoon when I walked out of there feeling deceptively strong but resigned to follow the doctor's orders. I had several more days to clear Camp Doha, mail my weapons back to U.S. Central Command Headquarters, coordinate my link-up with the Poles, and fly to Poland. I had lost the day, but I returned to my quarters relieved I was okay and fell asleep. It could all wait another day.

Clearing Camp Doha was an interesting adventure. I was several hours filling out paperwork that attempted to capture the details of my service in Iraq. I appreciated this was a good thing, particularly for young soldiers who would be monitored over time to ease their re-entry into a civil society. Someone told me that nearly every combat soldier suffers from some form of post-traumatic syndrome disorder. Like most professional soldiers, I was not inclined to think anything about it. I was happy to get my release form stamped and to be on my way.

A Miami-based charter plane painted a colorful Florida orange was parked on an isolated tarmac at the airport when General Kwiatkowski, 50 Polish officers and soldiers, and I stood by to board on the afternoon of 11 February. These soldiers were national heroes in Poland and they were anxious to go home. They awakened me with their cheers when the aircraft touched down several hours later in Szechen Province in northwestern Poland after our long but uneventful flight. I stepped aside to let the Polish boys get off to see their friends and loved ones, but General Kwiatkowski called me forward. As the senior officer on board, he was expected to report to the senior officer greeting the plane and he wanted me by his side. The senior officer on the tarmac was our own recently promoted Lieutenant General Andrzej Tyszkiewicz. A military band was playing as we walked down the steps where a large delegation of senior officers waited to greet us. General Tyszkiewicz returned his classmate's salute and hugged both of us as if we were his long-lost sons. We had come far together and I shared the pride of his accomplishments and his third star. Only the absence of my family kept it from being a true homecoming but standing with the official delegation was the U.S. Naval Attaché to the U.S. Embassy, Commander Yuri Tabach, USN. I had known Yuri since 1997 when we attended the Anti-Terrorist Course at Fort Bragg. Yuri was born in Soviet Russia and had come to the United States with his family as a young Jewish refugee in the early 1980s. A fierce American patriot and a brilliant foreign-area specialist, he had learned of my visit to Poland and had suggested to the American ambassador that an office call with this "Most unusual officer who Poland highly regarded" would be most appropriate. He had introduced himself to General Tyszkiewicz at my suggestion prior to our departure from Iraq, and his native Russian and background made him an instant hit with the great Polish commander. Yuri was a dear friend and his presence eased any discomfort I may have initially felt among the Polish and Russian-speaking senior officers who greeted us.

After a short reception in the terminal, we boarded a Russian-built An-26 transport aircraft and flew to Warsaw. A sedan sat by the tarmac that took the general, Yuri, and me to an apartment complex for military officers and official visitors where I was billeted for my stay in Poland's capital. We spoke a few minutes in the living room and the general told me to wear my combat uniform in the morning because I was to be decorated by the vice minister of defense. Smiling and genuinely happy to see me, he then suggested I get some sleep. I did not need to be told twice.

Major Magda, my military escort for the next couple of days, stood at the door of my quarters at 6 am sharp. Magda was a smart-looking officer who had served in the United Nations Iraq–Kuwait Observation Mission in 1999–2000. We shared our common experiences in the former demilitarized zone that separated the two countries over breakfast before driving to the Ministry of Defense. General Tyszkiewicz and Yuri had arrived a few minutes earlier and Yuri was beside himself; I laughed when he said, "Nobody gets an audience with Vice Minister Towpick. You are a great hero!"

A few minutes later, a young lady directed us into the vice minister's office and General Tyszkiewicz introduced me to Mr. Towpik. Andrzej Towpik was a good-looking man who spoke impeccable English. He was superbly dressed and I wished I had had a more appropriate uniform to wear to meet such an important Polish dignitary. He was smiling broadly as he shook everyone's hand and offered us all a seat at a small conference table. The general spoke first, describing me as his closest senior adviser during his tour in Iraq as commander of the Multinational Division (Central-South). I could not help being honored by his kind and, I sensed, heartfelt words.

"Roland was more than a liaison officer and adviser. He was a vital member of my staff who contributed significantly to the success of our operations."

The general also mentioned my service with the Polish and Ukrainian brigades which he knew was a source of great pride to me. Mr. Towpik thanked me for my contributions to Poland and the Coalition effort in Iraq and, over the next two hours, asked me a series of questions about my duties and experiences, the effectiveness of Polish troops, the future of Iraq, my thoughts on Iranian influence in Iraq, and the impact of the recent change of command of the Multinational Division. My responses were measured and honest. Poland's Army was gaining valuable combat experience in Iraq. They were learning lessons and contributing significantly to the Coalition's efforts to provide a more stable environment for the Iraqi people. The Poles had gained a tremendous appreciation for the Western way of warfare, a point that Commander in Chief of Polish Land Forces Lieutenant

General Edward Pietrzyk would make more than clear a year later when he said, "Fighting in Iraq has helped to transform Poland's Army into a more capable force with better equipment and hardier soldiers." He was particularly sold on the use of night-vision devices and the value of fighting at night.[1]

There was no denying the maturity the Poles and the other national contingents in the Multinational Division had gained in the first six months of their deployment in Iraq. I spoke passionately of my combat experiences with the Poles, Bulgarians, and Ukrainians who had adapted so well to both the desert and urban environment of Iraq. I told Mr. Towpik that "Serving with soldiers from eastern Europe was not anything I could have possibly anticipated as a young officer," and he smiled and nodded at my implied reference to the long years of the Cold War and the Warsaw Pact.

Mr. Towpik was genuinely interested in my observations concerning Iranian influence in Kerbelâ', Al-Najaf, Al-Kut, and the border region. I told him Iraq and the Coalition would suffer dire consequences if we did not do a better job of controlling the borders. I suggested the Coalition would be smart to step up the recruitment and development of Iraqi Security Forces and heavily reinforce its efforts to secure Iraq's borders. Given the condition we had found Iraq's military facilities in June 2003, I suggested greater investment in the infrastructure of its military and police forces would have to be made.

I also suggested that, even though Polish troops were performing well, force-protection requirements in Iraq's increasingly hostile environment would dictate a need for heavier equipment and weaponry. The Poles had suffered only a handful of casualties in their first rotation, but battlefield casualties in 2004 would rise significantly higher.

I spoke highly of the exceptional organizational and operational talents of General Tyszkiewicz. He had faced enormous challenges to establish the complex Multinational Division. The division had matured under his command and the transition to the second rotation under General Bieniek had been practically seamless. Mr. Towpik appeared somewhat relieved by the last point as I suspect he appreciated the difficulties of command in such a challenging environment.

Our time with Mr. Towpik passed quickly. He was a good listener who appeared to genuinely enjoy the conversation, but an aide reminded him of another appointment and he reluctantly excused himself. We left his office with a final round of handshakes and compliments. Yuri assured me the meeting had been exceptional and I had superbly represented the United States. He was thrilled and I was happy to have it behind me.

We drove to the "Citadel," a 19th-century fort built by Tsar Nicholas I, after a Polish uprising in 1830, to firmly establish Russian control of Warsaw. Stark but impressive looking, the fort's pentagon-shaped brick structure with high outer walls included some ninety acres of land and served as the headquarters of Polish

Land Forces. General Tyszkiewicz's position as the deputy commander of Polish Land Forces was considerably different from his combat assignment in Iraq, but he appeared to be very happy with his new office and position. Along with his numerous official duties, he was using his recent experience in Iraq as the basis of his doctoral thesis on counterinsurgency. His office was laden with books and souvenirs of previous assignments, not unlike most American senior officers and commanders. Over a cup of tea, he outlined his plans for the remainder of my visit.

"Roland, I regret that the decoration you are to receive is not ready. It will be presented to you in Kraków tomorrow. You will tour Warsaw today. Tomorrow you will drive to Kraków and tour the city. General Kwiatkowski will greet you there and serve as your host."

Yuri added one small detail that complicated things somewhat. The U.S. Ambassador to Poland, Mr. Christopher Hill, wished to meet me and General Tyszkiewicz later that afternoon. It was a surprise Yuri had pushed hard to achieve. General Tyszkiewicz took it in stride, adding he would meet us at the U.S. Embassy at the appointed time. I smiled at Yuri when he informed me I was now a "rock star" at the U.S. Embassy. I did not particularly care for another official call, but it was one of those things that came with the job. I was anxious to see Poland, but I was honored our ambassador would want to see me.

General Tyszkiewicz had often talked about his beloved Poland and his home in Warsaw. He personally arranged a tour guide of Warsaw for me and along with Major Magda we left the Citadel for a first-class tour of the capital city that bore the name forever identified with the "evil empire's" military pact. We enjoyed the city's statues, cathedrals, and government buildings, but there were three sites that totally held my attention. Warsaw had suffered tremendously during World War II. In the German blitz of 1939 and the uprising of the Polish Home Army in August 1944, Warsaw was nearly totally destroyed. In the 1970s, Poland reconstructed a portion of the city known as "Old Town" with as many of the original bricks and fixtures as possible that could be salvaged from the rubble. Now a beautiful tourist attraction with numerous shops, cafes, and restaurants, it is a romantic touch of Poland with its 13th-century cathedrals and fortifications. Major Magda had to push me along to stay on schedule. We drove to the area of Warsaw that had once been the walled Jewish ghetto. Its monuments, including one of several Jewish fighters emerging from a sewer, spoke of the horrors of the Nazi occupation and the triumph of the human spirit. Our last stop was the Tomb of the Unknown Soldier. The brave Poles of World War II were preceded in glory by Polish soldiers of countless campaigns in its long and often sad history. Poland contributed armies to both the Eastern and Western Fronts during World War II, fighting with distinction in the siege of Berlin with the Soviets as well as at Cassino, Normandy, and the Netherlands with the Western allies. The campaigns are engraved on tablets emplaced on the walls of the tomb that is guarded 24 hours a day, 7 days a week. I was fascinated by the rich history of this great country that has always identified with the West. Its loss to Soviet domination in the aftermath of the Yalta Conference in 1945 is one of the great travesties of the war.

At the U.S. Embassy, Yuri, General Tyszkiewicz, and I met with Ambassador Christopher R. Hill in a short but pleasant meeting. Ambassador Hill warmly welcomed us. He was no stranger to Poland, having served a previous tour in Warsaw. He had become ambassador in 2000 after serving as the Ambassador to the Republic of Macedonia from 1996 to 1999, and our special envoy to Kosovo from 1998 to 1999. He spoke Polish and several other eastern European languages. He congratulated us on the successful completion of our mission in Iraq. General Tyszkiewicz spoke briefly of the challenges the Coalition faced in Iraq, but the conversation quickly moved to recent efforts to sell Polish defense hardware, including the Honker transport vehicle, to Iraq. I was glad to hear that General Eaton's interest in the Honker during his visit to Camp Babylon had actually stimulated a possible sale to the Iraqi Armed Forces. It seemed appropriate the countries who sacrificed the most in Iraq should benefit accordingly. Our visit was curtailed by the ambassador's intense schedule of calls, but not before he thanked me for my long service to the nation. It was obvious he had squeezed our visit into an already tough schedule, and I was grateful for his interest and hospitality. A wonderful dinner with General Tyszkiewicz and Yuri at an upscale restaurant completed my day to remember in Warsaw.

A six-hour drive to the beautiful city of Kraków awaited me the following morning. Major Magda and a young captain joined me for breakfast. I was not particularly hungry, but I enjoyed their company and they were genuinely interested in me. Their appreciation for my service in Iraq was nearly overwhelming. Our continuous conversation about our experiences in the demilitarized zone before the invasion and the Iraq war seemed to make the long drive to Kraków go by much faster than the six hours it actually took. The long drive had the benefit of giving me a better appreciation for the Polish countryside. I enjoyed the view as much as I did the company. We interrupted our drive only once for a lunch break and entered the Royal Hotel in Kraków early that evening.

I was the guest of the 2nd Polish Corps and we were greeted by Brigadier General Kwiatkowski, its designated deputy commander. He greeted me as if we had not seen each other for months. Several beers later, he excused my two escort officers and we took a brisk walk to Kraków's magnificent town square, briefly toured a beautiful basilica, and had another round of drinks at one of the town square's numerous cafes. At the general's house, I met his lovely wife Kristina and daughter Camilla. Camilla spoke fluent Russian and English, an insignificant point that otherwise reminded me of the intelligence, education, and broad experience of the general population of this great country. Forced to deal with the vulnerability of its borders and the proximity and influence of the Russians and the Germans, the Poles struck me as very cosmopolitan. The ladies seemed very enamored with all things Western, particularly American fashion.

Dinner that evening with the Kwiatkowskis was a relaxing and enjoyable event. A private room in the Royal Hotel was arranged for us and I enjoyed responding to the ladies' questions of American life. My intentionally humorous thoughts about the Cold War were greeted with genuine interest and raucous laughter.

"American men," I joked, "thought that all Russian and former Eastern Bloc European women were like old grandmothers." I used the Polish word, "babushka" to describe the heavily bundled, fur-hatted old grandmothers that we used to see in documentaries of life in the Soviet Union. "We thought that you were all fat, boring, and unattractive." I suggested it was exactly what the Russians wanted and that the Cold War was all about keeping American men from appreciating the true beauty of eastern European women.

When the laughter subsided, General Kwiatkowski stood up and solemnly spoke of our tour of duty in Iraq and the value of my service to the Polish-led Multinational Division. When he finished, he turned to me, asked me to stand, and pinned to my shirt the Polish Army Medal in the First Degree. I thanked him for the recognition and the honor of having served with such noble and gallant soldiers. It was the perfect ending to a perfect day. I could not have been more proud as we called it a night and agreed to meet in the morning for breakfast and my continued tour of Kraków and the surrounding area.

Some fifty kilometers west of Krakow lay the facilities of the most notorious death camp of the 20th century. The Nazis had established the Auschwitz concentration camp in 1940 as a labor camp. Over a million people would be killed there by the spring of 1945. All over the world, it is known as a symbol of terror and genocide. General Kwiatkowski and I had often talked about his home in Kraków and I had told him about my interest in the history of World War II and the infamous concentration camp so near his hometown. My father's unit had liberated the German camp at Gunskirchen Lager near Lambach, Austria, in May 1945, and as a young boy I had looked at the gruesome pictures of death and brutality in his regimental history book. A visit to Auschwitz in the aftermath of the campaign in Iraq to eliminate yet another murderous dictator seemed appropriate to me and General Kwiatkowski had made the necessary arrangements.

A personal tour guide greeted us in the Polish town of Oświęcim that sat outside the infamous death camp. She brought to full understanding the horrific history of the massive concentration camp over the next several hours. We entered its gates marked by the infamous German words, *Arbeit Macht Frei*, or "Work will set you free," and toured the barracks with their displays of shoes, personal articles, and shorn hair from thousands of former inmates. The crematorium was particularly revealing of Nazi crimes to humanity. Its insufficient capacity led the Nazis to construct several others at adjoining camps at Birkenau and Monowitz. There were over forty other sub-camps. I was as fascinated by this massive display of inhumanity as I was sickened by it. Staring down on the maze of railroad tracks at the "Hell's Gate" entrance to Birkenau, I thought about Iraq and the tendency of our world to produce monsters typified by Hitler and Saddam Hussein. After we exited the crematorium in the main camp with the smell of death still in our nostrils, our guide pointed to a small scaffold where Rudolf Höss, the camp's former commandant had been hung in 1947. The general and I stared at it for what seemed like several minutes before he turned to me and said something I will never forget.

"Roland, maybe what we did in Iraq is a good thing. Perhaps soon there will be peace."

The visit to Auschwitz was the first time I had ever reflected on my activities in Iraq and the Middle East. Thoughts of destruction and death, the suffering and poverty of the Iraqi people, and the personal challenges I had experienced, not unlike my father had nearly sixty years before, raced through my mind. I walked away from Auschwitz proud of my service and hopeful that peace might someday be a reality for the people of Iraq and the Middle East.

Receiving the Ukrainian Order of Valor and Honor from Major General Harashuk, at MacDill Air Force Base, Tampa, Florida, 10 November 2004. (*Coalition Bulletin*, October–November 2004, courtesy of the U.S. Department of Defense)

CHAPTER 37

Epilogue

Hope is a waking dream.

—ARISTOTLE

On 1 March 2004, one year to the day since I went to Kuwait, I reported to U.S. Central Command (USCENTCOM) Headquarters with every intention of continuing to serve in some capacity either in the Joint Security Directorate or wherever else I could contribute to the war effort. I thought I was a perfect fit to work with the national contingents assigned to USCENTCOM and develop and coordinate Coalition plans. The nation was at war and it seemed logical to me that mandatory retirement and its associated bureaucratic necessities could be cast aside in the best interests of the Army and the nation. I was told, in no uncertain terms, to retire. Over the course of the next two months, I made several speeches in Washington, D.C., and Tampa concerning the war, and I was invited to attend the George C. Marshall Reserve Officers' Training Corps (ROTC) Award Seminar in Lexington, Virginia. This event brings together the top ROTC cadets from the nation to participate in roundtable discussions on major national security issues and hear from senior military and civilian officials about the challenges confronting our nation and the military. I was pleased to serve as the Middle East seminar leader. My military career ended rather inauspiciously the day before the long Memorial Day weekend, when I turned in the keys to my office and signed the necessary papers placing me on the retired list. A young, enlisted soldier handed me our nation's flag and thanked me for my service. I walked to the parking lot and drove home. I put my hopes of an extended military career behind me and looked to the future.

I became a civilian contract planner in USCENTCOM's Intelligence Directorate several days later. I had been encouraged to accept an available planner's position by several friends who had recently retired from the military and were now defense contractors themselves. Hardly two weeks had gone by when I was approached by a Bulgarian officer who informed me I had been cited by his minister of defense for my service in Iraq. A month later, a Ukrainian officer informed me his minister of defense had cited me for actions near Al-Kut and the Iran–Iraq border. In two colorful ceremonies in the fall of 2004, I was formally decorated by the senior representatives of these two great nations in the presence of the commanders of military contingents from over sixty nations that comprised the Global War on Terror Coalition. My comrades had not forgotten me; I was thrilled to be so honored. There were other honors from the Department of Defense, another award from Poland, and a certificate of combat service from El Salvador that arrived in the mail in 2006.

My duties at Central Command placed me in an excellent position to follow developments in Iraq. I was particularly interested in the developments impacting the Multinational Division (Central-South). Having aided the withdrawal of the Peninsula Shield Force from Kuwait in May 2003, I was somewhat dismayed by the withdrawal of countries assigned to the Multinational Division as early as 2004. Significant contributions by Arab land forces never materialized beyond the defense of Kuwait and it began to appear that European support was waning as well. The Najaf Governorate was passed back to American control in 2004 due to the reduction in strength of the forces under Polish command. The Multinational Division's Headquarters was moved in 2004 from Camp Babylon to Camp Echo near the town of ad-Dīwānīyah. Located in the center of Al-Qādisiyyah Province, Camp Echo was about sixty-five kilometers east of Al-Najaf and 170 kilometers south of Baghdad. This movement was due to the Spanish prime minister's decision to withdraw his forces from Iraq in response to the lack of public support in the aftermath of the Madrid train bombings in March 2004. The bombings were the deadliest terrorist attack in Spain's history. The official investigation by the Spanish judiciary found the attacks were directed by al-Qaeda in Iraq, allegedly to punish Spain for its involvement in the 2003 American-led invasion of Iraq. The other members of Plus Ultra withdrew at the same time, except for El Salvador, which sustained its combat presence in Iraq until 2009. The Thai contingent that had deployed to Camp Lima in Kerbelā' in September 2003 to provide engineering support, civil–military operations, and humanitarian assistance, withdrew from Iraq in accordance with its mandate at the end of September 2004. The Bulgarians would follow in December 2005, though they redeployed in 2006 and remained until the end of 2008. In January 2006, Polish troops transferred control of Babil province to American troops. The division's primary task by that point was to oversee the transfer of security in the areas under its control to the provisional Iraqi authorities.

The division began to switch from the stabilization tasks that defined the period I served with it to training the Iraqi Army and security forces, including the police and border police in 2006. The gallant Ukrainians continued to participate in combined combat operations focused on blocking illegal immigration and trafficking of weapons and drugs across the border, and to secure its area of responsibility during the Iraqi elections of 2005. Ukrainian soldiers prepared and conducted several joint operations with Iraqi armed forces, police, and border patrol along the Iraq–Iran border through 2006 and continued to provide personnel to the NATO Training

Mission-Iraq and United Nations Assistance Mission for Iraq until December 2008 when all its trainers were withdrawn.

The Poles commanded the division and provided command oversight of its force and mission transition. General Gruszka, who had commanded the Polish brigade late in my tour with the division, and my dear friend General "Bruno" Kwiatkowski, returned to command the division during the critical periods of transition in 2006–07. Bruno had been promoted to lieutenant general and was serving as the commander of the Polish Armed Forces Operational Command when, sadly, he was killed in the 2010 Polish Air Force plane crash that devastated the Polish government's leadership. The last of Poland's troops were withdrawn from Iraq in October 2008.

Command structure changes in Baghdad in the spring of 2004 led many to believe the United States was serious about stabilizing Iraq. The Multi-National Force-Iraq (MNF-I) replaced Combined Joint Task Force-7, in May 2004. General George Casey, USA, assumed command that summer from Lieutenant General Sanchez. General Sanchez returned to Germany and command of V Corps, retiring from the Army late in 2006. MNF-I was significantly reinforced during the troop surge of 2007 under General Petraeus, but never reached more than half of the original war plans requirements to stabilize Iraq. By the time the "surge" was initiated, Iraq was besieged by Iranian infiltration and influence, sectarian violence, al-Qaeda in Iraq, Islamic State in Iraq, the Mahdi Army, and other terrorist organizations opposing American and Coalition occupation. The aggressive actions taken by Coalition forces during his tenure of command, though admirable, were not enough to change the reality on the ground for any considerable length of time. By May 2011, all non-U.S. coalition members had withdrawn from Iraq. The American military withdrew in December 2011.

Reflecting on the crazy days of summer 2003 in the Coalition Military Assistance Training Team (CMATT), I was encouraged by the creation of the Multi-National Security Transition Command-Iraq (MNSTC-I) under the command of the newly promoted Lieutenant General David Petraeus in June 2004. This command consolidated the Civilian Police Assistance Team and advisory missions to the Ministries of Defense and Interior and, of course, the CMATT under Major General Paul Eaton that had, under great duress and limited support, initiated the development of the New Iraqi Army. The command would grow considerably over the next six years, a far cry from the "desperate men" of the summer of 2003, and be replaced by United States Forces-Iraq in 2010. MNSTC–I became U.S. Forces-Iraq, Advising and Training, commanded by a major general dual-hatted as Commander, NATO Training Mission-Iraq. The evolving nature of the training effort in Iraq and the increasing resources to enable the development of Iraqi security forces reflected the need for significant forces to stabilize Iraq in the aftermath of the maneuver phase of the invasion. The reality of the need for trained and equipped manpower was understood by all the senior commanders and yet, in the first year of the occupation, they settled for an ad hoc team of officers that literally begged, borrowed, and stole anything and everything they could to develop a force that ultimately proved to be ineffective. Only then were the resources provided. The 10 Iraqi divisions and other security forces envisioned by the senior commanders and war planners of the 1990s, reorganized, equipped, logistically supported, redeployed and appropriately advised in the summer of 2003, became a reality of sorts long after they were so desperately needed to stabilize Iraq, secure its borders, eliminate bad actors, and aid the country's reconstruction.

I grew increasingly disappointed, however, with the turn the war had taken. Our failure to secure Iraq in the aftermath of our charge to Baghdad and the fall of Saddam Hussein's regime, coupled with questionable decisions that alienated large portions of the population, allowed violent extremists from a variety of different groups including al-Qaeda, former regime elements, Jaysh al-Mahdi (Mahdi Army), and numerous other sectarian organizations with military wings, to orchestrate an insurgency that had grown considerably since I had returned to my home in Florida. The results were discouraging and our national hopes and objectives for Iraq modified accordingly. Millions of Iraqis were internally displaced or fled the country. Thousands were killed or wounded. The Iraqi Government failed to function effectively, beleaguered with sectarian bickering and selfishness. Its security forces evolved considerably since the desperate days of the New Iraqi Army's inception in 2003–04, with the vast resources that were dedicated to MNSTC-I and MNF-I for training, but the dedicated, professional, and combat-equipped force necessary to fight and win against Iraq's internal and external challenges remained a distant goal. American casualties exceeded 35,000 killed and wounded and national support for the war had declined considerably by the fall of 2010.

Nearly a decade after it entered Iraq, America's role was still a huge subject of national and world debate. The superb Army that crushed Iraq in March–April 2003 was visibly strained by long deployments that negatively impacted its overall readiness and manpower requirements. The modern U.S. Army was never built to sustain a long war and America's Army continues to pay the price for the decision to maintain considerable forces in Iraq for as long as it did. It calls into question the viability of the all-volunteer Army that saw its units continuously deployed, its professional officer and noncommissioned corps run into the ground, and the total force inadequately equipped and prepared to confront the larger, more symmetric threats that confront the nation in Asia and Europe. Whether or not Iraq eventually takes its place in the Middle East as an independent, powerful, and respected nation friendly to the United States in large measure still hangs in the balance.

After years of watching developments in the Arabian Gulf, serving in Iraq with the United Nations, and participating in several operations to counter Saddam

Hussein's aggressive policies and actions, I was convinced he was a "caged tiger" who could occasionally snarl through the bars of his cage and rattle the world. Like most soldiers, I wanted him gone. The reality, however, was that Saddam was the "glue" that kept a fractious Iraq from coming apart. It was clear to USCENTCOM war planners since the early 1990s that a probable consequence of Saddam's removal was civil war. The USCENTCOM war planners viewed Iraq as a short-term threat to our national interests in the Gulf. The long-term threat was, and continues to be, Iran. Iran feared Saddam despite Iraq's military weakness. Iraq was the Sunni-led Arab state that served as a bulwark against Iranian aggression. For over ten years, USCENTCOM commanders and Iraq war planners emphasized the need to quickly defeat, and then rehabilitate, the Iraqi Army to enable it to secure Iraq's borders if circumstances drove us to go to war. An occupation force that exceeded 350,000 troops in the original war plan was barely adequate to occupy, secure, stabilize, and reconstruct a broken country, but coupled with large Iraqi formations it could have done a credible job. Our intent was to disengage from Iraq as quickly as possible. A long-term occupation by a Western power was never in the cards. Even Douglas J. Feith, former Undersecretary of Defense for Policy, and one of the architects of the invasion, would later say a lengthy occupation was the single biggest mistake the U.S. made in Iraq.[1] As a planner who studied under some of the finest commanders and operational planners focused on the Iraq problem, I was disappointed by the realization the brain trust of such exceptional professional soldiers could be undermined by a powerful few and that a plan nearly ten years in development could be so vulnerable to the whims of those who never fought a battle and thought themselves to be of a superior intellect.

Military planning focuses on the accomplishment of carefully selected strategic and operational goals. Commanders and planners do not engage in political commentary or voice democratic ideals. They look at the threat, plan to contain or counter it, and, when necessary, destroy it. USCENTCOM war planners in the 1990s planned to quickly rearm the Iraqi Army as a credible defensive force, install a functional government, and withdraw our forces. Iraq was envisioned as a military power that would continue to provide an effective counter to our long-term threat in Iran. The civilian leadership in the Department of Defense at that time agreed with this logic. Democratic governance was not something military planners thought could be practically applied in Iraq or anywhere else in the Middle East given the region's history, culture, education, and general orientation of the people.

Our nation's senior leadership did not think through who would govern Iraq early enough and prepare him for a leadership role prior to the invasion. There were far more practical scenarios we could have taken. A number of planners thought that, prior to a relatively quick withdrawal of the bulk of Coalition combat forces from

Iraq, we would advise an Iraqi government installed in the aftermath of our initial operational success that had eliminated bad national and religious actors, and had redeployed the Iraqi Army, to abide by three fundamental national behaviors:

1. Do not support terrorism.
2. Do not develop weapons of mass destruction.
3. Do not threaten your neighbors.

Failure to adhere to these fundamental acts of behavior would result in bad consequences. Likewise, Iraq's neighbors would have been advised to stay out of Iraq and let it sort out its own problems. Not to do so would incur the wrath of American military might. This may appear overly simple to some, but the Iraqi political players would have likely moved quickly to negotiate and compromise an acceptable level of stability. The alternative would have been a war that would have eventually produced an Iraqi winner that would deal one way or another with Iraq's internal challenges. American concern with Iraqi democracy and its long-term involvement in Iraq's internal affairs, however noble, continued to drain its treasury, sap its military strength and credibility, weaken its international image, and diminish its capability to engage long-term threats. The occupation should and could have been ended in one or two years. Idealists are bothered by less-than-ideal solutions to the challenges the United States confronts. Their search for the perfect solution inevitably prolongs conflict and places soldiers in wars that cannot be won. "Mission creep" is nothing new to these characters and they have yet to learn the errors of such practice.

The conflict in Iraq was no surprise to those who studied the country before 2003. They were ultimately pushed aside by civilian actors and deferential senior military officers who were too willing to pursue a course of action they knew was ill-conceived.

By conducting a poorly resourced campaign that all but ignored the long-term work of professional military planners, foreign-area experts, and the commanders who preceded them, they invaded and occupied Iraq with minimal ground forces, failed to secure the country with martial-like, aggressive security measures, and redeploy Iraq's armed forces to secure its borders and eliminate selected actors like Muqtadā aṣ-Ṣadr. The absence of these measures allowed violent extremists including al-Qaeda and numerous Sunni and Shia sects to organize and fight Coalition forces and legal Iraqi authorities in an insurgency that grew significantly after the summer of 2003. General Shinseki, the Army chief of staff, as forces for Operation *Iraqi Freedom* were being deployed, publicly stated that 300,000 troops were required in Iraq for the postwar occupation and testified to that effect to the United States Senate Armed Services Committee on 25 February 2003. His testimony was rejected by both Secretary Rumsfeld and his Deputy Secretary of Defense, Paul Wolfowitz. General Shinseki was sidelined by Rumsfeld and, shamefully, no administration officials attended his retirement ceremony. General John Abizaid, USA, who assumed command of U.S. Central Command in July 2003, testified before Congress on 15 November 2006 that General Shinseki had been correct regarding the need for more troops. These military leaders, men of the highest honor and integrity, were superb examples for the young leaders of our military's officer corps, but sadly, the actions in large measure of many senior officers today appear to be overly deferential to policies and orders that threaten the martial culture, combat effectiveness, and overall readiness of our fighting forces and speaks to a sense of careerism that undermines soldiers' morale and ultimately the nation's confidence in its military.

Failure to adequately plan and resource the invasion's aftermath was compounded by pure arrogance that negatively impacted national policy and operations in Iraq well after the problems and solutions were identified. The fool's errand of the Bush Administration "to democratize" the Middle East was based on total ignorance of the religious, tribal, and clan culture of the Middle East. The facade of creating "elections" quickly crumbled. The American version of democracy would never work. First and foremost, the populace didn't want it or understand it; second, a democracy requires an educated people and rudimentary skills like reading were not significantly endemic to the culture. Planning gave way to a false hope that in time everything would stabilize even as the possibilities of a federalized Iraqi state and the merits of soft partition were contemplated. None of this detracts from the brilliant tactical successes of our combat formations that exemplified the excellence of the American warrior ethic of the day. The Iraqis will find their way without us; they would have as well in 2005.

Many countries that supported America's effort to stabilize Iraq in 2003, by providing peacekeeping forces, tired of the seemingly open-ended campaign of occupation. Their forces were ill-equipped for what awaited them. Few, if any, of them expected to engage in combat operations or sustain serious casualties. Several of these countries changed their manner of peacekeeping to a more aggressive, combat-oriented, realistic approach in time, but democracies are not prone to support wars of long duration. It is a characteristic our enemies exploit by simply waiting us out, bleeding our forces, and causing unacceptable opportunity costs. It was not surprising, in retrospect, that many of the supporting nations withdrew their troops within a year or two of their deployment. This point merits study as we examine the lessons of Iraq and derive the necessary strategies and tactics to address future challenges.

The United States Army will continue to bear the burden of sustained, unconventional combat that the next several decades promise to deliver not unlike the deployment of U.S. forces in response to the Northern Iraq offensive by the Islamic State as part of Operation *Inherent Resolve*. Schooled and oriented in the fast-moving, offensive operations of combined arms warfare, its officer corps can ill-afford not to study and plan the less-exciting and less-glorious campaigns that seek to secure and stabilize and set conditions for a reasonably quick disengagement. Given its experience in Iraq, perhaps the next generation of senior military officers will better serve the nation with realistic plans, objectives, and manageable goals, while simultaneously ensuring their civilian masters fully understand the risks, military necessities, and possible consequences of their actions. They must have the moral courage upon recognizing failures in planning and later in execution to strongly advance solutions. They must develop the stamina and the will to speak up even under the threat of being marginalized or punished. Only then will they not fail their nation and their troops on the ground. This is not just their job; it is their duty.

Reflecting on the challenges of the last 10 years of my military career, I am comfortable I fought a long, but "good war" that, as bad as it was at times, allowed me the opportunity to help a lot of good people and make a positive difference, however small, for my country and the multinational forces with which I served. I remain hopeful peace may yet come to the Middle East and America's efforts in Iraq and those of our fallen will not have been in vain.

Glossary of Acronyms and Terms

AO	Area of Operations
AOR	Area of Responsibility
ANGLICO	Air Naval Gunfire Liaison Company
BMP/BTR	Russian Heavy Infantry Transporter
C (Staff)	Designation of a principal staff officer on a Coalition or combined staff: C-1 (Personnel); C-2 (Intelligence); C-3 (Operations); C-4 (Logistics); C-5 (Plans); C-6 (Communications); C-9 (Civil Affairs)
USCENTCOM	United States Central Command
CFLCC	Coalition Forces Land Component Commander
CJTF	Combined (Coalition) Joint Task Force
CMATT	Coalition Military Assistance Training Team
CPA	Coalition Provisional Authority
DCSOPS	Deputy Chief of Staff for Operations
DDR	Disarmament, Demobilization, and Reintegration
DMZ	Demilitarized Zone
FEST	Forward Engineer Support Team
G (STAFF)	Designation of a principal staff officer at Division level (see C (Staff))
GCC	Gulf Cooperation Council
GERMED	German paramilitary medical unit assigned to the United Nations Iraq–Kuwait Observation Mission (UNIKOM)
GOSP	Gas Oil Separation Plant
GPS	Global Positioning System
HF	High Frequency
HUMVEE/HUMMER	Unofficial terms used by soldiers for the High Mobility Multipurpose Wheeled Vehicle or HMMWV
ICDC	Iraqi Civil Defense Corps
IMEF	First Marine Expeditionary Force
JCISE	Joint Counterintelligence Support Element
JDAM	Joint Direct Attack Munition
JSD	Joint Security Directorate

KB&R	Kellogg Brown & Root Inc
LNO	Liaison Officer
MFO	Multinational Force & Observers
MEDEVAC	Medical Evacuation
MEK	Mojahedin-e-Khalq
MEPS	Military Entrance Processing Station
MEU	Marine Expeditionary Unit
MNF-I	Multi-National Force-Iraq
MNSTC-I	Multi-National Security Transition Command-Iraq
MOD	Ministry of Defense
MND-CS	Multinational Division (Central-South)
MP	Military Police
MPRI	Military Professional Resources Inc
MRE	Meal, Ready-to-Eat
NCO	Noncommissioned Officer
NIA	New Iraqi Army
NIC	New Iraqi Corps
OMC-K	Office of Military Cooperation-Kuwait
ORHA	Office of reconstruction and Humanitarian Assistance
OPLAN	Operations Plan
ORP	Objective Rally Point
PERSCOM	United States Army Personnel command
PIR	Parachute Infantry Regiment
PSF	Peninsula Shield Force
PUK	Kurdish Patriotic Union of Kurdistan
QRF	Quick Reaction Force
RM	Royal Marines
RMC	Royal Marine Commando
RPG	Rocket-Propelled Grenade
RTCH	Rough Terrain Container Handler, pronounced "Wretch." A vehicle equipped with a crane designed to lift SEALAND containers.
S (Staff)	Designation of a principal staff officer at brigade and battalion level (see C (Staff))
SAIC	Science Applications International Corporation
SCIRI	Supreme Council for Islamic Revolution in Iraq
SHAPE	Supreme Headquarters Allied Powers, Europe
SOCCENT	Special Operations Command Central
SOW	Statement of Work
SUV	Sport Utility Vehicle
TAA	Tactical Assembly Area

TACSAT	Tactical Satellite
TOA	Transition of Authority
TOC	Tactical Operations Center
UN	United Nations
UNHCR	United Nations High Commissioner for Refugees
UNIKOM	United Nations Iraq–Kuwait Observation Mission
UNOSOM II	United Nations Operation in Somalia (1994–95)
USA	United States Army
USAR	United States Army Reserve
USAF	United States Air Force
USMC	United States Marine Corps
USMCR	United States Marine Corps Reserve
USMOG-W	United States Military Observation Group-Washington
USN	United States Navy
VHF	Very High Frequency
VMI	Virginia Military Institute
VOCO	Verbal Orders from the Commander
VTC	Video Teleconference

Endnotes

Chapter 2

1 Multiple Source History, *USCENTCOM, a War Fighting Headquarters, Know Your Heritage*, compiled by Mr. Keith Steltzer.
2 "Why Our Army is at the Breaking Point," *Time Magazine*, April 16, 2007, 4.
3 "Peacekeeping force could shrink in Sinai," *Army Times*, July 16, 2001, 18.

Chapter 5

1 Colonel Richard Stouder, interview with author, June 16, 2007.

Chapter 6

1 Comment attributed to General J. H. Binford Peay III, USA, addressing his war planners at U.S. Central Command regarding OPLAN 1002-96, circa February 1996.
2 Comments regarding need for ground forces to stabilize Iraq, personal interview with Colonel (Ret) Richard L. Stouder, USA, February 11, 2007.
3 Comments regarding General Franks's thoughts on OPLAN 1003-98, personal interview with Colonel (Ret) Mike Fitzgerald, USA, former chief, USCENTCOM War Plans Division, 2001–03, February 19, 2008.
4 General Keane's comment about Phase IV planning responsibility, John Barry and Evan Thomas, "Iraq: Blame the Top Brass?", *Newsweek*, November 13, 2007.
5 Planning guidance to USCENTCOM planners, personal interview with Colonel Fitzgerald, February 29, 2008.
6 Impact of Phase IV planning by USCENTCOM planners, personal interview with Colonel Fitzgerald, February 29, 2008.

Chapter 7

1 *The United Nations and the Iraq–Kuwait Conflict, 1990–1996*, The United Nations Blue Book Series, Volume IX (New York: United Nations Department of Public Information, 1996), 42.

Chapter 8

1 Authors notes in 2003 concerning numbers of British forces deployed at sea and in Southern Iraq in support of Operation *Telic*/Operation *Iraqi Freedom*.

Chapter 9

1   Quote by Major General Baba'eer, David Josar, "Troops from Six Arab Nations Guard Kuwait's Border with Iraq,", *Stars and Stripes*, European Edition, March 27, 2003.

Chapter 10

1   Comments and Quotes by LTC F. H. R. Howes, Situation Report ("Loose Minute"), Assessment of threat in Rumaylah, April 12, 2003.

Chapter 12

1   Iraq war planning, personal interview with Colonel (Ret) Richard L. Stouder, USA, former chief, USCENTCOM War Plans Division, 1992–96, February 11, 2007.
2   Reference to the Iraqi 51st Division, Ali A. Allawi, *The Occupation of Iraq, Winning the War, Losing the Peace* (New Haven: Yale University Press, 2007), 158.
3   Dissolution of the Iraqi Army, Ibid, 156–57.

Chapter 13

1   Transcript Interview with MG (Ret) Paul Eaton, USA, *CNN Late Edition with Wolf Blitzer*, February 19, 2006.
2   Northrup Grumman Announcement dated 2 July 2003, Titled: Northrup Grumman Awarded 48 Million Contract to Train the new Iraqi Army.

Chapter 17

1   Jona Lendering, "Babylon,", accessed 2008, http://www.livius.org/ba-bd/babylon/babylon.html.
2   Dr. Edmund Walendowski, Introduction-1a600907.us.archive.org GROM-Unit Profile.
3   "Poland," *Wikipedia, the free encyclopedia*, sections reference Polish–Lithuanian Commonwealth & Partitions, accessed 2008, https://en.wikipedia.org/wiki/Poland.

Chapter 18

1   Chart titled "State of Battle Groups (meeting with COL Tiso)" compiled by Colonel Viega, Chief of Staff, Spanish Brigade, Multinational Division (Central-South) on September 13, 2003.

Chapter 20

1   Reference to the City of Al-Kut, accessed 2008, http://www.globalsecurity.org/military/iraq/kut.htm.

Chapter 21

1   Reference to ICDC, accessed 2007, http://www.globalsecurity.org/military/world/iraq/icdc/htm.
2   "Border Security Expenditure," CPA Briefing with BG Mark Kimmit, Deputy Director for Coalition Operations and Dan Senor, Senior Adviser, CPA, Baghdad, Iraq, March 13, 2004.

3   Quotes from Allawi, Bremer, and Jaber, "Iraqis Graduate Training, 700 Soldiers make Up Core of Fledgling Army," *Stars and Stripes*, Mideast Edition, October 5, 2003, 9.

4   Ibid.

5   Transcript Interview with MG (Ret) Paul Eaton, USA, *CNN Late Edition with Wolf Blitzer*, February 19, 2006.

Chapter 22

1   Regarding the Iraqi Dinar, accessed 2007, http://globalsecurity.org/military/world/iraq/currency-reform.htm.

2   Andrew Garfield, "Executive Summary, Succeeding in Phase IV: British Perspectives on the U.S. Effort to Stabilize and Reconstruct Iraq," September 7, 2006, 2.

Chapter 26

1   Robert Asprey, *War in the Shadows, The Guerrilla in History*, Volume 2 (Garden City, New York: Doubleday, 1975), 1021.

Chapter 29

1   "ASP Security (1st Trip, 04 Dec 03-06 Dec 03)," Draft report by Major McKinney, USA, to the Director of Operations, Multinational Division (Central-South).

2   "History of Poland," *Wikipedia, the free encyclopedia*, accessed 2007, https://en.wikipedia.org/wiki/History_of_Poland.

3   Multinational Division Strategy and Division Commander's Intent, from undated draft copy of division fragmentation order (FRAGO) to subordinate commanders, circa November 17, 2003.

4   "All Quiet on the Polish Front," *The Polish Voice*, September 25, 2003.

Chapter 34

1   Lynne Olson and Stanley Cloud, *A Question of Honor, The Kosciuszko Squadron, Forgotten Heroes of World War II* (New York: Alfred A. Knopf, 2003), 29–34.

2   "Iraq Survey Group," *Wikipedia, the free encyclopedia*, accessed 2007, https://en.wikipedia.org/wiki/Iraq_Survey_Group.

Chapter 36

1   Nancy Montgomery, "Polish general: Iraq a challenge, opportunity," *Stars and Stripes*, September 23, 2005.

Chapter 37

1   Thomas E. Ricks, "Ex-Pentagon Aide says U.S. Abandoned Quick Iraq transition," *Washington Post*, December 11, 2007, 3.

Index

1st Corps Support Command, 17, 20, 307
1st Support Battalion, 16–20, 22, 24, 26–28
2nd Battalion, 16, 25, 28, 36, 146
3rd Battalion, 25, 36, 230, 285
3rd Infantry Division, 150, 156, 157
3rd Special Forces Group (SFG), 35, 26, 39
4th Air and Naval Gunfire Liaison Company
    (ANGLICO), 245, 246, 283, 319, 349
10th Mountain Division, 28, 71, 143, 150
16 Air Assault Brigade, 87, 104, 111
XVIII (18th) Airborne Corps, 15, 17, 37, 44,
    67
35th Kuwaiti Brigade, 120
82nd Airborne Division, 246, 261, 282, 285,
    298
87th Infantry, 28
101st Airborne, 13, 67, 130, 145, 179, 201,
    243, 275, 289
173rd Airborne Brigade, 25, 323
352nd Civil Affairs Command, 85–86
354th Civil Affairs Brigade, 86, 88, 89, 91,
    112, 137
505th Parachute Infantry Regiment, 16, 25

Abdullah, Colonel, 11, 98, 105, 109, 120–22
Afghanistan, xi, 10–12, 31–39, 42, 71, 86, 111,
    113, 116, 221, 317, 355, 366
Aircraft, 10, 17, 26, 27, 35, 41, 73, 104, 159,
    183, 184, 186, 199, 204, 207, 217, 225,
    231, 238, 279, 314, 330, 371, 372
    An-26, 373
    C-12, 130
    C-130 Hercules, 35, 132, 329
    F/A-18, 100
Air Force
    Iraqi, 167
    Polish, 381
    Royal, 10, 88, 112, 116, 176, 217

U.S., 9, 10, 32, 33, 36–38, 47, 49–54, 63,
    98, 104, 199, 245, 280, 323, 329, 358,
    371
AK-47, 146–47, 159, 238, 248, 249, 254, 256,
    301, 316, 341
Ali Al Salem Air Base, 94, 102, 104, 121, 124
Al-Kut, 178, 199–201, 208, 230–38, 245,
    267–74, 299, 301–07, 314–18, 328,
    335–43, 350, 362, 365, 366, 379
Al-Najaf, 178, 200, 207, 218–29, 230, 243,
    250, 254–59, 261, 271, 274, 294, 300, 314,
    331–35, 340, 360–67, 380
al-Qaeda, 27, 243, 366, 380, 381, 382, 384
Annan, Kofi, 41
Arab Peninsula Shield Force, xi
Arabs, 12, 16, 50, 79, 96, 100, 106, 116, 123,
    236, 249, 316
ARCENT, 50–57, 323
assault rifle, 61, 86, 146, 175, 200, 238, 248,
    316, 371 see also AK-47
Auschwitz, 377–78

Baath Party, 51, 57–58, 133, 134, 165, 250,
    327, 332
BaBa'eer, Major General Omar Ben Hassan,
    96–99, 107, 109, 120–24, 392
Baghdad, xii, xiii, 43, 55–8, 63, 66, 88, 99,
    124–28, 132–39, 140, 141–51, 155, 162,
    164, 165–70, 175–79, 186, 192, 195, 199,
    208, 213, 231, 234, 238, 242–48, 250,
    255, 257, 260, 268, 273, 282, 288, 291,
    295, 297, 300, 308–16, 327–28, 344, 349,
    366–67, 371, 380–82
    Battle of, 130, 246
    fall of, xii, 65, 104, 111, 119, 225, 251,
    331
Bagram, 33–39
Bahrain, 93, 105, 119

Bangladesh, 72, 73, 83, 232
Basrah, 55, 87, 88, 103, 139, 141, 145, 148–49, 159, 163, 166, 169, 204, 246, 333
battlefield, xii, 20, 34, 63, 67, 104, 134, 147, 165, 245, 278, 279, 281, 292, 314, 322, 330, 359, 374
Bedouin, 33, 79, 313
Benson, Colonel Kevin, 127–28
Bezluschenko, General, 199–201, 244, 265–69, 273, 300, 305, 307, 330, 337, 362, 363
Bieniek, General, 322, 352, 355, 359–64, 367, 374
bin Laden, Osama, 27
Blackman, General, 126–27, 133, 135
Bremer, Ambassador L. Paul, 57, 58, 134, 143, 149, 248, 257, 335, 393
Bronx, the, 3, 5, 7, 90, 140
Bush, George H. W., 47, 244, 322, 385

Cabeza, Colonel Javier, 197, 207, 208, 294, 317
Camp
    Arifjan, 86, 89, 90
    Ashraf, 146–7, 231
    Babylon, 176–78, 180–84, 202, 203, 209, 210, 212–17, 220, 223, 227, 229, 231, 238, 244–47, 250, 254, 259, 263–69, 271, 274–76, 280, 281–89, 296–97, 302, 307–20, 324, 328, 330, 336–38, 344, 349, 351–53, 359, 362–63, 365, 376, 380
    David, 14, 16
    Doha, 40–41, 62, 75–77, 85–86, 91, 94–95, 97–98, 103, 109–10, 124, 125, 129, 132, 139, 143–44, 166, 175–6, 371–72
    Fort, 232–33, 269–70, 301–02, 336, 338, 339, 341, 343
    Victory, 24, 121, 124, 144, 155, 166, 177, 179, 183, 188, 204, 210, 271–72, 283, 297, 323, 328, 365, 367
Canada, 21, 26
Carter, President Jimmy, 10
Cheney, Dick, 45–47, 52
Civil Affairs Brigade, 85–66, 88–89, 91, 112, 137
Civilian Observer Unit, 14, 15, 17
Clinton Administration, 46, 49, 132, 306

Coalition, The, xii, xiii, 43, 45, 57, 58, 75, 84, 88–89, 93, 95, 97, 110, 123, 125, 127, 129–33, 135, 138, 144, 155–56, 165, 175, 177, 179, 184, 193, 204, 213, 221, 226, 230–31, 242–43, 247, 248, 255, 257, 261, 272, 287, 291–99, 309, 312, 313–17, 327–8, 331, 334, 344–45, 350, 361, 368, 373–76, 381
Coalition forces, ix, 10, 58, 71, 79, 82, 88, 93, 96, 124, 242–43, 250–51, 261, 275, 293, 314, 327, 346, 355, 357, 363, 367–68, 381, 384
Coalition Military Assistance Training Team (CMATT), 128–30, 137–44, 147–54, 155–70, 175–81, 221, 242, 249, 250–51, 297, 309, 381
Coalition Provisional Authority (CPA), 57, 133, 144, 156, 165, 218, 234, 242, 261, 268, 272, 291, 309–12, 327, 333–36, 361, 368
Cody, Lieutenant General Dick, 14, 128
Cold War, 194–95, 200–01, 266, 287, 310, 330, 367, 374, 377
Combined Forces Land Component Command(er) (CFLCC), vi, 62, 63, 68, 71, 75, 78, 80, 82, 85, 91, 93–97, 102–24, 114, 120–30, 133–35, 138, 139, 175–76
Combined Joint Task Force-7 (CJTF-7), 24, 138, 155, 163, 177, 184, 209, 223, 229, 242, 255, 263, 272, 291, 299, 309, 314, 327, 333, 343, 360, 365, 381
communism, 193, 194, 254, 335
counterinsurgency, 288, 292, 375
counteroffensive, 49, 50, 55–56
criminal, 4, 104, 112, 114, 129, 165, 274, 291, 320, 327, 335, 357, 361
Crocker, General, 160–64, 167, 249
Cuscatlán Battalion, 254

DeGroff, Sergeant Major, 75–78, 80, 82–85
DellaJacano, Colonel, 120, 127
DeLong, Lieutenant General Mike, 31–32, 41
Delta Force, 40, 109, 189
demilitarized zone (DMZ), 11, 40, 71–78, 80–83, 87, 95, 97, 115, 185, 244, 373, 376
Deputy Chief of Staff for Operations (DCSOPS), 13, 14, 128, 177
Dominican Republic, 195, 207, 217, 218, 221, 315, 363

Eaton, General, xiii, 142–46, 149, 150–54, 157–69, 170–75, 241–50, 367, 376, 381

Egypt, xi, 11, 12, 14, 22, 27, 31, 45, 72, 191, 221

El Salvador, 195, 205, 207, 209, 215, 217, 218, 220, 254–57, 264, 265, 294, 331, 380

Eskan Village, 33, 39

Euphrates River, 178, 315

Figgures, Major General, 246, 263–65

Fiji, 14, 19, 21, 28, 258–59

First Gulf War, 55, 64–65, 68, 71–72, 80–81, 95, 109, 133, 139–41, 225, 259, 282, 313

Fisher, Chuck, 89–90

Fort
Benning, 14, 43, 141, 143
Campbell, 13, 67, 145
Knox, 43, 100, 167
Leavenworth, 14, 63, 100, 351

Franks, Lieutenant General Tommie, xi, xiii, 31, 32, 40–41, 53–56, 65, 129, 223, 327

French Foreign Legion, 26, 232

Fuller, Captain Geoff, 150, 161–62, 169–70, 311

Gas Oil Separation Plant (GOSP), 112–14

Gaza Strip, 17, 21, 27, 258

GERMED, 73, 74

Gingola, Master Sergeant Carl, 61, 303

Gogolewski, Sergeant 231–38

Great Patriotic War, 203, 306, 330, 338

Greer, Colonel, xiii, 135, 139–42, 146, 147, 153, 155–57, 162

guerrilla, 51, 57, 295, 319

Gulf War, 33, 43, 109, 233, 316 *see also* First Gulf War

Haiti, 86, 127, 189

Hawaii, 9, 21, 28, 30, 31, 132

Hawkins, Brigadier General, 66, 68

Hoar, General Joseph, 45

HUMINT (human intelligence) team, 294–95, 321, 355, 356, 358

Hungary, 22–24, 179, 195, 199, 261, 323

Hussein, Saddam, xii, 10, 31, 40–48, 50–55, 58, 63–64, 71, 77, 80, 83, 89, 93, 95, 97, 99, 106, 111, 114, 116, 122, 128–35, 141–42, 146, 160, 163, 177, 199, 205, 213, 229–30, 237, 248, 257, 261, 264, 296–97, 315, 319, 327, 331–32, 344, 351, 361, 378, 382–33

Illinois National Guard, 179, 212, 231, 316, 319, 330

Intifada, 16, 21, 27, 28, 100

Iran, 10, 22, 48, 51, 52, 57, 64, 80, 101, 124–25, 128, 129, 133, 141, 147, 160, 200, 213, 230–34, 236–39, 243, 253, 262–65, 267–80, 291–302, 310, 318, 328, 331, 333–39, 340, 343, 357, 361–66, 373–74, 379–83

Iran–Iraq War, 10, 80, 133, 141, 146, 165, 178, 230–32, 237

Iraqi Civil Defense Corps (ICDC), 242–43, 293, 299, 300, 317

Iraqi Oil Ministry, 112, 113, 297, 310

Islam, 50, 146, 230, 261, 272, 317, 381, 385

Italian, 3–6, 14, 22–24, 259, 263, 297, 344

János Isaszegi, Brigadier General, 179, 323

Jeffcoat, Lieutenant Colonel Marvin, 25, 289

Johnson, Major Trey, 169, 171, 311, 346

Joint Counterintelligence Support Element (JCISE), 33

Joint Security Directorate (JSD), 31–35, 57, 61–62, 183, 224, 317, 379

Joint Strategic Capabilities Plan (JSCP), 44–46, 48, 49, 51, 53, 57

Kanus, Lieutenant Alex, 231, 266, 267, 299, 302–4, 319, 338, 340–41

Kazakhstan, 189, 195

Kellogg Brown & Root (KB&R), 111–12, 130, 148, 159–60, 185, 211, 309, 313–14, 319–20

Kerbelaʾ, 178, 200, 203, 230–33, 242–43, 261, 274–78, 280–89, 291–98, 299, 300, 311, 314–17, 320–22, 330, 335, 337, 340, 343, 346, 349–50, 355–56, 357–60, 365–66, 374, 380

Kern, Brigadier General Jack, 36, 85–86

Khyber Pass, 34

King Khalid Military City, 93, 120, 123

Kingston, General Robert C., 10, 266

Kirkush Barracks, 144–53, 155–62, 167–70, 175, 241, 247–48

Krakow, 193, 375–77
Krystosik, Ambassador Ryszard, 211, 309–10, 335–36, 345–47, 362–63
Kunitskyi, Warrant Officer Antoliy, 306, 329, 343, 366
Kurds, 50, 51, 133, 135, 166, 170, 230, 249, 316
Kuwait, vi, xi, 10–14, 22, 31, 38, 40–55, 58, 61–66, 69, 71–79, 81–87, 90, 93, 94–97, 100–05, 110–11, 116, 119–24, 125–34, 141, 147, 150–52, 157, 166, 175, 185, 189, 192, 198, 224–25, 231, 244, 246, 257, 282, 310, 313, 316, 371, 373, 379, 380
Kwaśniewski, President Aleksander, 189, 322, 337
Kwiatkowski, General, 197, 211, 216–20, 253, 320–22, 337, 347, 352, 355, 356–63, 372, 375–77, 381

Landris, Colonel, 121
Laudes Inc, 164, 169
Logistics Center, 74–77, 82, 84, 232
Lowman, Captain Tom, xiii, 188, 192, 198, 208, 245, 253, 262, 265–67, 271, 281, 283, 286, 323, 328, 356, 359, 365

M60A3 tanks, 99–100
MacArthur, General Douglas, 13, 35, 313
MacDill Air Force Base, 9, 245, 323, 378
MacFarland, Colonel Sean, 179–80, 209–10
Magda, Major, 373–76
maneuver warfare, 21, 43, 123, 126
Marine Corps, ix, 10, 53, 79, 139, 296, 319, 320, 349
Marine Expeditionary Force (MEF), 45, 49, 50, 53, 64, 126, 138, 144, 178, 183, 210, 226, 243, 283, 319, 324
McDougal, Lieutenant Sean, 137, 141, 142, 148, 156, 159
McKiernan, General, 68, 126, 129, 134
Meating, Major General, 21, 25, 26
Middle East, xi, xii, 7–12, 26, 27, 30, 34, 50, 64, 71, 94, 96, 121–22, 133, 143, 163–64, 168–9, 171, 224, 230, 258, 260, 263, 349, 378–79, 382–86
Military Entrance Processing Stations (MEPS), 139, 141–42

Ministry of Defense, 127, 137, 156, 195, 329, 373
Military Police (MP), 23, 31, 33, 65, 120, 123, 137, 167, 190, 207, 243, 275, 280, 294, 335, 345
Mixon, Brigadier General Benjamin R., 37
Mohammad, Colonel, 98, 101–05, 116, 119, 120, 122–23, 255
Monterrozza, Colonel, 209, 211, 254–55
Mount Vernon, 3–7, 90, 140, 263
Mozan, Brigadier General, 99–100, 106
Mubarak, Muhammad Hosni El Sayed, 11, 22, 27
Multinational Division, xi, xiii, 24, 88, 144, 158, 170, 173, 179, 183–99, 201–27, 212, 218, 221, 225, 229, 239, 241–46, 253, 259, 261, 271, 280, 282, 291, 293, 311, 312, 318, 322, 327, 333, 343–44, 360, 365–67, 373–74, 377, 380
Multinational Force & Observers (MFO), xi, 12–20, 21–30
Muslim, 34, 230, 255, 317
    Shi'ite, 50–51, 135, 218, 229, 230, 233, 240, 274–75, 277
    Sunni, 50–51, 134–35, 166, 170, 229, 230, 327, 332, 383–84

Nairobi, 191–92
National Guard, 28, 71, 151, 179, 231, 266, 316, 319, 330, 349
National Intelligence Estimate (NIE), 45–46
National Military Strategy, 44, 47
National Security Strategy, 44, 46
NATO, 24, 45, 190, 194, 199, 215, 246, 287, 296, 322, 337, 345, 380–81
    Defense College, 24, 190
Navy, 23, 47, 50, 54, 88, 113, 186, 190–91, 247, 318
    SEALS, 190, 247
Nazi, 357, 375, 377
New Iraqi Army (NIA), xi, xii, xiii, 58, 88–89, 127, 132–37, 143–46, 149, 151, 153, 155–57, 160, 162, 163–67, 169–70, 175, 204, 210, 226, 241–42, 247–48, 250, 272, 295, 311, 361, 368, 381–82
New York, 3–7, 125, 140, 179, 263, 301, 339

Office of Military Cooperation (OMC), 36,
141
Office of Reconstruction and Humanitarian
Assistance (ORHA), 65, 130–32, 137, 144
Officer Candidate School, 188, 243
oil, 10, 46–47, 79–80, 88, 89, 109–17,
125–27, 152, 158, 190, 291, 296–97, 310
Ojrzanowski, General, 274, 276, 278–88, 290,
344–45, 355
Omani, 101, 120, 124, 274, 314
Ondul, Colonel, 38–39
Operation
Desert Storm, 10, 20, 44–47, 53–54, 86 152
Enduring Freedom, 11–12
Iraqi Freedom, xi, xiv, 30, 47, 57, 58, 150,
215, 221, 254, 384
Provide Relief, 10
Restore Hope, 10
Stuart, 255, 261, 264, 265, 271–73
Telic, 88
Uphold Democracy, 127
Vigilant Warrior, 44
Operations Plan (OPLAN), 9, 44–45, 49, 52,
65, 103, 189, 198
Orlando, Lieutenant Colonel Kim S., 243–44,
275–77, 288–89, 320

Pakistan, xi, 11, 12, 33–35, 42–43, 71, 191
Panama, 20, 73, 110, 143, 160, 219
Parachute Regiment, 246
Paulus, Dr Michael, 74, 83
peacekeeping, 11, 14, 19 20, 25, 29, 43, 71,
77, 113, 196, 207, 214, 264, 293, 315,
322, 334, 385
Peay, General J. H. Binford, xi, xiii, 11, 12, 44,
46, 48, 51, 52, 64, 129, 233
Pelham, 6–7
Peninsula Shield Force (PSF), xi, 58, 93–107,
109, 116, 119, 125, 143, 380
Pentagon, the, 13–15, 43, 45, 52, 55, 65, 132,
145, 296
Persian Gulf, 41, 296
Petraeus, General Dave, 145–46, 289, 381
Poland, 189, 190, 193, 194, 203, 231, 241,
273, 298, 319–24, 337, 349, 352, 356–58,
367, 371–77, 380–81
Port Authority, 87, 89, 90
Powell, Colin, 25, 45, 281

Purple Heart, 25, 307–08

Qatar, 53–54, 93, 97, 105, 119, 122, 225
Quick Reaction Force (QRF), 187, 200–01,
316, 321, 340

Rabon, Colonel Jim, 63, 66–67
Rashid, Colonel, 100, 105–06, 119, 120
Republican Guard, 45, 48, 55, 165
Roman Catholic Church, 4, 194
Roosevelt, Franklin D., 46, 193
Royal Marines, xi, 87–88, 103, 111, 112,
114–16
rules of engagement (ROE), 179, 187, 195,
198, 208, 214, 246, 264, 271, 272, 273,
291, 296, 315, 321–23, 334, 351, 359, 364
Rumaylah Oil Field, 88, 103, 109–17, 125–26,
152
Rumsfeld, Secretary Donald, 64–65, 384
Russia, 24, 46, 74, 98, 100, 146, 193–99, 200,
201, 216–18, 231–32, 238, 244, 248, 287,
330, 346, 372–74, 376

Sanchez, General Ricardo, 154–56, 167, 184,
194, 198, 212–17, 220–24, 227, 247,
264, 267–78, 280, 283– 85, 297, 299,
300, 302, 328–9, 337, 343–44, 360, 362,
364, 381
Saudi Arabia, xi, 22, 27, 31–32, 39–40, 44–49,
50–55, 71, 72, 93, 96, 113, 120, 151, 164,
178, 221, 244, 317
Saudi Arabian National Guard, 71, 151
Schwitters, Colonel James H., 34, 40
Science Applications International Corporation
(SAIC), 151, 165–66, 169
Scott Air Force Base, 35, 52
Scud missile, 87, 230
Semenets, Major Val, 232, 269, 270, 299, 300,
318, 338, 340, 343, 366
Sharm El-Sheik, 22, 24
Sinai, ix, xi, xv, 12, 13–20, 21, 22–24, 25–31,
100, 113, 168, 179, 199, 221, 258, 307,
323
Slocombe, Walter, 127, 129, 131–35, 139, 140,
142, 144, 154–56, 159, 165
Sobora, General, 197, 203, 231, 238, 244–45,
266–70, 273, 274, 299–308, 315, 319, 330,
337–41, 366

Somalia, xi, 10, 11, 14, 30, 43, 71, 86, 109, 112, 116, 143, 150, 162, 191–92, 199
Soviet Union, 11, 46–47, 190, 194, 203, 254, 287, 310, 366, 377
Spanish Brigade, 193, 195, 207 11, 215, 217, 220, 221, 225–27, 244–45, 262, 271, 294, 314–15, 317, 329, 360–64
Special Operations Task Force, 190, 331
Stalder, General Keith, 183, 186, 188, 195–96
Stanton, Colonel Marty, 71, 75–76, 85, 91, 105, 109
Stouder, Colonel Rich, xiii, 43, 44–50, 52–53, 56, 64, 124
Supreme Council for Islamic Revolution (SCIRI), 230–31
surveillance, 37, 72, 264, 317, 356, 358–59

Tactical Operations Center, 62, 79, 95, 283, 356
Taliban, 36
Tampa, 40, 61, 70, 143, 378–79
Tarvainen, General, 40, 74
Task Force IV, 62–63, 66, 75, 85, 176
terrorism, 11, 17, 27, 32, 34, 57, 66, 73, 96, 149, 190, 254, 260, 320–21, 343–47, 355, 372, 380–81, 384
Third Army, 41, 54, 139
Time Phased Force Deployment Data (TPFDD), 52, 56
Torglar, Major Jim, 131
Two Major Regional Contingency (2MRC), 45, 46, 48
Tyszkiewicz, Major General Andrzej, 45, 189–99, 200–04, 211–18, 220–24, 229, 241–45, 247–49, 254, 259, 261–64, 271–80, 282–89, 292–98, 310, 315, 319, 322–29, 330, 334, 338, 343–46, 349, 350–52, 372–76

UH-60 Black Hawk helicopter, 139, 209, 217, 224, 248, 263, 265, 314
Ukraine, 189, 195, 199, 238, 266, 302, 328, 330
Ukrainians, 195–200, 207–08, 213, 229, 230–39, 243–45, 266–68, 273–74, 299–301, 308, 316, 319, 328, 331, 337, 343, 357, 362, 374, 380

Umm Qasr, 72–76, 79–82, 85–91, 94, 103, 107, 111–12, 125, 137, 152, 166, 190, 231, 246, 263, 333
Underwood, Larry, 164, 169, 249
United Arab Emirates, 93, 97 98, 119
United Nations, ix, xi, 7, 11–14, 26, 29, 30, 43, 53, 55, 71, 94, 100, 191, 381–82
Iraq–Kuwait Observation Mission (UNIKOM), 13, 19, 38, 40, 71–79, 81, 83, 87, 94, 100, 111, 166, 185, 231, 244, 257, 295–96, 298, 373
Oil for Food Program, 79, 89
Operation Somalia II (UNOSOM II), 191–92
United States Task Force Sinai, 12, 30
Uruguay, 19–20, 22, 73, 143, 219
U.S. Army War College, 9, 12, 43, 52, 152, 192
U.S. Central Command (USCENTCOM), ix, xii, 9–12, 31–35, 40–52, 53–65, 71, 113, 125–29, 135, 193, 223–25, 225, 280, 316–17, 327, 333, 366, 372, 379, 383, 385
Joint Security Directorate (JSD), 31, 57, 61, 148, 183, 224, 317, 379
U.S. Congress, 62, 223, 224, 244, 250, 385
U.S. Embassy, 33, 36, 39, 40, 372, 375–76
USS Cole, 27

Verge, Colonel Peter, 76 78, 82–83
Vietnam, 10, 25, 27, 67, 262, 305
War, 150, 177, 253
Vinnell Corporation, 150–51, 155–60, 164, 167, 168, 249
Virginia Military Institute, 19, 36, 75, 150, 210

Waldhauser, Colonel Tom, 79–80, 82, 85
War Plans Division, xiii, 11, 12, 43, 44, 52, 64, 71, 127
Warsaw, 190, 193, 358, 373, 375–76
Pact, 194, 199, 266, 330, 346, 374
Weh, Colonel Al, 150, 157–58, 166
Whitley, British Major General Albert, 68, 71, 85, 103, 116
Williams, Brigadier Bob, 166–67
Williams, Colonel Mike, 66–67, 116
Wilson, Major Dave, 94, 126

Wojdkowski, General Walt, 141, 144, 155, 177–78, 272, 366–67
Wolfowitz, Paul, 45, 296, 384
World War I, 5, 80, 124, 230, 232, 287, 320, 357
World War II, 3–5, 61, 89, 110–11, 147, 189–94, 217, 203, 287, 295–96, 298, 346, 357–58, 375–77

Yugoslavia, 100, 141, 144, 146

Zinni, General, ix, xi, xiii, 9–13, 23, 34, 41, 51, 53, 55–56, 64, 66, 98, 111, 129, 141, 145, 165, 223, 225, 296, 320

About the Author

Colonel (Retired) Roland J. Tiso Jr., USA, graduated from the Virginia Military Institute in 1973 and was commissioned a second lieutenant of Infantry. Retired from the U.S. Army in 2004, his last assignment was as the senior adviser to the Polish-led Multinational Division (Central-South) in Iraq. He is widely traveled throughout the Middle East and Central Asia. Colonel Tiso was selected as a Distinguished Member of the 506th Infantry Regiment in 2022. He resides in Valrico, Florida, with his wife Judie.